RICHARD WOODS (1715–1793)
Master of the Pleasure Garden

A contemporary of the famous landscape designer 'Capability' Brown, Richard Woods has never received the recognition he deserves: in contrast to Brown, he emphasised the pleasure ground and kitchen garden, with a more pronounced use of flowers than was general among the landscape improvers of his time. He liked variety and incident in his plans and, where he was employed on a larger scale, the encroachment of the pleasure ground into the park created the Woodsian 'pleasure park'.

In this important work of detection and biography, Fiona Cowell analyses his designs, and explores his actives as a plantsman, a determined amateur architect and a farmer. In particular, she shows the difficulties he found as a Catholic living in penal times, examining the difficulties encountered by both Woods and his Catholic patrons, and placing the man and his work in their wider social and economic context. Unjustly neglected in the past, he is here given his rightful place among the creators of the English landscape style.

Garden and Landscape History

ISSN 1758–518X

General Editor
Tom Williamson

This exciting new series offers a forum for the study of all aspects of the subject. It takes a deliberately inclusive approach, aiming to cover both the 'designed' landscape and the working, 'vernacular' countryside; topics embrace, but are not limited to, the history of gardens and related subjects, biographies of major designers, in-depth studies of key sites, and regional surveys.

Proposals or enquiries may be sent directly to the editor or the publisher at the addresses given below; all submissions will receive prompt and informed consideration.

Professor Tom Williamson, University of East Anglia, University Plain, NORWICH, Norfolk NR4 7TJ

Boydell & Brewer, PO Box 9, Woodbridge, Suffolk, England, UK IP12 3DF

RICHARD WOODS (1715–1793)
MASTER OF THE PLEASURE GARDEN

RICHARD WOODS
(1715–1793)

MASTER OF THE PLEASURE GARDEN

FIONA COWELL

THE BOYDELL PRESS

First published 2009
The Boydell Press, Woodbridge

ISBN 978–1–84383–524–0

The Boydell Press is an imprint of Boydell & Brewer Ltd
PO Box 9, Woodbridge, Suffolk IP12 3DF, UK
and of Boydell & Brewer Inc.
668 Mt Hope Avenue, Rochester, NY 14620, USA
website: www.boydellandbrewer.com

The publisher has no responsibility for the continued existence or
accuracy of URLs for external or third-party internet websites referred
to in this book, and does not guarantee that any content
on such websites is, or will remain, accurate or appropriate.

A CIP record for this book is available
from the British Library

This publication is printed on acid-free paper

Designed and typeset by Tina Ranft
Printed in Great Britain by
CPI Antony Rowe, Chippenham and Eastbourne

CONTENTS

For Emily
nemo mihi amicior

The publishers acknowledge the generous support of the
Marc Fitch Fund in the production of this volume.

LIST OF ILLUSTRATIONS

Illustrations are reproduced by the kind permission of the organisations listed by each image. Copyright of all images is vested in the owner. Images without a location come from the collection of the author or the library of F. R. Cowell.

Title page: black and white version of Plate 10:
Part 1 title page: detail from figure 2
Part 2 title page: detail from figure 6
Gazetteer title page: detail from figure 11

COLOUR PLATES

ACKNOWLEDGMENTS

MY HUSBAND ADRIAN, my former supervisor Professor Tom Williamson and my editorial mentor Emily Lane have all given me support and encouragement beyond that which anyone has the right to expect.

Andrew Westman has patiently and skilfully redrawn many of Woods's plans which are too faded and indistinct to reproduce photographically, and Jane Furse has not only helped me over the years with her analysis of the Cannon Hall landscape, but also allowed me to reproduce her meticulous tracing of Woods's plan.

My friend and colleague Marion Swetenham accompanied me on many of my site visits and gave me the benefit of her fine eye for the lie of the land. She has also recently acted as an invaluable *alter ego* in England.

Nancy Edwards (then Briggs) and Hugh Prince must also be acknowledged as the first people to recognise Woods as a landscaper of significance and initiate research into him. They have both given me generous guidance and advice.

I have been helped by a great number of individuals and institutions, to all of whom I am extremely grateful. All specific contributions have been acknowledged where they occur in the text, but I should particularly like to thank the following: Father Alexander of St George's College, Lady Armytage, Sarah Bendall, Sir Simon Benton Jones, Sir William and Lady Boulton, David Brown, John Clark, Susan Campbell, The Canonesses of the Holy Sepulchre, Mike Cousins, Stephen Daniels, John Drake, Fridy Duterloo-Morgan, Sarah Fitzgerald, Esther Gatland, Peter Goodchild, Keith Goodway, Mike Hall, John Harris, Brian Harrison, Julie Harrup, David Jacques, Susan Kellerman, Mark Laird, Bryan Maggs, Jennifer Meir, John Phibbs, Anne Rowe, Alister Sutherland, Ian Sutton, Michael Symes, Edmund Thornhill, Deborah Turnbull, Rosamund and John Wallinger, Elizabeth Whittle, Barry Williamson, May Woods and Stephen Wright. All these have answered queries at length and added to my knowledge and understanding of their specialist subjects. All the County Gardens Trusts have contributed information and encouragement.

I should like to express my gratitude for the help and kindness I have been shown at all the record repositories, public and private, and in particular Essex Record Office, my local refuge and source of inspiration. Philip Winterbottom at Drummonds and Pamela Hunter at Hoares Banks have allowed me unstinted access to their ledgers; Gareth Hughes at Audley End opened the English Heritage archive to me; and Gerardine Mulcahy of the Burton Constable Foundation provided me with invaluable photocopies. The Beineicke Library at Yale University, the Folger Shakespeare Library in Washington DC and Kansas University Library were extremely accommodating to a foreign researcher.

Finally, I am deeply grateful to Professors Timothy Mowl and Tom Williamson for supporting my application to the Marc Fitch Fund.

ABBREVIATIONS

BL	British Library
BRO	Berkshire Record Office
CBS	Centre for Buckinghamshire Studies
CaRO	Cambridgeshire Record Office
CaROH	Cambridgeshire Record Office, Huntingdon Branch
CKS	Centre for Kentish Studies
CRO	Cornwall Record Office
DA	Doncaster Archives
DHC	Dorset History Centre
ERO	Essex Record Office
GRO	Gloucestershire Record Office
HALS	Hertfordshire Archives and Local Studies
LMA	London Metropolitan Archives
LRO	Lancashire Record Office
NLW	National Library of Wales
PRO	Public Record Office
SA	Sheffield Archives
SHS	Surrey History Services
SRO	Staffordshire Record Office
SROB	Suffolk Record Office, Bury St Edmunds Branch
WoRO	Worcestershire Record Office
WRO	Warwickshire Record Office
WSHC	Wiltshire and Swindon History Centre
WSuRO	West Sussex Record Office
WYAS	West Yorkshire Archive Service (followed by relevant branch)

NOTE

It became obvious in the early stages of research that 'Woods' and 'Wood' were virtually interchangeable spellings, possibly due to confusion in the eighteenth century, as today, over the squiggle frequently found at the end of a word. The name is sometimes written both ways even within single account books, and the absence of the final 's' has not been considered necessarily relevant in identifying Richard Woods.

Original spelling, punctuation and syntax has been retained in quotations throughout.

Properties given in bold type in Chapter 3 are listed in the gazetteer at the end of the volume.

GENERAL EDITOR'S FOREWORD

A VERY GREAT DEAL HAS BEEN WRITTEN over the years about Lancelot 'Capability' Brown; so much, indeed, that the achievements of other landscape gardeners working in England in the second half of the eighteenth century have been greatly neglected and largely misunderstood. Such individuals have often been described, if associated with Brown himself, as 'lieutenants' or 'foremen'; and if not so associated, as his 'imitators'. Yet while Brown was the most well-known and financially successful landscape gardener of his age, several of these men were gifted and original designers, who arguably contributed as much to the dominant styles of the period as Brown himself, and who could be considered by the wealthy arbiters of taste as perfectly acceptable alternatives to him.

Richard Woods was one of the most important of these landscape gardeners, and in this meticulously researched yet extremely readable volume – as much a work of detection as of scholarship – Dr Cowell describes his life and work. She investigates his origins, dissects and characterises his influences and style, and charts in detail his career, providing a comprehensive gazetteer of the places at which he worked. Yet this is more than a work of art history, for Dr Cowell is at pains to place Woods firmly within his wider social and economic context. This is one of the most important contributions to landscape and garden history to appear for many years.

PREFACE

RICHARD WOODS WAS ONE OF SEVERAL LANDSCAPE IMPROVERS practising in the second half of the eighteenth century, during and around the time that Lancelot Brown held sway. He, like all the others, designed within the framework of a fashion now loosely called 'Brownian', with a strong emphasis on the naturalistic and artfully informal, but to a greater degree than his peers Woods developed his own particular style that did not follow the lead of their celebrated contemporary. A comparison of themes provides an effective way to evaluate his contribution to eighteenth-century landscaping. Woods's relatively sparse biographical details are contained in the first section, setting the context for a Catholic who worked for both Protestant and Catholic patrons in a period of important political and economic developments.

In the years following the appearance of garden history as a valid field of study, it was for some decades considered that any successful landscape design was by definition Brown's creation, as (although it was realised that he had a scattering of 'followers' or 'pupils') there was nobody else practising at the time deemed to have enough skill to produce anything remotely comparable. As research on the shadowy sideline practitioners progressed – William Emes, Adam Mickle snr and jnr, Nathaniel Richmond, Thomas White snr and jnr, Richard Woods, and others – a different picture began to emerge.[1] While it remained clear that Brown was pre-eminent in success and talent, and that as a single designer he was responsible for more than anyone else, he nevertheless produced a minority of the total number of designed landscapes of the eighteenth century, perhaps as few as 5 per cent.[2] With the passage of time, the relative merits of the considerable number of improvers available for work at various periods from the middle of the eighteenth century have become more easily discernible, but to contemporary eyes this crystallisation was less obvious. It comes as a surprise to find that at the time these men were regarded to a certain extent as interchangeable: Brown took over from Woods at Wardour and Wynnstay, Woods followed Brown at Chillington and Audley End, Emes followed Brown at Ingestre and replaced him at Eaton Hall, White replaced Woods at Goldsborough. Richmond, as an ex-foreman of Brown's, successfully built up his own business and thereafter worked in a style generally difficult to distinguish from that of his erstwhile mentor. It is even more unexpected to discover that names almost unknown now were recognised in their day: such men as Thomas Leggett, at some time a foreman of Emes, who had his own landscaping business and was acknowledged in retrospect as having been 'quite the fashion'.[3] Some of

Woods's foremen also later branched out on their own, with unrecorded results. The final story of these men has yet to be written.

This evaluation of relative merits, and indeed the realisation that the landscape style had several aspects and variations, is not only an interesting study in itself but also serves to put Brown into an increasingly realistic context. It is now accepted that Brown was not the only player in the field, albeit he was the most successful, but it has been generally supposed that all the other improvers of the mid–late eighteenth century were taking Brown, directly or indirectly, as their model. To find in Woods a competitor with his own very idiosyncratic style is a salutary reminder of the diversity of eighteenth-century attitudes.

[1] See bibliography and references *passim* to this research: Goodway for Emes; Turnbull for the Whites; Brown for Richmond. The Mickles are discussed in David Jacques, *Georgian Gardens* (London, 1983) pp. 142–3.

[2] David Brown, 'Nathaniel Richmond 1724–1784, "Gentleman Improver"' (unpublished PhD thesis, University of East Anglia, 2000) p. 1.

[3] Entry by Patrick Bowe in *Oxford Companion to Gardens* (Oxford, 1986) and pers. comm. by Keith Goodway.

PART 1

WOODS
THE MAN

CHAPTER 1

WOODS IN CONTEXT

'Every thing that could be desired in a moderate space.'

NOTHING BETTER SUMS UP THE ACHIEVEMENT of Richard Woods than this comment by John Claudius Loudon in 1822 on the landscape at Cusworth Park, and nothing better illustrates the complete disregard into which Woods had fallen than the fact that Loudon does not acknowledge him as the designer.

Two generations can be a long time in the evolution of historical attitudes, and prior to Dorothy Stroud's seminal biography of Lancelot Brown, first published in 1957, there was limited understanding or appreciation of the designed landscape. The respected and influential garden historian Christopher Hussey, writing in 1930 of Wardour Castle, displayed the sort of attitude that Stroud had to counter when she started researching Brown. Wardour Castle was designed by Paine in 1770 as a mansion on a new site, and placed in the landscape setting designed for it by Woods, and yet Hussey could deplore the grounds 'as pastoral as those of a byre', and the fact that

> Wardour finds itself incongruously surrounded by meadow
> land, with which it has less connection than the most humble
> cottage. Had there been an axial approach into a considerable
> forecourt, enriched with piers and gates, or terraces and
> flights of steps, or any formalised outworks to soften its
> impact on the sod, the great grey pile would have had some
> apparent connection with its setting and the balanced
> simplicity of its design be accentuated instead of lost.[1]

By the time that Hussey wrote the preface to Stroud's original edition, he admitted that ignorance about Brown represented a gap in our understanding of garden history 'as regrettable as it can now be perceived to be large', and we have long since been conditioned to consider a landscape setting for an English Palladian mansion as being not only perfectly correct but also aesthetically satisfying.

At one stage Woods was to some people a respectable alternative to Brown, yet his death was not even reported in the local newspaper, let alone causing dryads to go into black gloves.[2] In spite of a reasonable amount of surviving material, in many respects Woods remains an elusive figure. The fact that he was a Catholic has made it impossible to trace his birth and upbringing; there is scarcely any extant correspondence to him, virtually no contemporary comments about him, and – a very great loss – the record of his bank account with Wrights disappeared when the bank failed in 1840. Woods also had a short-lived account with Hoares, from April to December 1767,[3] and just this single page in a ledger threw up an important piece of information.[4] Even at a time when cash still played a great part in the settling of accounts, a full banking record can reveal a range of clients and extent of employment, as it did for Brown, White and Richmond, all of whom banked with Drummonds and whose account ledgers still survive.

At the time that Woods would have been starting his own practice, in the 1750s, there were still a few older men available for landscape improvement: Robert Greening, who died in 1758; Thomas Wright, 'the Wizard of Durham', who was very active through the 1750s but more or less retired after 1763 apart from a few important commissions;[5] and Sanderson Miller (who only advised friends on a non-commercial basis), who was out of action through mental illness after 1760.[6] Francis Richardson was still in good business until his death in 1761,[7] although his practice was restricted to the north. Through the early 1760s – with the notable exception of Brown – there were fewer improvers available than before or after, although several who later went into business on their own account were already working as foremen of Brown. Among the oldest of the new wave was Nathaniel Richmond, born in 1724 and with the advantage of having worked for and with Brown, practising on his own from 1759. William Emes (b. 1729/30) left his post as head gardener at Kedleston in 1760 but initially worked almost exclusively in the midlands and west.[8] Thus in general terms, until the late 1760s, Brown, Emes, Richmond and Woods were the only significant players in the game. Thereafter there was an explosion of improvers as a new generation, and in many respects a new type, came on the scene. They included other foremen/associates of Brown such as Thomas White snr (1739–1811), Samuel Lapidge (c.1740–1806) and Adam Mickle jnr (1747–c.1810); foremen of Woods such as Anthony Sparrow; foremen of Emes such as John Webb (1754–1828) and Thomas Leggett (fl. 1761–1810); John Haverfield (c.1740–1820); and Samuel Driver (d. 1779) – all ready, willing and with varying skill able to design and lay out grounds.

This proliferation of improvers towards the latter part of the century was largely the result of the fashion for naturalism filtering down the social scale, combined with the fact that the eighteenth century saw the emergence of a new class of wealthy would-be gentlemen, happy to spend on acquiring the status of a gentleman.[9] One of the most clearly visible signs of gentility was a fine house in a fine setting, the two usually going together,[10] but neither the careful squire nor the *nouveau riche* would have entertained the idea of approaching the fashionable and charismatic Brown, any more than he would have condescended to landscape their relatively modest acreage. There was room for Brown at the top, a handful of first-rate designers just below him, and then a flurry of lesser men – and many of these are found combining landscape improving with another livelihood, such as surveying or the nursery trade. Where the early proselytisers of a more natural style, Charles Bridgeman (d. 1738), Stephen Switzer (d. 1745) and William Kent (d. 1748), found their employers in the higher ranks of society, by the end of the eighteenth century modest naturalistic landscapes, of greater or lesser artistic worth, had become commonplace.

The gradual but inexorable rise of artistic naturalism in landscape design through the eighteenth century has been explored and discussed sufficiently often not to need repeating here. In the context of Woods, due consideration must also be given to the reverse argument: the resistance to the wave of modernisation that is obvious not just in the tenacity of the old styles, but also in the surprising willingness even of well-placed patrons to commission designs which, with the judgement of hindsight, we would describe as old-fashioned. Tom Williamson has commented on the danger to the study of garden history of concentrating exclusively on the greatest and grandest new layouts, created by the most powerful, rich and articulate in the land.[11] These were indeed influential pointers to the direction of a trend, but it must not be forgotten that the mass of gentry and successful new men thought long, hard, and probably for many years (if at all) about giving their grounds the latest treatment. The much-quoted comment of Sir Thomas Robinson in 1734 that 'the celebrated gardens of Claremont, Chiswick, and Stowe are now full of labourers, to modernize the expensive works finished in them, even since everyone's memory'[12] is an observation not on the generality of gardens but on three of the most famous of the time, and it would be many decades before that movement became general for many a 'polite' but modest country estate at gentry level. Gardens which, with the disdain of hindsight, would look old-fashioned were being proudly depicted well past 1750, and frequently escaped alteration into the third quarter of the century or beyond.

THE CATHOLIC BACKGROUND

As the eighteenth century opened the Glorious Revolution and reclaimed Protestant succession were still recent memories, and the persistence of anti-Catholic feeling can be readily explained not only by a general English xenophobia but also by the fact that papism carried political as well as religious connotations. Popes consistently supported the deposing of the Protestant monarch when there was a Catholic alternative, thus making Catholicism axiomatic with potential sedition.

However, by the mid century, and in spite of the second Jacobite uprising of the Forty-five, the tide of opinion was turning. By this time most of the

Catholic families, while dutifully praying for the Stuarts, had no real ambition to substitute them for the Hanoverians. It was noticeable, when it came to the point during the Forty-five, that Prince Charles Edward failed to enlist the support of more than a handful of English families on his march south, and Protestant Tories and the Catholic community alike held back from the attempt to overthrow the government. Repression and revenge followed in Scotland after both Jacobite risings, but there were few lasting repercussions in England. Astonishingly, when the Young Pretender visited London officially incognito in 1750, it did not even cause a political ripple on the water.

Nevertheless, it has to be remembered that the penal laws against the Catholics remained on the statute books, and on whatever pretext any or all of them could suddenly be imposed or more severely interpreted. Even the greatest families were still treading on unstable ground, with the memory that for 160 years (with some periods of brief respite) the whole force of the state had been directed at coercing them to deny their faith and refusing them the opportunity to prove that a papist could in spite of his religion be a good citizen and a loyal subject. Thomas Sheldon, serving King George in the Hanoverian army as the English service was closed to him, wrote to his mother that 'being born a Catholic was something he would not wish on his worst enemy'.[13]

A breakthrough came with the death of the Old Pretender in 1766, when Pope Clement XIII refused to recognise Prince Charles Edward (the 'Young Pretender') as the new legitimate king of England following his conversion to Anglicanism during his visit to London in 1750. This was the defining moment of disentanglement of the political from the religious aspects of English Catholicism, and dealt the final blow to the faded dream of a Catholic Stuart restoration. Only then could the possibility of a measure of official toleration start to gain ground. At the same time, by the second half of the eighteenth century there was a growing sense in the upper echelons of society that religious tolerance was the mark of civilised behaviour and gentility, although pockets of religious bigotry and hatred lingered on, mainly at the level of the labouring masses or uneducated provincial squire.[14] Sporadic anti-popery panics peppered the eighteenth century, usually caused less by genuine religious fervour than by an unformed but obstinately held belief echoed in the mob cry of 'No popery, no slavery, no wooden shoes'.

By a strange coincidence, the period of Woods's life-span of 1715/16 to 1793 neatly covers this last stage of persecution – albeit much reduced – suffered by English Catholics since the Reformation. By this period, providing that they did nothing to raise political suspicions or excite religious passions, Catholics were generally able to lead a quiet and normal life, although still suffering discrimination in respect of worship, education and official or military employment. This paradoxical position accounts for many of the apparent contradictions in the position of Catholics and their ability to act with freedom. It may also be relevant in the attempt to place Woods in context.

WOOD'S BIRTHPLACE

If the unlikely possibility that Woods was a convert sometime in later life is discounted, he was born a Catholic in 1715 or 1716, just around the time of the last major anti-papist scare. No record has been found of his baptism in any of the very sparse recusant registers that survive,[15] and it is only the information that he died aged seventy-seven, given in the *Laity's Directory* for 1793, that allows a supposed birth year of 1715/16. Considering the penalties suffered by a Catholic priest caught serving his flock, it is hardly surprising that records of Catholic baptisms for this period are so scanty. The same is true of marriages before Hardwicke's Marriage Act of 1753 made weddings unlawful unless conducted by an Anglican minister, and Woods was already married by 1751.

In principle it should be possible to trace a Catholic from one of the series of head-counts of papists periodically undertaken through the eighteenth century in the wake of every papist scare, real or imagined. However, even the very full list drawn up following the Jacobite rebellion of the Fifteen includes very few named humbly born, and only the Returns of Papists of 1705–6[16] contain enough detail, although this is not consistent throughout the country, to suggest a tentative birthplace and parentage for Woods. Out of the relatively few Catholic families recorded in England called Wood or Woods, the most likely candidate for Richard's father is one Richard Woods, miller, listed with his wife in Hatherop, Gloucestershire, among the seventeen papists in the diocese. Nothing more has come to light about this man, but it is interesting that Richard Woods (the landscaper) was employed at some time before 1778[17] by Sir John Webb, the leading Catholic of the Hatherop district,[18] to draw up a plan of improvements for his estate, and that Webb was one of the guardians of the 9th Baron Petre during his long minority between 1742 and 1760. Woods was employed by this Lord Petre as his surveyor at Thorndon Hall near Ingatestone (Essex) for the last ten years of his life, a position which the account books suggest was created for him.

Unfortunately these Returns of Papists have not survived for Norfolk, where a Richard Woods of Oxburgh, 'gardner', took an apprentice in 1741.[19] Oxburgh Hall was the seat of the Catholic Bedingfeld family, but this Woods was not necessarily a co-religionist. There is no Woods among the Catholics listed in the returns for 1767, although Richard would anyway have moved away by that date.

Another possibility is to see Woods born and brought up in or near Thorndon or Witham in Essex, within the sphere of the closely allied Petre and Southcote families. When Robert James, 8th Baron Petre, was born posthumously in 1713 with a full twenty-one years of minority ahead, his guardianship was given not only to Sir John Webb but also to Sir Edward Southcote, whose main residence was Witham Place, some twelve miles from Ingatestone, seat of the Petres. In spite of being seventeen years his junior, Robert James remained close to his guardian's son Philip, who was the owner of Wooburn Farm,[20] one of the most renowned *fermes ornées*, which he created from 1735 in Chertsey (Surrey). Both Petres and Southcotes were ardent Catholics. There is considerable stylistic evidence to connect Woods with Southcote and Wooburn Farm, as we shall see: the integration of husbandry with gardening finds an echo in Woods's designs to the very end of his career, just as his concentration on the use of flowers seems to follow Southcote's precedent. However, there is no evidence in the Returns of Papists for Witham or Ingatestone to suggest that Woods originated in the same county as Southcote or Petre, and the fact that Woods moved to Essex in 1768 and spent the rest of his life there may be no more than coincidence. Unless further information comes to light, Woods's place of origin and parentage remain speculative.

CATHOLIC EDUCATION

The degree to which Woods was educated, and in what subjects, is also open to conjecture. Second only to worship, the question of education was a major irritant under the penal laws, and was aggravated by the exaggerated claim of popish proselytising. The great Catholic families such as the Arundells and the Petres were able to send their sons openly to an English Catholic school like Old Hall Green Academy (Hertfordshire) or to employ a tutor who would give appropriate religious instruction, as alternatives to sending their children to be educated in one of the Catholic schools abroad.[21] For those below gentry status, as Woods obviously was, the options were more restricted. Grammar and village schools were available to those with modest funds, but were usually connected with Anglican clergy, and such Catholic village schools as existed were, by their clandestine nature, generally of short duration. It is probable that Woods received his early education from such a school, where he was given a grounding in literacy but not to a very polished standard. His grammar, syntax and spelling remained idiosyncratic to the end of his life, but on the other hand he must have been sufficiently well educated to have become a competent surveyor and adequate draughtsman.

The fact that during his career Woods produced at least three straight surveys with no indication of proposed improvements strongly suggests that he was trained primarily as a surveyor,[22] and came subsequently to improving, at the same time practising his other skills (possibly gardener, nurseryman, architect, even farmer) as required. The profession of surveyor was given great impetus in the eighteenth century by the general surge in prosperity and progress, which brought in its wake recently acquired estates to map, or additions and improvements to the lands of the older established families. Although the account books for Woods's first known commission in 1758 enter him as 'Mr Woods ye Gardiner or Surveyour', the description 'surveyor' cannot be taken at face value since it was the word commonly used for landscape improvers. Mathematics and associated technological skills such as surveying and cartography were being widely taught by the early eighteenth century, but it is possible that, after a reasonably sound early schooling,

Woods managed to acquire his technical knowledge through private study. Nicholas Hans cites a number of examples of self-taught professionals.[23] Among the books sold by Woods in 1783[24] were titles relevant to the gaining of skills of this sort: Stone's *Construction and Principal Uses of Mathematical Instruments*, a 1723 translation of a French work, is a good example of the kind of teaching manual available. It contained detailed information supplemented with clear engravings on every aspect of the branch of mathematics needed for surveying, plotting, gauging and measuring. Instructions were given for the construction and use of the theodolite, surveying-wheel, compass and other instruments, and the contents page even lists 'taking Plots, measuring or laying out Lands, taking Heights, Distances etc' as skills that could be learnt from the text. Technical books being published at this time were usually advertised as 'For the Use of Schools and private Gentlemen'.[25] Other volumes owned by Woods on the same or associated subjects (as described in the sale catalogue) included 'Stone's Mathematical Dictionary' (1726); 'Pardon's Practical Arithmetick' (1738); 'Ward's Mathematics'; 'Leybourn's Dialling' (1700); 'Leadbetter's Dialling' (1737) and 'Euclid's Elements'.[26] Whether this reading list was supplementary to formal teaching or an alternative to it, it indicates a determination in Woods to apply himself to the study of surveying, a subject that was crucial to his success as a landscape designer.

CATHOLIC WORSHIP

To study a Catholic during the penal times is to study the incidence and distribution of Catholic centres in England. For the obvious reasons of communal support and provision of facilities to worship, the Catholic communities were either in towns or clustered round one of the remaining great Catholic families. Throughout the bad or less bad times, aristocrats and gentry (for a number of whom Woods worked during his career) such as the Petres in Essex, the Arundells in Wiltshire, the Throckmortons in Warwickshire, the Southcotes and Westons in Surrey, the Molyneux and Blundells in Lancashire and others like them were able to provide their neighbouring co-religionists with regular worship, often employing a private chaplain for their own family and a priest for the local community. Mass might also be locally available through the services of a priest relying on a hiding place in the house of a co-religionist, or as a last resort through the occasional visit of the circuit priests who ministered to 'great numbers of the lower sort of men of two hundred & a hundred a year in severall parts of England'.[27] If Woods was not within reach of a family with a regular chaplain, he might have had to rely on the services of such an itinerant priest. The life of the mission priests was unenviable, even when under the protection of one of the great families, and Bishop Bonaventure Giffard complained of 'a persecution which obliges me to scamper about and seek hiding holes',[28] forcing him to flee his lodgings no less than fourteen times in a half year.[29]

For the priests serving urban centres the likelihood of a quiet life was even more remote. 'Mass houses' were usually to be found in back rooms and, as a report covering the period February and March 1767 shows,[30] there was a high probability of an informer sending round the officers: three mass houses were suppressed in those two months in Southwark, St Giles and Kent Street, and the officiating priest caught, tried for 'unlawfully exercising the functions of a popish priest' and condemned to life imprisonment.

Some of the richer and more devout not only kept their own chaplain but also provided a priest in an outlying estate; at her mission at Cheam in Surrey,[31] for example, the Dowager Lady [Catherine] Petre intermittently maintained a chaplaincy which had been started in the mid seventeenth century. With the arrival in Surrey of Philip Southcote and the establishment of the mission at Wooburn Farm after 1745, a new centre of worship was opened. The registers of Wooburn Lodge Chapel[32] show a Richard Wood standing sponsor at a Catholic baptism in 1755.

When Woods moved to London Stile in 1762 (see below, p. 27), the nearest centre of Catholicism was at the Earl of Shrewsbury's mansion between Brentford and Richmond. Although the family ceased to live in Isleworth soon after 1761, the priest's lodging and chapel were still maintained for some years in the house.[33] From the lodgings he took at about the same time near Leicester Fields, Woods had a greater choice of places to worship, and the chapel of the Portuguese Embassy in Golden Square might have been an obvious option in view of its association with Lady Petre's mission at Cheam.[34] Woods's move to North Ockendon in Essex in 1768 brought him within range of the well-established missions at Thorndon and Ingatestone, and it must be considered whether this was one of his reasons for choosing that part of the country. By this date, with the first Catholic Relief Bill only ten years away, toleration of the papists had advanced sufficiently for both Lord Petre and Lord Arundell to be able to include a Catholic chapel in their new building programmes, at Thorndon Hall and Wardour Castle respectively. Admittedly these chapels were an integral part of the mansion and not free-standing structures, but they were fitted up and used without any need for secrecy. The '1st Xstening in the new Chapel of New Thorndon' was performed in July 1770. Far more surprising is the appearance on the designs for the remodelling of Old Thorndon Hall in 1733 of a room openly designated a chapel.[35] On the other hand, the Welds of Lulworth, with whom King George III was on friendly visiting terms, asked him whether they could build a chapel instead of using their dining room for worship, and were told 'he felt he could only suggest a family mausoleum which could be fitted up as a chapel'.[36] The law was clear enough, but the extent to which it could be flouted with impunity was not.

The passing of the first Catholic Relief Bill in 1778 – the most momentous event for the English Catholic community since the Reformation – happened while Woods was living at North Ockendon Hall. In practical terms it did little more than give official recognition to practices which had quietly been gaining ground for decades, but for the first time in 200 years it was no longer a punishable offence for a Catholic priest to exercise and teach his religion, and Catholics were at last able to inherit or purchase property freely. Many indeed had already been doing so, but as late as 1772 the inheritance of a Catholic had been seized under the law by her Protestant kinsman.[37] He lost the case, but it was a reminder of how the law still stood, and prudent Catholics had for many generations bought and bequeathed their lands through Protestant friends or trustees, as Philip Southcote did in respect of Wooburn Farm. It is possible that this would account for the fact that Woods never owned freehold property.

The bill required Catholics to register at Quarter Sessions and take an oath of allegiance, the wording of which allowed them for the first time to demonstrate their loyalty to the Crown and thus emphasise the fact that they were no political threat. Lord Petre, who had worked tirelessly to persuade and cajole the king and government to accept this small measure of toleration for his faith, was anxious that he, his friends and family, and anyone over whom he had influence, should be among the earliest to register.[38] It is significant that Woods was among this first batch of twenty-six signatories in Essex, at the first available session of the court in Chelmsford on 14 July 1778,[39] suggesting that he was already in contact with Lord Petre in some way. Although Lord Petre continued to campaign for further toleration, for a man in Woods's position the issue of his faith probably became less pressing after this date. Even the Gordon Riots of 1780, although a disagreeable reminder that anti-papist hysteria could still be whipped up at street level, had little to do with the general attitude towards Catholics, and the fact that the riot soon degenerated into unfocused mob disorder enabled government troops to be used to re-establish order without loss of face. The second Catholic Relief Bill of 1791 was certainly an important step towards full emancipation, but many, including Woods, did not bother to register a second time.[40]

WOODS'S CATHOLIC PATRONS

It is possible that the fact that Woods was a Catholic influenced some of the Catholic patrons who employed him. Of his forty-seven[41] known commissions eight were for Catholic families, which does not sound a high proportion until it is considered that, out of Brown's 200-odd, he also worked for eight Catholics. On the other hand, the 9th Lord Petre (for whom Woods worked at the end of his life as the Thorndon surveyor) called on Brown rather than Woods for the major remodelling of his park in 1766, and a number of other Catholic landowners who could have employed Woods chose not to.[42] Except where he knew it would not cause offence, Woods is unlikely to have flaunted his religion, and it is even possible that some employers were not aware of his Catholicism. Moreover, it is significant that neither the Anglican Church Commissioners nor the Chancellors of Oxford and Cambridge Universities had the slightest hesitation in using the architect James Gibbs, a Catholic working in the troubled times following the Fifteen.[43]

There is also the question of how many land-owning Catholics there were at this date, and, of those, how many were in a financial position to embellish house or grounds. Joseph Berington stated that in 1780 there were 'but eight Peers, nineteen Baronets, and about a hundred and fifty Gentlemen of landed property' and also pointed out that 'the eldest sons of our gentry never think of trade, and the younger children have seldom a sufficient fortune on which to ground any prospect of success'.[44] Given these numbers, the employment of Woods by eight Catholic patrons seems a fairly high percentage. Catholics (as well as Jews) were denied public and political careers, simply because it was unacceptable to them to take the oath required of anyone in an official position. In being denied political office, they were at the same time denied the possibility of making a fortune, or even a living, in government employ, and had to rely on prudent management of their estates, a fortunate marriage or some sort of entrepreneurial activity if their status allowed it. Mineral extraction, for example, was seen as a socially acceptable way of augmenting the income from an estate. A Catholic landowner hoping to spend money on his house and grounds was more likely than his Protestant counterpart to have leisure to do so, but shorter funds. There were some exceptions: Lord Arundell was in a position to lavish a fortune on Wardour, his own ample funds augmented as a result of marrying an heiress, although bad estate management and a lavish lifestyle brought the family to the verge of financial disaster, from which it never entirely recovered. Lord Petre was fortunate in his mother, who ensured that his estate during his long minority was carefully managed, leaving him with a fine fortune to enjoy when he came of age.

The commission for which the Catholic aspect probably had most importance for Woods was Wardour Castle in Wiltshire: the devoutly Catholic 7th Lord Arundell had already employed Brown in the 1750s, and there was no reason for the 8th Baron not to have resumed contact where his father had left off. Joseph Spence (and it should be noted that he was an Anglican clergyman) gave the newly wed Arundells advice on their house and grounds in 1763 and referred to the plan (now missing) that Brown had made. Why did the Arundells turn to Woods? Perhaps they were not impressed by Brown's plan; perhaps they wanted to give a co-religionist an opportunity; or just possibly this is another tenuous link with Southcote through Spence, giving a helping hand to an ex-protegé. However, when the relationship with Woods was turning sour from 1771, Lord Arundell had no hesitation in bringing in Brown to replace him. All in all, it seems that being a Catholic made little or no difference when a potential employer was reviewing his options, except perhaps where all other considerations were equal.

CHAPTER 2

INFLUENCES

EARLY TRAINING AND PRACTICE

NOT EVEN THE GREATEST GENIUS in horticultural design and practice achieved prominence without training and experience. What was true for Brown was certainly true for Woods and all the other improvers of the eighteenth century, and it has also to be remembered that Brown and Woods, who were slightly older than the rest of the new generation of landscape practitioners, would have been absorbing knowledge and learning design techniques in the decade from 1735, when a large number of new gardens were still being made in a late geometric style. At this date the new design principles were being put into practice only at the most advanced and fashionable level by such as Pope and Kent, and although Brown may have gained his horticultural skills in the garden of Sir William Loraine, it was not until he arrived at Stowe in 1741 that he was fully exposed to the new attitude to landscaping.

The decade 1750–60 probably saw the period when Woods was establishing himself as a surveyor and improver. This most important phase of Woods's life, when he would have been laying the foundation of his entire later practice, is at present entirely open to conjecture. In whatever part of the country Woods was born, his first recorded appearance is in the court books for the manor of Chertsey Beomond (Surrey)[1] where, on 15 January 1750/51, Thomas Cussings (the clerk's misspelling of Cousins) surrendered to Richard Woods of Chertsey, gardener, a copyhold plot of thirty-five rods (about a quarter of an acre; one tenth of a hectare) in Gogmore Lane, Chertsey, at a rent of 4d and a fine certain of 4d. It has been argued that the description of Woods as 'gardener' is a strong indication that he was a nurseryman,[2] but it is also conceivable that he was (if only at this period) a gardener in the more literal sense, and, given the proximity of Wooburn Farm less than 2 miles (3km) away, it is quite feasible that he was working there under Philip Southcote. It may be significant that there is no entry for Woods in the Poor Rate assessment before his occupation of the Gogmore Lane house in spite of him being called 'of Chertsey' in the manor court book; a possible reason for this would be that he was being housed by Southcote while working for him.

THE *FERME ORNÉE*

As the regularity in garden design of the opening years of the eighteenth century began to give way – very slowly and very unevenly – to a greater naturalism and informality, there was a period in which a variety of landscape styles were acceptable. Designers and owners alike were to some extent learning as they went, playing with new ideas and reaching towards an appreciation of them. Until Brown's ascendancy was firmly established by the late 1750s there was no single undisputed way even for the higher levels of society to exhibit 'correct' taste in garden design. That this change in perception (if not in universal practice) was gaining ground, however, is neatly shown by comparing two editions of Philip Miller's renowned *Gardener's Dictionary*. In the first edition of 1731 he writes: 'In a fine Garden, the first Thing that should present itself to the Sight, is a Parterre.' This advice stands in the 1752 edition, but by the 8th edition in 1768 the passage reads: '… the first Thing that should present itself to the Sight should be an open Lawn of Grass which, in size, should be proportionable to the garden.' Similar amendments were made to all the sections dealing with design and layout.

All this quiet turmoil was taking place during Woods's early years as an adult, and even if concentrating primarily in those years on surveying he cannot have been unaware of it. At the same time, what might be described as a tributary to the main stream of new garden design was being developed by Southcote in his *ferme ornée* at Wooburn Farm. The idea of combining pleasure and use – *dulci et utile* – had been expounded in books and practised in gardens even before Joseph Addison adumbrated the *ferme ornée* in 1712 in *The Spectator*[3] or Stephen Switzer gave it the first expression in print in the 1742 edition of *Ichnographia rustica*.[4] The latter had already aired the idea in the first edition of *Ichnographia* of 1718, in which he took the satisfaction to be gained from admiring a well-ordered and productive estate a step further by claiming that agriculture and gardening were 'inextricably wove', and described 'mixing the useful and profitable Parts of Gard'ning with the pleasurable in the interior Parts of my Designs, and Padducks, obscure Enclosures etc. in the outward'. This early form of *ferme ornée* integrated agriculture and horticulture by placing the farming activities of cornfields and grazing in and among the decorated walks of a mainly formal layout. Switzer described the engraved plans in his second volume as being 'as easy and natural as possible, adorned with Corn-fields, and other Rural Plantations',[5] illustrating Riskins (Lord Bathurst's property in Buckinghamshire), where a number of 'Promiscuous Kitchen Quarters' were scattered among the regular compartments. This theme was developed by Lord Bolingbroke on his return in 1725 from political exile when he bought Dawley Manor (Middlesex) and promptly renamed it 'Dawley Farm'. Here he played the patriot–statesman–farmer and ostentatiously combined hayfields (where Pope described him reading a letter 'between two Haycocks') with still-extensive formal gardens, avenues and plantations.[6] Horace Walpole, writing decades later, commended Bridgeman for 'dar[ing] to introduce cultivated fields' into the royal garden at Richmond during his work there in the 1720s.[7] Batty Langley, in his *New Principles of Gardening* of 1728, also adopted some of Switzer's suggestions for inclusion within the 'serpentine Meanders' of the groves of 'small Inclosures of Corn, open Plains, or small Meadows, Hop-Gardens … Vineyards, Orchards, Nurseries, … Paddocks of Deer, Sheep, Cows &c with the rural Enrichments of Hay-stacks, Wood-Piles &c.', although the designs he illustrates are still firmly within a formal setting.

The idea of the ornamented farm was thus established during the first quarter of the eighteenth century, but the slightly later *ferme ornée* at Wooburn Farm was differently conceived, as was William Shenstone's at The Leasowes (Shropshire) and a handful of others. These later versions differed from what had gone before not least because they were in a naturalistic setting, which arguably suited the style much better: at Wooburn and the Leasowes farming activity was not scattered among garden compartments, but carried on centrally with the garden aspect flowing round and through it, taking in little incidents on the way, for instance the 'ruined chapel' at Wooburn, and Virgil's Grove at The Leasowes. The fact that the earlier and later groups of examples were so dissimilar might explain the claim of Joseph Spence, Southcote's friend and collector of his sayings, that 'Mr Southcote was the first that brought in the garden farm, or *ferme ornée*.' This Observation (no. 1125) is one of a number of comments which, taken together, constitute all that is known of Southcote's views and precepts.[8]

WOOBURN FARM

Philip Southcote[9] was a younger son and had to look to his own career. He enjoyed a colourful youth, soldiering in France and womanising everywhere, and eventually made a highly surprising but financially advantageous match with the Dowager Duchess of Cleveland, by then seventy years old to his thirty-six, and with the proceeds bought the land for Wooburn Farm at Chertsey in Surrey. After the death of the Dowager in 1745 Southcote married Bridget Andrew, who at his death in 1758 was left the estate for her lifetime with the reversion, in the absence of direct heirs, to the 9th Baron Petre. This legacy to the son of Robert James, the 8th Baron, Southcote's old friend and kinsman, reflects their close association during the creation of Wooburn Farm, documented by Spence in his Observations.

Wooburn Farm was created by Southcote between 1734 or 1735[10] and his death, and was thereafter maintained by Bridget until she died in 1783. When Lord Petre inherited Wooburn Farm many of the papers relative to the property – which would have included any evidence of Woods's presence there – were sent to Thorndon, and presumably perished in the disastrous fire of 1878, together with much of the Petre archive for the eighteenth century. There is very little surviving documentary evidence relating to the creation and maintenance of the *ferme ornée*, and even the earliest estate map is of 1834. Little of its design remains in the grounds of what is now St George's College, but fortunately its place on the tourist route resulted in a number of contemporary descriptions and illustrations, from which it is possible to deduce the concept behind Wooburn Farm and the aspects of its design that seem to find an echo in Woods's work.

Southcote's initial aim at Wooburn, as stated by Spence, was 'to have a garden on the middle high ground and a walk all round my farm, for convenience as well as pleasure: for from the garden I could see what was doing in the grounds, and by the walk could have a pleasing access to either of them where I might be wanted' (Observation no. 1127). This is a strong indication that Southcote was keeping an eye on the productive aspect of his property as well as enjoying the aesthetic. In spite of being well-connected he was not a wealthy man by eighteenth-century standards and, moreover, as a Catholic he was debarred by his faith from a number of career options. His

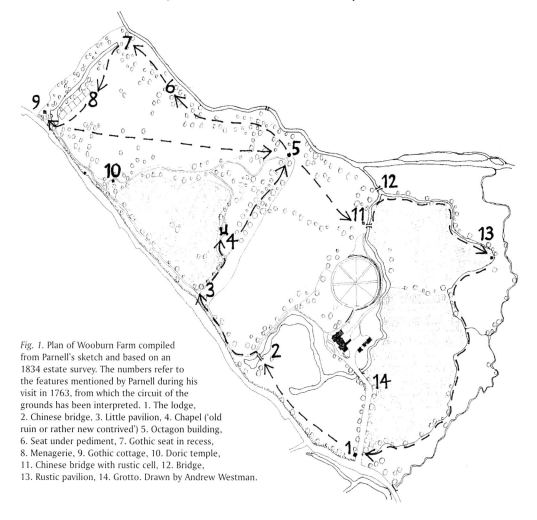

Fig. 1. Plan of Wooburn Farm compiled from Parnell's sketch and based on an 1834 estate survey. The numbers refer to the features mentioned by Parnell during his visit in 1763, from which the circuit of the grounds has been interpreted. 1. The lodge, 2. Chinese bridge, 3. Little pavilion, 4. Chapel ('old ruin or rather new contrived') 5. Octagon building, 6. Seat under pediment, 7. Gothic seat in recess, 8. Menagerie, 9. Gothic cottage, 10. Doric temple, 11. Chinese bridge with rustic cell, 12. Bridge, 13. Rustic pavilion, 14. Grotto. Drawn by Andrew Westman.

marriage had brought him the funds to purchase the land for Wooburn Farm, but this was a project that presumably had to make a serious contribution to its own upkeep. In the absence of accounts it is impossible to judge how successful he was as a farmer, but at least he was able to hand on the property to his second wife who continued living there until her death. This is in contrast to Shenstone, whose enthusiasm for poetry and indifference to agriculture led to the failure of The Leasowes as a viable venture. Southcote's 'convenient' layout was also a vehicle for his skill in planting, no doubt learned from his friend Robert James Petre, one of the foremost plantsmen of his day, and a place where he could indulge his talent for placing trees and flowers to the greatest possible effect, threaded through a flourishing mixed agricultural landscape.

Fig. 2. The only near-contemporary view of Wooburn Farm, a drawing from which Luke Sullivan's engraving of 1759 was made. Some of the 'pretty pavilions' seen by James Parnell can be indistinctly seen, including the rock arch with a bench on it, which is echoed in Woods's designs for Cusworth and Copford Hall.

The two fullest accounts of Wooburn Farm come from the travel notes of the Irish visitor (later Sir) John Parnell in 1763[11] and from the description by Thomas Whately in *Observations on Modern Gardening*, written in 1765 but not published until 1770. Whereas Shenstone at The Leasowes feared that planting flowers in Virgil's Grove might make it 'look too like a garden' and was uncertain whether he should preserve the flowers he was placing beside a small stream,[12] Southcote used flowers extensively – to border the paths, fill in the angles, cluster in 'spots and studs' and generally enliven the scene throughout. Both Parnell and Whately comment on the presence

of flowers and flowering shrubs, the walks 'enriched with woodbine, jessamine, and every odoriferous plant, whose tendrils will entwine with the thicket' (Whately); 'a fine meadow which is separated from you by low green pales within which are clumps of flowering shrubs, flowers &c' (Parnell); 'the shrubs and flowers which used to be deemed peculiar to [the parterre or the fields] have been liberally transferred to the other' (Whately); 'you pass through fine old forest trees scattered irregularly, and amidst them some plots of flowers' (Parnell). This insistence on flowers had been noted in 1757 by Richard Pococke, who wrote that the 'walks are adorn'd not only with plantations of wood but with spots and beds of flowering shrubs and other flowers to fill up angles, and other shrubs to diversifie the scene'.[13] Woods was pre-eminent among the improvers in his use of flowers within the designed landscape, possibly being influenced in this by Southcote, who is described as prevailing on Kent in the much-quoted phrase 'to resume flowers in the natural way of gardening, in a natural way' (Observation no. 1128). More particularly, an early – albeit short-lived – feature of Wooburn Farm was a 'rosary' which had been designed with Petre's help (Observations nos 1123 and 1134), and at a time before a special garden for roses was a common feature, Woods included one on at least three of his plans.

The most compelling evidence to link Woods with Southcote, Spence and Wooburn Farm lies with three tantalising documents in Spence's hand:[14] 'Mr Wood's design for New Cut from Canal, 1749'; a fence design 'from Mr Wood', 1749; and an 'Order of Planting after Mr Southcote's manner'. This last is virtually duplicated in a copy entitled 'Plantation fro' Mr. Wood' in a different hand, but endorsed by Spence. Parnell's account refers several times to the flower-adorned walks (as well as spots and clumps) round Wooburn Farm,[15] which probably relate in some degree to this plan. Mark Laird has described the views that these plans would have created:

> Thus visitors stepping along the five-foot [1.5m] wide 'Sand walk' would have enjoyed two types of view. On one side, looking beyond a 'Fence' (presumably the three-foot-[1m] high 'Fence from Mr Wood'), they would have cast an eye over expansive meadows full of livestock (such as the 'beautiful spotted cows' Sir John Parnell encountered at Wooburn in 1763). On the other side and close up, the visitor's gaze would have been drawn to a flower 'border' (two-an-a-half-feet [0.75m] wide). This was backed by a plantation of shrubs and trees (five feet [1.5m] wide), all set out against 'The Old Hedgerow'. The neatness of the border would have contrasted with the rusticity of the farm, for the border was edged with pinks and filled with garden flowers.[16]

This echoes vividly the impression created in the mind's eye of a plantation designed by Woods at Cusworth in one of his most successful commissions (see pp. 45–46 and gazetteer), where the path, edged with pinks and bordered by a railing, gave a view on one side over the grazed lawn and on the other to a plantation screening walled enclosures, with 'roses honeysuckles and jessamins towards the front'. Even though this was in a park rather than agricultural setting, the similarity is striking.

The only other obvious contender for the 'Mr Wood' of these plans is Thomas Wood, whose 'prettily ornamented farm' at Littleton on the north side of the Thames was admired by Parnell in 1763,[17] but if Spence had been on friendly terms with him, it is surprising that there is no letter to or from Thomas Wood among the copious Spence correspondence. A 'new cut from canal' also suggests surveying and engineering skills, far more likely to be

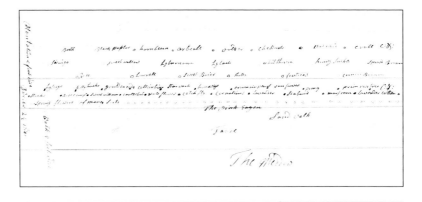

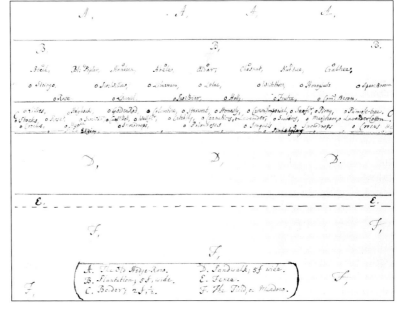

Fig. 3. Two planting plans among the Spence papers, probably linking Woods with Southcote and Wooburn Farm. (Top) 'Plantation fro' Mr Wood' 1749, which is almost replicated by (below) an 'Order of Planting after Mr Southcote's manner'. The collection also includes 'Mr Wood's design for New Cut from Canal, 1749' and a design for a fence.

found in Richard Woods than in the gentleman Thomas Wood. Perhaps Spence, on one of his visits to Southcote, had been given an idea by Woods for the enlargement of the little canal at his property at Byfleet, which he then drew up himself; alternatively, either of the two canals at Wooburn Farm, one by the menagerie, the other curving round the house (see Figures 1 and 2), might have been the subject of a 'new cut' which was not executed.

The issue is confused by the fact that at Littleton a long thin piece of water was made in front of the house – possibly by Richard Woods himself who was employed there in the late 1760s – with an 'appendix' at one extremity very similar to the 'new cut from canal'. It is possible that Richard Woods might have been responsible for both.

SOUTHCOTE'S PLANTING

Whately was impressed by the larger-scale planting at Wooburn: 'the clumps and groves, though separately small, are often massed by the perspective, and gathered into considerable groups, which are beautiful in their forms, their tints and their positions.' Southcote had indeed set out to achieve this effect: his views on the potential of perspective to be achieved in planting, and on the importance of foliage colour and variety, are reported by Spence in various Observations. Southcote's ability to create prospects has already been mentioned, and is confirmed by George Mason: 'Mr Southcote taught us to form other [vistas], through the branches of a single tree only; and shew'd us how the opening might be made natural and easy, and (as it were) perfectly accidental.'[18] This is related to one of Spence's Observations (no. 1130), in which he reported Southcote's view that 'perspective, prospect, distancing, and attracting, comprehend all that part of painting in gardening.' Spence goes on to explain Southcote's skill in teasing a view from a plantation: 'by perspective he meant looking *under* trees to some farther object (under-view); by prospect, looking *by* trees, but the line open at the top (clear-view).'

Arthur Young, in his *Six Months Tour through the North of England* (1769), commented on Shenstone's use of borrowed views to enlarge The Leasowes visually,[19] and Southcote also achieved this by bringing in a vista stretching to 'the Duke's new building on Shrub Hill on one hand, to Richmond Park on the other' (Observation no. 1085). Switzer had advocated opening up views into the country from the garden – part of his 'extensive gardening' – and indeed practised it where he was employed as a designer.[20] Southcote was praised by the Prussian visitor Friedrich von Erdsmansdorff for using a similar stratagem at Wooburn Farm with 'small irregular avenues affording views of the prettiest countryside in the world'.[21] Whately wrote that 'the brow of the hill commands two lovely prospects', and, even today, although hardly anything remains of the landscape of Wooburn Farm, the sudden vista from the site of the Octagon down a steep drop to the little River Bourne and extensive country beyond is almost breathtaking.

If this was the garden in which Woods formed his ideas of style and composition, one would expect to find examples in his work of Southcote's planting ideals. Woods's written legacy is almost all concerned with prosaic instructions to his foremen and with overcoming practical problems, but in at least one instance his awareness of the effects that could be achieved by colour grouping clumps of trees strongly suggests such an influence. This is at Cusworth in Yorkshire, the only commission for which a full set of working instructions survives, and here his precision over the species to be used, and their combined impact, indicates a considerable knowledge of a Southcote style of planting. The clumps at Cusworth are small, but were obviously arranged with a collective effect in mind, in exactly the spirit described above by Whately (see pp. 44ff).

By the 1760s it was so much a normal desideratum to call in views and take advantage of distant vistas that it was less remarked upon than earlier. However, at Wardour in Wiltshire, one of Woods's few commissions for which visitors' comments are recorded,[22] praise was forthcoming for the effect of his arrangement of groups of trees on the park side of the walk along the Great

Fig. 4. Woods's ambitious proposal for the improvement of Wormsley, 1779 or 1780. This plan covers aspects of a *ferme ornée* in the bottom left section, and includes an intriguing arrangement of circular gardens behind the house. See Figures 68 and 69 for a redrawing and detail.

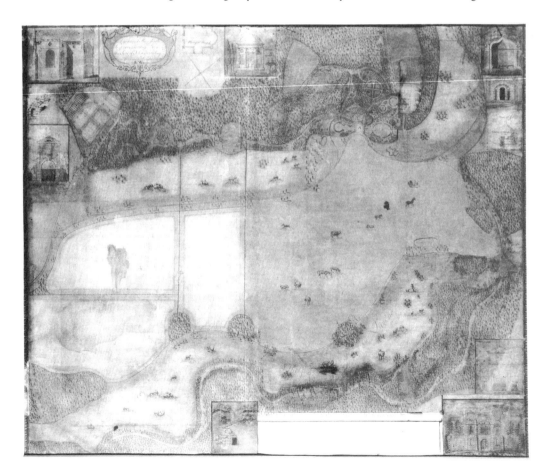

Terrace, so that the magnificent view west was alternately hidden and seen. Beyond these two executed examples, many instances can be found in his plans to show how fully he understood the effect of perspective and judicious placing of plantations. An excellent example is provided by his proposals for Wormsley, Buckinghamshire, where on rising ground south-west of the house he made a break in the woodland path to form a view from a wide curving vantage point across the open flat ground of pasture and arable towards two clumps, again on rising ground, like scenery wings leading the eye into a prospect of further pasture and plantation. Although not executed, this was a very skilful and carefully considered piece of perspective improvement to a naturally rather formless piece of landscape.

Various comments by Southcote in the Observations make it clear that he valued a hilly ground for a garden, or failing that, some movement in the landform provided it was not made in 'a vain endeavour toward helping it out' (no. 1080), and realised that 'even the least risings and falls in a bank make some variety of lights and shades' (no. 1145). Wherever there are surviving instructions in Woods's commissions for forming the ground it is obvious that he was very aware of the effect of some irregularity, insisting in several places on giving a piece of flat ground some undulation.

GARDEN BUILDINGS AT WOOBURN FARM

Parnell and Whately both mention the number and diversity of little buildings at Wooburn Farm and the skill with which they were incorporated into the design. This might explain Woods's fondness throughout his career for little buildings in his park designs, which contrasts with the other improvers, who were, in general, using such ornaments with more economy by the 1760s. At Wooburn Farm some seven structures, as well as a menagerie and bridge, were scattered through the design in the space of about 116 acres (47ha); one example is the grotto arch that still survives in the garden around St George's College. This is illustrated on the drawing by Luke Sullivan of c.1759 (see Figure 2), topped by a bench in just the same way as Woods suggested for Cusworth and Copford Hall (Figure 40 and Plate 6). Other buildings at Wooburn (see pp. 74–75) were also of a sort being used by Woods on plans as late as 1780. More generally, it is not so much that particular buildings in Wooburn appear to have been copied by Woods, but rather that his continued use of architectural features to close short views and provide interest on the line of the walk looks back to this style of garden layout.

WOODS'S USE OF THE *FERME ORNÉE*

Opinions differ over the demise of the concept of the *ferme ornée*, and the name itself by the end of the century was shifting in meaning towards 'model farm', as exemplified in John Plaw's *Ferme Ornée* of 1795. Given the suggested evidence for connecting Woods with Wooburn, it is striking that he – unlike Brown, Richmond, White, Emes or any other contemporary improvers – created a number of designs which appear to be firmly in the *ferme ornée* tradition, in a form that would have been understood by Southcote: a ribbon of garden, wide or narrow, through or encircling hedged fields, whether grazed or arable. For at least three commissions he used the form outright: Hatfield Peverel Priory (Essex) was a new house on a new site, and Woods's plan incorporates some of the presumably pre-existing arable fields into the design while arranging the grazing within sunk fences and throwing a walk round the whole property. There is no attempt to plant out the agricultural activity, which instead is brought into the designed landscape by the path following the eastern boundary, passing through two clumps of trees before it turns to join the park. The plan for Wormsley encompasses arable fields within the perimeter walk; the house and gardens look out over parkland (depicted by Woods as grazed by horses) sandwiched between arms of 'sheep lawn' and enclosing fields, at least one of them arable.[23] Brizes (Essex), even more surprising for the date of 1788 (see Plate 5), retains the pasture field boundaries with incidental ornamentation and, again, the perimeter walk. An immediately striking aspect of Woods's plan is that although the design immediately proclaims *ferme ornée*, all the field boundaries are disguised with sunk fences and quick hedges (remnants of which are still visible) so that from the house the view would have been more or less one of integrated parkland.

Fig. 5. Woods's plan for Hatfield Peverel Priory (after 1765) before the building of the new house a few years later. The old Priory looks west over the ornamental ponds, with arable fields retained within the designed landscape.

The fact that large portions of Brownian landscapes were farmed – a crop of hay followed by stock grazing, or permanent pasture – makes it very difficult to disentangle completely the strands of thought contributing to the idea of the *ferme ornée*, and even in 1786 William Mason could write that 'Beauty scorns to dwell/ Where Use is exil'd'.[24] Woods's proposal of 1764 for Old Alresford House (Hampshire) well illustrates the fine dividing line between *ferme ornée* and naturalistic park: in a small property of some 20 acres (8ha) he created what could be described as a *pré orné*, a single grazed field contained on three sides by a ha-ha, within which the ornamental walks and a bowling green or saloon were laid out. The enclosures for farm-like activities (rick-yard, cow-yard, poultry court, pigsty), as well as the usual offices, are tucked away behind walls and planting. This results in a very small but perfectly polite park, in which only the fact of the grazing being contained by an ornamented walk suggests a connection with the *ferme ornée*.

An apt pupil absorbs only so much from his teacher as corresponds with the development of his own ideas, and it would be a mistake to look for exact parallels between Woods's style and Wooburn Farm. However, there is

Fig. 6. The plan for Old Alresford Hall, 1764. The south boundary was kept open to take in a view over Alresford Pond, a large piece of water created in the Middle Ages. This property is undergoing an extensive restoration, and where necessary creation, of Woods's plan.

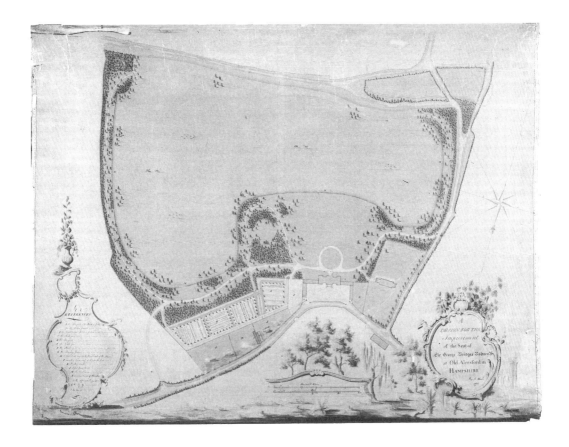

enough similarity between the two, both in Southcote's stated principles and in what was observed by others on the ground, to suggest more than coincidence. The relatively small estate of Wooburn Farm, full of variety in both planting and building, borrowing views into the surrounding countryside and incorporating well-managed farming, finds echoes in many of Woods's commissions and, whatever the perceived status of the *ferme ornée*, it is rare to find the style so prominently displayed by one of the improvers. Some of White's extensive plans include fields,[25] but more as an adjacent block of farmland than an integrated part of the designed landscape. Woods never lost sight of the advice expressed by Spence and followed by Southcote in the layout of Wooburn Farm regarding the need 'to study variety, as nothing without it can be pleasing'[26] – a vital component of the layouts of the 1740s and 50s, but later allowed to slip in favour of a greater naturalism. Whereas Brown may have 'set up on a few ideas of Kent and Mr Southcote'[27] he quickly developed his own style, while Woods largely stayed with the vision of paradise[28] created at Wooburn Farm.

CHAPTER 3

IMPROVER, FARMER, SURVEYOR

I N SPITE OF AN INTENSIVE SEARCH by the present author,[1] Woods's earliest recorded commission remains **Buckland House** in Oxfordshire, where he was employed by Sir Robert Throckmorton from 1758. Throckmorton – not surprisingly, given the restricted nature of Catholic society – had ties of marriage and friendship with most of the great families still professing the old faith, and references occur throughout the Buckland archive to Southcote. Unless more precise evidence comes to light, this seems the most likely reason that Woods was asked to landscape Sir Robert's new mansion.

Probably while work was continuing at Buckland, Woods was employed by Sir William Lee in 1759 at **Hartwell House** in Buckinghamshire, where he designed the greenhouse and pinery and devised a new flower/kitchen garden of a very unusual type, for which he supplied a long and varied list of plants. He probably also planned some if not all of the surrounding small park.

In 1760 Woods embarked on a series of Yorkshire commissions which went on until 1765, starting at **Cannon Hall** for John Spencer, who probably introduced him to a number of his friends and neighbours. Cannon Hall was a full-scale landscaping which in addition to considerable park planting and a new kitchen garden included making two flower gardens and building a pinery, bridges, cascades and the park wall.

From December 1761, while work at Cannon Hall was in full swing, Woods was employed by John Battie Wrightson for a major commission at **Cusworth Hall**, a short distance away. The subtlety and sophistication of this landscaping places it among Woods's greatest successes, while the memoranda he sent to the foreman in charge of the operation, revealing all the details of the creation of a landscape design, are unique in the documentation of this period.

Various other smaller Yorkshire commissions came Woods's way between 1760 and 1765: John Spencer records in his diaries a visit by Woods to Sir George Armytage at **Kirklees Hall** in 1760 and thereafter two other visits the following year. Possibly there were others not mentioned by Spencer. Daniel Lascelles, brother of Edwin (later Lord Harewood), employed Woods at **Goldsborough Hall** in 1763, but the work stagnated under an unsatisfactory foreman, and also probably owing to Woods's patent lack of interest in the commission. The single memorandum detailing the first phase of work contains illuminating information on Woods's planting practice, but the majority of his plan was unexecuted. Woods was also consulted by Daniel Lascelles's cousin Edward at **Stapleton Park**, possibly just to design and supervise new carriageways through the park, and by Edwin Lascelles at **Harewood House**, where he achieved a limited amount of work apparently near the new house in the pleasure grounds. Here too the commission ended on a sour note, with Woods obviously concentrating all his attention from 1764 on an exciting new commission at Wardour Castle in Wiltshire.

His involvement at **Bretton Hall** in 1764 for Sir Thomas Wentworth, recorded by Spencer, certainly included a bridge and possibly more extensive landscaping. A minor commission at **Haigh Hall** for Thomas Cotton is implied by the entry in Spencer's diaries that 'Mr Cotton gave Mr Woods orders to come to him on Monday', but Spencer provides no further information about what Woods did for his friend. He provided a plan in 1765 for Thomas Stapleton for the improvement of **Carlton Hall** (now Carlton Towers), but probably executed only a small portion of it, whereas an alternative plan submitted by White some fifteen years later was largely implemented. No documentation is available to show whether other visits mentioned in Spencer's diary – to 'Mr Farrer' at Barnborough Grange and to 'Mr Walker' at Puill Hill – resulted in any work.

In addition to the fifteen journeys to Yorkshire recorded in letters and accounts for those years, some of which kept him from home for several weeks, Woods also had work during this period in other, widely spaced, parts of the country. In 1761 he was in Buckinghamshire at **Little Linford Hall**, where he designed for Sir Matthew Knapp an attractive treatment of the 30 acres (12ha) of pleasure ground around the house, and in 1763–64 he was in Cambridgeshire at **Shudy Camps Park** for Marmaduke Dayrell, another of John Spencer's circle – all that is known of this commission comes from two letters Woods wrote to Spencer to inform him in the briefest terms about the agreed plans. In 1762 and 1763 Woods is recorded in Hertfordshire at **Newsells Park** for George Jennings, where the surviving evidence on site, and an estate map of 1788,[2] suggests a limited amount of work in the pleasure ground and possibly the kitchen garden. No documents survive to provide any further information.

Also in 1763 the first of Woods's Essex commissions started at **Boreham House** for Richard Hoare of the banking family. This continued until 1772 under Woods's foreman. In 1764 he was in Hampshire at **Old Alresford House** for Admiral Sir George Rodney, and in 1765 he was back in Essex at **Hatfield Peverel Priory** for John Wright, a coachmaker who had recently joined the ranks of the gentry.[3] Woods produced a plan for the improvement of **Wivenhoe Park** in 1765 for Isaac Martin Rebow, although the main work did not start for ten years. He even travelled as far as Northumberland that year, probably for Matthew White Ridley at **Heaton Hall**. This is the most northerly of Woods's known commissions.

SIDNEY'S ALLEY AND LONDON STILE

With his growing success, Woods must have felt that a more central address would be advantageous. The earliest record of this is on the first Cusworth memorandum of late 1761 or early 1762, where he signs himself 'Woods Surveyer at Chertsey in Surry, In Sidneys Alley Leicester Fields London', but there is no way of knowing whether he had a residence there before this date. The name of Woods does not appear in any of the tax and rate assessments for St Anne's Soho,[4] which suggests that his lodging was not large enough, or not on a lease sufficiently long, for him to be responsible for paying the levies. However, as he refers in a letter of 1770[5] to sitting down quietly to do some work after his return to London, it is probable that he kept his foothold in Sidney's Alley even after his move to Essex in 1768.

Sidney's Alley, on the site of what is now New Coventry Street, had been part of a gradual development of Leicester Fields from 1630. By the time of Woods's residence the square had been turfed and planted, with the smarter houses in Leicester Fields itself (Joshua Reynolds bought a property there for £1,650 in 1760), while those in Sidney's Alley were intended for shopkeepers and tradesmen.[6]

Within a year of taking a property there, Woods also moved from Chertsey to Chiswick, an area well within the centre of fashionable society, and not very far from Capability Brown's base at Hammersmith. Woods rented a property in London Stile, a small area round the junction of Turnham Green Lane (now Wellesley Road) with Brentford Road,[7] and appears in the rate books under Strand-on-the-Green from 1762, for a 'house and gardens' at a rateable value of £20, and an acre (0.4ha) of orchard at £7.[8] A student walking through that part of Middlesex in 1774 wrote of 'the gardeners' gardens with fruit trees all in full bloom, which make it like the seat of paradise',[9] and a glance at Rocque's map of ten miles around London of 1741–45 shows that the triangle of land contained by the river and Brentford Road was almost continuous garden of one sort or another.

This raises the question (which, again, cannot be answered decisively) of whether Woods had a nursery here. The rate books do not give any detail about land use, but it is known that at that date there were at least two nurserymen in the area.[10] James Scott (brother of Henry Scott, who had a nursery in Weybridge[11]) appears in the rate listing for Turnham Green for 1756 with a modest holding to which he gradually added, until by 1759/60 his house and various parcels of land amounted to a rateable value of £28. Henry Woodman, who had supplied trees to Joseph Spence, among many others, was in the same area as Woods until his death in 1758, after which his business was continued by his widow or son. The rateable value of his nursery was £32 in 1768. Both of these figures are comparable with Woods's rating of £27.

John Harvey argued very strongly in *Early Nurserymen* that because Woods sent a bill for the plants for the improvements at Hartwell in 1759–60, it proves that he grew them. It is also, however, possible that Woods was acting as a middleman and only arranged for them to be sent, perhaps from a nursery such as James Scott's which he certainly used later in his career.[12] The sparse correspondence for the Hartwell commission reveals that Lowe's nursery at Kingston Wick supplied the fruit trees,[13] if nothing else. If Woods grew the plants sent to Hartwell, he had in 1759 – that is, while still in Chertsey – a very considerable nursery, capable of producing over a hundred varieties of ornamental plus commoner trees in some quantity, and succession and fruiting pineapple plants.[14] It is possible that the acreage to supply such an order was not assessed for Poor Rate (the only tax books available for Chertsey at that date), but it is unlikely.[15] Perhaps more significant is that the plants for Buckland in 1758, comprising a very similar selection, had been supplied by Hewitt's Brompton nursery on Woods's orders,[16] and that Hartwell is the only known instance of Woods providing plants while living in Gogmore Lane. In short, it is debatable whether Woods owned a commercial nursery in Chertsey.

It seems far more likely that his residence in London Stile in Chiswick did comprise nursery ground, possibly managed during his prolonged absences by his wife Hannah in the same way that Widow Woodman ran her late husband's business. A sentence written in December 1768, shortly after Woods had moved from London Stile, is revealing: 'The magnolias was dissposed of before I rec'd your Lordship's letter, as I was oblig'd to remove them that very week … the time being expired that was agreed upon for my clearing the ground'.[17] In addition, one of the invoices for plants supplied for Wardour shows that the stock came partially from Egham, but also from London Stile.[18] This is the closest to firm evidence of Woods as a nurseryman that has come to light.

The only indication of any children of Richard and Hannah Woods also comes during his time in London Stile, when on 2 June 1765 a daughter Martha married James Ansell of Hammersmith.[19] Ansell was taken on by his father-in-law as an assistant within a year,[20] but no references to him in this capacity have been found later than 1774, after the Wardour commission had ended. It is possible that Ansell subsequently joined James Christie in establishing Christie's auction rooms, a possibility strengthened by the fact that 'Messrs Christie and Ansell' conducted the sale of Woods's household effects in 1783.[21]

It was during this period, when Woods was settled in Chiswick with a lodging in central London, and engaged on work all over the country, that he embarked on the major commission of his career, at **Wardour Castle** in Wiltshire for Lord Arundell. Woods obviously had high hopes of this employment, both in terms of the landscaping and of his own position, and it may have been the commencement of work at Wardour in 1764 that caused a cooling of his commitment to his Yorkshire patron, Daniel Lascelles. From January 1764, when he received his first payment for Wardour, to the last payment in November 1772, Woods was primarily, although by no means exclusively, concentrating on work for Lord Arundell. His status at this time is shown by his employment of Ansell as his assistant, the fact that he travelled with a servant, and by his obvious use of at least one professional draughtsman, if not a studio.

In 1768, when Woods started on the improvement of Arundell's other estate of **Irnham Hall** in Lincolnshire (part of Lady Arundell's dowry), nothing had been decided about the architect or design of Arundell's principal seat of Wardour Castle, and when the family went to stay there they were still living in a relatively modest house attached to the old castle walls. The refurbishment of Lady Arundell's family home at Irnham, involving little upheaval, delay or expense, must have seemed an attractive proposition as an alternative.

FARMER WOODS

In 1768 Woods was at the height of his career. He had some eighteen of his known commissions behind him or in hand, and was still handsomely employed at Wardour Castle, with the prospect opening before him of improving Irnham. But he was in his fifties and was quite often ill, and even in 1766 he had given an indication that he was looking for an alternative way of earning his living. In June that year he wrote to Lord Arundell (and it is noticeable that the letter was copied in a fair hand, presumably by his newly appointed assistant James Ansell, and is not in Woods's own spidery writing) hoping for the position of land steward, recently left vacant. He emphasised, 'I do not make this application for the want of Bread, as God be prais'd I'm in good Business', rather he acknowledged that he wished for 'a more retir'd Course of Life, and that with some worthy Nobleman, where I might insure myself, upon acting right, of being happy the remainder of my days, which have hitherto been attended with immense toil and incessant labours'.[22] Lord Arundell's reply to this request has not survived, but as there is no further reference to the subject it is clear that Woods's application was unsuccessful. It is perhaps surprising that he did not pursue similar employment with another great family but instead, two years later, made what seems a surprising move in taking the tenancy of a sizeable farm in south Essex.

In September 1768, Woods signed an agreement with Richard Benyon snr for a twenty-one-year lease at £230 per year on North Ockendon Hall, Essex,[23] where he had apparently been living by at least July in that year.[24] The North Ockendon estate had been acquired in 1767 by Richard Benyon, who reorganised the tenancies within it to provide four farms of differing sizes. North Ockendon Hall Farm, the holding taken by Woods, was 260 acres (105ha) of mainly arable land, and although it was only by a narrow margin the largest in the estate, it was obviously considered the most prestigious as the mansion house went with it.

The previous tenant at North Ockendon had died in November 1767, leaving some years of the original lease to run. The mansion and farm were not advertised in the *Chelmsford Chronicle* following that date, which suggests that Benyon was making enquiries among friends and acquaintances for a new tenant. A possible source of contact between Woods and him at this date was Christopher Griffith, for whom Woods had drawn a survey of his estate at **Padworth** in Berkshire in 1767, and who was a close friend and neighbour of Powlett Wrighte of **Englefield**, Benyon's step-son and eventual heir.

A farm of this size, on productive Essex soil, was a serious agricultural exercise, and would not have been undertaken by Woods without due consideration. A survey of North Ockendon Hall Farm taken c.1775[25] shows a typical medium-to-large Essex farm, of acreage quite sufficient to support a full-time farmer. This apparent change of direction for Woods raises a number of questions, not least whether he was intending to sub-let it, employ a bailiff to farm it for him, or farm it himself with the help of a farm manager, and indeed whether he had the qualifications to be a farmer. Woods at least thought himself capable: 'In regard to the nature of land, timber, Coppice wood, repairs, improvements and farms etc I hope I may be allow'd to understand as well as most men from my close application and long experience'.[26] Although this is the language of a surveyor rather than a farmer, it is clear that Woods was fully aware of the practical aspect of farming life, even if he is only referring to knowledge acquired on the sidelines of a career in surveying and designing 'new work'. It has been pointed out that 'the chief concern of Essex landlords was to secure a body of tenants, possessed of both considerable capital and farming skill',[27] and Benyon was unlikely to have accepted Woods as the most important tenant on the estate unless he was satisfied with his credentials, and unless he was convinced that Woods intended at least to supervise the farming closely, as an absentee farmer working through a bailiff was thought detrimental to good management. The inclusion of 'John Woods of North Ockendon' in the subscription list for Hutchins's *History and Antiquities of Dorset* of 1774 raises the possibility that Woods also had a son, who might have acted as a bailiff. This hypothesis adds credibility to the farming venture, but no further information on John has come to light, and the name may have been the result of a clerk confusing Richard with the better-known John Wood the architect.

Other pieces of evidence point to Woods's personal involvement in the farming of North Ockendon Hall. The terms of his tenancy precluded him from sub-letting the mansion house, and whereas the 'small house' on the farm might have been adequate for a farm manager, it would almost certainly not have been for a sub-tenant of such a sizeable farm. Another reason to suppose that Woods was farming himself lies in the 'Composition for the tythes of the Parish of North Ockendon' for 1775, which shows Woods paying £44 7s 0d (the highest in the parish).[28] Although not impossible, it would be unlikely that Woods would be paying on behalf of a sub-tenant. Of even greater significance is a letter of October 1769, in which Woods refers to taking home ewes he had bought in Dorset when there on business,[29] and in April 1770 he referred to being at home until 'I get my spring harry over'.[30] Another letter of December 1777 shows that Woods was in personal touch with 'the merchant, who bought my pease', as he gives his correspondent detailed instructions on how to find the right wharf and what to expect from the transaction.[31] A memorandum of about 1768 to Lord Arundell gives precise instructions and quantities for making a 'proper mixture or dressing for his meadow' and 'an other composition of manuer proper for soure course soyls', information which falls into the province of the farmer rather than the landscape designer.[32]

However, correspondence and other clearly dated material relating to Woods's commissions between 1768 and 1783 show that he was away from North Ockendon in different years and at various times during the critical farming months of May to July, and the possibility must be considered that the prime mover in the farming venture was Hannah (or John if he existed) rather than Richard. It is also significant that Woods apparently did not give up his lodgings in London until at least 1770.

THE LIFE OF A TENANT FARMER

Surprisingly, in view of his flourishing practice, it appears that Woods was hoping that he could make a sufficient living from the farm to enable him to ease gradually out of 'improving', or at least to regard the farm as his retirement employment. Writing to Lord Arundell in September 1771, he pointed out, 'I am … content to get a genteel subsistence for my self and family, & while I can do that, will follow business, but no longer; but will retire to my farm, & garden, & drawings, at home'.[33] Woods obviously had in mind a quietly comfortable and gentlemanly existence for his twilight years.

The assumption of making a modest living from the farm was not over-optimistic at the time, and Woods might reasonably have expected to achieve a profit in the region of £200 a year. He would have had to bring capital of about £1000 with him to pay for the first year of residence before a harvest; to purchase implements, livestock and seed; and to fund agricultural improvements. The Chertsey property, which had been mortgaged for £160 and sub-let since 1763, possibly to fund the move to London Stile, was not finally sold until October 1770, but the surrender of the London Stile property in 1768 must have released some capital, with the remainder raised through borrowing, inheritance or savings. Woods's reference in 1780 to his creditors suggests that he had been lent the money, which was a very common way of funding the acquisition of a tenanted farm.

In addition to providing for his retirement, Woods may well have seen the farm as a way up the social ladder. At a time when the difference between 'Mr' and 'Esq.' was clearly defined (although not static), Woods firmly belonged in the former category and is unlikely to have expected contact with Benyon except through his steward. Nevertheless, the position of nearly-gentleman tenant farmer on the most prestigious farm in the parish would have commanded a certain position in the locality, especially at a period when the more successful farmers were coming to be seen as a 'lesser gentry'.[34] Mordaunt viewed farming in this light in 1761, and foresaw that 'farmers will vie with their landlords'.[35] The position of Woods as the superior tenant in North Ockendon is illustrated in the subscription list of the 'Barstable and Chafford Association against the Depredations of Divers Loose and Disorderly Persons', set up by Benyon in 1779.[36] This gathering of 'the Gentlemen and Farmers' of the district for 'the preservation of their property' had seventy-four subscribers altogether, numbering two barons, a sprinkling of esquires and reverends, and a majority of plain farming misters. Woods was the only North Ockendon tenant included in the list.[37]

During their tenancy, Hannah and Richard Woods filled the house with furniture and fittings of some elegance, as evidenced by the catalogue of the sale in 1783 following Hannah's death:[38] there are no fewer than eleven bedsteads, some with cotton hangings but most with different sorts of fine woollen cloth, a mahogany dining table with 'ten handsome chairs', a considerable number of assorted pieces of furniture, Wilton and other carpets, prints and pictures, some 'elegant blue and white china' including twenty-four plates, and eighteen wine glasses. The sale lasted two days. The quantity and perhaps quality of the household contents suggest either an inheritance, or that Hannah Woods had been deliberately acquiring the trappings of gentility. To take the supposition a step further, it may have been the desire of his wife to cut some sort of a figure in country society that, added to his weariness with the discomfort of life as a self-employed surveyor, induced Woods to embark on the North Ockendon venture. Certainly, the speed with which he sold up and moved following her death suggests that he was only staying on there, when he could no longer really afford to do so, for some reason connected with her.

FARMER OR MARKET GARDENER?

The sale of Woods's effects when he left North Ockendon included several items of farm machinery. Most were what would be expected on any farm but a few of the implements suggest a modern, progressive attitude. 'A double-breasted plough compleat' was a fairly recent phenomenon, which had been proved at a local demonstration to give far superior results over the ordinary plough.[39] The 'spike roller', which was described in the sale catalogue 'as of singular utility in breaking the large clods of earth in a dry season', had been discussed and illustrated in 1771 by Arthur Young who thoroughly recommended it as a most desirable innovation,[40] and it is noticeable that even in 1783 its purpose had to be described. A 'tilted cart on steel springs, very useful in rough cross roads' was another unusually sophisticated item to find in the farm shed. Woods's library included Gent's *Epitome of the art of husbandry*[41] and Nourse's *Improvements of Husbandry*,[42] suggesting an interest in the theory of farming to supplement his knowledge gained as a surveyor.

A significant change in the arrangement of the farm was made after 1769. Park Field (8 acres [3.25ha]) had grown its share of crops in rotation until the first year of Woods's tenancy, when the word 'garden' was pencilled in beside it. Thereafter, it is described as 'nursery', a change of use suggesting the raising of plants (although there is no indication of this in any of the documentation of his later commissions) or a market garden of some sort. Woods's kitchen garden equipment in the sale catalogue suggests a more intensive production than required by a single family, and includes 'A well constructed hot house for forcing early fruits, 42 feet [12.8m] long, 8 feet [2.5m] wide and 9 feet [2.8m] high, with iron doors and grates'; 'a range of 68 feet [21m] of framing and glass for a peach wall'; 'a frame and ten large lights for a Dutch melon pit, 42 feet [12.8m] long'; and a *chaise marée* (probably a clerk's error for *chaise marine*) which was described as being 'calculated for the safe and easy conveyance of choice and tender fruits'. This produce could have been transported to Romford, 6 miles (9.5km) away, or might even have been destined for London at a distance of 16 miles (25km), although this seems less likely. The probability that Woods was involved in fruit production is strengthened by a chance remark in a letter of 1780 to a current client: 'After the weather braks and the are softer [*sic*] I will send you the Colmar pears &c'.[43] Woods the market gardener as well as Woods the farmer.

LATER COMMISSIONS

During the 1770s Woods had work at seven Essex estates, and was beginning to be seen as the local man. The Chinese Temple at **Alresford** was nearing completion in 1772; at **Hare Hall** in Romford he designed a strip of pleasure ground round two sides of a 70-acre (28ha) park as the setting for a new villa by James Paine; Lord Waltham employed him at **New Hall** in Boreham to make a small piece of water behind the house, and a new garden with greenhouse; Lord Dacre, who had employed Brown intermittently for years at **Belhus** in Aveley, nevertheless used Woods to give the final form to the Long Pond there; he was at **Great Myles's** in Kelvedon to widen part of the little river in front of the house and design a bridge for it; and at Wivenhoe near Colchester the landscaping he had suggested in 1765 was finally put into execution from 1776. Correspondence with Colonel Rebow of Wivenhoe suggests that Woods was engaged at **Mark's Hall** during this period, and there is an entry for an ice-house design for **Gidea Hall**, the property of his landlord Richard Benyon.

Woods was also travelling considerable distances to other estates: in

1768 to **Diddington Hall** in Huntingdonshire, although there is no information about his work there; from 1768 to 1772 to **Wavendon House** in Buckinghamshire, where he designed the piece of water; in 1769 and 1770 to **Nuthall Temple** in Nottinghamshire, for probably minor alterations to Thomas Wright's garden layout; from 1769 to 1771 to **Lulworth Castle** in Dorset for unspecified work in the park including an ice house and probably a kitchen garden; until 1770 to **Littleton House** in Surrey for improvements to the pleasure grounds; and in 1770 to **Chillington Hall** in Staffordshire, probably to provide designs for a garden building. There is reference to a plan he produced sometime before 1778 for the joint estates of **Hatherop and Williamstrip** in Gloucestershire, although there is no evidence that this was executed. His creation of a garden around **Wyndham House** in Salisbury probably dates from this period, although it is usually assigned to c.1780. Until late 1771 he was still employed by Lord Arundell at Irnham Hall in Lincolnshire for both building alterations and pleasure-ground design, and at Wardour in Wiltshire. A promising commission in December 1770 at **Wynnstay** in north Wales lasted only a short time and achieved little, but he was more successful at **Brocket Hall** in Hertfordshire for Lord Melbourne, reshaping the river and creating a pleasure garden and probably a kitchen garden.

It is clear that from the late 1770s his practice was slowing down. He provided ambitious plans for **Hengrave Hall** in Suffolk in 1777 and for **Wormsley Park** in Oxfordshire in 1779, but neither resulted in large-scale work, and after the mid decade the only important improvements being undertaken under his supervision were at Wivenhoe. A design he produced in 1780 for the Elysium Garden at **Audley End** in Saffron Walden did not result in any further employment.

FINANCIAL DIFFICULTIES

If Woods had moved into North Ockendon Hall with high hopes in 1768, there are signs that as early as three years later he was coming to the realisation that he could not successfully combine two careers. A letter to Lord Arundell of September 1771 suggests the considerable weariness of a man 'for ever upon the tatter, allways from home neglecting his domestic affairs and wareing his life out by fateagues'.[44] In spite of a reasonable flow, if not torrent, of work, by February 1780 Woods's financial situation was obviously causing him concern, and he wrote to Colonel Rebow, for whom he was working at the time, 'I have had [an] … allarme wch I cannot get the better of, unless I could have the good fortune of getting in some cash … If it could be convenient to send me a draf for 40 or 35£ … it wou'd releve my present distress.' He also pointed out that he could no longer afford to hire a post chaise, but had to travel on the common coach. There is no hint about the cause of the 'allarme', but it appears that he had fallen into debt, and he wrote again to Rebow in December on a more peremptory note: 'The Time is now nigh, for settling with my Creditors and am therefore oblig'd to address myself to all my worthy Employers, to enable me, to keep up my payments'.[45]

It is possible that the cause of Woods's particular financial distress in 1780 was connected with the second year of very low wheat prices,[46] which for a man who had probably borrowed money to set up farming, and who was always paid considerably in arrears by his clients, might well have caused him – in modern parlance – a cash-flow problem.

THE LAST LAP

The change in Woods's way of life following Hannah's death in February 1783 was swift and dramatic. In September the contents of North Ockendon Hall were auctioned by Christie's. They included (in addition to the furniture) a collection of books which gives a precious insight into Woods's choice of reading, although he kept back 'many valuable books, on several subjects', which were sold after his death in 1793.[47] His stock was presumably sold separately or possibly to the incoming tenant. By early November he was established as surveyor at a salary of £100 a year to Robert Edward, 9th Lord Petre, for his main estate at Thorndon Hall in Essex,[48] a position he may have been given as a member of the local Catholic community, probably even worshipping at the Thorndon mission.

Some time between September and November he moved to Ingrave, a village on the boundary of Thorndon park and conveniently situated for his new employment. There on 22 November he married Mary Gorst, spinster, with both of them being described as 'of this parish'. Unfortunately there is a long gap in the manorial records of Ingrave, as no court was held for twenty-one years from 1770, and in the welter of catching up during the proceedings of 1791 no clear dates are given for intervening events.[49] Richard Woods is recorded as having purchased of John Stacey Esq. 'a Messuage or Tenement called Maxes' which had been divided into two but 'lately rebuilt and converted into one Messuage', with the evidence of the Land Tax suggesting that this was not until 1786.[50] The manorial records continue to call the house Maxes, but Woods renamed it New Cottage, and addressed all his correspondence from there until his death. Whereas North Ockendon Hall was taxed (on a rate of 4s in the £) at £15,[51] Maxes cost Woods only 8s, rising to 12s after he enclosed a piece of waste in front of the house. It seems clear that after a period of being seriously overstretched financially, Woods had recovered his position with a new, far smaller house, a new wife, and a new situation which was probably entirely congenial to him.

WOODS AT THORNDON

It is clear from a tetchy letter written by Woods to Lord Petre's steward in 1784 that part of his duties at **Thorndon** lay in checking and measuring building work, and he did not deny himself the pleasure of being censorious about the render on the new lodge at Thorndon: 'I never had to do with any of that kind of Stuco before, or ever will again if I can avoid it, for it is sad pick-pocket business indeed'.[52] However, the main purpose of his retained position was apparently to design and supervise some minor amendments to the landscape designed by Brown some twenty years earlier. Although Woods's name is not mentioned in the accounts, his foreman Joseph Golding was in charge of the 'groundworks' and no other improver is named.

FINAL COMMISSIONS

In addition to his duties as surveyor, Woods was allowed to take on outside work, and in the ten years before his death he undertook two full-scale commissions. He had no studio at his disposal by this time, and must have worked from the 'large writing desk, completely fitted up' which was sold with the rest of his effects by his widow.[53] The plans for improvement for **Copford Hall** near Colchester of 1784 and for **Brizes** at Kelvedon Hatch of 1788 (both in Essex), are executed in a charmingly naïve and less polished style than his earlier maps, which are more precisely detailed and were presumably drawn by an employee.

At the time of Woods's death in May 1793 he was working on an extension at **Stanway** to the Copford estate, and his widow Mary was obliged to wrangle over his outstanding bill. As his executrix, she was given the administration of his modest estate of less than £300,[54] and the notice she inserted in the *Chelmsford Chronicle* a few days after his death announced 'The House to be Let, and the Furniture disposed of by Private Treaty', although she was still paying Land Tax on Maxes until 1803. Her death in 1814 was noted the following year in the Ingrave manor court book.

PART 2

WOODS
THE DESIGNER

CHAPTER 4

PLANTS, PLANTING SCHEMES AND PLANT SUPPLIES[1]

UNLESS MAJOR EARTH MOVING WAS BEING CONTEMPLATED in an improvement – either the re-forming of contours or the excavation of a large piece of water – the main impact, and sometimes the main expense, of a new landscape design would be provided by planting.[2] The improvers were frequently judged more by their skill in setting out plantations than by any other single criterion, and it was a considerable compliment to Woods that a visitor to Wardour in 1801, Richard Warner, wrote that between the old castle and the house 'the ground is broken by plantations, suggested by Mr Wood of Essex, the judiciousness of which Brown himself had the taste to admire and fortitude to applaud'.[3] The pre-eminence of the easy but artful arrangement of trees emerged as formal layouts declined and naturalism advanced. A geometric design used trees as bold statements, with solid woodland through which rides or vistas were cut, stupendous avenues constructed as far as the ownership of land would allow, and 'cabinets' or 'rooms' cut out of blocks of planting. As the naturalistic landscape gained favour, trees came to be used in a subtly different way, as apparently uncontrived screens, clumps, waves of planting, to inform the space in which they were placed. Plantations were needed to entice the eye to a particular feature – where an avenue had marshalled it – to hide unwanted objects, to form a backdrop, to frame a vista, to demarcate a boundary without seeming to do so, in short to become architectonic components in the view. This change in attitude towards the role of trees in a landscape was unfolding as Woods grew up.

Hardly surprisingly, species used *en masse* as architectural aids were the easily available and inexpensive forest trees, while the new and exotic varieties were more likely to be disposed as ornamental focal points or part of a tree collection. Joseph Spence, walking round the Duke of Argyll's famous garden of Whitton (Middlesex) in 1760, some twenty-five years after its creation and little altered since, noted specimen trees of American introductions planted at the centre of 'rooms' in the grove-work, while the majority of the plant rarities were kept in 'an enclosure for the more curious trees'.[4] Only planters on the 8th Lord Petre's scale, with an estate of 1000 acres and in possession of thousands of American trees, could afford to use exotic new species as massed effects.[5] This was certainly still true in the 1750s, when Woods may be presumed to have started in serious practice, and recent introductions were still displayed as single specimens in the shrubbery.

However, by 1760 planting practice indicates that a number of the earlier introductions were freely and relatively cheaply available, and many former novelties were sufficiently affordable to be absorbed into the more visible parts of grove-work and mass planting in the pleasure ground. It is difficult to be precise on this subject, as the earliest priced nursery list was Telford's in 1775, and lists of plants supplied by or for the improvers seldom specified size. On Woods's priced list for Hartwell of 1759, the difference in cost seems to reflect relative ease of propagation rather than date of introduction; for instance, 'Agnus castus' was priced at 2s and 'Arbor judae' at 1s (both sixteenth-century introductions), while persimmons (1629) were 1s 6d and Diervilla (1720) was 6d. At the expensive end of Woods's list was the Weymouth pine (1705) at 5s (but size unspecified) and the Balm of Gilead fir (1697) at 4s. The main point is that at Hartwell introductions as recent as 1740 (e.g. *Thuja orientalis*) were considered to be within the price range of a mixed pleasure-ground planting, but there is no sign of very new material like *Ailanthus altissima* (1751) or *Euonymus atropurpureus* (1756). The progress of trees from rarity to general distribution can be charted through the various gardening manuals: for instance, in the first edition of Philip Miller's *Gardener's Dictionary*, of 1731, 'Lord Weymouth's Pine' was to be found in a few noble gardens, but the 1768 edition notes that 'there are a much greater number of these trees now in England'; and in Richard Weston's *Gardener's and Planter's Calendar* of 1773 Weymouth pines are classed among the ordinary timber trees, alongside oak and Scotch firs, at £10 per hundred for 4ft (1.2m) plants.

THE 'PLEASURE PARK'

During Woods's working life, it was the accepted norm that despite the disguise of a ha-ha there should be a clear division between park and pleasure ground, both physically and stylistically. Nevertheless this was occasionally questioned by authors on gardening style, even if there is little evidence on the ground that the distinction was ignored.

At a time when fashions and attitudes in garden design were in a state of flux, flexibility seems to have existed over what was meant by what – as indeed it still does. Whately, composing his *Observations on Modern Gardening* in 1765, was uneasy about too precise a division between park and garden, considering that 'the affinity of the two subjects is so close, that it would be difficult to draw the exact line of separation between them: gardens have lately encroached very much both in extent and in style on the character of a park.' He felt that there usually were, or should be, differences in treatment between the two, 'but whatever distinctions the extent may occasion between a park and a garden, a state of highly cultivated nature is consistent with each of their characters; and may in both be of the same kind, though in different degrees.'

Thomas Mawe and John Abercrombie took the idea further in *The Universal Gardener and Botanist* (1778), suggesting that 'Pleasure-ground may be said to comprehend all ornamental compartments, or divisions of ground and plantation … consisting of lawns, plantations of trees and shrubs, flower compartments … &c whether situated wholly within the space generally considered as the Pleasure-garden, or extended over ha-ha's to the adjacent fields, parks … or other out-grounds.' Samuel Fullmer, in *The Young Gardener's Best Companion* (1781), also felt that the pleasure ground could include 'not only the space within the limits of the garden, but all the ornamental plantations extend[ing] to any adjacent out-grounds, parks, paddocks etc.' and reinforced this by advising 'always to plant some large hardy perennials in the shrubbery compartments on the boundaries of the main lawns and principal walks, as also in the running shrubberies extending round paddocks, parks etc.' – the ornamented hedgerows that had been a feature of Southcote's Wooburn Farm had metamorphosed, not disappeared.

The division between parts of the grounds in Woods's work is often imprecise, a trait particularly noticeable in his relatively small-scale layouts, where this merging of parts might be described as a 'pleasure park' rather than a designed landscape divided into pleasure ground and park. Cusworth, for example, is difficult to divide into neatly named areas. Although 'the park' is referred to – as indeed was usual even where a modest area was being landscaped – the different parts of the grounds mingle to such an extent that the whole 100-acre (40ha) layout can be seen as pleasure ground or rather pleasure park in the manner referred to above, in which the hanging lawn bordered by plantations and walks descends to the 'great river' and then blends imperceptibly with meadows beyond, also bordered by plantations and walks. The ha-ha for which instructions were given was to keep stock off an ornamental hill plantation, not to divide pleasure ground from park.

Before concluding that Woods was unskilled in park planting on a larger scale, we should remember the favourable comment by Richard Warner (quoted at the beginning of this chapter) on his work in the 800-acre (325ha) Wardour park, even referring to a compliment by Brown. But it remains true that of the forty-seven estates with which Woods is known to have been associated in one way or another, only six were of a size to have even the potential for planting on a truly Brownian scale.[6] In the great majority Woods's activity was limited to an area of around 100 acres (40ha) or less, sometimes representing small sections of a larger park, and frequently with an obvious and emphasised pleasure ground or pleasure garden.

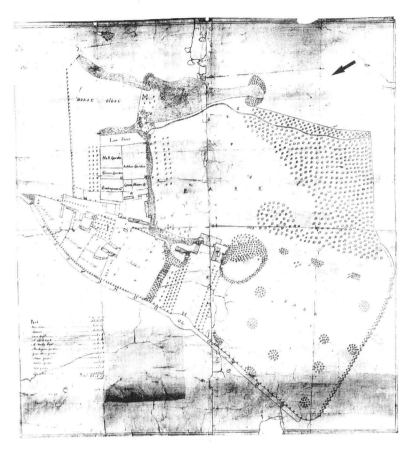

Fig. 7. A survey of Cusworth, probably mid 1760s, showing most of Woods's improvements but omitting the third piece of water. The flower garden is one of the rectangular enclosures on the left, and not part of a pleasure-ground circuit.

Some commissions were even more restricted. At Goldsborough it is noticeable that Woods's plan covered only about 17 acres (7ha) round the house, making it essentially a pleasure-ground design in the more restricted sense, whereas White who followed him there produced a plan for roughly 80 acres (32ha) which included large-scale clumps and plantations. Woods's design for Audley End was specifically for a pleasure garden, while he produced one plan for a town garden, around Wyndham House (now Bourne Hill) in Salisbury.

WOODS'S PARK PLANTING SCHEMES

The shape and disposition of Woods's park plantations, where relevant, can be seen wherever a plan for improvements or a near-contemporary estate map survives, but the documentary evidence for the species he used is scarcer. Only at Cannon Hall, Wardour and Irnham is there information about his planting beyond the ha-ha or in the wider landscape, and for all these it is noticeable that he made lavish use of firs, pines and other conifers. The planting instructions make it clear that for the most part he was not intending them as nurse trees but as decorative species in their own right. The evidence for planting at Cannon Hall comes from the laconic diaries kept by Woods's employer John Spencer.[7] The most relevant entries are for March and April 1762: in these two months he recorded the planting of 'Spruce Firrs [*Picea abies*][8] in the Park' and a plantation by the newly finished park walls of 'alternately oaks, elms, beech, firs, chestnuts, oaks, firs, beech' with more beech and sycamore elsewhere in the park, and four small fir plantations, while four Weymouth pines (still classed here as relatively exotic) were put 'upon the slope in the Pleasure Ground'. This bald statement of the species gives no idea of the way in which they were arranged, but the first edition 25-inch Ordnance Survey map of 1890 shows the mixed planting along the park wall and various conifer clumps. The overall effect can be judged from the panoramic view of Cannon Hall painted before 1794 (Plate 2).

Although no plan was made for Lord Arundell's secondary seat at Irnham, Woods referred in a letter of 1770 to not having enough 'scotch and spruce firrs, for six of those clumps in the park, wch. was designed for those sorts'.[9] However, he was obviously open to the idea of filling the clumps with trees available from the Irnham nursery, rather than buying the necessary 450 evergreens of his own preference: 'In case you wou'd not chuse to plant any more firrs, I have given directions to fill up the clumps with such plants as you have enough of in your nursery, viz. young oaks of last year's sowing, & some Spanish chestnuts, & you have some elm & beech, plain, and Burch layers, enough to plant two clumps, & then four clumps with the young oaks & chestnuts.' It is interesting that as an economy measure trees as small as year-old oak seedlings were contemplated within the clumps. The park at Irnham was also planted with specimen cedars of Lebanon, although Woods suggested that, as only eight were available, it would be best for Arundell himself to tell the foreman where he wanted them.

Among the various estimates and correspondence for Wardour, only for the clumps bordering the new south approach is there a planting specification: each clump, previously raised into a little mound with the spoil from digging out the road, was to be planted with '4 large Scotch or spruce firrs' (*Pinus sylvestris* or *Picea abies*) and then the space was to be filled with 'smaller scotch, spruce, silver firrs [*Abies alba*] and larches … and by way of underwood with holley, privet and nutwood'.[10] The taller specimens were presumably to give the clumps some authority before the rest of the planting caught up. Woods made a 'sample' of how he wanted the trees arranged, and probably for this reason did not specify the measurements, but at a rough guess scaling up from the survey made by George Ingman in 1773[11] the clumps had an approximate diameter of 60ft (18m), while the turf borders between them were scattered with unidentified 'forest trees'.

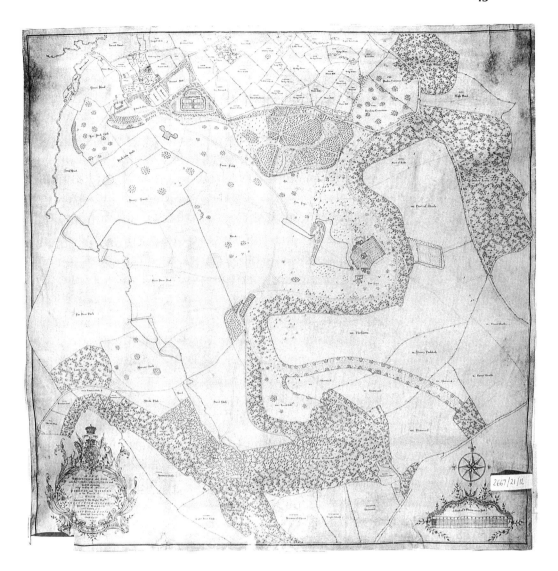

The differing habit and tone of the conifers would have made a very lively combination, although they would have been only just reaching maturity when the line of the approach was moved by the 10th Lord Arundell in the early nineteenth century.

Other estates where Woods planned a new approach bordered with planting were Cusworth and Wivenhoe. At Cusworth, Woods suggested an unusual arrangement of elm and beech bordering the new 'coach road or tarrice', where the trees are set in triangles of alternate species, resulting in a zig-zag. The reason for this quirky pattern is not mentioned, and there is nothing similar either in Woods's work elsewhere or in that of the other

Fig. 8. Ingman's survey of Wardour 1773, showing clearly what Woods had achieved before being dismissed in 1772. Brown's first visit for the 8th Baron Arundell was not until 1774.

Fig. 9. The unusual planting arrangement suggested by Woods to border a carriageway in the park at Cusworth. Sketch from Woods's memorandum to the foreman of September 1765.

improvers. Woods's plans for Wivenhoe (1765) and Hengrave (1777) both show projected new approaches through the park but with dispositions of clumps bordering the carriageway far looser than at Wardour. However, there is no evidence that either of them was constructed and Woods's ideas for the planting are unknown.

PLANTING IN CUSWORTH

A rough plan of the Cusworth estate which is generally attributed to Woods and is claimed to show his planting plans for the park boundaries is now known to have been made while Richardson was still employed there, before Woods's first visit, and is anyway more likely to be a survey of standing timber.[12] Woods's planting for Cusworth is the subject of numerous references in his memoranda to the foreman, and can be considered equally

Fig. 10. Plan of the planting round the stables, wood yard and drying ground at Cusworth, and section of the planting to screen the drying ground. The section is a sketch by Woods in the first memorandum for the foreman, late 1761 or early 1762.

as park, grove or perimeter walk. The earliest of these references occurs in the first memorandum (probably 1761) and concerns the need to conceal the areas of everyday activity crowding in on the house. Setting out and planting a screen around the drying ground was described in detail and accompanied by a useful plan showing the desired effect.[13] From these it is clear that the screen, which adjoined the house to the west, was visualised by Woods not just as a means of hiding the drying ground but as a decorative feature in its own right. The memorandum includes a sketch plan of the section through the plantation, as well as his instructions for planting: two staggered rows ('put em tryangle') of dark green spruce firs (*Picea abies*) concealed the drying ground itself, and then working outwards, in clusters of three of each species, came soft bluish green Weymouth pines (*Pinus strobus*), light bright green larches (*Larix decidua*), and silver firs (*Abies alba*) with needles of dark glossy green above and white bands on the underside. The 'internal parts of the plantation' were to be filled up with 'any sorts of young firs by way of nursery', and laurel and holly 'wch will not only help to thicken the plantation, but will afford a fine variety of shades'.

This use of evergreens, not just as an efficient year-round screen, but in an assortment carefully chosen for the overall aesthetic effect, marks Woods out from the other improvers, and even from a strand of contemporary opinion: George Mason in his *Essay on Design in Gardening* (1768) condemned an 'injudicious application of Fir-trees', and while Horace Walpole could concede an evergreen plantation 'as a screen to conceal some deformity or as a shelter in winter' he had apparently never seen, or perhaps would not admit, that such a screen could be attractive in itself.[14] Brown's planting at Sherborne to conceal the stables and kitchen garden, where he used predominately beech with holly and yew underplanting, approached the same problem from a different angle, giving a more naturalistic and less self-consciously decorative treatment.[15] If Woods had indeed gained his experience at Wooburn Farm, he might well have absorbed some of the attitudes on the niceties of colour blending in trees as practised by Lord Petre and commented on by Southcote: Petre, he said, 'understood the colours of every tree, and always considered how he placed them by one another' (Spence's Observation no. 1124).[16]

The screens around the drying ground and stables, although scarcely groves as such, were nevertheless part of the flow of a continuous plantation cut through with a walk (memoranda 2 and 3) which was shown on a plan of probably the late 1760s;[17] it ran from the east side of the house to below 'Low Piece'. The stables were enclosed by a stone wall masked by a thick plantation 'of firrs and pines fill'd up with all kinds of low evergreens … Plant each sort of firrs or pines by themselves in long groups, you may interspearse some Roses honeysuckles and jessimens towards the front among the evergreens.' The long plantation, decorated near the outer edges, was bordered by a 4ft (1.2m) band of turf separating it from the 7ft (2m) gravel walk, which on the park side had an 'opin grove'. This allowed glimpses of the lawn between the trunks of the beech, elm, chestnut, larch and a few tulip trees, with 'some few groups of evergreens and the sweets' which would break the monotony and 'have a fine affect from the Lybrary windoor'. All this was contained within a railing, with a scattering of single trees outside it 'to coraspond with the opin grove'. The turf border between the thick plantation and path had a few trees planted in it, with 'here and there a honeysuckle planted to climb up', but once the path turned the corner into the narrower plantation beside the kitchen garden wall, 'ye walk must be only edged with pinks or thrift or something low as there is not room for any other sort of work.'

Similar in feeling was the major plantation 'under Mr Copley's park walls', where Cusworth adjoined the Sprotborough estate, south of the pieces of water. The basic plan was repeated (wall/thick plantation/turf border/gravel walk/turf border/open grove), but here an extra ingredient was added in the form of 'differant large clumps of forest trees … downwards towards the meadows'. The position of the seven clumps was indicated by stakes, and each had a specific characteristic. The first was of 'any kinds of decedious forest plants' in front of which (i.e. north, in the direction of the house) was to be placed a smaller clump of firs 'nearly operset the center of ye back clump'. The second clump was planted the other way round, with the main grouping of firs or pines and the subsidiary clump of 'decedious plants about 12yds [11m] long'. The third clump was different again, being composed of deciduous trees in the centre with evergreens at each end, but of two separate sorts – Woods suggested scotch firs at one end and spruce firs at the other. In front of this third clump was a grouping of 25yds (23m) of larches. This alternation of evergreen, deciduous, and mixed clumps continued for the remainder of the seven stakes. Finally, the article of the memorandum ends with the instruction that in the thick plantation 'all the intermeduit spaces are to be filld with short planting such as will only rise high enough to cover ye wall, and may be composed of any sorts of underwood, and the whole next the wall to be fronted with shrubs mixt with evergreens, but to observe to bring forward all short and sweet kinds of plants.'

PLANTATION STYLES

With the exception of the drying ground screen, these Cusworth schemes were in the style of what might be called grove plantation, whether considered as outlying pleasure-ground or park planting. In this context, Woods's boundary plantations, interspersed with flowers or flowering shrubs, were standard practice by that time. Batty Langley as early as 1728 and Philip Miller in 1731 were already suggesting planting along these lines, but as part of wilderness-work in a fairly formal setting rather than in a boundary plantation. Southcote, over ten years later, was the first to adapt the idea for use in a naturalistic perimeter walk. This is recorded in the two similar plans illustrated in a previous chapter (see p. 18) which show an 'Old Hedge-Row' with a plantation 5ft (1.5m) in width composed of graduated trees and shrubs in front, and then a 2.5ft (0.8m) border for three rows of flowers directly beside the sand walk. The effect has been drawn by Mark Laird (Plate 10) and it is immediately noticeable that this is not a gradual slope of plants arranged by height from forest trees to the edging of pinks, but a steep drop from the highest to the lowest, leaving a very narrow border for the flowers. Although the spacing and graduation of the plants scarcely looks informal to modern eyes, at the time it was part of what Spence calls the 'making pleasure-grounds [as] an imitation of "beautiful Nature"' (Observation no. 1070). From the 1740s to the 70s the general principle behind this sort of planting was widely accepted for grove-work, not least by Spence, whose design for 'Mr Rudge's Pleasure Ground' (probably at Wheatfield in Oxfordshire) was 'a carefully arranged mixture of sandwalks, winding in the approved manner among "close grove works" of the "best flowering shrubs and trees and the lowest and best evergreens" backed by large trees.'[18] John Byng, far readier to find fault than to praise, criticised The Leasowes in 1781 for being 'insufficiently *orné*', and wished that 'honeysuckles and sweet-smelling shrubs (of which at present there is a total want) were trained round the trees and planted by the walks'.[19] Cambridge Park, on the Thames at Twickenham, was described by Henrietta Pye in 1760: 'the grove … lies not in a strait line but winding in and out … and fenced on each side by thick bushes of roses, orange-flowers, honey-suckles, lilacs, and sweet williams, and shaded by fine tall trees.'[20] This arrangement sounds far more floriferous than Woods's at Cusworth, but at Buckland in 1758, where from the map evidence there seems to have been a similar fusion of pleasure ground and park,[21] the list of plants supplied by Henry Hewitt on Woods's orders strongly suggests a walk through an ornamented plantation.[22] The range of trees and shrubs is far more varied than for Cusworth, and includes many exotics, but no recent introductions. Among the 'scarlet maples' (*Acer rubrum*), 'triple-thorned acacias' (*Gleditsia triacanthos*), 'scarlet horse chestnuts' (*Aesculus pavia*), 'sweet gums' (*Liquidambar styraciflua*) and similar, with several varieties of oak, were flowering trees such as 'double blossomed peaches' (*Prunus persica* var.), pears (*Pyrus communis* var.), cherries (*Prunus cerasifera* var.), a number of different thorns (*Crataegus* var.), 'white arbor judae' (*Cercis siliquastrum alba*) and 135 roses of 27 varieties.[23] It may be guessed that the plantation was partly to border the pieces of water, as Hewitt, perhaps uncertain of the gardeners' expertise in this area, had obligingly marked the plants with a 'D' or 'W' to signify whether they should be planted in dry or wet positions. There is no way of knowing whether the roses, five of each sort, were destined as a border for the walk or for a rosery elsewhere in the grounds.

The client, Sir Robert Throckmorton, was presumably interested in knowing what plants were available for the pleasure ground, as just a month before employing Woods he had bought a copy of John Hill's *Eden* (1757), a lavish folio containing sixty plates of flower illustrations with descriptions and cultural instructions, which is unusual in also including advice on the construction and maintenance of a garden.[24] The advance of the modern taste in gardening was still new enough in 1757 to be worth a comment: 'We have thrown down our nine-foot [2.7m] Walls, and opened the Prospect by Ha-ha's.' In the composing of walks through groves he follows much that Isaac Ware had said in his *Complete Body of Architecture*, published the previous year, and particularly advised the planting of flowering shrubs to border the paths.[25]

Variety and flower-bordered walks in perimeter belts were keynotes of the style of gardening developed and popularised by Southcote who, as noted above, was a friend of Throckmorton's and probable employer of Woods. It is a tempting possibility that Throckmorton was attracted to this style of gardening, with an emphasis on flowers within the new-style belts and walks, and that his friend Southcote might have recommended Woods as a practitioner trained in this fashion.

Wardour was the location of yet another ornamented plantation walk, known as the Great Terrace.[26] This spectacular walk along the foot of a steep wooded bank called the Hangings, started by Woods in February 1765, can perhaps be considered the greatest achievement of this commission. Taking as his starting point a narrow path running tight to the boundary between park and wood, shown on a 1753 survey,[27] Woods contracted to 'form and sow with grass seeds and finish all the Ground relating to the [first section of the] great Terrace', with the specification for a later section referring to a walk 50yds (46m) wide, and to 'fill up all the Plantations … from end to end'.[28] The required plants had been supplied two months earlier: a mixture of 1718 forest and ornamental trees with 550 flowering shrubs (including 'common roses in sorts' and sweet briar). Woods here applied the usual formula, with a slight variation due to one side of the walk meeting the steep wooded hill, while on the park side an irregular arrangement of clumps was attached to the Terrace. From the number of each species supplied, it may be guessed that the clumps were mainly composed of larch, oak, beech, sweet chestnut and hornbeam, possibly underplanted with laurel, while the more decorative trees were artfully set out along the walk, with a border of them on the hillside blending with the established wood. The selection included varieties of oak (*Quercus alba, coccinea, ilex, nigra, prinus, rubra*), two sorts of 'acacia' (*Robinia pseudacacia* and *Gleditsia triacanthos*), Weymouth pines (*Pinus strobus*), striped sycamore (*Acer pseudoplatanus variegatum*), arbor vitae (*Thuja occidentalis*), spruce fir (*Picea abies*), American ash (*Fraxinus americana*) and others. These were interspersed with ornamentals such as althea frutex (*Hibiscus syriacus*), Spanish broom (*Spartium junceum*), 'laylocks' (*syringa vulgaris*), 'syringoes' (*Philadelphus coronarius*), phlomis (*Phlomis fruticosa*), striped hollies and a scattering of roses. Woods doubtless disposed them with as much care for effect as shown in the Cusworth plantations, and it is no surprise that the Great Terrace, with the double advantage of the planting and of occasional glimpses into the magnificent countryside, was a showpiece of the Wardour landscape. Richard Sulivan reported in 1778 in his *Tour through Parts of England* that 'the beauties of this walk, as we were given to understand [by the housekeeper] before we left the house, have met with general admiration' – praise repeated by later visitors.[29] The 1773 survey of Wardour Castle estate by Ingman shows the Terrace bordered on the rising ground to the east by open planting and on the park side by a series of irregularly placed and sized clumps.[30]

Woods's commission at Boreham House (Essex) included making a pleasure-ground plantation from the house down to a new 'river', for which the nurseryman Spencer Turner supplied a mix of evergreens for the framework (*Prunus laurocerasus*, *Ligustrum vulgare sempervirens*, *Laurus nobilis* and *Viburnum tinus*) along with some ornamentals to border the path or to place in some other more prominent position (*Phillyrea latifolia variegata*, *Rhamnus alaternus variegata*, *Spartium junceum*, phlomis and jasmine).[31] Lists of flower roots and seeds to enliven the scene, sent by Christopher Harvey and John Mearns between 1765 and 1771 (although their exact destination is unknown), are relatively rare documentary survivals. There is no map evidence that the pleasure ground, staked out in 1763,[32] included a separate flower or pleasure garden, so possibly the sweet peas, lupins, double poppies, China asters, French marigolds, white candy tuft and double larkspur were destined for spots incorporated within the plantation, or even to border the path. Either way, it is illustrative of the way that a plantation would have been diversified by colourful flowers, and another instance of the difficulty of keeping strictly separate the divisions of the designed landscape.

Woods's choice of plants for this sort of ornamented walk, as documented for Buckland and Wardour, is very similar to Brown's selection for his redesigned wilderness at Petworth, where attractive but common shrubs such as guelder rose (*Viburnum opulus*), Spanish broom (*Spartium junceum*), tamarisk (*tamarix gallica*), syringa (*Philadelphus coronarius*) and lilac (*syringa vulgaris*), with a number of different rose species and just two adventurous exotics ('3 Catalpha'; '5 Oriental Collutea'), mingled with the forest trees at the edge of the walks. An extensive collection sent by Nathaniel Richmond for Compton Place in 1780 is rather more adventurous, specifying eight different honeysuckles, for instance, as well as a yellow horse chestnut (*Aesculus flava*) and four dogwoods, but the majority of the plants are still the standard choice for groves and similar situations.[33]

Pleasure-ground planting did not necessarily include flower-ornamented walks. An example of this can be seen at Wivenhoe, where from 1776 Woods was landscaping the central section of the park. By 1780 his association of some fifteen years with Colonel Rebow was drawing to a close, and there is evidence that Rebow was by then directing his own landscaping, with the workforce still nominally under Woods but on piece work rather than day wages. In February 1780 Woods wrote relating to planting at the head of the new piece of water and by the kitchen garden, enclosing a priced list of plants typical for close planting, with a slightly terse covering letter suggesting that 'Your self, will not probabley, know how to determine about getting the proper plants without a little advice, as being (I presume) rather unacquainted with that part of the business … I will put down the number [of plants] wch I suppose youl. want this spring, to plant about the head of the river, the bank by the long canall and the plantation by the pales on the east side of the park', which was also to act as a nursery. At the foot of the list he wrote, 'I don't know, that you can get the plants at the above prices, without I order em but in that youl. please yourself, & try elsewhere.'[34] The

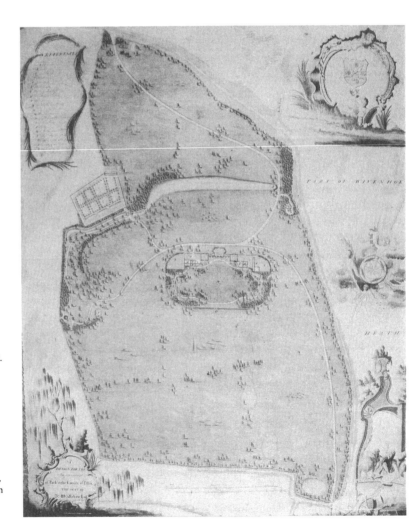

Fig. 11. Woods's plan for Wivenhoe, produced in 1765, although work did not start for eleven years. Although the design covers the whole park, Woods's work was concentrated in the central section, with the creation of the piece of water and landscaping around the house. The original of this plan has been lost for many years, and it is known only from this old monochrome photograph.

mix was a standard conifer selection of spruce fir, Weymouth pine and larch, with a smaller number of 'Newfound land spruce fir' (*Picea glauca* or *mariana*), 'Cypress' (probably *Cupressus sempervirens*) and 'Red cedars' (*Juniperus virginiana*), underplanted with cherry laurel, Portugal laurel, laurustinus and holly. Constable's painting of 1816 (Plate 9) suggests that the planting behind the boathouse on the eastern boundary of the park was rather deciduous than evergreen, and indeed he described the scene he was painting as 'a grotto with some elms, at the head of a peice of water', indicating that Rebow did not adopt Woods's suggested selection of trees.[35]

The long plantation at Cusworth came down to the bank of the 'great river' (the main piece of water) and the foot of the mount, where the character of the planting shifted slightly from the ornamental mix bordering the path. The middle of each plantation near the cascade was of firs and larches with the shorter plants in front – laburnums and weeping willows, but mostly unspecified 'short evergreens and shrubs'. Later planting in 1765 included cypress (*Cupressus* var.) and red cedars (*Juniperus virginiana*). The island in the great river was planted in 1763 with 'a pritty many' weeping willows placed 'near the edges', interspersed with 'little clumps of

Fig. 12. Detail of Figure 7 to show, in a naïve style, Woods's planting round the head of the 'Great River' or first piece of water. The cascade is at the top left, and the grotto–boat house at the bottom left.

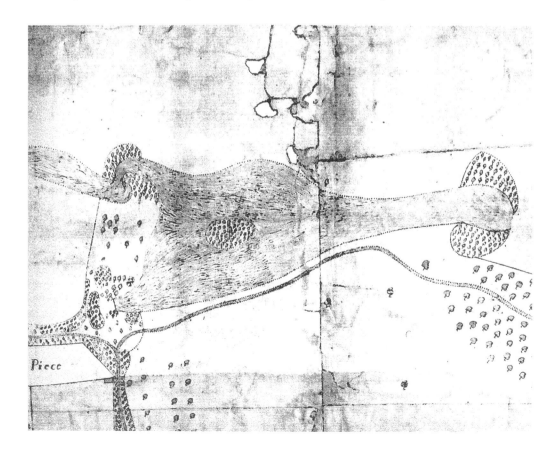

evergreens where the short Bowes [boughs] are placed, wch may be cheefly of Laurels and Laurestinus and pursline trees [*Atriplex halimus*] and perrywinkle and plant 5 or 6 plants for each clump so that the Ducks may harbor therein'. A year later (September 1764) some extra vegetation was needed on the island: 'plant about 2 plains 2 white poplars and 2 black with some more laurels and some common shrubs to make it thick'.

The study of existing planting in Woods's plantations is, sadly, unrewarding. Very few of his landscapes survive in anything like recognisable form, and even where the odd specimens of long-lived species remain where he is known to have designed a plantation they can give no impression of the finished effect in the eighteenth century. The chance survival of a few oaks or pines – the former by now magnificent and the latter straggly – without their supporting cast and out of proportion with each other, is of arboricultural but not aesthetic interest.[36] In general, a clearer idea of his planting style can be gained from his written instructions, combined with evidence of the position of clumps or plantations on early editions of the Ordnance Survey maps and a knowledge of the contours of the site.

PLEASURE-GROUND AND PLEASURE-GARDEN/ FLOWER-GARDEN PLANTING[37]

As we have seen, 'pleasure ground' can be interpreted to include features beyond the ha-ha, such as plantation walks or groves, pieces of water, even an entire small park, but it is nevertheless most commonly taken to be a particular area of garden, as described by Philip Miller in the 1768 edition of his *Gardener's Dictionary*: close to the house lies 'an open lawn of grass, properly bounded by plantations … Where flowers are desired, there may be borders continued round the extent of the lawn, immediately before the plantations of shrubs; which if properly planted with hardy flowers to succeed each other, will afford a pleasing prospect.'[38]

Mark Laird has irrefutably shown that the use of flowers was ubiquitous in mid-eighteenth-century pleasure grounds, following on in an unbroken continuum from the formal parterres and beds of the early eighteenth century. The garden manuals had no need to make a particular point of it as it was accepted practice: John Hill in his instructions for the pleasure ground in *Eden* (1757) advised that in February the gardener should 'examine the condition of those hardy Spring Flowers which are planted in the Ground among Flowering-Shrubs', and under October he assumed that 'the flowering Shrubs are planted with some Trees perhaps, and certainly with Roots of Flowers among them'. Brown's contract for Petworth of 1754 includes 'proper preparations for flowers' in the walk through the laurels and by the new terrace,[39] and the 1769 edition of Philip Miller's *Gardeners Kalendar*[40] observed that many flowers which for some time after being introduced were 'nursed up with the greatest care … are now commonly planted in the open borders of the Pleasure-Garden'.

At Cusworth there is no reference in the memoranda to borders, clumps or beds for flowers, but a walled flower garden next to the kitchen garden was allowed to remain from the earlier layout (see Figure 7). Brown even created a new walled kitchen and flower garden at Tottenham as part of the 1763–64 alterations round the house.[41] The term 'flower garden' could be used either in this sense, or synonymously with 'pleasure garden', although the latter could conversely denote what came to be known (from about 1750 onwards[42]) as a shrubbery, in direct contradistinction to a flower garden. On these definitions too there was no consensus in the eighteenth century. Hill has much to say on the laying-out of the pleasure ground, 'the most delicate Point and the least understood of all', insisting that the flower garden and pleasure garden should be distinct from each other. A flower garden should be 'a particular Piece of Ground for the Beds of the select Kinds', whereas in the pleasure garden 'the finest Kinds that bear the open Ground must be planted here with the same regard to Light and Shade, Harmony of Colours, and Variety, that we have recommended in the Choice of Greens for the Grove.' In the pleasure garden 'Flowers will be a great Ornament to it, but they must not be considered as the principal Object; nor must … the Disposition be subservient to them.'[43] John Rutter and Daniel Carter in 1767 also felt that the flower and pleasure gardens were necessarily different:

> These two things have been confounded, but they are absolutely distinct in their nature; for the finest of flowers … require certain articles of shelter and defence, and other management, which must not come in sight of a view of pleasure. … Those selected for the common service of the borders in the pleasure-garden, are large, and of a more distinct appearance. … Indeed if there be no particular regard paid to the express flower-garden, yet [fine flowers] should be raised for the farther decoration of the clumps and borders. Where there is a particular spot for fine flowers, the inferior kinds will still be beautiful enough for the pleasure-garden.[44]

In the flower garden the garden was for flowers; in the pleasure garden the flowers were for the garden. Some of the other manual writers make this point specifically, but even where it is not mentioned the texts of the month-by-month 'kalendars' make it clear that two separate parts of the garden are meant. In short, confusion of terminology was rife, and whereas some estates had a walled flower garden, probably adjacent to the kitchen garden and used either for cutting or raising special blooms, others used part of the kitchen garden for this purpose, and possibly as a nursery as well where this was not a separate area – all this in addition to a shrubbery or similar pleasure ground.

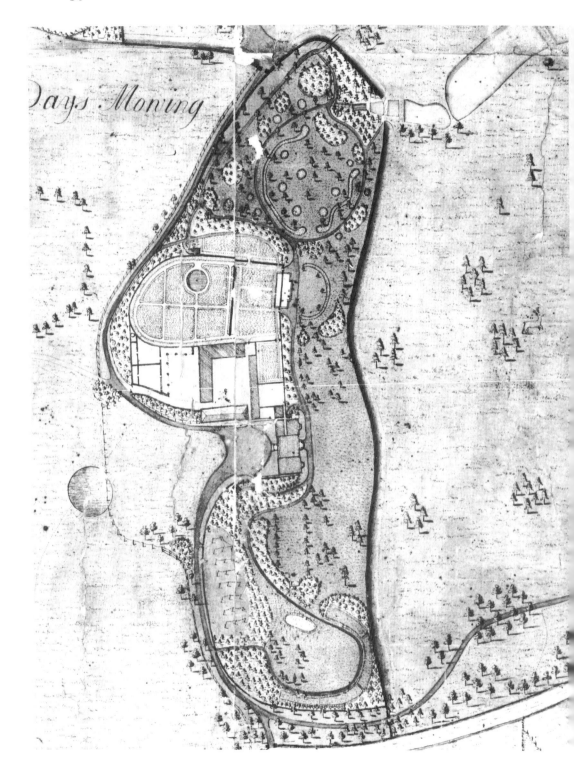

Days Moning

Woods's plan for Cannon Hall, where he was working at almost the same time as Cusworth, well illustrates the diversity of meaning attached to the terms of 'pleasure ground', 'pleasure garden' and 'flower garden'.[45] It is highly unusual in showing and referencing both an *ornamental* flower garden and a shrubbery: the former is described as 'the Belt in front of the Pinery, to be richly adorned with the choicest flowers and low Exoticks', conveniently close to the shelter of the kitchen garden, where (following the advice in Rutter and Carter) these blooms could be 'produced in seed-beds with great care, and afterwards planted in their particular beds.' Almost next to it, but screened by planting, was 'the Shrubbery or Best Flower Garden adorned with clumps of greens and Shrubs and beds and borders of Roses and all sorts of common and sweet flowers'. Two plant lists relating to this period supply the form and colour of the woody material in the gardens: the shrubbery was obviously full of variety, with many of the species present only in twos or fives.[46] There are no similar references on the plan for Hengrave of 1777 to describe the shrubbery, but it is clear that the pleasure ground west of the house was to have long serpentine beds very similar to those at Cannon Hall, and which in the same way must have contained flowers. The

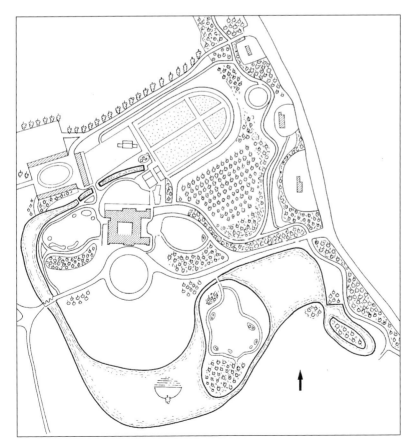

Opposite: Fig. 13. The pleasure ground from a survey of Cannon Hall 'with improvements by Richard Woods'. The pinery is at the bottom of the kitchen garden, but facing into the garden and looking over an elliptical lawn bordered with 'exotic' flowers. The shrubbery, or 'best flower garden' is to the right, with serpentine flower borders and round studs. See Figure 14 for a similar shrubbery designed for Hengrave ten years later.

Left: Fig. 14. Detail of the plan for Hengrave, redrawn by Phillip Judge, showing the shrubbery to the west of the house with similar studs for flowers and serpentine beds as at Cannon Hall.

56

RICHARD WOODS
(1715–1793)
MASTER OF THE
PLEASURE GARDEN

painting by William Tomkins of the Elysium Garden at Audley End, for which Woods supplied a plan in 1780, perfectly illustrates the effect of eighteenth-century pleasure-ground planting, where the dark structural bank of shrubs at the back of the borders brilliantly sets off the mass of flowers in a narrow margin in front[47] (Plate 3).

A typical memorandum entry, for laying out the pleasure garden at Goldsborough, may be taken as an example: the foreman was told that 'the winding Lines of Stakes are ye Boundrys of Each Border, quarter or Clump Let there be a margin left for flowers about 3 or 4 feet [approx. 1m] wide in which margin let there be a few roses Jessamines & HoneySuckles planted … to intermix with the flowers.' The little rectangle denoting a bench placed at

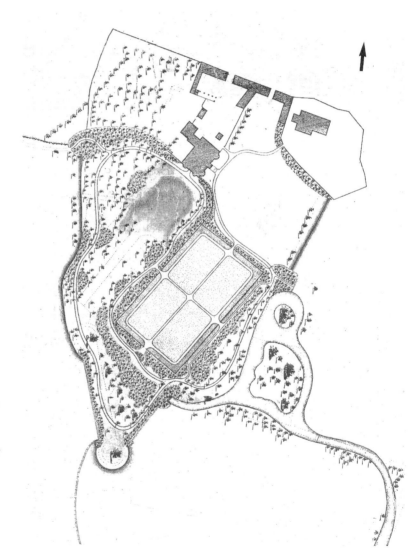

Fig. 15. The main portion of Woods's plan for Goldsborough of 1763, with its emphasis on the pleasure garden, piece of water and kitchen garden. One of the bastions from an earlier layout has been left to give a viewing platform overlooking the parkland.

a corner of the pleasure ground becomes a charming garden feature, illustrated by a rare sketch: 'At the back of the Seat upon the little mount … let it be princepally Evergreens with some Honey Suckles mixt with them to Clime up' – backed, according to the sketch, with 'filberts &c.' The positions for the trees scattered through the rest of the pleasure ground lawn were marked by whitened stakes denoting species 'such as Oaks, Elms, Beech & Chestnuts &c with some flowering trees mixt with them, such as Double Blossom'd Peach Do. Almond Do. Cherrys Arborjuda Tuliptrees &c Thorns &c, & where the short stakes stand upon ye turf near the borders, are to be short choys growing plants, such as portingall Laurels, arbutus stripd holleys D^o Laurustinus D^o Phillereys Chenia arborvitae Sistus several sorts &c sumacks'.[48]

Fig. 16. 'Section of ye little mount or platform'. A sketch by the foreman William Stones, illustrating Woods's instructions 'to carry on ye Improvements at Goldsborough'. Stones made a fair copy of Woods's scribbled memorandum.

A detail of a painting of New Hall where Woods was working in the period 1767–76 shows the effect in a pleasure ground of the kind of varied planting he is known to have implemented elsewhere (Plate 4). For the pleasure ground at Irnham Woods ordered 226 plants 'proper to help fill up the borders'. A hundred privet were to 'fill up the middle of the quarters', with 'swedeish juniper' (*Juniperus suecica*), Spanish broom (*Spartium junceum*), 'Luca broom' (*Genista tinctoria* 'Elatior'), rose (two of 'each sort'), portugal laurel (*Prunus lusitanica*), arbutus (*Arbutus unedo*), 'tamorask in two sorts' (*Tamarix gallica* and *Myricaria germanica*) and 'sistus of each sort' (any of *Cistus albidus, crispus, ladanifer, laurifolius, monspelianus, populifolius*). He does not specify whether a margin is to be left for flowers, but this is a reasonable assumption.

The survival of Woods's plant list for Hartwell,[49] taken with a near-contemporary map of 1776–7,[50] makes it possible to speculate that many of the large number of evergreens (laurestinus, phillyrea, holly, pyracantha, Swedish juniper etc.) and common flowering shrubs (phlomis, Spanish broom, lilac, philadelphus etc.) were for the thick plantations round the perimeter of the new garden, while the more costly trees and flowering bushes (scarlet oak, Carolina poplar, oriental colutea, candleberry myrtle, double pomegranate etc.), mainly ordered in twos, were to be placed in prominent positions.[51] The existence of the map and the fact that Woods had supplied a design for 'a new garden' suggest that this display must have been intended for the garden-within-a-garden overlooked by the greenhouse, foreshadowing the flower garden in front of the pinery at Cannon Hall, and

Fig. 17. Detail showing
the park and pleasure
ground at Hartwell
House in 1776. Woods's
'New Garden Greenhouse
and Pinery' are in the
walled enclosure on the
left, with the greenhouse
facing a little lawn, and
the pinery (or stove)
above it looking over
Hot-house Piece.

the half-functional, half-ornamental kitchen gardens at Wardour and
probably Brocket. Mark Laird has pointed out that Woods's planting at
Buckland, Hartwell and Cannon Hall shows a 'selection characterised by
unusual exotics … not present, for example, in bills associated with
Capability Brown at Petworth or Tottenham Park',[52] and more adventurous
than the palette used by Robert Adam at Kedleston – another instance of
Woods standing out as the improver with a unique interest in, and probable
knowledge of, the finer points of adornment of the pleasure ground,
showing that it was possible for the standard framework of planting to be
given an exotic gloss by the inclusion of rare, expensive or interesting
specimens in salient positions.

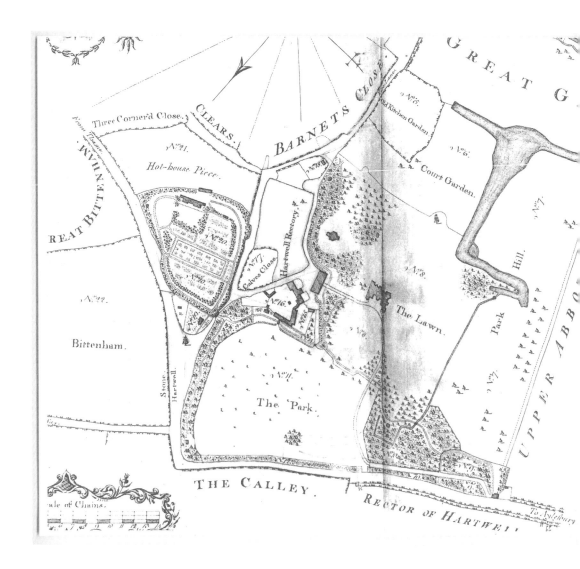

THE AVAILABILITY OF FLOWERS

As the eighteenth century advanced, flowers were increasingly assumed to be the specialist concern of the gardener or the lady of the house, making the improver's role in this area more tentative. It is scarcely surprising that the selection and arrangement of plants from so many in circulation had become separate from the overall design of the improver, and that it was enough for him to indicate where a margin should be left for flowers without making the choice himself. Because so many of the pleasure-ground blooms were propagated on the estate, or through the exchange of gifts between families, few figure on nurserymen's bills, leading to a misunderstanding of the numbers grown. As Weston advised under the month of August in *The Gardener's and Planter's Calendar* (1773), the gardener must 'pass over the Shrubs and Flowers frequently, to gather the seeds as they ripen; by this method you will save double the quantity from the same plants', and this advice was given in other manuals. The fact that the flower lists for Boreham include only one or two of each variety (lupin, sweet pea, double larkspur, lavatera, candy tuft, nasturtium, sunflower, lychnis, stock, chrysanthemum, tobacco, china aster, double poppy and tagetes) suggests that in future years it was expected that enough seed would be collected from them to supply the garden.

Whether the choice of border plants was at the instigation of improver, lady of the house or gardener, the variety available by the 1770s is remarkable. While Robert Furber's nursery catalogue of 1730 offered a total of 285 flowering bulbs, annuals and herbaceous plants,[53] Richard Weston's *Flora Anglicana* (1775) lists 359 species of herbaceous plants alone, most of which have several varieties. The diversity of spring bulbs is staggering, with over a thousand hyacinths listed in 1776 by Robert Edmeades's *The Gentleman and Lady's Gardener*.[54] John Hill's *Eden* of 1757 shows the range of colour, height and form of the flowers from which the pleasure garden and shrubbery displays could be created[55] – the various manuals and catalogues prove that there was no lack of choice for the flower beds. Although Switzer (no great lover of flowers) was exaggerating when he wrote in 1718 in *Ichnographia rustica* that 'in the latter part of the Year … the Beauty of Flowers is gone, and Borders are like graves',[56] it is nevertheless true that from the 1730s the flood of introductions provided a far wider choice through the season. This very wealth of plant material made the gardener's task of choosing and arranging – and then in subsequent years, propagating – far more demanding as well as more exciting. Hill noted that 'the Gardener's Task is indeed become very easy by the Nurseryman doing the greatest Part of it for him, but … a Seminary [nursery] will be necessary for many of his flowering Plants'.

Woods is unique among his contemporary improvers in actually showing on his plans a clear differentiation between clumps of tree and/or shrub planting, and clumps additionally planted with herbaceous material, which are dabbed with what might be called 'herbaceous dotting'. In some places, as at Goldsborough, this merely reinforces the written instructions for laying out the borders, but for other commissions where only the plan survives it gives a whole new dimension to the final effect of the landscaping. Perhaps the most spectacular example is Brizes (1788) (Plate 5), for which Woods suggested an ornamented walk which he called on the plan 'The Lady's Walk inrich'd'. This was in most respects an unexceptional winding path bordered on both sides by plantations. However, halfway down a swell has been made in the plantations and a bench placed in the middle of one side; directly opposite, on the other side of the path, an oval bed lies in front of the bench, planted with shrubs but also full of herbaceous dotting, which extends to the narrow band of plantation beyond and to the side of the bed. It is easy to

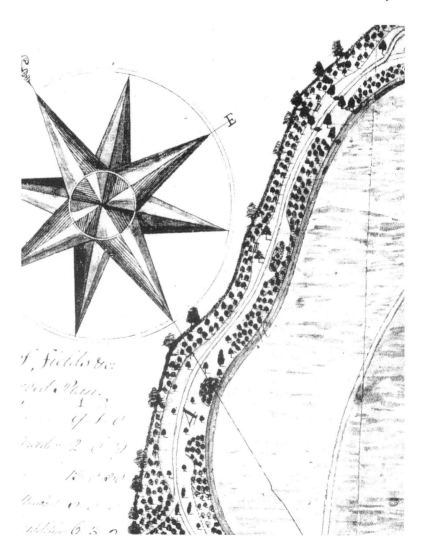

Fig. 18. A section of 'The Lady's Walk Inrich'd' from Woods's plan for Brizes, showing the oval bed set into a swell in the plantation with the 'herbaceous dotting' denoting flowers among the shrubs.

visualise the view from the bench into the park beyond the ha-ha over the top of a flower-planted bed.

Evidence of beds planted with herbaceous material can be seen on several of Woods's plans, although the very precise dotting is missing in some places where it might be expected. The walk along the canal at Little Linford has a winding plantation on one side, and three large beds without dotting on the other side of the path, which may therefore be assumed to contain only graduated shrubs (see Figure 64). A similar arrangement of beds is found beside the river at Brocket Hall, but in the absence of a plan by Woods his planting intentions remain unknown. However, at Hatfield Priory, where the pleasure garden has also been laid out beside the water, a triangle of ground contains oval beds which include dotting (see Figure 5). At Wivenhoe just two small round dotted beds have been inserted into spandrels on the south side of the house wings, near the apex of the pleasure-ground lawn (see Figure 66). The pleasure garden shown on the 1771 plan for Wardour, which included a menagerie, had four round beds in the lawn which, judging from the way they are drawn, might have been for flowers alone without shrub support (see Plate 11). The plan for the 1784 improvements at Copford (see Plate 6) gives a particularly clear insight into

Fig. 19. Detail from Woods's plan for Copford Hall, showing the flower border along the side façade of the house and oval beds with 'herbaceous dotting'.

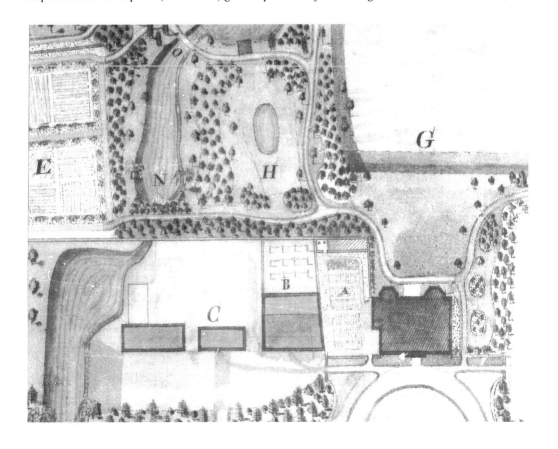

the effect Woods sought in the pleasure ground. The garden façade of the house looks over a lawn towards the distant view, while under the windows on the south side a long flower bed has been laid out. Across a path is another small lawn with three oval beds of shrubs and 'herbaceous dotting', bordered by a winding line of ordinary plantation.

WARDOUR OLD CASTLE FLOWER GARDEN

In addition to the beds and borders for flowers shown on his plans, Woods supervised a far more unusual exercise in the reorganisation and replanting of the flower garden in front of Wardour Old Castle, to which the Arundells' residence was still attached until the new mansion was finished in 1777. The formal terraced layout around the castle, illustrated in an engraving of 1735 by Buck, had probably been to some extent re-worked during the following thirty years, but further modification was undertaken at the beginning of Woods's commission.

The accounts record trenching and levelling in the castle garden between 1764 and 1766, including digging 'all the ground within the Limits of the Staks … and lay it in order for sowing and planting, & to take up the Turff & lay it again where the Walks are to be'.[57] A collection of 'herbacious flowering Plants', for which the castle garden was the only possible destination at that date, was delivered in December 1765, at the same time as a collection of 'Plants for the Nursery'.[58] The end result is clearly illustrated in an engraving of the 1770s,[59] which shows the ruins of the west front with two roughly rectangular plats scattered with low trees or bushes and surrounded by a border of flowers – a hybrid picture of formal parterre quarters but with a very loose structure. It is feasible that Lady Arundell wanted a flower garden near at hand, and Woods produced a layout that would not seem too out of place with the formal wilderness that is shown surrounding the Old Castle on his plan.

Whatever the reason for this most unusual garden, in planting terms it is significant as a very rare example of a collection of herbaceous flowers provided directly by one of the improvers.[60] The plants in the list are typical of the 'sweet and common flowers' that would be found in a pleasure garden, although a few are priced relatively high as single specimens ('double rose campion', 'iron colour'd Fox-Glove', 'yellow broad leaf loose-strife', 'double dutch William', 'Arabis Alpina'). The only one of these that had been recently introduced was the loosestrife (*Lysimachia ciliata*, 1732), so presumably the price reflects a well-grown specimen useful for propagation as well as show. In considering this list, it must be remembered that £3-worth of unspecified 'annual and perannual Flower seeds' were included, which makes it difficult to visualise the total effect of the garden planting. No very recent introductions are included (unless there were rarities among the seeds), but, as already stated, expensive 'choice flowers' would have been displayed in the flower garden rather than the pleasure garden.

ROSES

While Cannon Hall had a flower garden and a separate shrubbery, at Copford the pleasure ground also included a 'rosery saloon', with beds and plantations grouped round a small pond. This is one of three commissions which specifically included such a feature – the others are Wardour (1765) and Audley End (1780), while Buckland is a further possibility (1758). It is clear that Woods also intended roses as a major component of planting schemes elsewhere; they feature on all his surviving plant lists, even if only in general terms, as at Hartwell, where he supplied fifty 'American Roses' and fifty 'Second best Sorts'. For Buckland he ordered from Henry Hewitt's nursery five each of twenty-seven kinds of rose which represented a large number of the identifiable species available at the time. The list of the trees and shrubs at Cannon Hall in the 1760s already mentioned,[61] almost certainly representing Woods's planting in the shrubbery and elsewhere, contains 112 roses of twenty-one varieties.

Woods was certainly not on his own in having a penchant for this most delightful of flowers, which was in wide demand throughout the eighteenth century (and not just at the cutting edge of garden fashion) in spite of the restricted range of colour and form before the new introductions and revolution in breeding in the early 1800s. Richard Bradley in *New Improvements of Planting and Gardening* (1717) claimed that 'we have more Variety of Roses propagated by our Gardeners, than of any other Flowering-Tree or Shrub';[62] the Perfects' nursery in 1755 sent the Countess of Oxford at Welbeck Abbey eighty-eight roses of thirty-two varieties;[63] while Brown included nine on the famous Petworth wilderness list[64] and supervised the planting at Tottenham Park of 'a good Supply of Rose Trees, Sweet Brier dwarf Honey Suckles & other sweet smelling Shrubs' on the sides of the Serpentine.[65] More detail about these roses comes from the estimate of the nurseryman William Pendar, sent just after Brown's instructions, which lists '100 Moss Red Provence, Damask Provence Hundred-leav'd, Blush, Monthly, Double Yellow, York and Lancaster and Velvet Roses 2 sorts', as well as '100 Roses 10 sorts'.[66] The Rev. William Hanbury, horticultural practitioner as well as author, listed and discussed some sixty roses ranging in height from 3–4ft (approx. 1m) to 10–12ft (3–3.5m) and with a flowering season 'from May to the end of the summer months', with a few even 'continuing to exhibit a succession of flowers until the frost puts a period to the blowing'.[67] It is clear from nurserymen's invoices around the mid century that roses were readily available and not outrageously expensive, while the first priced catalogue in 1775 of the Telfords' York nursery listed forty-one varieties at prices ranging from a hefty 5s to a reasonable 4d, comparable to prices for varieties of that pleasure-ground staple, the jasmine.[68] Hill wrote in 1757 that the gardener in October 'directs his Eyes to the Roses and Honeysuckles, and those other flowering Shrubs which are fragrant among Flowers, and mix well with them in the Borders', while the first edition of Mawe and Abercrombie's *Every Man his Own Gardener* in 1767 gives instructions for pruning and propagating roses in a way that makes it obvious that they are expected to be represented in the garden.

In spite of a general recognition and use of roses, however, it was not common until near the end of the century, when roses had become available in far greater variety than before, to devote a space or garden entirely to them. Certainly Emes was reported to think that 'the roses and any other prize shrubs … had better be scattered promiscuously in the front borders than put all in one or two.'[69] Nevertheless, the term 'rosery' or 'rosary' was in circulation, even if uncommon, and the *Oxford English Dictionary* gives the fifteenth-century translation of Palladius's *De re rustica* as the first use of it in the sense of 'a piece of ground set apart for the cultivation of roses; a rose-garden'.[70] Probably the first rosery alluded to in the eighteenth century was that at Wooburn Farm, but the earliest known designs are those by Thomas Wright for Becket Park in the 1750s.

Mark Laird has raised the question of whether a 'rosery' was indeed a garden just for roses, and suggests that the word might have been used synonymously with 'flower garden'. The main evidence for this reading derives from the title of one of Wright's two designs, 'Construction of a Rosery or Flower Garden', and the fact that Spence appears to call the 'close and disagreeable rosary' at Wooburn (Observation no. 1134) a 'flower garden' in another Observation (no. 1123). But there is an equal, if not greater, weight of evidence to suggest that a rosery was primarily for roses: Wright's 'rosarie' for Badminton[71] in 1750 bears no resemblance to the geometrical flower-shaped parterre or garden for Beckett, but is rather along the lines of Woods's 'rosary saloon' at Copford or 'rosery' at Audley End – a garden compartment enclosed by plantations with beds in a loose grouping within it. It is also noticeable that Whately makes a distinction between a rosary and a bed of flowers in his description of Wooburn Farm, remarking that 'in every corner or vacant space, is a rosary, a close or open clump, or a bed of flowers'.[72]

A possible explanation for this confusion lies in the habit of old roses, many of which are of sprawling or floppy growth, and it may be guessed that some sort of foliage framework was provided for them.[73] If the height and spread of each variety of rose used by Woods in two commissions (Buckland and Cannon Hall) is noted, it will be seen that with some support a stud of roses could be arranged for a high mound – from ground level to 6ft (1.75m) or higher – of assorted blooms in the short but spectacular flowering season. It would seem logical to suppose that the supporting shrubs made their own contribution to extend the period of interest, possibly being interspersed with herbaceous flowers. This must remain speculation, as virtually no guidance has come to light on the planting of a rosery in spite of so much praise for the beauty of the flower and information on its cultivation and propagation in the gardening manuals. Spence's directions for the estate of

'Mr Dashwood' in 1761 described 'studs of roses, honeysuckles and jessamins', giving the impression that the studs were far smaller than those shown on Woods's plans, or indeed on Wright's design for the rosarie at Badminton.[74] But perhaps the principle was similar: Spence goes on, 'Here a damask rose with 2 or 3 jessamins; there a Provence rose with a couple of miserions; cabbage rose with a couple of dwarf Dutch honeysuckles, in a third'. He also observed that the colours could be mixed: '2 white [roses] with a red … and 2 red with a white'.

It should be noted that the studs and clusters apparently forming Woods's rosaries have a different pedigree from the rosary by Wright for Beckett Park where the beds were arranged around a petal design. This formation is logically part of the flower garden laid out in radial 'petals', seen as early as 1649 in Pierre Morin's garden in Paris, leading to Brown's plan for Brocklesby in 1772 and culminating in Repton's design for the rose garden at Ashridge in 1813.[75] Whatever form the planting of the rosery took, there is no reason to suppose that Woods was using the word to mean 'flower garden', and indeed at Copford it is clear from the plan that both a flower garden and a rosery saloon were included within the pleasure ground. Woods and Wright are rare examples of mid–late eighteenth-century designers who proposed this form of garden.

NURSERIES AND PLANT COLLECTORS

The ready exchange of seeds and plants between estates has already been mentioned, but the main supply of plant material, above all for new work, came from commercial nurseries.[76] The few large nurseries of the early eighteenth century,[77] and most notably that of London and Wise at Brompton, were supplying on a national scale vast quantities of forest trees for plantations, low evergreens for topiary and avenue trees for the grand approach through the park, as well as nursery garden produce and exotics.[78] Although small-scale regional nurseries certainly existed before the beginning of the eighteenth century, only after the third decade, with the decline in the organisation and management of Brompton nursery, was there a gradual proliferation of nurseries capable of supplying more than their own local estates, while in about 1730 in the London area the number had risen to around thirty.

From 1722 the Apothecaries' Garden in Chelsea was in the care of Philip Miller, under whose aegis it developed from a simple physic garden into one of the collecting centres for new introductions, many of which found their way from there into the important private gardens'.[79] Miller was one of a group of friends and associates whose enthusiasm for the introduction of new species opened a momentous chapter in the history of plant collecting in England. A friend and correspondent of Miller's, Peter Collinson – a cloth merchant whose heart was in horticulture – set up a syndicate to sponsor plant collecting in America by a Pennsylvania farmer, John Bartram.[80] The two men had initially exchanged plants on a friend-to-friend basis, but from 1736 Collinson engaged the interest and wealth of Robert James, 8th Lord Petre, to commission regular consignments of seeds and even plants. Petre was joined in 1740 by the Duke of Norfolk, and in 1742 by the Dukes of Richmond and Bedford, who were among the principal purchasers of Petre's prodigious collection of rare American trees after his untimely death at the age of twenty-nine.

Although Philip Southcote was not one of the syndicate, he was demonstrably interested in the new planting possibilities, and included ornamentals in Wooburn Farm which by 1838 were listed as 'one of the largest liquidambar trees in Britain, a remarkably fine hemlock spruce, very large tulip trees, acacias, hickories, pines, cedars, and cypresses, and a magnificent cut-leaved alder'.[81] Certainly he seems to have absorbed some of Petre's modern attitudes to the disposition of trees in the landscape, even though his planting tastes tended to a greater use of flowers than Petre practised at Thorndon. Lord Petre and his friends were not the only enthusiasts for plant collecting, and Blanche Henrey has pointed out that many private persons encouraged and paid for plant introductions during the early years of the eighteenth century: a list of these people was published by John Cowell in his *Curious and Profitable Gardener* of 1730, and another in the *Catalogus plantarum* of the Society of Gardeners in the same year. As the century progressed, the role of introducer, raiser and disseminator of new plants gradually passed to the more progressive nurserymen,[82] many of whom were also authors of garden-related titles. There was a general proliferation of publications on horticulture and botany from about the middle of the century,[83] with books describing and illustrating botanical and horticultural innovations pouring off the presses – titles on plant collections, on new introductions, on the culture and management of exotics, pleasure-garden flowers, forest trees, fruit trees and vegetables.[84] Scarcely an issue of a newspaper, local or national, failed to carry an advertisement for some new publication for an increasingly literate and enquiring public, and a good number of the new titles were of a gardening nature.

At the same time a mushrooming of nurseries large and small took place, many of them still unrecorded except for a passing reference in an estate account book. In c.1760 a calculation was made by the Society of Gardeners that England contained 100 nurserymen, as well as other plant-related categories of tradesmen. The main reason for this explosion in the number of nurseries, as in the number of publications, was the impetus given to plant-collecting by the flood of introductions from the New World, in addition to plant material that had been reaching this country for the previous 100 years from other quarters of the globe, mainly through trade and exploration. Between 1731 and 1768 the number of plant species cultivated in England doubled.[85]

Woods's location in south-east England, and particularly from c.1762 in the Kew area, where he probably owned a nursery himself (see p. 28), was admirably situated for access to two nurseries on his doorstep. James Scott was in Turnham Green and Henry Woodman in Strand-on-the-Green, while Lowe was only a short distance away at Hampton Court. At a time when transport for bulky and perishable goods was slow and expensive, it was obviously a considerable advantage to be able to source plants locally: John MacClary, writing in 1740 about Rousham, assumes that General Dormer 'will have no common ones [plants] from London for the carriage of the seven Bundles of flowering Shrubs came to £3 7s 6d'.[86] In October 1769, Woods ordered plants for Irnham Hall from a nursery in Sleaford (possibly Samuel Benson), less than 20 miles (32km) away, with the suggestion that two teams of horses should be sent to collect them 'by which means they can help each other out of the slows'. However, it is also noticeable that a surprising number of distant estates were supplied – or partially supplied – from London nurseries, possibly owing not only to a greater variety of stock, but also to the ease with which plants could be conveniently inspected during polite society's annual sojourn in the capital. This is illustrated by Woods's request to Lord Arundell in 1771 to look over the orange trees reserved for Wardour at Mr Sesarego's in Piccadilly before they were despatched.

It is not noticeable that Woods favoured one particular nursery above others. Irnham was supplied not only by the Sleaford nursery but also by another at Newark (probably Michael Noble), both of whom sent bills dating from the period of Woods's employment (1770–1). For some commissions he used the obvious firm, like the Perfects for the Yorkshire estates of Cannon Hall and Cusworth; but even with a nursery of this reputation so close, it seems that Cusworth was supplied with Weymouth pines in 1762 by Thomas Emerton (or Emmerton), a nurseryman of South Mimms.[87] Lowe of Kingston Wick supplied fruit trees to Hartwell in 1759 and Cannon Hall in 1762, and 'Mr Scott' was criticised by the Cannon Hall steward in 1763 for repeatedly promising and failing to send 'the plants'.[88] This might refer to pineapple plants for Cannon Hall's new pinery from Henry Scott of Weybridge,[89] specialist in pineapples and brother of Woods's nurseryman neighbour in Chiswick, James Scott. Woods does not name the nursery he used for Wivenhoe, but it may have been the well-established firm of Robert Agnis a short distance away in Colchester.

These few names have been taken, or guessed, from surviving correspondence covering Woods's career, and must represent only a few of the nurseries whose plants clothed his designs. Entries in accounts or comments in letters make it clear that Woods made a personal visit to the nursery he was using for a particular commission, suggesting that the critical eye of the improver was a necessary preliminary to placing an order.[90]

HOW DID WOODS DIFFER FROM HIS PEERS?

Brown is now recognised as a designer of pleasure grounds, but his plans often show only the referenced position of such a garden, without any layout detail, quite unlike the minutiae of Woods's designs for this area; exceptions are where he was specifically asked for a pleasure ground (for instance, 'Lady Griffin's garden' at Audley End, the pleasure grounds at Heveningham and Weston and, perhaps most significantly, the formal flower garden at Brocklesby). Emes's only known flower garden design was for Lord Harrowby at Sandon Park, but its existence reasonably suggests that he might have designed others for which evidence is lacking. Richmond, who worked both with Brown and on his own much in Brown's style, is known to have supervised the creation of pleasure grounds for several estates and was praised by Repton in the Lamer Red Book for knowing 'how to dress walks in a pleasure garden'.[91] However, no documentation survives on his precise ideas for plant material within the layouts, and where there are planting lists they not surprisingly concern only trees and shrubs, with no hint of a leaning towards herbaceous flowers. White was *par excellence* a planter of forest trees, and indeed won medals for the great numbers he established.[92] Although he was known as a man 'who lays out pleasure grounds and rides',[93] very few of his forty-two surviving plans indicates a pleasure, shrub or flower garden, although a notable exception was at Scone Palace, for which his extensive list of plants in 1784 certainly included pleasure-ground material – a great range of flowering shrubs and ornamental trees in small quantities, with thirty-eight different roses and six assorted honeysuckle varieties.[94] Unfortunately there is no indication, either on the plan or in correspondence, of the destination of these plants.

Woods stands out from his competitors as essentially a pleasure-ground/pleasure-garden designer. Where information survives about such park planting as he implemented there is an even more noticeable difference between his style and that of his contemporaries. The detailed planting instructions for Cusworth (see pp. 44–52), although rare survivals among archives relating to Woods, are likely to be typical of his practice: the plantation along the Spotborough boundary of the small park indicates a highly contrived arrangement, where informality vies with a very studied effect. Brown also used scattered specimen trees and outliers beyond the line of the plantation,[95] but the overall result must have been quite different and far more naturalistic, with a less artful planting mix and arrangement. Brown was also mainly working on a different scale from Woods, and whereas planting designed to be admired from a distance benefits from a simpler, less intricate, treatment, the majority of the parks in which Woods worked would have been seen at closer quarters – what Hanbury in his *Complete Body of Planting and Gardening* (1770) described as 'within the vortex of a morning walk'. This point is even made by Woods when he gave instructions at Cusworth to finish all the gravel walks in the garden, 'and then the walk through the park and field, to meet the walk along Sprodborough [sic] Park wall, and then Mr Wrightson will be so far compleat in a fine range of walk'.[96]

John Phibbs has demolished the idea that Brown did not plant evergreens,[97] and makes the point that 'eighteenth-century plantations that today are dominated by over-mature broad-leaves were often described by eighteenth-century travellers as fir woods.' However, the evidence for those few estates where Woods designed clumps and plantations within the park is that he used evergreens to a far greater extent than Brown. The explanation written under his little sketch for a circular fence 'proper to inclose clumps of Firrs pines & Cedars, where such are planted in parks near walks or coach roads' suggests that this is a common practice of his, which is also particularly noticeable at Cusworth. The memoranda contain several references to clumps or plantations containing only or mainly evergreens. For instance, to the north of the stables up to the intended lodges were groups of first firs[98] and pines mixed, then larches, then Scotch firs, then silver firs, then spruce firs, then Weymouth pines, 'and then begin with larches again and so on alternitely to the end'. Forest trees were scattered the other side of the fence enclosing the evergreens. Further instructions were to 'Finish all about the mount … that is to say to fill up the close planting … with Scotch spruce and silver firs and larches, and fill in with laurels and hollys'; 'About the cascade … plant nothing taller than laurels except a few larches and weeping willows … but on the south side may plant some firr with the other evergreens'; and 'The clump about the rock [arch] may be firrs filld up with other greens'.

It is also true that there are references to more usual planting mixes, such as the 'loose plantations in defferant places' composed of beech, elm and chestnut (near the library window) and 'arbeals' (*Populus alba*) with elms on the south side of the piece of water, but the overwhelming impression is of a remarkable insistence on evergreens. This was noted in 1787 by Angus in his description of Cusworth for his *Seats of the Nobility and Gentry*, although he does not name Woods in connection with the property: 'the Plantations in the Park contain a great Variety of different kinds of Firs, esteemed in as high a State of Perfection as any in the Kingdom'. It was obviously sufficiently uncommon a planting practice to be worth mentioning.

The unrelieved evergreen plantation mix suggested by Woods for Wivenhoe would not have found a place among Brown's designs, and the question also remains over how many firs Brown intended as nurse trees. He is recorded at Burton Constable as objecting to too many firs in the clumps,[99] whereas it is obvious from the Cusworth evidence that Woods was using the firs as part of a decorative mix. It is noticeable that Woods's sketches for garden buildings all include flanking bottle-brush trees, whereas the supporting vegetation in Brown's drawings was usually deciduous. Even the title vignette from the survey of Brown's own manor of

Fenstanton shows only deciduous trees.[100] Possibly our perception of Brown as planter of deciduous native trees has been influenced by the number of contemporary or near-contemporary views of his landscapes which appear to prove the point.

It is now recognised that all the improvers assumed the presence of flowers in their pleasure grounds to a greater or lesser degree, or at the very least were not averse to them. Yet for many decades it was the mistaken belief that in the mid eighteenth century flowers were banished from the landscape, and were allowed space only behind the walls of an enclosed garden – and this in spite of William Mason observing in the 1770s that 'the ornament which a variety of flowers gives to edges and borders, & clumps of shrubs, in small pleasure-grounds, is great & universally acknowledged'.[101] The explanation may lie in the role of the improvers, which was usually to transform an outmoded formal garden into a naturalistic landscape (or occasionally to create one on a new site) with contracts or correspondence concerning the large and expensive items that this entailed. The pleasure ground was a chronologically uninterrupted feature, whose rectangular beds left over from an earlier taste could be rounded or serpentised, or even grassed over, by the home workforce to bring them into line with fashion. Unless a newly positioned or designed garden within the landscape was commissioned, it did not necessarily enter the improver's remit even to mention it in correspondence. Naturally, exceptions can be found: as part of large-scale improvements at Sherborne (Dorset), Brown contracted in 1771 'to make and alter all the Garden Ground Enclosed, planting trees, shrubs and flowers'.[102] 'Lady Griffin's garden' at Audley End, which Brown contracted to make in 1763, shows oval beds on his plan which probably contained flowers, although there is no documentary evidence for it.[103] Brown is sometimes seen adding flowers with his own hand, as at Tottenham Park where the 'Minutes of Mr Brown's Proceedings 1 May 1766' record that he ordered 'a good Variety of Flowers planted to the front of the Shrubberys'.[104] A chance survival of the diary kept by Lord Harrowby shows Emes making suggestions for the new pleasure garden at Sandon Park (Staffordshire) in 1782:[105] '[Emes] has marked out a border for the flowering shrubs. Thinks a few laurels and other evergreens might form a background [then other shrubs] … and then a border of about three feet of flowers'. Lady Elizabeth Compton, for whom Richmond was working in 1778–9 at Compton Place, Sussex, wrote to her bailiff that she hoped to find 'a great profusion of all sorts of sweet Flowers about the House, Sea Seat & Paradise'.[106] Although Richmond and Emes and White snr all produced designs including pleasure grounds – indeed, Richmond at the latter end of his career specialised in this area[107] – where detailed documentation survives the evidence is for shrubs, even though the gardener would have added to the effect where appropriate with a margin of flowers. The emphasis on references specifically to flowers within the improvements, denoted by 'herbaceous dotting', puts Woods into a slightly different category from the other 'Brownian' practitioners. The inclusion of informal flower studs, beds and borders within the new style of gardening was a strand of eighteenth-century design started by the Hon. Richard ('Dickie') Bateman in the 1730s at Grove House, Old Windsor, at the same time that Southcote was setting out similar features in his *ferme ornée*. John Harris has pointed out the connection between Bateman, Southcote and Thomas Wright[108] (one of the few of that period to produce designs for roseries, as Woods did), and it is logical to see Woods continuing in this tradition linked to Southcote. It is not the same starting point as Brown's – the successor to Kent and creator of the ultimate naturalistic designed landscape – and this may be one of the reasons why Brown's and Woods's designs diverged as much as they did.

Woods has left no remark outlining his principles as revelatory as Brown's on the disposition of colours and shades in planting, with 'so much Beauty depending on the size of the trees and the colour of their leaves to produce the effect of light and shade so very essential to the perfecting of a good plan'.[109] As all Woods's surviving written comments and instructions were of a highly practical nature, mainly to foremen, it is rare to find an example such as the Cusworth memoranda, where he comments that the trees chosen for the screen 'will make a fine variety of shades', but just this one remark reveals him as a man who knew his trees, and had a definite visual result in mind.

CHAPTER 5

WOODS THE ASPIRING ARCHITECT

WOODS WAS AN ENTHUSIASTIC WOULD-BE ARCHITECT, although only once in the documentary record is he actually described as one. The entry in the estate account book for a visit to Chillington (Staffordshire) in 1770, apparently relating to a five-guinea design for the Gothic pavilion, was originally written 'Paid Mr Woods Designor &c of London' and was subsequently altered with the words 'Architect & gardener' inserted superscript.[1] The extent to which an improver was also expected to be able to supply architectural ideas, designs and building instructions varied. Capability Brown's position, in this respect as in so many others, was paramount, having had the invaluable start as clerk of works at Stowe through the 1740s, supervising the construction of some of the most fashionable and influential garden buildings going up at that time. As early as 1750 he had already designed the house at Croome, which was not just an elegant façade but also 'a model for every internal and domestic convenience',[2] and went on to become an accepted architect throughout his career, working either on his own or in conjunction with, *inter alios*, Henry Holland.

None of Brown's competitors in the field of landscape design could pretend to Brown's excellence in architecture, although all were expected to be proficient in the design and setting out of a kitchen garden and its associated structures. Apart from his work in this area, Richmond put forward only a few proposals for garden buildings, of which possibly only the Sea Seat at Compton Place and an alcove seat at Lamer were executed.[3] White included the occasional temple or summer-house on his plans, and referred to 'a thatched building', a 'handsome building or temple' and a garden house on his design for Belle Isle, but this was the exception rather than the rule.[4] Emes's architectural work was similarly slight: lodge designs for Attingham (probably not built), an unexecuted design for an orangery at Margam and for a greenhouse at Penrice, and a signed plan for a pinery at Kelmarsh make up the total.[5]

Compared with these, Woods's architectural output, even if mainly on paper, was considerable. From the evidence of the surviving documents alone he produced some forty designs, either included on a plan for improvement or as loose drawings; in addition there are another thirteen buildings specified on plans but for which the design was either not supplied or has not survived. Of that combined number only seventeen are known to have been built, and all that remain now are eight buildings, four bridges and some architectural elements built into new constructions.[6] Included in this list are greenhouses and pineries, plus any rockwork arches which formed part of a boathouse.

In reviewing the possible influences on Woods's architectural style, only those sources which could have been available to him have been considered: that is, pattern and other text books, contemporary guide books, and such gardens as were open to all comers.

PATTERN BOOKS[7]

Responding to the burgeoning market for both domestic and garden buildings, and at the same time feeding it, architects of differing skill rushed into print with designs. An early architectural pattern book to be published, and one of the most academically correct, was James Gibbs's *Book of Architecture* of 1728, which was partly an advertisement for what he had achieved and partly an invitation to 'Gentlemen as might be concerned in Building, especially in the remote parts of the Country, where little or no assistance for Designs can be procured [who] may be here furnished with Draughts of useful and convenient Buildings and proper Ornaments; which may be executed by any Workman who understands Lines, either as here Design'd, or with some Alteration.' However, the preface ends with a warning against 'any material Change' being made in the designs 'by the Forwardness of unskilful Workmen, or the Caprice of ignorant, assuming Practitioners'. Later and lesser pattern books were not so demanding: the preface to William Pain's *Builder's Companion* (1758) claims that all the examples illustrated in the book 'are immediately adapted to Workmen, and may be executed by the meanest Capacity'.

The quality of design and of advice varies enormously from book to book. Some contain no text to speak of and are scarcely more than pretty picture books,[8] while others give serious and detailed guidance: Isaac Ware's *Complete Body of Architecture* of 1756 (issued initially as a part work) claims to 'instruct rather than amuse', and contains information on a range of architectural subjects from mansions to garden temples, including the orders, drainage and cesspools, roofing, bridges and much else besides. The tone is practical and didactic, the format large, and the engravings finely executed. Robert Morris was another of the superior breed of pattern-book author, who in his long preface to *The Architectural Remembrancer* (1751) pointed out that many are taught the rules of architecture but few rise to greatness in its practice. He also noted that one of the signal uses of the pattern book was to help the patron decide on exactly what he wanted from a commission by showing a variety of examples and thus avoiding disappointment in the finished building.

CLASSICAL, GOTHIC AND EXOTIC

Garden buildings in the form of gazebos and banqueting houses had been a feature of garden design from the sixteenth century. Throughout the seventeenth century statues, urns and fountains were regularly found scattered in garden designs, with columns or pavilions to give focus to a vista, but while the earlier Grand Tourists commented delightedly on the waterworks and grottos they saw in Italian gardens they made little reference to the temple ruins that so excited a later generation. Timothy Nourse in *Campania Foelix* of 1700 (a book owned by Woods), the aim of which was to encourage his readers to improve their estates from both an agricultural and aesthetic aspect, wrote of fountains, statues and a shell-work grotto, but no garden buildings.[9]

By the 1740s the scene had already shifted and was changing rapidly. The popularity of the classical temple or pavilion was a direct result of inspiration from the Grand Tour,[10] which by the second quarter of the eighteenth century was coming to be regarded as an educational necessity for a great number of well-bred young Britons.[11] William Kent's influence was paramount in promoting not just a more naturalistic style of gardening but also a leaning towards the Italy he had grown to love during his ten-year residence there. Kent's ideas, implemented via and with Burlington and then on through polite society, were eagerly taken up by the fashion-conscious, and Palladianism (or a vaguer classicism) became the exciting new style, whose seed had been germinating since Inigo Jones had practised it with such panache in the 1620s. The enthusiasm for the reinvention of Italy in England spread and flourished, both in serious architecture and for the more ephemeral and frivolous decoration of the new landscaped garden, with the demand gradually spreading outwards into a slightly lower layer of society as the style became popularised.

However, most practitioners of the new style of gardening sought variety as eagerly as classical correctness and, while classical temples and alcoves were tentatively invading the English designed landscape in the 1730s[12] (and ultimately were never supplanted in overall popularity), other imported styles were finding their apologists from the 1740s. By the mid century, a proliferation of garden buildings could be found in classical, Gothic or Chinese form, with a sprinkling of such fancies as Turkish, Indian and Egyptian, and various emanations of rustic and grotesque. Wooburn Farm had been no more than an unadorned stretch of farmland when Philip Southcote bought it in 1734, but James Parnell on a visit to the famous *ferme ornée* in 1763 (five years after Southcote's death) noted that the scene had been enlivened with 'several pretty pavilions'. These included a 'new-contrived' ruin, an 'octagon building', a 'seat under a pediment supported by four Doric columns', a 'Gothic seat in a recess', a menagerie 'with a fine gothic front … wch makes a pretty seat', a 'Rustic Cell' decorated with quite a heavy rustication, a 'Gothic hut, thatched' (a hermitage) and a 'little

Chinese bridge'. By this time such an eclectic collection was standard, and Tobias Smollett in 1766 considered that 'arbours, grottos, hermitages, temples and alcoves' were what an Englishman expected to see 'in a fine extensive garden or park'.[13]

Any of the prevailing styles could be commandeered for ornamental garden buildings, irrespective of their relevance to the purpose of the construction. Unlike the perceived correct iconography for the placing of statues (Neptune presiding over a basin, Flora in a flower garden, etc.), there seemed to be no such rule attached to garden buildings, with the single – and not invariably applied – exception of the 'rustic' to express the idea of a hermitage or grotto. Walpole complained of the Gothic ruin at Painshill that 'The Goths never built summer houses or temples in a garden', although this was a purist attitude that did not stand in his way when building the castellated villa of Strawberry Hill on the banks of the Thames,[14] and it was certainly not a generally held view. This is noticeable in the pattern books, where different versions of a building are presented one after the other, with no indication of a change of setting. A Chinese alcove seat was as acceptable as Gothic or classical in exactly the same place, and even design hybridisation was illustrated in the less serious publications. This eclecticism could easily get out of hand if insufficient screening were provided between China and Greece. Parnell, commenting on the other gardens he visited in 1763, saw the absurdity of cramming together buildings with quite different connotations. He was enthusiastic about Kew, but regretted that

> nothing prevents the Eye from taking in all the Buildings at one View, or at least the greater Part, which, tho' pleasing to the last degree in themselves; as they are of Different Orders, or rather the orders of Different Nations, is an amazing absurdity. Where Different Nations are thus introduced into an Improvement they shoud at least be hid from one another by an hill, wood, or clump of trees that, as we walk from one, before we have a View of the other, the Fancy may have room to change to that Country, where the Building supposes us to be, but thus to exhibit a Grecian Temple within one hundred yards of a Gothic which comes again as near a Chinese is as irreconcilable to Fancy as to Nature or Reason.[15]

SOURCES

The study of Woods's essays in architecture is complicated by the fact that there is no single style, either of drawing or of the built result, that is clearly his own. This is compounded by the facts that he obviously employed one or more draughtsmen (the collected drawings over his career are not all in the same hand or style) and that those drawings which are annotated in his own writing, rather than just signed, are far cruder in execution than the others. There are examples of both in the Wardour archive. He certainly had recourse to pattern books, and used them exactly as intended, for construction advice and to provide suggestions and sources of detail rather than as designs to be lifted complete from the pages. Robert Morris, whose overall style seems to have had a considerable influence on Woods's designs, hoped that 'to a fertile Genius' his drawings might be 'an Assistant, in adapting any Part of them to a Variety of Purposes for Utility or Ornament'. There are also similarities between a number of Woods's designs and those of Isaac Ware, whose book may have been another that he consulted.

Among the books known to have been owned by Woods, which were sold in 1783, are William Chambers's *Civil Architecture* (1759) and James Leoni's *Architecture [of Alberti]* (1726), both expensively produced folios rather than pattern books as such. Lowlier volumes were Sebastien Le Clerc's *Treatise of Architecture* (English edition 1724), William Salmon's *Palladio Londoniensis or the Art of London Building* (1734) and William Halfpenny's 'Architecture' – probably his *New and Compleat System of Architecture* (1749) or *Useful Architecture* (1752). In addition, Woods had Batty Langley's *London Prices* (1750), a blow-by-blow guide to pricing building work down to the cost of the last nail. These books alone would have given him a full range of diagrams, designs and information on all aspects of the orders and the uses to which they could be put; detailed advice on a wide field of construction, from foundations to roofs; much information on brickwork and on the construction of bridges, and on mensuration and pricing; there is even a useful chapter in the Leoni on the conveying of water and how to keep canals well supplied. They also all included examples of general architectural details, such as window and door architraves, which could be easily adapted to garden buildings. After Woods's death his widow sold his remaining volumes, which are likely to have included a number of pattern books whose titles will probably never be known. It seems that Woods, who had probably learned much of his surveying techniques from text books, had branched – albeit at a superficial level – into the art of architecture by the same method.

A complementary way to absorb information on new styles and trends in garden design was by studying examples. Whereas Brown actively worked at Stowe, the only way Woods had access to this much-celebrated garden was by joining the throng of visitors, and/or by studying one of its guide books. The earliest of these, Benton Seeley's *Description of the Gardens …at Stow*, which first came out in 1744, contains several pages of fairly crude images of the features to be seen. One of them, the 'Obelisk', bears a striking resemblance to a design of 1767 by Woods for Wardour, where he combined it with a rustic base and a dove-house.

The little architectural drawings that appear on some of Woods's plans show a considerable variety of approach. The only composition that reappears throughout his career – albeit spasmodically – is a façade with

Fig. 20. Benton Seeley's drawing of the obelisk at Stowe, 1744 (right), and Woods's drawing for a garden building at Wardour, 1769 (left). This is one of several instances where Woods seems to have taken ideas from pattern books or engravings.

rather heavy rustication, often including vermiculation, and associated with piers or pilasters interrupted by blocks of rustication.[16] It appears, for instance, in his built structures at Wardour of the 1760s and in a design as late as 1780 on a plan for Audley End (see Figure 61). Even at the earlier date this style was looking old-fashioned (except when adapted to the sort of 'rustic' designs of Thomas Wright's *Grottos*, in his *Universal Architecture* of 1758), and these are not features that appear commonly in the pattern books. Ware in 1756 shows a sparing use of vermiculation and architraves with intermittent blocks, usually as a minor part of a major building. Robert Morris is the only architectural writer who was illustrating large expanses of vermiculation in the 1750s, and there is a strong similarity of feeling between his design for an octagonal pavilion in *Rural Architecture* (1750) and the almost solidly vermiculated surfaces of Woods's ice-house portico at Buckland (1758+) – see Figs. 21 and 22 below. It is very likely that Woods owned and used books by Morris, since there are other clues that he borrowed from both *Rural Architecture* and *The Architectural Remembrancer*.

The slight shift in emphasis from solid vermiculation towards blocks of vermiculation alternating with ashlar, prefigured at Buckland and exhibited in Woods's work at Wardour in the 1760s, can perhaps be traced to an example lying not far away. As Woods approached Wardour from London, his road crossed the grounds of Fonthill Redivivus (as it was then

RICHARD WOODS
(1715–1793)
MASTER OF THE
PLEASURE GARDEN

Above: Fig. 21. The ice house at Buckland, after 1759. Note the similarity of treatment to Robert Morris's design in Figure 22.

Right: Fig. 22. Design for a garden building by Robert Morris, 1750.

called) and passed under the splendid gateway which still stands at the entrance to the park.[17] The vermiculated detailing on the arch, even to the ears on the grotesque head keystone, is so close to Woods's cold-bath façade at Wardour that it suggests more than coincidence. The only examples in the pattern books for a part-vermiculated arch with grotesque keystone can be found in bridge designs published by Ware (Figure 43), which might have reinforced Woods's leaning towards the style.

Above: Fig. 23. The gateway into the park at Fonthill. Woods would have passed under this on his way to Wardour, and might have taken the decoration around the arch as inspiration for Lord Arundell's cold bath (see photo right).

Right: Fig. 24. The entrance to the cold bath at Wardour. Photo Michael Cyprien.

WOODS'S GOTHIC

Woods's approach to Gothic was characteristically magpie-like, as is clearly seen from an alcove on the Wormsley plan for an improvement of c.1779. The design is an adaptation and simplification of two drawings from William Halfpenny's *Rural Architecture in the Gothick Taste* (1752). The remains of one of Woods's earliest known buildings, the 'Gothick alcove' of c.1761 at the head of the canal at Little Linford in Buckinghamshire (Plate 8), suggest that it was probably similar to that at Wormsley. A Gothic alcove was also marked on the plan for Cannon Hall (Yorkshire) but no design was included.

The 'Gothick tempel' in the Lady Grove at Wardour is important in Woods's oeuvre inasmuch as it was actually built, is dated and documented, and survived long enough to be photographed, although in a very dilapidated state. There is an entry in the 1766 accounts for 4 guineas for a design, but in common with the drawings for the other features that were built (not just suggested), it was probably used on site as a working plan and has not survived. The agreement to start work on the temple – part of the complete reorganisation of the Lady Grove – was signed in 1768, Woods undertaking to have finished it by midsummer 1769 at a cost of £46. Photographs taken before its collapse (too faded to reproduce) suggest that the design, which originally incorporated a decorated stone parapet, can be traced to Batty Langley's seminal *Ancient Architecture* (1742),[18] again as an amalgam of several plates giving a different and original result.

Woods's Gothic was a substantial, even slightly ponderous version of the style, with none of the lightheartedness of Strawberry Hill. This trait is

Figs 25 and 26. The Gothic alcove on Woods's plan for the improvement of Wormsley Park, redrawn by Andrew Westman. The inspiration for this design seems to have been taken from two of Halfpenny's plates (see Fig. 26 on right for one of them) in *Rural Architecture in the Gothic Taste*. The remains of the Gothic alcove at Little Linford suggest that it was also similar.

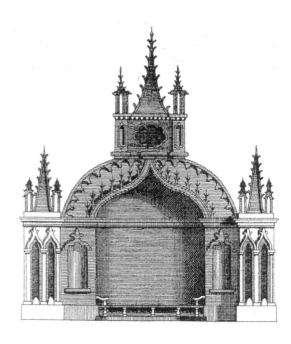

Figs. 27 (left) and 28 (below). The 'Gothic tempel' in Lady Grove at Wardour in 1983, shortly before further collapse. It has since been dismantled and re-erected (with some alteration of the design) in the grounds of Hatfield Peverel Priory. Woods's inspiration again came from Batty Langley, as an amalgam of two plates in *Gothic Architecture Improved* (Fig. 31 on page 84 shows a pierced stone parapet and octagonal pitched roof, and Fig. 49 on page 105 has the ogee arches, both features of the original form of the 'Gothic tempel').

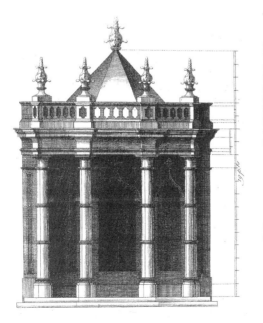

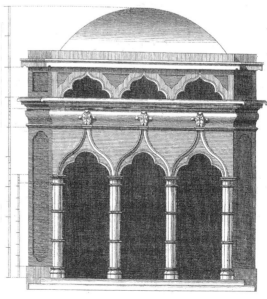

Fig. 29. The now demolished Gothic belvedere at Chillington Castle, probably to Woods's design. He drew two versions of this form of building (see Fig. 30 [left and below left]), following various pattern books by taking details from each rather than lifting a design wholesale.

Fig. 30. (left) The Gothic belvedere referenced on Woods's plan for Wardour (1764); *(below left)* design for 'Tower or Castle' from Woods's plan for Stanway (1792); *(below)* Batty Langley's 'Gothick *Pavillion*' from *Gothic Architecture Improved*, 1747, illustrating some of the aspects of the Chillington belvedere. This work contains another very similar design.

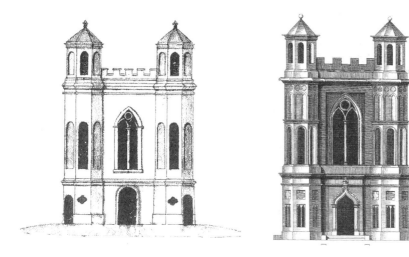

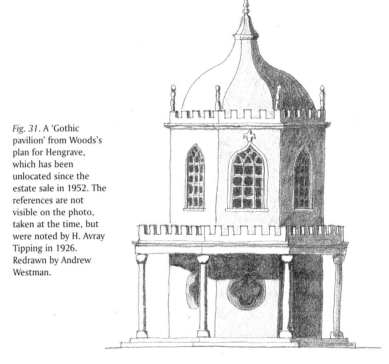

Fig. 31. A 'Gothic pavilion' from Woods's plan for Hengrave, which has been unlocated since the estate sale in 1952. The references are not visible on the photo, taken at the time, but were noted by H. Avray Tipping in 1926. Redrawn by Andrew Westman.

evident again in the Gothic pavilion at Chillington, which has been ascribed to Woods on the grounds that it was built shortly after his visit in the guise of 'Designor and architect', and because of its similarity to the 'Castle or tower' he suggested for Stanway, his last plan for improvement, in 1792. There is also a loose drawing among the Wardour papers of a Gothic belvedere, which probably relates to a feature of that name on Woods's plan of 1764. The plan for Hengrave of 1777 includes a 'Gothic Temple' of a rather different design, which although lighter in feeling lacks balance between the top and bottom halves.

When putting together a 'Skitch for a ruin'd Gateway' for Wardour in 1770 (not executed), Woods seems to have taken as his model one of the 'Façades to place before disagreable Objects' from Lightoler's *Gentleman's and Farmer's Architect* (1762).[19] But he was sensitive enough to the *genius loci* to adapt his drawing to the style of the real ruin within the grounds, and inserted into the arch the tripartite round-headed Gothic windows from the side of Old Wardour Castle, clearly shown on the Buck engraving of 1735. This was in true Gothic style, far removed from Batty Langley's fantasies, and throws into relief the eclecticism of the age. For the single estate of Wardour, Woods designed Gothic and Gothick, classical in both early and mid-century style, rustic and Chinese.

CHINESE

George Mason, writing in 1768, observed, 'Little did Sir William Temple imagine, that in about half a century the Chinese would become the fashionable taste in this country.'[20] Following in the wake of early examples of 'Chinese' pavilions,[21] the craze took off at a galloping rate, and by 1750 had attracted even Horace Walpole, who toyed for a short time with the idea of building a Chinese summer-house at Strawberry Hill.[22]

Precisely what was understood by a 'Chinese' house is not very clear. Japan and China were usually confounded in the popular mind, and it was apparently not thought incongruous that the interior of the Stowe pavilion was, in the words of the Marchioness Grey, 'quite wainscotted with Japan [i.e. lacquer panels]; … a great many Screens have been cut to pieces (I fancy) to make it.'[23] As William Chambers wrote in his preface to *Chinese Architecture* of 1757, 'Our notions of [Chinese] architecture are very imperfect', an observation fully justified by some of the whimsical and fantastic creations to be found in the pattern books. Whereas Chambers's drawings are a serious attempt to record a style of architecture that he had seen while in the service of the Swedish East India Company, the concoctions of Charles Over included identical structures that could be Gothic or Chinese by the addition of a crenellation here, a bell and dragon there,[24] and even Thomas Wright could produce a drawing for a 'Chinese Gothic' temple.[25] Chambers looked on Chinese buildings as 'toys in architecture', and, with a handful of long-lived exceptions, most of the pavilions in this taste were probably constructed of wood, which quickly deteriorated once the fashion was past and they were no longer maintained. This is borne out by Thomas Pennant's scornful dismissal of most 'Chinese' structures as a 'mongrel invention of British carpenters'.[26] Bridges became 'Chinese' through a simple lattice balustrade – as in the 'Chineas Bridge and Cascade' on Woods's Hengrave plan of 1777 – and boats by the addition of a dragon-head prow and curlicue stern, as seen sailing on the Great Pond in Woods's plan for Wardour. The design for gates into the rosery or 'entrance to the wood' at Wardour was similarly only Chinese at the most superficial level, with 'rustic' piers supporting Chinese lattice panel gates.

Woods's only known built essay in the Chinese style is at Alresford (Essex). The commission, of 1772–6, was for the adaptation of a small building in the grounds of the Hall near the bank of the pond (which appears on a survey of 1730 and therefore owes nothing to Woods) and the construction of a 'Chinese Temple', consisting of an ante-room and passage leading to an octagonal banqueting room, with a little gallery over the water for fishing. The design bears a passing resemblance to a little pavilion built on the bank of the Thames at Petersham, near Richmond, by the Duke and Duchess of Queensberry, known as Gay's Summer House (they had housed the poet John Gay for much of his adult life).[27] As it was presumably built before Gay died in 1732, there is a possibility that it was seen from the river

Fig. 32. Engraving of 'Gay's summer house' on the banks of the Thames at Richmond. It has affinities with Woods's Chinese Temple at Alresford, Essex, and could have been seen by him while he was living at London Stile.

by Woods, living at Kew in the 1760s, and that he liked the style and stored it in his memory. If a Chinese connection was needed, only a little further upstream was the Chinese pavilion in the grounds of Crossdeep House.[28]

The estimate for the Alresford 'Chinese Temple'[29] gives an insight into the construction as well as design details: the 'caps and all flatt parts of ye roof' were to be leaded, and the rest covered with 'tarpoling straind upon the bording and painted on both sides so as to turn the water'; under the eaves of the gallery was a 'sweeping sofate' (Woods may have borrowed from pattern books but did not extend his debt to spelling), and 14ft (4.25m) of Chinese railing were to go round the gallery and under the two side windows. The oriental effect was diluted by the '4 Gothick cullums' holding up the gallery roof – a perfect example of insouciant design hybridisation. There is nothing Chinese suggested in the fold-down plan of the interior, and the end result looks more like an engaging cottage with an intriguingly styled roof than anything out of the Orient, although the estimate does hint at the 'ironwork [that] may be wanting weathercock bells etc'. The instructions and section for the making of the foundations of the gallery[30] again show Woods in the light of a structural engineer, with specifications for the 'carcass frameing' to be supported by two oak girders with struts bolted on to it and resting on a ledge in the brickwork. Flanking buttresses, mainly below water level, provided the necessary stability, and a drain was inserted between the water line and the gallery floor to prevent flood damage when the sluice at the end of the pond was insufficient. This little house, which survives in good heart,[31] was given immortality in a painting of 1816 by Constable.[32]

The only other reference by Woods to a Chinese temple is on the plan for Wardour, but a drawing for it is lacking in the archive. Perhaps this was another influence from the park at Fonthill, which in the 1750s had a 'Chinese rotondo' on one of the hills in front of the house.[33]

A design for Fishing inside of Banqueting Room

Left: Fig. 33. One of two fold-down plans for the interior of Woods's Chinese Temple at Alresford. The vaguely Chinese treatment of the façades was not repeated indoors.

Below: Fig. 34. Oil on canvas by John Constable of Woods's Chinese Temple (now Quarters House). This painting, with a companion canvas of Wivenhoe Park, was commissioned by Colonel Rebow as a favour to the artist who was trying to make sufficient money to marry Maria Bicknell. Constable described his painting as 'a scene in a wood with a beautiful little fishing house'.

GREENHOUSES AND PINERIES

The combination of utility and ornament in a garden feature is typical of the eighteenth-century attitude. The functional aspect of greenhouses was nothing new: oranges and other tender greens had been protected by movable timber housing from the sixteenth century,[34] and by more permanent structures in brick and slate from the seventeenth.[35] By the end of that century, and trailing the Continent, some effort was being made to give the over-wintering of tender plants some aesthetic importance, as can be seen in the engraving of the Versailles-inspired Bretby with a seven-bay pedimented greenhouse,[36] or the still-extant greenhouse of 1704 at Kensington Palace in London. From the eighteenth century, the ornamental greenhouse had arrived. It was still tile- or slate-roofed,[37] and received sunlight and natural warmth only from the large south-facing windows, while in the cold weather flues carried heat round the building from a stove. The pineapple, which required a greater level of light and heat to fruit, had to be housed in a different sort of building, closer in feeling to the modern greenhouse, with sloping glass panes rising to a ridge roof, and provision for tan beds to provide warmth below the plants.

It is rare to find a functional pinery, as distinct from an ornamental greenhouse, on its own in a position of visual prominence,[38] but the novelty of the luxury nevertheless sometimes allowed it a place in full view in the first half of the century. Pope's villa at Twickenham had pineries on unashamed show flanking the raised portico on the river front of the house after the alterations of the 1730s.[39]

A pinery by Woods was to be similarly on display at Cannon Hall. A letter to Woods in May 1760 from John Stanhope, friend and brother-in-law of John Spencer, for whom Woods was designing the pinery, sheds rare light on Woods's real or perceived competence. Stanhope, who had been asked to comment on Woods's suggestions, queried the 'arched Cavities … under the Walks round the Pits or Bark-beds' which he thought would keep the tan too dry; he found the 17ft (5m) bearings of 'an extraordinary length … that no Timber will ever carry'; he could not understand why the glasses sloped backwards and thought them too large at 6ft (1.8m), 'wch. is too high for any Man to manage' let alone with the extra weight of covers (to shade the glasses when necessary), and told Woods: 'whether you intend any Covors or not, I cannot say, but this from my own Experience I am sure of, that none are necessary.'[40] Having demolished most of the essentials of Woods's pinery, he concluded, 'I woud. not have you imagine, I find fault with your design in ye main'. Neither the plan for the Cannon Hall pinery nor Woods's reply, received by Spencer in June, have survived but the building of the Cannon Hall pinery proceeded without delay and was complete that August. The diary of John Spencer records its progress in economical terms, culminating in the laconic but triumphant, 'Cut the first Pineapple out of my Hot House'.[41]

A plan and elevation for a pinery – although not as built – produced by

Woods for Wardour a few years later shows arched cavities beneath the walks, 6ft (1.8m) glasses and long bearings. For covers, Woods suggested nothing so archaic as wooden shutters to be lifted on and off, but 'Tarpalion fix'd wth. rowlers'. Woods was probably ahead of Stanhope in understanding the limits to which glasshouse design could be taken; he had previously designed and built at least one pinery, at Hartwell, and it appears from the evidence at Wardour that he was not impressed by Stanhope's remarks.

In spite of the examples at Cannon Hall and Pope's pineries on the villa façade, it was more usual for pineries to be placed in the kitchen garden. Examples on Woods's plans are at Copford, Little Linford and Wormsley, although there is no evidence that these were built. At Hartwell, although Woods's design has not survived to confirm it, the greenhouse is obviously a feature in a decorative garden within the kitchen garden while the pinery is in a less prominent position behind it (see Figure 17).

Woods's design for the whole complex at Wardour, built in 1769 – ornamental greenhouse[42] flanked by pineries, with hot walls and back sheds, in a new walled kitchen garden – was a typical approach to the interrelation of the functional and ornamental. A design for an elaborate greenhouse in the Wardour archive is not the one used, which like that for the Gothick temple was probably the site plan and was thrown away once it had served

Fig. 35. The greenhouse designed by Woods in 1769 for the new kitchen garden at Wardour, flanked by pineries which have now been converted into bungalows.

its purpose. The estimate specifies 'the front of Ashler-stone, and the back of Burr-stone, the floor of smooth paving stone to be covered with Devonshire slate, the sashes made of Wainscot Oak and glazed with Crown Glass, a stone cornice Outside and light stucco cornice inside, the roof framed of good elm and fir timber the Wall plates and bond timbers of oak, the whole to be completed, finding all materials &c. for £320.' In February 1770, with the interior plaster not yet started, sixty orange trees in three different sizes were chosen and bought by Woods on Lord Arundell's account from 'Mr Sesarego' at the Olive Tree in Air Street, Piccadilly, and transported to Wardour. The greenhouse has recently been restored as part of enabling development, with the pineries converted into bungalows which visually overpower it and destroy the architectural balance between them.

When associated with – usually flanked by – pineries or stoves, the place of the greenhouse was in the kitchen garden, even where it had been given some architectural pretension. When standing on its own, however, it was more likely to be located in the pleasure ground, as in Thomas Robins's celebrated view of the garden at Woodside;[43] on two plans where no pinery was commissioned, Woods gave the greenhouse a prominent position within the pleasure ground. His greenhouse at Brizes faced the beginning of the main ornamental circuit from the house, with a little lawn in front of it probably for orange trees in tubs and suchlike during the summer months (see Plate 5). At Wivenhoe the plan for improvement shows that the greenhouse was incorporated into a symmetrical arrangement of ancillary buildings flanking the mansion, but looking straight over the pleasure grounds (see Figure 11): no design seems to have been supplied for this. A greenhouse of similar design to the one at Wardour can just be glimpsed in the pleasure ground at the edge of a painting of New Hall (Essex), where Woods was working in the late 1760s (see Plate 4).

ICE HOUSES

The early ice houses were no more than pits dug in the ground and lined with straw, with the insulation process achieved by alternating layers of ice or packed snow with more straw, and yet more straw covering the surface. By the middle of the eighteenth century the idea had filtered down to gentry level, although it was still considered quite extravagant and exotic, and had developed into a brick-lined structure which was sometimes given an architectural embellishment, either an ornamented doorway or a portico almost doubling as a grotto.[44] The technology remained the same, although applied in a more sophisticated way.

Woods designed at least three ice houses, at Buckland, Wardour and Lulworth. Of these, that at Buckland is still standing (Figure 21), the one at Wardour has been demolished, and the structure at Lulworth is known only from Woods's plan for its construction. To gain a clear idea of Woods's work in this area, a composite picture has to be made from the evidence provided by these three examples. For the earliest, that at Buckland, built for Sir Robert Throckmorton sometime after 1758, there is no documentary archive but the completeness of the structure, comprising portico, ice chamber and thatched roof, makes a happy comparison with the desolation of the remains of the Wardour ice house shortly before its final demise.

For Wardour, the memorandum of the agreement between Lord Arundell

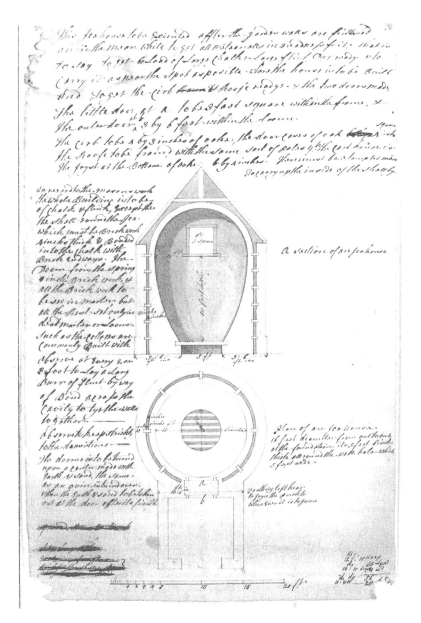

Fig. 36. Woods's instructions for building the ice house at Lulworth, c.1770. A porch (probably ornamental) was envisaged, although no design was left for it.

and Woods, in May 1765, makes it clear that Arundell paid for the materials but Woods was responsible for the cartage of bricks and lime, and of stone from the quarry. Woods contracted to 'Digg the foundations to make the Earth Centers to turn the Arch upon, to saw out the whole Rofe [roof] to make the two Door and Door Cases ... to thatch the rofe of the Ice house and Tile the rofe of the porch the whole to be completed for forty pounds'. The portico, priced at an extra five pounds, was described as a 'Grotesk front to the porch'. The style was similar to that of the cold bath (see Figure 38) which lay a short distance away, with a pedimented arch of vermiculated blocks alternating with smooth ashlar. Instead of two open side arches within the portico, as at Buckland, there were two shallow arched recesses or seats flanking the door to the ice chamber.

The design for Lulworth (c.1770)[45] provides more details of the building process, and shows that Woods was well aware of the problems of construction and did not just hand the drawing to the workmen and expect them to know what to do. If he took his architectural ideas from pattern books, his knowledge of construction techniques in all their complexity must have been learnt at the same time as his surveying, probably again from the available instruction books. He gives all the dimensions of the supporting timbers, advises that 'there must be a templet [template] made to carry up the inside of the shell by' and specifies that 'the shell round the Ice ... must be brickwork 4 inches [10cm] thick and bonded into the chalk with brick endways. ... Observe at every 2 or 3 feet [60–90cm] to lay a long Burr of flint by way of Bond across the Cavity to tye the walls together. Observe to keep stricly to the dementions.' Although no design was left for it, apparently an ornamental porch was planned for a future date, as the instructions by the doorway on the plan read: 'Toothing left here to joyn the porch to whenever it is to go on'.

Brown is known to have designed a few ice houses, for instance at Beechwood Park (Hertfordshire)[46] and at Castle Ashby (Northamptonshire), for which his account book records building a new ice house 'in a very Expensive manner and Plan £68 0s 0d'.[47] However, considering Brown's output, there are surprisingly few surviving designs or structures on record, although this might reflect a lack of research on the subject.

COLD BATHS

The notion that bathing in cold water was good for mind and body had been urged in print since the mid sixteenth century,[48] but again became common practice only in the eighteenth. John Floyer, writing of the history of cold bathing in 1702, considered that it 'rendered the limbs strong, musculous and lively' but did not recommend it for anyone under twenty years old or 'of thin Habits'.[49] An essential part of the therapy was the coldness of the water, and he dismissed cold baths 'made in a Tub, so not cold enough for the purpose design'd'. Hence the fashion, at least until the later eighteenth century, for the cold bath as part of the garden rather than as an interior design improvement, since only outside would there be access to a good supply of really cold running water, preferably a spring. The comment of Greville that the water in the bath at Oatlands was 'clear as crystal and cold as ice' neatly summarises the two necessary qualities.[50] One of the earliest cold plunge baths to be associated with a pleasurable activity was built in Rusthall (Kent) in 1708 and was 'at first adorned with amusing waterworks, and a handsome house over it'.[51] The Bagnio at Chiswick, built about 1717, was a more substantial and architecturally important building than the term 'cold bath' implies, and doubtless added to the growing popularity of the idea of cold bathing. Stowe had a cold bath by about 1723; Kent gave one to Rousham in the 1730s in the form of an open-air octagonal pool with a little cavern-like building for dressing; and a plunge pool had been included in the Painswick layout by 1748.

The very idea of bathing – whether in the sea, a public bath, or one's own plunge pool – was regarded by some with hesitation as late as 1778: letters from Mary Rebow to her husband at that time relate her resistance to the idea of trying the nearby Wivenhoe Baths, and then her delight when she found that there 'is a pretty little room to dress in, the water is perfectly clear'.[52] Woods was working for the Rebows at this time, laying out their grounds at Wivenhoe Park, but there is no suggestion for a cold bath among the improvements, in spite of the fact that a spring is marked on the plan.

The only cold bath known to have been executed by Woods was at Wardour, but he left a plan and elevation for one on the design for the Elysium Garden at Audley End (Figure 61), while a 'Cold bath and grotto' is among the references for Cannon Hall and the plan for Hengrave includes a 'Cold Bath'. It is also likely that one of the little buildings on the plan for Wormsley (now missing the references) was a cold bath.

Fig. 37. A drawing by Woods on his plan for Wormsley Park, 1779 or 1780. Judging by its 'rustic' style and similarity to his designs for cold baths at Wardour and Audley End, this probably was intended for the same purpose. The references for this plan are lost, and the purpose of the little buildings has to be guessed. Redrawn by Andrew Westman.

The association of bathing with streams and nymphs made the grotesque a very suitable style for a bath house, and Woods's building instructions for Wardour stipulate that the outside was to be 'rough built'. The rugged was not to stray inside, however: the two rooms, one for the pool and one for a dressing room with fireplace, both 12ft (3.6m) square and top-lit by lanterns, were to have walls 'flooted like stone', a coved ceiling and 'plain stucco

Top: Fig. 38. Design by Woods for the Cold Bath at Wardour, c.1766. The portico was slightly changed for the built version (see next figure) but the tumbling cascade remained the same.

Right: Fig. 39. A photograph of 1958 showing the Cold Bath before the portico was moved to the side. The upper storey was added in the nineteenth century.

cornice'. Woods instructed the foreman to 'observe that round the dressing room you must lay some rough stones to keep the earth from tuching the foundations, which will otherways make the room very damp, these stones lay'd in the manner of a stone drain without mortar will do very well.' The pool itself, the 'Cistern', was 10ft long, 8ft wide and 5ft deep (3 x 2.4 x 1.5m) with stone steps down and stone-paved floors. Lead pipes and brass cocks were supplied 'to let the water in and out' from the stream over which it was built. The impression left by the elevations and construction detail is one of a slightly whimsical but neat building, with none of the high ornamentation of the grotto bath house at Oatlands, but a sufficient rustic elegance for its surroundings.[53]

The Audley End design is for a 'Bath and Tea Room'. The elevation is in a similar stolid rustic style, but there is a little more fantasy in the plan of the octagonal tea room, where apsidal niches have been set into four of the walls (see Figure 61); a fireplace is also shown. Little of Woods's plan for the Elysium Garden was adopted, but the notion that the garden would be a pleasant place to take tea at the end of a stroll from the house was translated to the bridge eventually designed by Adam, now called the Tea Bridge. Possibly this aspect of the Elysium Garden was specified by Sir John Griffin Griffin on commissioning the plan from Woods, or possibly it was Woods's own idea that was taken up and developed.

The baths designed by Brown at Corsham Court, Burleigh and Beechwood Park had architectural qualities far beyond Woods's competence: they were obviously intended to have a far higher profile in the landscape, and would have been commensurately more costly to build.

GROTTOS AND ROCKWORK

The grotto as an architectural form was introduced to England in the early seventeenth century as an elaborately decorated basement room, richly patterned with arabesques of shellwork and designed as a parlour rather than a place to meditate or seek inspiration. This form of grotto continued to be popular through the eighteenth century in the slightly altered guise of a shell house, a little building in the grounds frequently decorated by the ladies of the family. At the same time, a different version evolving from the same initial inspiration appeared in the early eighteenth century as a cavern fashioned from rough-hewn boulders, dripping with natural or piped water, with or without decoration of minerals, spars and ores. Pope's celebrated grotto at Twickenham, started in the 1720s and still being elaborated at his death in 1754, falls into this category and it is noticeable that by this time the grotto's stated purpose had shifted from a purely social venue to a place of half-serious reverence for a nymph or deity. The rugged aspect now associated with such a structure is illustrated by Pope in a letter to Ralph Allen in 1741: 'I told you my grotto was finished, and now all that wants to the Completion of my Garden is the Frontispiece to it, of your rude Stones to build a sort of Ruinous Arch at the Entry to it on the Garden side.'[54]

It is extremely doubtful whether Woods appreciated any of the classical connotations associated with 'grotesque' forms of building, but it was certainly a style that attracted him, whether or not he had seen Thomas Wright's *Universal Architecture* of 1758, with its section on grottos. Unfortunately no design has survived for the 'grotto over the spring' marked on the Little Linford plan, and the 'cold bath and grotto' on the plan for Cannon Hall also lacks a drawing. A grotto marked on the plan for Wardour is depicted as a low rocky mound surmounted by scrubby planting, adding up to hardly more than a rough rock arch. Such a rock arch in various forms was used by Woods on several occasions: there is documentation of examples adapted to a boathouse entrance, a cascade or a terminating point for a piece of water. It is possible that he might have seen a version of this at Stowe, on the ground or from the pages of Benton Seeley's guide book of 1750, where it is described as 'An Artificial Piece of Rock-work'. A print of 1749 was also in circulation, depicting the cascade at Belton with the water gushing under a rough central arch.[55]

Woods recognised the potential for the concealment of a simple summer boathouse by a rocky arch blending perfectly into the artfully natural waterside. Whereas his design for such a boathouse at Wardour, c.1764 and illustrated by a very amateurish sketch, was not executed, the concept had been most successfully realised at Cusworth in 1762. Here the finished product survives, together with the plan and elevation, and with comments on the construction in Woods's memorandum of 1762 to the Cusworth foreman.[56] As usual, his instructions are grammatically unpolished but contain a wealth of practical advice:

> You are to observe that the boat house should be built this
> autumn otherwise it will be attended with great
> inconveniences affter the river is full of water, for you are to
> observe, that in turning this arch no wood center must be
> used, but affter the walls are got up to the plenth that a flat
> scaffel of bords is to be made upon the plinth, and upon that
> a mould to be raised with earth to the shape of the arch,
> wch will much better answer the purpose. In seting the arch,
> some of the stones may be let down 5 or 6 inches some 3 or
> 4 inches, and some stand flush upon the mould, by wch
> means the arch will apear very rough and craggy.

The plan and elevation drawing for this grotto shows a bench perched on the mount behind the arch. Some twenty years later, in Woods's plan for Copford Hall, a bench is similarly positioned above a rustic arch which was the frame for a cascade (see Plate 6). Both echo the placing of a seat on the grotto arch in Wooburn Farm, illustrated in the engraving by Luke Sullivan (see Figure 2).

Left: Fig. 40. Woods's design for the boat house at Cusworth, 1762. Note the similarity to the rock arch with bench on the engraving of Wooburn Farm, Figure 2.

Below: Fig. 41. Cusworth boat house in 1985. It has since been restored, and most of the planting behind it has gone. From the tail of the pond, and anywhere along the bank, the boat house appears as the terminal focal point, whereas the cascade to the right, invisible until the last moment, takes the overflow to the second pond and a different scene.

The boathouse at Wivenhoe in Essex, part of the improvements started in 1776, is described in Woods's estimate as 'a Rustick arch' and appears on his plan as 'A Rock Arch for a Boat House'. However, stone is not a material found in Essex, and here the rustic effect had to be achieved with brick, although from Constable's painting, in which it features in the background (see Plate 9), it seems that flints may have been used to face the side walls.[57] No memoranda to the foreman survive, but on returning home after a visit to Wivenhoe in October 1777 Woods found a letter from his employer 'with the disagreeable account of the Boat house falling down, at which I am both mortifyed and surprized, as it all seem'd to stand very firm when I was there'. He considered that if the arch had not been 'covered over with clay as I directed before the rainfall' that would account for the collapse, but if it had been protected in this way, the only possible reason must have been 'a defect in the workmanship, in not being well filled with mortar'.[58] Perhaps the comment he made relative to Irnham in 1770 was also the case here: 'I think it is very hard and straing that nobody is to be rely'd upon after my back is turn'd.'[59] If this incident caused any ill-feeling it is not recorded in the correspondence. The bricklayer was paid for repairing the damage and work continued on the improvements.

BRIDGES

Damming a stream to form a fine pond or lake, or widening it to make a 'river', was an almost essential aspect of the improvement of any grounds. A bridge thus often became a practical necessity, and frequently also fulfilled an ornamental function, providing a focal point for the new piece of water or deceiving the eye into believing that the far bank was not a dam but simply a crossing-point. A bridge was considered an important piece of architecture, and it is noticeable that although Woods built three reasonably substantial bridges as part of suggested improvements (two at Cannon Hall and one at Great Myles's), at the grander commissions of Wardour Castle and Brocket Hall the designing of the bridge was given to James Paine, the architect in both cases in charge of building the mansion.

Woods's bridge at Bretton Hall of 1764 ended in disaster: the diary of John Spencer of Cannon Hall, where Woods was working at the same time, records on 15 December: 'Sir Thos. Wentworth's new Bridge was carried down this day by the Violence of the Flood. Mr Woods is generally blamed for his unskilfull direction about the Construction of it.'[60] Whatever the truth of the assertion, it should be pointed out in Woods's defence that this area of Yorkshire suffered severe and unusual flooding in the 1760s and 1770s,[61] and also that a similar fate befell Repton at Stoneleigh Abbey, where a terrible storm swept away his newly completed bridge over the Avon. From the evidence of building instructions left by Woods for other properties, it seems uncharacteristic that he should have failed to leave proper instructions at Bretton Hall, whether or not they were carried out.

Although Woods was not given the commission to build the bridge at Wardour (a project which was eventually abandoned), he produced two designs, both borrowing heavily from Isaac Ware and both illustrating a poor grasp of the art of shading: the wings appear to swing backwards instead of curving forwards as shown on the attached plan. Woods's bridges at Cannon Hall were less ambitious and more successful. The first and visually more

Figs. 42 (below) and 43 (bottom). Woods's drawing for an unexecuted project for a bridge at Wardour, c.1769 and one of Isaac Ware's bridge designs of 1757.

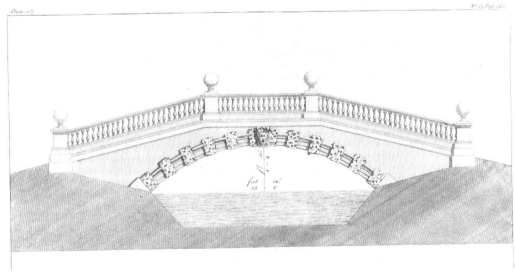

Fig. 44. The 'rustic Stone bridge' at Cannon Hall by Woods, finished in 1762. Compare with his project for Wardour and Ware's bridge design (Figures 42 and 43).

important was again in the 'rustick' style, while in 1764 a second bridge was built in what Woods called 'Palladian' style, although this would more properly be described as merely classical.[62]

The bridge-cum-dam was a device twice used by Woods to manage a change in water level where there was an insufficient flow for a cascade under the bridge. The effect of such a bridge in the landscape is seen in the painting by Constable of Wivenhoe Park (Plate 9), while instructions for building the dam at Cusworth are given in a memorandum to the foreman, with a section drawing. Woods, with his habitual insistence on practical

Fig. 45. Sketch by Woods of the section through the bridge-cum-dam at Cusworth, from the memorandum to the foreman of 19 September 1764. In addition to the annotations on the drawing, he gave detailed directions for the construction. The bridge at Wivenhoe was built in the same way.

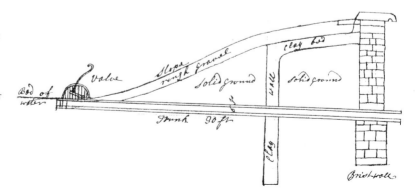

detail, and giving equal attention to the soundness of the construction and to the finished appearance, wrote:

> get the foundation of the Bridge built according to the plan,
> and the clay wall made in the front as described … and be sure
> to sink to the natural clay bottom each way from the Bridge to
> the Double stakes, and from thence may begin to run out to
> the uper strater of clay or strong loame, and so to raise the
> whole about 6 inches [15cm] above the water levil. In raise[ing]
> the Banks, you'l observe to carry it out on the north side farr
> enough to coraspond with the natural surfice of the meadow,
> and on the south side at such distance as to make it appear
> very easey, and at the Stake No. 1 make a gentle swell the top
> 1ft 8is [5cm] above the surfice of the water and all the other
> parts of the Banks about 10is or at most a foot. … Let the
> trunk be made 30ft [9m] long and 6 inches [15cm] wide in ye
> core and let it go through the brick wall about a foot [30cm],
> and let the valve be made according to the modal.[63]

Richmond used the same stratagem for a napped flint bridge to hide the dam at Hitchin Priory.[64]

The bridge built by Woods as a major part of his commission at Great Myles's in Essex in 1771 is unlike any of his other designs. It carried the road over the water and created the focal point for the new 'river' (made by damming the stream), but Woods took advantage of its purpose as a screen and not as a way through for boats by giving it an unusually long, slim outline with a low arch. As the mansion was demolished in 1835, its

Fig. 46. Woods's bridge at Great Myles's, built in 1771 at a cost of £250. After the demolition of the mansion, the bridge sits slightly incongruously in an agricultural landscape.

relationship with the bridge can no longer be judged, but it can certainly be argued that a more robust design and a higher arch would have detracted from the view from the house down to Menagerie Wood.

Woods even made an attempt, late in his career, at a bridge with superstructure. One of the disadvantages of the site for the Elysium Garden at Audley End was the proximity of the road, which skirted the piece of ground for its entire length. The problem could be solved by planting, except where a long pond left the property to run under the road. Here Woods (perhaps with echoes of the Palladian Bridge at Stowe in his memory) suggested a 'Doric Arcade', with solid back, to sit on the old bridge and create a screen and focal point for the end of the garden (see Figure 61). An alternative plan tamely suggested that the front of the bridge should be 'ornamented and the Parapet rais'd so high as to prevent People from looking over it'.[65] The bridge eventually commissioned from Adam is no more than an up-to-date interpretation of Woods's old-fashioned design for the arcade (see Plate 3).

STABLES AND MORE SUBSTANTIAL BUILDINGS

In his work for the 8th Lord Arundell at Wardour Castle and his Lincolnshire seat Irnham, Woods came nearer than with any other commission to building serious architecture. For both properties he designed stables, executed at Irnham in 1769/70, 'very plain but strong and convenient'[66] and surviving with a crenellated porch added in the nineteenth century. Also at Irnham he proposed a new chapel, which would have been equally plain. As at Wardour, where the drawings for any executed building have not survived, only the design for the chapel is extant.

His real bid for architectural fame was made at Wardour. Here Lord Arundell spent some time after his marriage in 1763 debating whether to restore Old Wardour Castle, reduced to a shell by Cromwellian soldiers in 1644, or to build on a new site.[67] When Woods was first commissioned in 1764 to prepare plans for the wholesale improvement of the park, Arundell was still inclined to the former option, or perhaps to rebuild in the same position, although by February 1765 he had decided to build on a new, higher site and there is a reference in an estimate to a 'great Screen in north of the intended new house'. He took a little longer to decide on his architect, and one of the items on a bill from Woods covering work in 1766 is 'To a set of drawings for a mansion house in the Castle stile'.[68] Among the various papers relating to this period the only drawings which answer to that description are four unsigned designs of lamentable quality. They are not in the style of draughtsmanship of any of the other drawings in the collection, whether signed by Woods or not, and it must remain an open question whether his talent could fall so low, or his self-delusion rise so high. Whether these are Woods's designs or not, it was obvious that he was not going to be the architect of the house, and in January 1770 he wrote in a rueful tone,

'Your Ldship is pleased to observe, that you intend having plans from other people and shall take that wch you like best. I much commend yr. Ldsp. in making the best choice you can in a good design for yr. new house at Wardour ... If I have not the good fortune to please you in a plan for that purpose I am resign'd to my fortune'.

In April 1770, after Paine had won the commission, Woods was given the task of drawing in the outline of the new house on his 1764 plan, and even had to re-draw it to rectify the position. He agreed to 'call on Mr Pain for the outlines of the House that I may not make any mistake'. Being obliged to humble himself in this way must have been distasteful, but a man in Woods's position could not afford to take umbrage.

By this date, building work at Irnham was well under way; the stables were nearly complete and Woods had also produced estimates 'to take in pieces the present breakfast parler and stewards room and passage and lay em all into one noble drawing room'. Lord Arundell would have been in a position to judge Woods's ability to undertake building on a larger scale than summer-houses, although work on the house was alteration rather than construction. The Irnham correspondence does not cover this period, and Woods's classical range (demolished in the 1880s)[69] attached to the Tudor

Fig. 47. Two of a set of designs for the new mansion at Wardour. These probably constitute the 'set of drawings for a Mansion House in the Castle Stile' for which Woods charged in 1766.

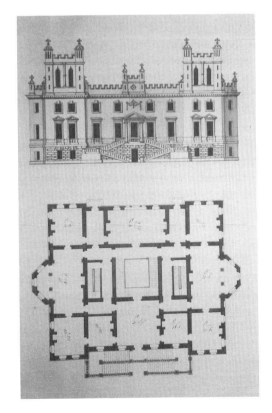
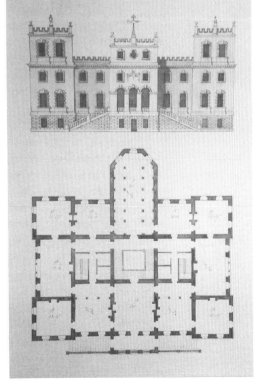

Fig. 48. The drawing room at Irnham Hall, built by Woods c.1770 out of the old steward's room, breakfast parlour and passage. It was destroyed by fire in 1887 and replaced by a Tudor-style range. The vignette is from an estate survey of 1850.

house must be judged from a vignette on an 1850 estate map. The interior, with high ceilings and lit by two large Venetian windows, was doubtless splendid,[70] but the façade is no more than mediocre.

It is difficult to come to an unequivocal assessment of Woods's architectural achievements. In some respects he was an uninspired dabbler, largely dependent on pattern books for his ideas, and yet occasionally he proved capable of producing an attractive and well-balanced design, even if not in the class of great architecture, as in the Great Myles's bridge or the Chinese Temple at Alresford. The fact that so little of his built work survives makes it all the more difficult to judge the whole output, but nevertheless the overall impression of Woods's efforts in this field is one of being behind the times. The single architectural style that he produced with any consistency, although he certainly used others, involved heavy rustication apparently adapted from buildings of the 1740s and pattern books of the 1750s, which he was still using as late as 1780 on the Audley End plan.

Woods seems to have formed his ideas early in his career, and thereafter was either unwilling or unable to move with the times, or was given insufficient incentive to do so. An explanation for this failure to adapt, which is also apparent in his landscaping in general, may lie in his presumed early assimilation of the ideas behind Wooburn Farm, in conjunction with an inflexibility of character. It is also possible that after 1768 and his move to North Ockendon he was too stretched trying to combine a farming and a surveying career to keep fully abreast of changing fashions. He was adept at recycling his designs; a good illustration is the alcove seat designed for

Wardour but not used there, which reappears in an almost identical version on the plan for Hengrave.

Woods was probably on firmer ground as a structural engineer than as an architect, in spite of his two recorded mishaps. Where the documentation has survived, the detailed building instructions he gave suggests that it was his normal practice to ensure that the workmen knew exactly how to proceed. Whereas Brown would have gained this sort of expertise from his years as clerk of works at Stowe, Woods seems to have acquired it through reading and then practice. The fact that he was prepared to venture into large-scale architecture, even if he was never given the opportunity to prove himself, shows a considerable self-confidence.

Woods was aiming on behalf of his employers, and presumably sometimes with their guidance, for a landscape that made a pleasing visual ensemble, which from his surviving designs obviously included little buildings in their 'proper places' (as he sometimes specified on his plans). The passionate classical ideal of the highly educated Grand Tourists, and their delight in the delicious intricacies of an esoteric iconography, was not for Woods. He was obviously neither a trained architect nor brought up in the serious classical tradition provided by the grammar schools. On the other hand, he showed he was well able to absorb information from books, and must have had an inventive mind in addition to a good eye. He was in fact exactly the sort of audience to whom the authors of the architectural pattern books were playing: and, after all, Dr Johnson defined an architect simply as 'a contriver of a building'.

Fig. 49. One of the many examples of Woods's re-use of garden building designs. The unexecuted alcove seat (*left*) produced for Wardour c.1769, is virtually replicated on the plan for Hengrave of 1777, redrawn for clarity by Andrew Westman (*right*).

CHAPTER 6

THE WOODS LANDSCAPE

A MONG THE IMPROVERS AVAILABLE FOR WORK in the second half of the eighteenth century there is no argument over Brown's pre-eminence. It is clear from correspondence that a plan from Brown became an object of desire (as was later the case with Repton's Red Books), with success feeding fame and further success; nevertheless, it is probably true to say that, given the same specifications for a commission, the various more competent landscapers might well have produced designs difficult to assign to any one of them in particular without documentary support. Indeed, if all mid-eighteenth-century plans were redrawn by the same hand on the same scale, many instances would be found where attribution would be uncertain if not impossible. As David Brown has pointed out, all the improvers were 'working in a design language that was widely known and well-established by 1760 at the latest',[1] and all of them, even the minor practitioners, were to a greater or lesser degree capable of a design that fell within the parameters of the fashionable designed landscape, even though there is a great gulf between the least and the most skilful examples.

It is also an open question whether Lord Arundell, for instance, who asked Brown for a visit to Wardour in 1773 'having seen several specimens of yr. fine taste',[2] would have recognised the difference on the ground between the master and Emes or Richmond. Brown's work for Lord Petre at Thorndon Hall between 1766 and 1772 at a cost of some £5000 – dates and expense comparable to Woods's work at Wardour – does not appear from Spyers's survey of 1778[3] to have been the unified, magnificent landscape one might expect from Brown. Did the perceived excellence of the landscape lie as much in the name of the man as the result as executed? In the absence of estate papers for this period, there is no record of Petre's satisfaction with the result.

With the increasing flow of research into various aspects and practitioners of eighteenth-century garden improvements, it has become apparent that there was not just one naturalistic landscape style but rather a variety of interpretations of this theme. Some of the variations were extremely subtle, and are probably more easily discerned with hindsight than they were at the time. However, that there is a clear difference between Brown and Woods – as distinct from any other Brownians – is easy to grasp by comparing the plan produced by each for Wardour.[4] Brown's plan of 1775 is specifically a design

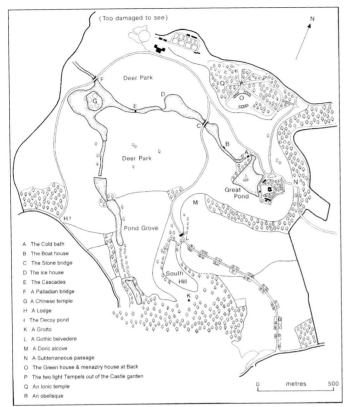

(Too damaged to see)

N

Deer Park

F

G

E

D

C

B

A

Deer Park

Great
Pond

N

M

Pond Grove

L

South
Hill

K

H?

A   The Cold bath
B   The Boat house
C   The Stone bridge
D   The ice house
E   The Cascades
F   A Palladian bridge
G   A Chinese temple
H   A Lodge
I   The Decoy pond
K   A Grotto
L   A Gothic belvedere
M   A Doric alcove
N   A Subterraneous passage
O   The Green house & menaziry house at Back
P   The two light Tempels out of the Castle garden
Q   An Ionic temple
R   An obelisque

Q

O

P

0   metres   500

Left: Fig. 50. Woods's plan for Wardour, 1764. The size, complexity and faded condition of the original makes it unsuitable for photographic reproduction, and it is here redrawn for clarity by Phillip Judge. Of the various features referenced, the only ones to be built were the cold bath (A), the ice house (D) and the greenhouse (but in a different position, in the new kitchen garden).

Below: Fig. 51. Brown's plan, specifically for alterations, of 1775. Note the different orientation from Woods's plan, possibly intended to make a direct comparison less obvious.

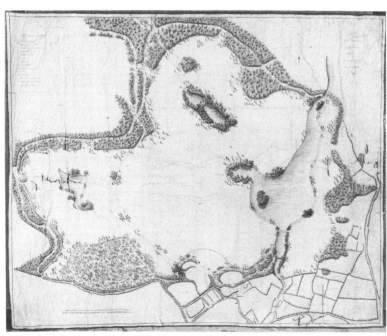

for alterations, and omits not only the old castle, which he is unlikely to have suggested should be demolished, but also everything done by Woods between 1764 and 1771, leaving his intentions for this recent work open to interpretation. The most striking and immediate difference between their two plans is that of cartographic style. Possibly one of Brown's great achievements was the realisation that a relatively bold and simple layout, almost always presented in monochrome, had more visual impact than Woods's detailed, sometimes even fussy, coloured presentations. Brown's plan for Wardour is bold, masterly, ignoring inconvenient details and presenting an easily grasped overall view of the park; Woods's by comparison is intricate, elaborate and covered in tiny items that need to be magnified for full appreciation. The shapes and curves on Brown's are graceful and satisfying to the eye (although this would not necessarily have been so apparent on the ground), whereas there is no very obvious pattern emerging from Woods's. Even if Woods's plan were to be redrawn in Brown's style, and only including such landform details as Brown showed, there would still be a striking contrast between the ideas of each. Their handling of planting provides just one example: Brown worked here in blocks of trees, building them up to create curving screens or serpentine-fronted expanses of green which informed a landscape already rich in beauty. Woods appears to have relied on woodland already present – there is no evidence on his plan or from the accounts to suggest a major programme of new plantations, and the west side of the park has no new planting at all. His executed scheme along the Great Terrace was extended pleasure-ground planting, mixing forest trees and ornamentals.

Nothing demonstrates more clearly than the comparison of these two plans the fact that Woods's particular skill in pleasure grounds on an intimate scale did not translate so convincingly on paper into a spectacular, unified landscape on the scale of Wardour. Nevertheless, if executed in its entirety, Woods's plan would have created a landscape full of variety and incident, not without grandeur, and arguably more interesting to walk around than Brown's boldly conceived and far simpler layout of 1775. The specific reason for Arundell's dismissal of Woods is not known. Did his dissatisfaction lie with Woods's plan itself, or had he become convinced that he was falling behind in terms of fashion, that the upper echelons of society in which he moved were singing the praises of Brown, not of Woods?

Woods's characteristic approach to the design of a landscape is also apparent when his plan for Goldsborough is compared with White's. Woods's plan (see Figure 15) is typical of his work, with great emphasis on the pleasure ground and on a small, detailed piece of water; while White, asked for an alternative plan only two years later, produced something on a more generous scale combining aspects of park and forest, with little in the way of a pleasure ground and no lake. This reflects Woods's interest in the pleasure ground, and White's in large-scale tree planting. The diversity of scenes and arrangement contained in many of Woods's designs were desiderata in the 1740s and 1750s, but by the 1760s and 1770s were perhaps starting to look fussy to contemporaries compared with Brown's assertive expanses of water and sweeps of planting.

Although Woods's life and career are far less well documented than Brown's, White's or Emes's, the study of the way in which he set about creating his landscapes is greatly facilitated by the survival of the set of

Fig. 52. White's plan for Goldsborough, submitted two years after Woods's plan (see Figure 15) and very different in scope and emphasis. North is roughly to the bottom of the plan.

memoranda written to the foreman at Cusworth between 1761 and 1764, which set out precise instructions on all aspects of the work in hand.[5] The detail contained in these documents is unique in the study of the entire 'English landscape garden', and when supplemented by instructions to foremen at other estates and correspondence relating to various commissions, it allows one to construct a very clear picture of the working methods and range of skills of one of the better-known improvers. As a practitioner of his times, Woods worked in much the same way as all the others to execute his plans, but the features and aspects of his designs which can be described as peculiarly his may be distinguished from the methods he employed that conform to the general practice.

CLIENT RELATIONSHIPS

The necessary preliminary to any work on a new landscaping was a site visit, a walk around the grounds probably accompanied by the client and a drawn plan or verbal discussion to decide on the objectives of the commission. In broad terms these steps were common to all the improvers, and where correspondence survives (mainly for Brown) it becomes clear that the critical aspect in a successful landscaping was the ability to think visually, to see immediately the 'capabilities' of the site which would then be transferred to paper after a survey had been taken. To make an attractive formal layout on a flat piece of paper or fairly level piece of ground certainly required imagination and skill, but to create a naturalistic landscape which was severely determined by the lie of the land, to use contours instead of ignoring them, to capitalise on a wandering stream rather than trying to minimise its impact, to include if topographically possible all the features expected in an idealised landscape, and to visualise it all in the course of a few hours needed both talent and training at the least.

It is also important to remember that the historian has to judge the success of a design by prioritising the 'plan for improvement' followed by what remains of the landscape after 250 years, whereas the client had the benefit of hearing from the improver himself a description of his vision. Nevertheless, irrespective of the spoken picture it seems that the drawn plan was considered a valuable reference tool, if nothing else, and Repton repeats a criticism of Richmond often heard from his employers 'that they seldom understood what were his intentions till they were executed'.[6] This comment reinforces the theory that the name of the improver was as important to the client as his improvements.

From the improver's point of view the financial and psychological success of the project depended largely not just on his skill in seeing at a glance what might be achieved, but also in enthusing and encouraging the prospective client, who did not necessarily have the same gift for envisaging a landscape in his mind's eye. Flattery was necessary as well as assurance: every landowner wanted to hear that there was something special about his property. Virtually all surviving correspondence relating to Woods is from him and not about him, but he can be seen at work on public relations in the comment made by Mary Rebow about his improvements at Wivenhoe, when he told her that at his next visit 'he should just beautify and put the finishing touches to one of the most pleasing pictures in England'.[7] Brown could exaggerate just as transparently, as when the Earl of Shelburne cynically reported that he 'twenty times assured me that he does not know a finer place in England than Bowood Park'.[8]

Some clients were opinionated, others malleable; in the 1770s Christopher Sykes at Sledmere rejected designs by White and Brown but incorporated some of their ideas in a plan of his own devising, whereas the Earl of Abingdon, one of Brown's most uncritical clients, wrote to him, 'I pay so great Deference to your Taste, Prudence, and Judgment, that I never make the least Inquiry concerning the Improvements at Rycot.'[9] At the opposite end of the scale stands Edwin Lascelles, who claimed that Brown left the ground at Harewood 'scandalously lay'd, and beggarly sown, and … several other parts slovenly run over and badly finished'.[10] In a profession which relied heavily on initial personal contact and subsequently on supervision by others, it was inevitable that all the improvers had successes and failures in their client relationships.

SETTING OUT THE GROUNDS

The initial assessment of the grounds usually took an improver two to four days;[11] following that, a surveyor might be sent to take measurements from which the plan would be drawn;[12] and once the outline of the design and the terms of employment had been settled (possibly with signed contracts between the parties) the improver himself would visit again to set out the grounds for the first stage of the intended works. This process is exemplified at Wardour, where Woods is first entered in the house accounts in January 1764 for six guineas, suggesting a three-day session. 'Mr Sparrow, Mr Woods'es Surveyor', charged for ten days in March and April;[13] the plan was probably delivered in late April;[14] and Woods with his servant spent twelve days at board wages in May to set out the grounds. By the end of that month the accounts show the first action in the park, with labourers 'cuting and grubing wood in Lady Grove'. The length of time spent on measuring by a surveyor obviously depended on the extent of the grounds and size of the commission: Brown's surveyor Spyers took '3 weeks and 3 days' at Tottenham Park[15] but it does not seem that all Woods's improvements were preceded by a preliminary survey or plan – a number of his minor projects would not have required such formality or expense. Whereas Wardour had received the full (and costly) treatment, Woods embarked on improvements at Lord Arundell's other property at Irnham after just a site visit and agreement on the work involved, specified in articles signed on the same occasion in June 1768, but leaving a fair amount of the aesthetic detail to Woods. As well as forming the Bowling Green, he was 'to rectify and form all the other Ground and walks in such parts as shall be judged proper by Richard Woods in order to make the whole in good Taste … within the Limits of the Pleasure Garden'. The visit, discussion and signature of articles appear from the accounts to have taken only two days.[16]

Although Woods was paid for 'surveying and setting out the Grounds' at Cusworth, no drawn plan survives. Before leaving Cusworth on his first visit, Woods may have had access to the two rough sketches, with viewlines and a survey of standing timber, probably made by Richardson in early 1761[17] to enable him to crystallise his thoughts, just as White wrote to Thomas Grimston in 1782: 'I have your plan of Grimston Garth now before me and shall before I leave home draw a rough draft of the improvements to be made there whilst they are upon my memory.'[18]

GROUND FORMING

The various clauses in a contract or articles of agreement relative to making or improving a landscape were likely to cover work on ground forming; creation of a new piece of water, or conversion of a formal canal or fishponds into a naturalistic lake; building or reorganising a kitchen garden, sometimes with pinery and/or greenhouse; new drives and approaches; planting everywhere appropriate; building ha-has and making a pleasure ground and/or pleasure garden. None of Woods's commissions is known to have required moving serious quantities of earth on the scale of Lord Walpole 'moving the hill' in front of Houghton Hall[19] or Repton's proposals to excavate the rising ground in front of Catchfrench.[20] Emes lowered the incline in front of Chirk Castle,[21] and White at Harewood created a mount to the south of the house, reported by the steward Popplewell: 'We have had six carts and above thirty men sinking and raising the ground.'[22] But even minor changes in the flow of the land can make a great difference to a view, and Woods required a degree of ground shaping in most of his improvements.

The reason for altering the existing lie of the land near the house was frequently to give a better view of the piece of water. Similar instructions were given at various times by all the improvers: for example, Brown at Syon sloped the ground down to the Thames and at Chatsworth excavated some of the land west of the house to the Derwent, in both cases to enable the river to be seen better.[23] At Cusworth Woods was anxious that his new piece of water should be seen not just during the walk around the grounds, but clearly from the house. He directed that 'having leavel'd and formed the water line next the park, you must then … cut down four other pateron lines and let them be so shaped as to let you see the edge of the water from the house' (Memorandum 3); a short time later, with reference to the second pond 'in pertucler be suer to scoop out a fine hollow in front of the cascade so as to see the lower water very fairly from the seat which will be upon the mount, and may also be seen from principle floor of the House' (Memorandum 4). At Boreham House he was similarly concerned that the new 'river' should not be hidden, and in spite of having cut a preliminary pattern line for excavation it was necessary to lower 'another large piece at upper end of the great bank on the lawn that the River may be the more efectualy seen'.[24] The Wivenhoe estimate specifies levelling the lawn between the house and the pond 'so as to see the Water from the House'.[25] The climate of Britain being 'delightful when framed and glazed, that is, beautiful through a window' as Horace Walpole aptly observed,[26] underlines the importance of ensuring the water could be seen from the comfort of the drawing room.

However, a good view of the water was not the only reason for moving earth: an idealised landscape required gentle swells and curves in the land to break monotony and add subtle contrasts. This is particularly relevant for work on Woods's usual modest scale, and seems to hark back to Southcote's views and Spence's dictum that 'if the ground be all flat one should make risings or inequalities in it; very small swellings will help much if properly placed'. At Cusworth Woods left directions very much in line with Spence's ideas: when writing about the slope to the lower water, he instructed that 'in order to make it more beautifull some soft swells may be left or formed where the difforant stakes are for that purpose, which will make the whole appear finely waved' (Memorandum 5); and again 'in forming the mount you'l use all your engineowitty [ingenuity] to give the ground as much variety and life as possible by rowling and waveing it about in the manner I described to you' (Memorandum 4). At Goldsborough, in forming the lawns of the pleasure ground 'you'l observe to make soft swells where the stakes are placed marked No.1 but at the stake No.2 the ground is to be raised a yard [0.9m], with a platform at the top not less than 15 feet [4.5m] wide and to fall in a concave slope … and on each side to form swelling banks with their bases running farther out than the bass of the concave, so that the whole side of the wilderness towards the house may appear a waved bank.'[27] The pleasure-ground lawn behind the house at Newsells (where Woods probably worked in 1763) bears such a striking similarity to this shape that, in spite of the absence of supporting documents, there are reasonable grounds for ascribing it to his design. At Hatfield Peverel, again without any documentation, it is obvious that the spoil from the creation of the ponds has been used to make just such swells and curves in the ground as specified for Cusworth and Goldsborough. Even at Wardour, with a potential 800 acres (323ha) as his canvas, Woods contracted to improve the lawns by filling up 'all such hollows as are awkward and disagreeable so as to lay all in a soft and easey waves'.

Interfering with the natural lie of the land had to be undertaken with care, and did not always have the desired result. Walpole considered that at Moor Park Brown had 'undulated the horizon in so many artificial mole-hills, that it is full as unnatural as if it was drawn with a rule and compasses'.[28] The client was sometimes aware of the desirability of a little alteration of the topography before an improver told him so, and Lord Stormont recorded in his diary that 'the ground about [Scone Palace] lies prettily and might very easily be laid out on a gentle slope to the river',[29] a suggestion included in White's contract eight years later.

Woods was concerned that while the ground was being moulded into pleasing contours, the eventual ability to maintain it should not be forgotten. Following his exhortation to 'rowl and wave' at Cusworth he added, 'In all this waveing you'l always consider the scythe, for if ground is so formed that it cannot be easily mown it is imperfict' (Memorandum 4). The admiration accorded smooth grassland is exemplified by Parnell's description of Bushy Park: 'One vast beauty, I must not omit, the ground under the trees, which are very close together, is as finely clothed with grass and free from any Roughness as the mow'd Plots in a Pleasure Garden.'[30] He was obviously not expecting a fine sward in this position, but was delighted with it.

At both Cusworth and Goldsborough the house stood high enough to require a hillside ('hanging') lawn on the garden side, and in both places Woods left a sketch of the exact profile he had designed, bringing the lawn down in easy stages. A terrace was made in front of the façade of both houses, followed at Goldsborough by the ground falling 'downwards in a fine bold O G [i.e. ogee] slope'. Cusworth was given a more complex arrangement with a gentle concave slope to a lower line of stakes, 'then revirse it to a convex for a considerable space and then fall into the natural concave below' (Memorandum 2). Whereas at Goldsborough it appeared that the effect could be achieved merely by using the spoil from the pond excavation, at Cusworth the process was more complicated and needed Woods's detailed instructions:

> In order to persue this work right, you must first plow up
> the whole, then opin a wide line down from top to bottam,
> throw half the top earth on[e] way and half the other, let this
> line be made at least 30 feet [9m] wide, then work it down
> to the true shape, and the rock being carryed of, throw back
> the two ridges of top spitt to form the surfice; then opin
> another 30 feet stripe in the same manner and so on, and by
> this method of working you'l avoid carting of the top and
> carting it back again.

It is tempting to imagine that Woods might have read and absorbed Switzer's admonition in his *Ichnographia* (a book he possibly owned): 'People are generally in such a Hurry and Amaze, and Gardeners take so little Notice of this one Particular, that I have often seen [them] … tumbling their Earth backward and forward, when it might have been dispos'd in its proper Place at once.'[31]

PIECES OF WATER

Often the most important feature in the landscape, even its focal point, a new piece of water was also likely to be the single most expensive item. The ease of harnessing a sufficient body of water and the nature of the soil beneath it naturally affected the cost considerably. At its simplest, a stream with a good flow through a valley of clay subsoil could be dammed and result in a passable lake. However, in practice it seldom proved so easy, not least owing to the difficulty of diverting or retaining the necessary flow, and because a more sophisticated shape was usually demanded. Even when the outline had been decided a certain amount of leeway was accepted, as the Wivenhoe estimate indicates: 'The Shape and Limits of those two pieces of Water, are nearly determined by the lines of Stakes set out for that Purpose, or as near that as the Falls, and Shape of the Ground on both sides will admit of.'[32] The first steps involved locating the stream or spring which was to act as the base for the new 'river', 'pond' or (less used at this date) 'lake', and taking levels to confirm the viability of the project. Woods or his surveyor made a basic error at Wivenhoe, where the original plan of 1765 shows a single long piece of water, created out of a stream and two existing ponds (compare Figures 53 and 11), which would have been impossible owing to

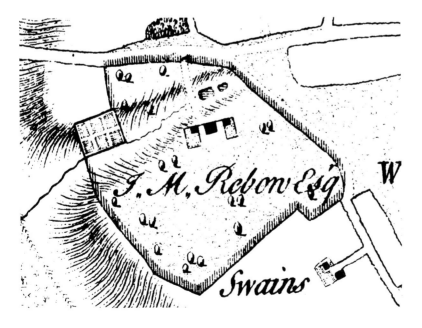

Fig. 53. Wivenhoe Park just prior to Woods's landscaping, from Chapman and André's *Map of Essex* of 1777. Note the two fish ponds and stream from which the long piece of water was made.

the lie of the land. If the surroundings of a new piece of water were marshy, drainage was necessary both to help feed the pond and to create firm lawns round it. As White's foreman at Scone observed, he could not 'dress up the ground until the drains are first made'.[33] If a spring was to be the source of water, laborious digging or boring and testing of pressure would be necessary. Milton Abbas is a very rare case where even after the expenditure of vast sums and all the skill at Brown's command, the success of a piece of water could not be achieved.[34]

The three ponds at Cusworth provide a microcosm of Woods's approach to creating pieces of water. By the time they were completed, a stream, a spring, marshy land and finally a pump had all been pressed into service. Although the largest pond (known as the Great River or Upper Water) was the first to be started, all three were planned and mapped as an ensemble from the outset. When Woods wrote his second memorandum to the foreman (probably early 1762) the outline had already been 'staked and lockspitted', although one section of the bank was still to be finalised and was marked

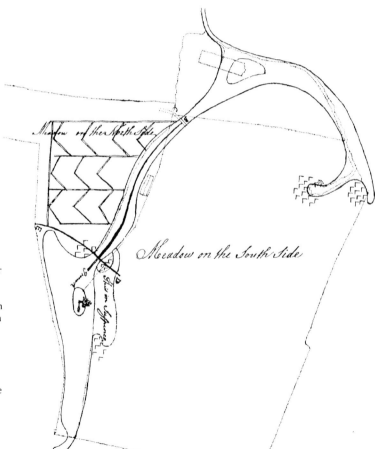

Fig. 54. Woods's plan for the excavation of the pieces of water at Cusworth, referred to in his second memorandum to the foreman, probably early 1762. An associated set of plans in section show 'the naturall surfice of the ground', followed by 'the surfice of the Water when made and full', and finally 'the Bed of the river & shape of the Banks on both sides'. From these plans the foreman would be able to calculate 'the quantittys of earth to be removd'. The extra curl at the end of the third pond was not made.

'This in Susspence'. Before starting to dig the shape of the Upper Water, the 'very boggey and course ground' beyond the projected north bank was drained in a herring-bone pattern down towards the water line. Making the head was an elaborate and time-consuming undertaking, and the most likely place for future maintenance problems. Woods insisted that the trench across the head (the line DE on the plan) which would be required to hold back the weight of water must be

> sunk till you come to a solid and firm bottam either in a close gravel or sand or clay, and in case you should be obliged to sink 3: 4: 5: or 6 feet [1–2m] below the bed of the water before you come to such a bottam you must have patience, and persue it till you are sure you are safe … Let the clay be put in thin courses not more than 6 or 7 inches [15–18cm] at each course, and well ramed … and as you advance in height with the clay keep filling up on both sides with earth wch. must also be as well ramed.

These instructions are virtually repeated on the estimate for 'executing the several Pieces of Water' at Wivenhoe some fifteen years later.[35] His instructions for Goldsborough in 1764 were more cursory, merely directing that the lower side of the head should be made up 'with a good ribb of clay'.[36]

The head of Brown's lake at Croome did not give trouble for some twenty years,[37] but that at Harewood started to leak while it was still under construction. The comments of the Harewood steward on that occasion are significant, as they explain Woods's insistence on a thorough foundation for the work: 'Upon the strictest examination we found no remedy but opening the head to the bottom where the trunk lyed; … we found that the water has made it's way through the clay wall close by the south side of the trunk.'[38]

Once the source of water had been secured and the shape of the banks staked out, the laborious task of excavation could begin. Woods obviously examined the soil structure wherever he planned a pond, and left instructions for disposing of the various qualities of spoil as the men started digging. At Cusworth the good earth was to be kept on one side for final touches in the landscape and used to fill in the furrows in the old meadow; the sub-soil ('dirty stuff') for raising the ground round the head; and the gravel to be taken straight to the new road under construction. At Wivenhoe Woods noticed 'that in the Hollow Ground where the second Water is to be … there is some good Earth which it would be wrong to bury and therefore is proposed to be taken out at least a full spit deep and to be carried up the Hill, in order to improve the Lawn'. The spoil from making the pond at Hare Hall was used to form a small raised pleasure ground between the water and the boundary of the small property (Plate 7).

A trunk was usually laid through the pond for ease of draining when necessary. In the main pond at Cusworth, 'about the middle of the head, there must be a trunk of wood laid under in wch. there is to be a valve or plugg, in order to let out the water to the bottam, whenever it may be required'. Woods directed the carpenter that the trunk 'must be made of plank 2 inches [5cm] thick, either of oake ellem or beech, and 6 inches [15cm] square in the cleare within'. He sent a sketch when the second head at the bridge was under construction, showing the position of the trunk and valve (see Figure 45).

At Cusworth it was obviously decided early on to use the spring at the tail of the Third or Lower Water to make a curving arm outside the power of the stream. This piece of water was also visible from the upper floors of the house and, as Judith Roberts has observed, 'was a vital element in creating the desired illusion of a meandering river running through the grounds'.[39] To form the spring into a reservoir large enough to feed this third pond meant raising it by 3ft (1m), and in August 1763 Woods gave a sketch of the section of the basin to contain this higher level of water. However, the memoranda show that the water supply from the spring continued to give problems, including 'boyling in the meadow', and it was finally decided that an 'engine' or pump was needed to secure the water supply. Woods located John Whitehurst, 'Watchmaker and Engineer of Derby' (at the time 'puting up an Engine for Lord Lincoln at Clumber Park'), who estimated for a wind- or hand-operated pump with sufficient power to feed not only the pond but even to carry water up to the house. The engine required at Wivenhoe in 1779 was designed by Woods himself, suggesting that he may have carefully observed Whitehurst's design and operation.

At both Cusworth and Wivenhoe precautions had to be taken against the deer in the park crossing the water and encroaching on the pleasure ground. Woods's solution at the former estate – whether effective or not is not recorded – was to build a ha-ha wall in the pond on the house side, just below water level. To prevent the deer and/or cattle poaching the banks on the other side, rough gravel was incorporated into the puddled clay and well rammed.

With such detailed instructions extant for making the Cusworth ponds, supplemented by information from Wivenhoe, the method of construction for all Woods's pieces of water can be deduced. Quality of clay was obviously an issue: at Cusworth the correct sort was at hand and only needed to be put aside where found, but at Hatfield Peverel the local orange clay, which occurs in large lumps and seams in the garden soil, was insufficiently viscous to line the ponds securely, and a grey clay was imported from outside the estate.[40]

With minor differences, this method of pond construction was adopted by all the improvers as common practice and well-established technology. It nevertheless required considerable skill, and at times needed more than directions left with a foreman. During the period of uncertainty over the ultimate force of the spring at Cusworth, Woods instructed that if after various experiments it looked unlikely that enough water pressure would be realised, 'you'l let me know by a line, when I will come over and settle the

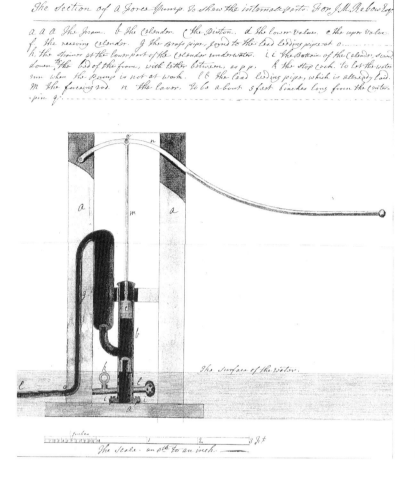

Fig. 55. Woods's design for a pump for Wivenhoe Park, associated with raising water from the spring to the house. It was made by 'Mr Hadley' in London, who also supplied Woods with a 'fire engine' for his own use at North Ockendon.

matter, as no certain directions can now be given how to proceed in that difficult case'. It has recently been suggested that at the outset of his career Brown was primarily a water engineer,[41] and gained his experience in this field at Grimsthorpe (Lincolnshire) with the making of the dam-cum-causeway before his employment at Stowe. If Woods learned his trade at Wooburn Farm, he would have lacked any experience from that estate in creating a great piece of water, and initially might have had to rely on books such as Switzer's *Introduction to a General System of Hydrostaticks and Hydraulics* (1729), which dealt with springs as well as ways of conducting water and organising engines for water features.[42] How or where an improver acquired his knowledge of water engineering, there is no doubt that it was an essential part of his repertoire, and it is no mean feat that apart from a few instances of heads needing repair, the vast majority of ponds and lakes created in the eighteenth century stand as sound today as they did then.

Whereas the method employed in forming water features may have been fairly standard, the resulting outlines varied considerably, and none of the improvers consistently designed any one shape. As stated above, this can to a great extent be explained by the landform of the estate, but the fact that topography was not necessarily the only determining factor is well illustrated by again comparing Woods's and Brown's plans for Wardour (see Figures 50 and 51). They both proposed making use of a chain of pre-existing fish ponds on the west side of the park: Brown designed a single great piece of water dominating the entire west section of the park, and yet giving the south front of the house a lively view of a curving bank and wooded inlet, whereas Woods joined the upper two ponds[43] and incorporated them into his encircling necklace of small pieces of water of varying shapes. Woods typically preferred an arrangement of small ponds, evident again at Buckland where the potential for a large unbroken piece of water was ignored. The

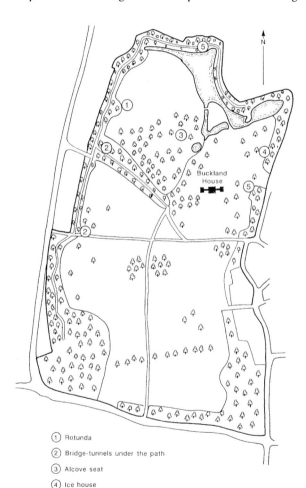

Fig. 56. A redrawing of Buckland House and park in 1803 by Phillip Judge. This map is the first to show Woods's work (from 1758), concentrated in the north section of the grounds and including a layout of pieces of water reminiscent of his plan for Wardour in 1764 (see Figure 50)

1 Rotunda

2 Bridge-tunnels under the path

3 Alcove seat

4 Ice house

5 Possible positions for a rosery

emphasis is always on variety and charm rather than magnificence, and particularly where these modest water features are on different levels, as at Cusworth or Hatfield Peverel, the result is extremely happy. Woods surprisingly often also favoured a piece of water more akin to an informally shaped canal, sometimes straight and sometimes curved, over one with a naturally occurring outline. This was sometimes the main water feature, as at Wivenhoe; on a smaller scale, as at Hare Hall; on a very small scale, as at Brizes; or in addition to another pond, as at Hatfield Peverel or Little Linford. It is also noticeable that at Wivenhoe the pond as made was given a more distinctive shape than that on the plan and, in addition, a short 'strait canal' was placed under the kitchen garden walls.

Apart from the canal form, Woods made no repeated use of any particular shape of pond. At Wavendon (1768) the line of the water supply necessitated the new pond being at a right angle to the house, but Woods turned this potentially awkward arrangement to advantage by giving his pond the form of a thin pear or droplet with a long tail winding away down a view to a plantation at the end. At Cannon Hall some of the more frantic natural twists of the river below the house were incorporated into a wider bed, but he left the watercourse in a series of varied shapes. At Brocket Hall, on the other hand, the tortuous line of the river, left over from a previous design, was

Fig. 57. Wavendon House, from the 1885 6-inch Ordnance Survey. The form of Woods's ponds are clear on the Ordnance Surveyor's Drawing of 1815, although at a much smaller scale.

Fig. 58. A view of Brocket Hall, looking down the Broadwater towards Paine's bridge, in an engraving by William Angus after Paul Sandby, 1787. The text, which is repeated in the *Copperplate Magazine* of 1795, praises 'Mr Wood of Essex' for his work in the grounds.

smoothed out into three elongated swelling shapes (see above and Plate 1). New Hall and Boreham House, almost facing each other at a distance on opposite sides of the road, were given similar very short stretches of 'river' with swelling centres (Figure 73). For Hengrave Woods proposed an imaginative scheme involving the adaptation of a pond and moat into an informal piece of water embracing the house and dovecote island, while his improvements at Copford involved hardly more than softening the outlines of the formal ponds he found there. In short, Woods used any and all shapes when planning his pieces of water, but had a fondness for a curved swelling canal or a chain of small ponds, and an aversion to a large lake.

CASCADES

A cascade at a change in level was one of the most popular devices for adding a point of interest or sparkle to a piece of water, whether on the scale of the small but highly effective arrangement of rocks at Cusworth or Brown's Grand Cascade at Blenheim. The Cusworth cascade is a component part of a particularly subtle visual trick: from the west extremity of the Upper Water, itself hidden in plantation, the boathouse-grotto (see p. 96 and Figures 12 and 41) appears as the terminal of the pond. Only once the mount over the grotto

Fig. 59. Redrawing by Andrew Westman of Woods's plan for Hengrave, 1777, omitting the buildings round the edge. From a photograph of the lost original in the possession of the RIBA (see Fig. 79).

Below: Fig. 60. One of the cascades at Cannon Hall, which according to John Spencer's diary played for the first time on 30 October 1763.

Opposite: Fig. 61. Woods's design for the Elysium Garden at Audley End, 1780. Note the 'rustic' façade of the cold bath, top right, and the bridge with superstructure which was developed by Adam into the Tea Bridge. The cascade was built and survives.

has been reached is it revealed that the water is flowing down the cascade, invisible at the higher level, into a second pond and towards an entirely new scene. The Cold Bath at Wardour had water tumbling down a 'Rural Cascade', treating the outflow from the bath in a decorative manner in front of the building (Figure 38). Among his unexecuted plans for Wardour, Woods designed a cascade under a bridge in the form of steps, a device which maximised the sound and impact of rushing water. The widened river at Cannon Hall had three cascades, one of them directly below the house, visible in a panorama of the landscape painted shortly after Woods had worked there (see Plate 2). His best-known cascade was part of a project for the Elysium Garden at Audley End in 1780 and now stands as a dramatic feature in a garden that in other respects no longer exists as an entity. The design is echoed by that for Copford Hall four years later (Plate 6), which was constructed but never enjoyed the flow of water depicted on Woods's plan and now remains as the arch alone.

Woods was much attracted to this form of rustic arch, with or without cascade or boathouse, in a form reminiscent of Kent and his designs for Chatsworth and Rousham.[44] Whereas Woods would not have had access to these, Stowe could be visited by the general public, and the guide book by Benton Seeley was widely available; in addition perhaps to borrowing the design for an obelisk at Wardour (see p. 77), he might have liked and copied the 'Cascade which running under the Ground falls down … through several artificial Craggs and Rocks'.[45]

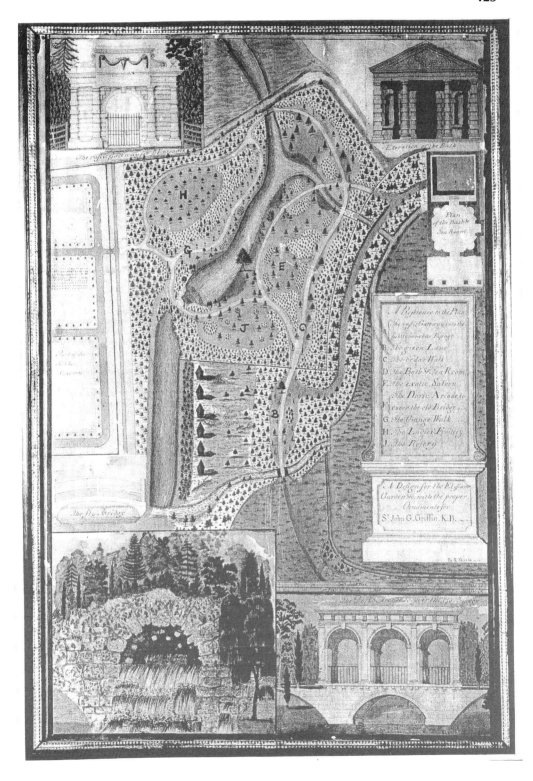

The rustic Gate way into the Entrance

Elevation of the Bath

Plan of the Bath & Tea Room

A Reference to the Plan

A The rustic Entrance into the subterraneous Passage
B The green Lane
C The Cedar Walk
D The Bath & Tea Room
E The exotic Saloon
F The Doric Arcade to cover the old Bridge
G The Orange Walk
H The Ladies Flower Garden
J The Rosery

A Design for the Elysium Garden, &c. with the proper Ornaments for Sr. John G. Griffin K.B.

The old Bridge

The Doric Arcade to cover the old Bridge

Woods was denied his most dramatic fall of water when his plans for Wynnstay were cancelled, and all that remains of his proposals is the description of his intentions in a letter to Lord Arundell. His excitement was obvious: 'the place is Truly Noble indeed, being struck out by nature extreamly romantick, & great, both in soft & rough features. The Lawns, & water, about the house, will be soft and dillicate, & at a farther disstance, extreamly rude & wild, we shall have many falls of water to move thru a hundred feet, with banks, or cliffs, more than 200 ft above the water.'[46] It is ironic that the creation of this scene, which was deferred until the early nineteenth century but is assumed to be to Brown's designs, is largely along the lines imagined by Woods. The Welsh volumes of *The Beauties of England and Wales* state that 'the waters of several brooks and rills were made confluent, to as to form a torrent; which dashing over a lofty ledge of artificial rock-work, covered with mosses and lichens, assumes the appearance of a natural cascade.'[47] This magnificence would have been at the other end of the scale from the many modest little tumbles of water between one pond and the next drawn on virtually every plan for improvements by Woods, or indeed by many of the other practitioners of the time.

DRIVES AND APPROACHES

One of the consequences of a new design for the grounds was that the previous approaches to the house were almost certainly inadequate or in the wrong place. In addition, many a public road running close to the house, which in earlier days might have been thought an advantage, was found to be a great hindrance to newly desired privacy and an expansive park layout. Hardly a contract or agreement made with any of the improvers failed to include a clause concerning new coach roads and approaches, reflecting the fact that, although of no artistic merit in themselves, they were absolutely necessary for the appreciation of the recently created beauty through which they ran. For any estate where fairly large-scale maps exist (manuscript or printed) preceding and following improvement, the importance of the proper siting of the approach can be readily seen.

Brown's approaches were in general designed to show off the park as a prelude to showing off the house, and famously gave tantalising glimpses of the building as it came into view and then was hidden again. Repton disliked this teasing as much as he abhorred a straight approach line; his ideal was a pleasingly curving but short approach, which initially hid the house but left it visible from the time that it came into view. He argued that the purpose of the approach was to gain the house and the route was therefore apparently to be the shortest, although a little cheating was permissible where for aesthetic or practical reasons this was necessary.[48] Woods's approaches were essentially pragmatic; in the few places where he was working on a extensive scale, as at Wardour, his new approach could be described as Brownian, leading the visitor from an entrance at the furthest point from the house up through the new park, curving through plantations and over bridges, finally with a clear view of the magnificent south front of the mansion. There was also, not surprisingly, a necessary short direct service route to the house, as is the case with most Brown landscapes. For other commissions, Woods's attitude seems to have been very flexible, possibly reflecting the fact that he was usually working at smaller properties. In some places he had no objection to a straight, and quite short, drive to the house: this can be seen at Hatfield Peverel, Copford and Brizes. On the other hand at Old Alresford he suggested (unsuccessfully) turning the old entrance court with its direct access to the road into a service area, and making a new and scenic approach from the side (see Figure 6). At Carlton Hall his plan suggests that he intended retaining the trees of the old avenue leading straight from the house to the road while altering the approach to a gently curving line entering from the south-west. Even where a slightly longer approach through the park was possible, he seldom attempted anything other than a gentle curve, and the approaches on

Fig. 62. The plan for Carlton by Woods, 1765. Although the eventual landscaping mainly followed White's design of c.1780, there is some cartographic evidence that the plantation and walk on the west boundary (at the bottom of the plan) were executed as shown here.

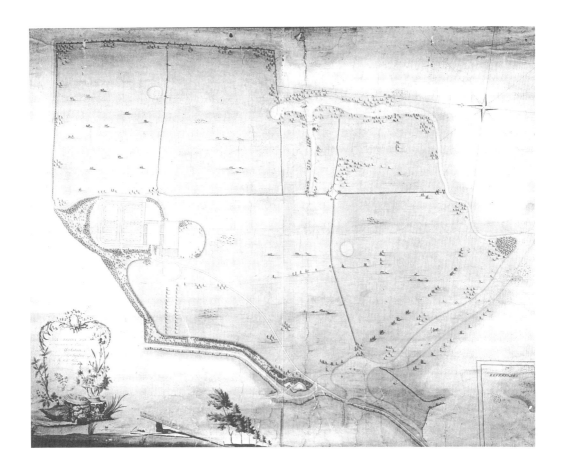

the plans for Little Linford, Hengrave and Wivenhoe either run virtually parallel inside the park to the public road or cut almost straight across the grounds. Here, as in every aspect of the design process, the wishes of the employer were surely paramount and must have accounted for a number of changes to and omissions from the plan for improvement.

Just as the creation of the piece of water required practical as well as aesthetic skill, so the coach road needed far more than the ability to draw a well-placed line on a plan. Wherever documentation survives for a Woods commission, his care over every aspect of road-making is apparent. The first Cusworth memorandum provides directions for the coach road through the park:

> When you begin this road, you must first dig out all the top earth at least a full spitt deep, and dispose of this earth to fill up the hollows on both sides the road for a certain distance so that there may be even margins of turff on each side. When you have taken out the good earth then bottom the road with stone from the most convenient place. If gravel should prove scarce, use the less for example 4 or 5 inches [10–12cm] of gravel over a good stone bottom woud be suficient [but] be suer to keep the top of the road to the leavel of the surfice of the park otherwise it will look very ugly if it was to swell up like a turnpike.[49]

It is interesting that it was thought important that the road through the park, however well constructed, should avoid looking like a public thoroughfare. If gravel was found during excavation for the pond it could be taken straight to the new coach road, but sometimes the source of supply was less obvious. During his work at Irnham in 1769 Woods went to inspect gravel on the nearby Grimsthorpe estate, but was able to report to his client, 'I find yt. your own is very good and full as good as the Duke of Ancasters, and is a full half mile [800m] nearer carrage.'[50] Where gravel or stone was lacking on the estate, other materials could be used instead: White wrote to Lord Stormont while working at Scone that the road he was constructing would 'afford the nearest receptacle for the rubbage of the walls to be led off … in that part'.[51]

The Wivenhoe documents provide no detail beyond the bare statement in the estimate of the cost of making the roads, but a letter to Woods's employer Colonel Rebow from his wife reports that the rain had enabled Woods to 'Plough up part of the Lawn before the House, in order to set [the men] a Pattern, both of that, & of ye Roads leading to ye House, which was a nice busy Day, & I assure you gives one a very good Idea of how it will be when its finished'.

Evidence from a number of Woods's plans indicates that he was not averse to leaving or even creating quite formal planting bordering his carriageways. The general attitude to avenues in the second half of the eighteenth century is difficult to gauge exactly. It has in the past been claimed that Brown removed or broke the line of all avenues where he worked, but this is as demonstrably untrue of him[52] as it is of Woods. Whereas at Cusworth Woods had some of the trees moved out of the north court avenue to 'brake the lines' (Memorandum 2), whole or partial avenues were left in place on his plans for Little Linford, Carlton Hall and Wormsley, and there is a section of avenue within the pleasure ground at Cannon Hall. In the same way, Richmond's attitude to avenues was ambivalent: he is reported as wishing to destroy the fine avenue at Gorhambury, but partially retained and incorporated several at Marden Park.[53]

HA-HAS AND FENCES

The ways of containing or separating parts of the grounds were the nuts and bolts of the design, and accorded a degree of importance by owner and improver alike. Probably the first ha-ha built in this country was at Levens by the French gardener Guillaume Beaumont in 1694,[54] followed more famously by Bridgeman at Stowe in the 1720s.[55] Thereafter the ha-ha was used ever more widely as the concept of naturalism progressed. Early ha-has (like the one at Stowe) frequently included a *cheval de frise* or row of pointed stakes set at an angle on the inside of the bank as extra reinforcement against stock. This was described by Parnell as the original fencing at Wooburn Farm, and was obviously still extant in 1763.[56] However, by that date it was less common than the other two forms: wall-and-ditch (near the house), and ditch with wall or hedge through the middle (usually at a further distance, and known as a sunk fence).

Whately insisted that the ha-ha was only a hedge which did not impede the view and was not intended 'to blend the garden with the country',[57] but Walpole (who called it a 'simple enchantment') saw it as the means by which 'the contiguous out-lying parts [beyond the garden] came to be included in a kind of general design: and when nature was taken into the plan, under improvements, every step that was made, pointed out new beauties and inspired new ideas'.[58] The primary function of the ha-ha was of course to contain stock in its proper place, which by extension presented the possibility of turning the whole of the park-plus-garden into a unified design without apparent divisions. It was this gradual dissolving of the precise boundaries between different parts of the garden that led to the possibility of the 'pleasure park' described in Chapter 4, of which Woods was so skilful a practitioner.

Brown's 'Hints' for Burton Constable in 1772 and 1773 were written up by the agent Robert Raines, who included sketches following Brown's directions for a ha-ha and sunk fence[59] which differ only slightly from those supplied by Woods for Cusworth. Although by the mid century the ha-ha and

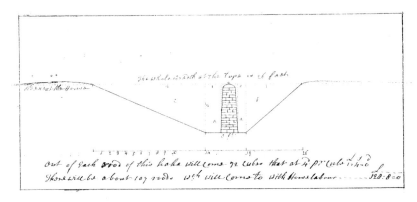

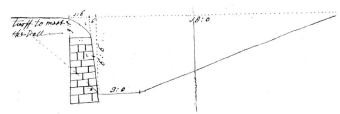

Fig. 63. Two sketches by Woods for the landscaping at Cusworth: (top) a ha-ha of the 'sunk fence' type, but with a central wall, and (right) a normal ha-ha with turf-topped wall and a single slope.

sunk fence had been in use for some twenty years, their construction obviously still required some explanation.

Where the ha-ha was too expensive or unnecessary, fencing took over. The construction of a ha-ha of any sort was costly, and when White discovered that at Scone a total of 10,224yds (9349m) of sunk fence would be needed in his proposals, he reduced his ideas and admitted that 'some other mode must be taken, such as a sod bank with post and rail on the top'.[60] Although fencing was a minor component of the landscape as a whole, it was nevertheless part of the improver's remit to provide suitable designs. Richmond's work at Compton Place included a drawing for the fence, which the bailiff reported in 1779 'is all put up and the ground finished'.[61] It is clear from this correspondence and much of Woods's that fencing was usually painted green, presumably in an attempt to make it merge as much as possible with the planting it contained. Woods left sketches and specifications for different kinds of fence for Wardour, Irnham and Wivenhoe, and references to it on at least two plans: 'light green rails' continued the line of the ha-ha at Old Alresford, and a 'light green rail fence' bordered the Elysian Grove at Wivenhoe ('light' would refer here to the style of railing rather than to the colour). The fences for Wardour and Irnham were of various sorts: a 'light iron fence proper for the Boundrys of Lawns to defend plantations etc' was illustrated side-by-side with 'the iron fence in front of the Queen's palace' (which would cost four times as much), presumably to show what good value his suggestion would be. Three variations of design are shown together, annotated by Woods's foreman as a 'rail fence', obviously wood; 'a pannil of wyer fence … with wyer standards', and a third panel 'with a yew standard in the middle'. A 'light Railing proper to divide Park &c or to inclose plantations' at Irnham had an optional extra rail at the top of 'tar'd rope'; while clumps of firs, pines or cedars were given 'a light circular fence … to be painted olive green'.[62] The 'railing to inclose the lower end of the River' at Wivenhoe was specified in minute detail with measurements, spacings and even the nail positions visible on the accompanying sketch. A drawing was included of an iron cap 'to put upon the top of the post, to prevent from splitting' with a handle to hold it straight and keep it from twisting.

KITCHEN GARDENS

The walled garden for produce and ornament, or produce alone, was of paramount importance in the running of a country estate, where self-sufficiency in fruit and vegetables was taken for granted. Whereas it was standard for the improver to advise on the location of a new kitchen garden, and possibly submit an outline design for it, this feature assumes a place of great importance in the study of Woods's practice in that he often brings it into a prominence not suggested by the other improvers.

A kitchen garden was naturally illustrated on all of Woods's plans for improvement, but documentation makes it clear that he was not responsible for building or altering all of them. At Wivenhoe, where the kitchen garden had been newly constructed with the house only some twenty years before Woods's involvement, there is no mention in any of the letters or accounts of any change of design or layout. Nevertheless, Woods had to address the problem of one of the blank brick outside walls being clearly visible from the house. His solution was to make a narrow canal along its length, with the spoil used to form a slightly raised 'Border along by the Wall & a Walk between that & the Water'. Woods intended this 'long bank' to be planted with roses, gooseberries, currants, raspberries, and filberts – that is, a mixture of the useful and beautiful – with an initial cleansing crop, as the foreman reported: 'Mr Tomson thinks to plant it with potatoes'.[63]

Woods's plan of 1763 for Goldsborough (see Figure 15) left the prominently positioned kitchen garden as marked on a survey of 1738,[64] enclosed it in plantation and fitted the pleasure ground round it. However, the interior was to be completely reorganised, and was the subject of part of the memorandum sent to the foreman supervising the improvements.[65] The directions make it clear that the kitchen garden was not draining properly, and Woods wrote that 'the ground must be so formed as that it may lye with such decents to prevent the water hanging as the bottam is a could clay soyl'. A main stone drain was to be made down the middle, connecting with cross drains to draw surplus water into the ha-ha at the east end, and in spite of this precaution the fruit trees were to be set 'upon the top of the Border &

so raise hillocks round them, otherwise in a few years they will draw themselves down too deep'. None of this work had been started before White took over in 1765 and submitted a very different plan which included the repositioning of the kitchen garden clear of the pleasure ground area. The Ordnance Survey shows that White's kitchen garden was built exactly where he suggested.

At Goldsborough Woods's concern was only with the proper functioning of the garden, not with the planting or design within it, but at Kirklees his new kitchen garden included 'altering borders, walks etc.' as well as building a garden house and hot walls.[66] Where the kitchen garden was not relocated, it was often extended: that at Copford Hall, lying conveniently next to a vacant small field,[67] was to be enlarged and (to guess from the ground-plan on the map) provided with a greenhouse possibly flanked by pineries, although this refinement was not built. At Old Alresford, where there was a complete lack of ornamental buildings in the design of the layout, Woods merely advised adding to the kitchen garden to provide space for a melon ground, but keeping all the enclosures out of sight of the pleasure-ground circuit.

It is with the kitchen gardens known or surmised to have been designed by Woods, and not just reorganised or extended, that we enter an area of unusual interest. Whereas a plain rectangle, or possibly a rectangle with rounded corners, was the norm for new kitchen gardens in the eighteenth century, Woods proposed a curved or apsidal north wall at Cannon Hall, Hengrave, Wardour, Wormsley and probably Lulworth and Wynnstay, with a lozenge shape at Newsells possibly to his design. This suggests that he was acutely aware of the advantage of maximising a warm south- or south-west facing back for fruit trees, a practical detail not widely practised until the end of the century. In addition, in other commissions (Hartwell, Wardour, Little Linford and probably Brocket) he proposed a merging of kitchen garden and pleasure garden that was quite outside normal practice at the time.

One of Woods's most distinctive and attractive kitchen garden designs appears on his plan for Little Linford, where in an awkwardly sited triangle he fitted a semi-circular kitchen garden with quadrant beds and a melon ground attached to its back wall. The long straight side of the kitchen garden was left open to a walk through the pleasure ground, with a greenhouse sited in the middle of the curved wall as a focal point. Whereas a freestanding greenhouse in the pleasure ground was not unusual, to position it right at the back of the kitchen garden and yet in full view from the ornamental walk along the canal was a signal departure from the norm. A semicircle was also a very uncommon shape for a productive garden,[68] not least owing to the awkwardness of cultivating and transporting the crop through wedge-shaped beds, and in terms of arrangement it would have been easy enough to fill the available plot with a rectangle flanked by small triangular slips. The choice of a semicircle appears to have been a deliberate part of the design of the garden as a whole;

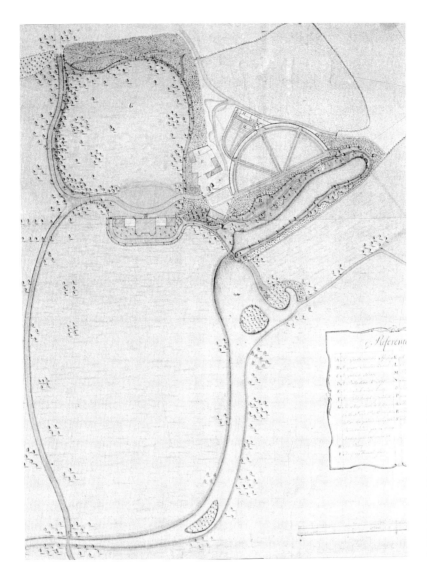

Fig. 64. Woods's plan for Little Linford, 1761. Typical Woods features are the unusually shaped kitchen garden with open access to the pleasure ground, the informal canal with a Gothic alcove seat at the top end and the 'sheep lawn' (top left) with a position for a 'light Doric or Ionic alcove' in direct view of the house.

it even poses the question of whether Woods was influenced by Southcote's circular kitchen garden at Wooburn Farm commended by Parnell, who described it as 'surrounded with shrubberies which connects it with the pleasure ground about the house which is at this time [June] spread over with several trees brought out of the greenhouse which has a most elegant effect in that part of a fine-kept piece of ground'.[69] Here at Little Linford was a kitchen garden not placed discreetly out of the way but positioned adjacent to the pleasure ground and indirectly part of it.

The merging of ornament and utility in the kitchen garden is particularly noticeable in Woods's work. Admittedly, it was widely accepted that the kitchen garden could be considered one of the destinations in a walk round the grounds,[70] and its often ambiguous position as a place of combined functions is aptly and charmingly illustrated by the frontispiece of the first edition of Mawe and Abercrombie's *Every Man his Own Gardener* (1767), where against a mixture of flowers, vegetables and cold frames polite company is seen in the background of the walled garden approaching a very utilitarian-looking greenhouse. As discussed in Chapter 4, if only one walled garden was available, it could and often did combine the functions of a productive garden and a sheltered place to raise rare and expensive flowers. It should also be noted that coarse produce – potatoes, cabbages and root vegetables – was usually grown in a field somewhere on the estate rather than in the kitchen garden.

THE KITCHEN-CUM-PLEASURE-GARDEN

Little Linford is an example of bringing the kitchen garden visually into the pleasure ground, but in three other commissions Woods took this a stage further by making the new kitchen garden a discrete part of it. At Wardour the kitchen garden for the Old Castle was sited a little to the east of the house, but was not in a convenient position for the new mansion on the crest of the hill. A new kitchen garden was marked on Woods's plan for improvements of 1764, and the agreement for building it and all it contained was signed in 1769. The building specification and the design on the separate plan of 1770 for the grounds around the house (Plate 11) show that this was not intended as a simple enclosure for produce alone. The pedimented greenhouse, freestanding but flanked by pineries set back from its façade (see pp. 89–90 for discussion of the architecture), was made the focal point of the main area, while the two subsidiary paths running the width of the garden continued into an apsidal extension comprising the hot walls and melon ground. The most unusual part of the agreement is that Woods contracted to 'lay out and plant the new Kitchen Garden' as well as being responsible for the built structures, the whole to cost the considerable sum of £1149 5s 6d. The relationship of this garden to the pleasure ground as a whole is immediately visible from the plan: various paths lead into the kitchen garden from the front and sides, while only the back is screened by thick plantation. Instead of normal slips, fruit trees were planted beyond the east and west walls in such a way as to make the overall shape of the whole composition into a round-pointed triangle.

A remarkable example of the fusion of kitchen garden and pleasure ground is found at Hartwell House, where in 1759 Woods submitted a 'Design for the new Garden Greenhouse and Pinery' for Sir William Lee.[71] The layout as recorded on an estate survey of 1776,[72] while obviously including beds of produce, places unusual emphasis on its other function as a pleasure garden (see Figure 17). The perimeter path was flanked by plantation, probably high on the road side and low towards the interior, and led past the brick walls of a rectangular garden-within-a-garden to nurture and ripen fruit.[73] Beyond this, the pleasure-garden aspect took precedence: a small building, possibly an alcove seat,[74] was positioned in the spandrel of thicker planting where the path turned east to follow the boundary, with a view into what the head gardener Lapidge called 'the Lawn before the Green House'. This was a levelled and slightly raised platform (converted to the 'bowling green' by the Victorians and still visible today), enclosed by ornamental planting with the greenhouse forming one of the sides, and it may be imagined that some of the exotics on the list of plants supplied by Woods were destined for this position. The lawn and planting in front of the greenhouse would have given a necessary softening to the aspect from the building, which otherwise would have looked out to the brick walls of the fruit garden. The pinery (referred to by Lapidge as a 'stove') was doubtless the separate building shown on Weston's map behind the greenhouse, looking out over 'Hot House Piece'.[75] The path continued around, dropping to the lower level east of the platform into a section with full view of produce before looping back into a narrow lawn enclosed by plantations and ornamented with another little building, and so back to the entrance. This arrangement almost presages Repton's attitude to a kitchen garden in his assertion in *Fragments* (1816) that 'a *jardin orné* may be made one of the most interesting luxuries of a country residence'.

A new head gardener contracted in 1798 to 'keep in as good Repair as it is now in the Kitchen Garden, Flower Garden & Pleasure Grounds from the entrance at the Arch up to the Boundaries of the fence of the Whole',[76] and the fusion of these usually separate divisions is confirmed in *Aedes Hartwellianae* (an account of Hartwell in 1851): 'even under banishment, vegetables and orchard-fruits may be so managed as at least to constitute part of, or to communicate with, the pleasure-ground … The Hartwell kitchen-gardens, though kept at a distance, are not wholly in Brunonian guise; for neither the lady's private flower-garden[77] … nor the aviary are omitted, – while tastefully-serpented walks among trees and shrubs of varied descriptions afford all the recreation which can be yielded by the most exclusive pleasure-grounds.' The planting is also mentioned: Portugal laurels of 25–30ft (8–9m) in 1851 and 'some fine hawthorns, several of them upwards of 35ft [10m]' – Woods had supplied *Prunus lusitanica* and a number of varieties of *Crataegus*.

There is less documentation to determine exactly the nature of Woods's commission at Brocket Hall in 1770, but cartographic evidence suggests that he was commissioned to alter some of the landscape specifically in the area close to the house, including the pleasure and kitchen gardens and the water, and plantations near the new approach, but not to redesign the whole park. An estate survey of 1798[78] illustrates what looks like a garden very much in his style bordering the newly shaped river, with direct access to a walled kitchen garden of a typically Woodsian irregular shape, containing hot-house and pinery on an ambitious scale forming a canted corner to one of the extremities (Plate 1). The significant aspect here is that these buildings are included not in the accounts for the kitchen garden (which looks like the wedge shape positioned further north) but under 'Pleasure Garden'. This is probably another example of a half-productive, half-ornamental garden.

THE PINERY GARDEN: THE CANNON HALL EXAMPLE

Fig. 65. A detail from the painting of Cannon Hall, showing the very plain and functional pinery in a position of importance and not hidden in the kitchen garden. The undated canvas was probably painted in the late 1760s to celebrate Spencer's building of the new house by Carr, and landscaping by Woods.

The kitchen garden at Cannon Hall (see Figure 13) was presumably planned as a round-ended rectangle but was forced by the curve of the road into an asymmetrical shape, with an additional small rectangular garden (possibly for fruit) at right angles to it. Here it is not a greenhouse which is of particular interest but the pinery, and more specifically, the position of the pinery. Woods's plan for improvements shows it close to the house, outside its customary kitchen-garden enclosure, and furthermore looking over a little oval lawn enclosed by a belt planted with 'exotic' flowers – that is, not the common sort – adjacent to the shrubbery. It has been mistakenly assumed that the substantial building now in the position of the pinery was designed

by Woods,[79] but a painting recently discovered by Jane Furse, showing Cannon Hall after Woods's improvements, reveals the very different picture of a lean-to glasshouse (see Plate 2 for the whole painting), which presumably also provided space for the 'low exoticks' when they needed shelter from the elements.[80] Although the elliptical garden in front of the pinery is indistinct on the painting, an estate map of 1839 shows it very much as designed by Woods.[81] To the modern eye, the juxtaposition of a plain glasshouse with an ornamental lawn might well seem incongruous, but the social status gained by the possession of a pinery was still enormous at this date and correspondence shows that Spencer was very proud of his. During Spencer's visits to London, Dutton the steward regularly wrote that 'a Brace of Pineapples' had been sent up to town on the carrier, with which expensive rarity Spencer could regale his London circle.

WOODS'S LANDSCAPE STYLE

The question remains of how the various component parts of Woods's landscapes were assembled, and in the process reflected his particular style. Within the wide variety of designs mentioned at the beginning of this chapter, three tendencies frequently reappear: a liking for a form of *ferme ornée*, a wide variety of incidents in the layout, and above all a strong emphasis on the pleasure ground/pleasure garden (sometimes even embracing the kitchen garden). Whereas Brown's style developed over the course of his career, Woods's later plans are indistinguishable from his earliest in design terms, in spite of a considerable shift in attitude to the designed landscape in the thirty years of his working life. There is nothing in the plans for Brizes (1788) or Stanway (1793) to distinguish them from Little Linford (1761) or Hatfield Peverel (1765), no less detail or greater feeling of the Picturesque. By contrast, Brown's plans for Ingestre and Badminton (both 1750s) could almost be taken for the work of Robert Greening at Wimpole around that date, whereas that for Heveningham of 1782 reveals a very different treatment of a long, wide stretch of land. It looks as though all Woods's predilections, possibly learnt at Wooburn Farm in the 1740s, were obstinately clung to through the intervening years.

Woods's plans in general cannot be grasped at a glance in the way that White's or many of Brown's can. To gain the feeling for a Woods landscape needs a particularly close scrutiny of the detail, an ability to visualise the impact of a certain little building, an opening in the planting, or even just the placing of a bench. For example, White's designs for Blyborough (1767), Burton Constable (1768) and Grove (1773) rely for their effect on the shape of the piece of water, the outlines of planting and the sweep of parkland. This is equally true of Goldsborough, whereas Woods's plan for the same estate (see Figures 15 and 16) comes to life only when such details as the planting behind the bench in the pleasure ground and the little bastion overlooking the parkland are considered. In addition (as with any improver's work) a knowledge of the lie of the land is essential in order to translate a two-dimensional design on paper into a picture complete with contours. The plan for Hatfield Peverel is a good example of this: a layout that on paper looks simple to the point of dullness relies for its success on topography, both that of the natural landform which allows a splendid borrowed long view, and that created by Woods on a small scale within the park with the spoil from the ponds.

The plan for Wivenhoe (Figure 11) combines many of Woods's characteristic features, and the central section which represents the executed portion neatly contains in 30–35 acres (12–14ha) the piece of water and different aspects of pleasure ground where Woods was so successful. The deer park comprising the south half of the property, which still retained vestiges of tree lines from old field boundaries, was left virtually untouched in his plan, except for some perimeter planting and the informally clumped approach up to the house. By contrast, the pleasure garden (referenced on the plan as a bowling green) in front of the house, overlooking the pasture and separated from it by a ha-ha, was both detailed in plan and curvilinear yet formal in outline. The path makes a symmetrical, cartouche-shaped circuit of the round-cornered rectangle which contains all the offices as well as the pleasure garden, winding through irregular plantations at the sides

Fig. 66. The pleasure garden at Wivenhoe Park. Although the plantations are scattered, the overall effect is of symmetry and formality. The only flower beds are set into the spandrels in front of the wings of the house.

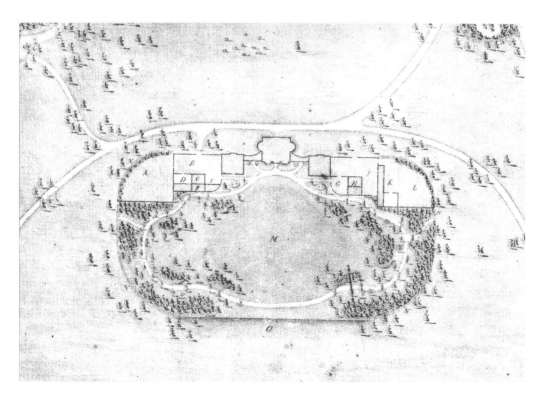

where it is fenced, and open behind the ha-ha in front. Two flower studs are placed in spandrels of lawn near the house, and a greenhouse borders the path in much the same way that it does at Brizes (see p. 90 and Plate 5). A subsidiary path leads out of the garden through the park and towards the Elysian Grove, a little walk fenced off from the deer, as in tune with the times as the 'bowling green' is unexpected for the period. The path wanders beside plantations and past a temple and a crescent of water until it arrives at the kitchen garden wall and a little straight canal.

Cannon Hall has already been discussed with reference to the planting in the shrubbery and pinery lawn to the east of the house, both of which were typically and peculiarly Woods, but the entire plan is equally characteristic of his style. The design covers 90-odd acres (36ha) comprising the central portion of the deer park,[82] and unlike Cusworth there is a clear division, marked by a ha-ha, between park and pleasure ground. Woods introduced clumps and intended a tree-scattered corridor between his new approach (not executed) and the west boundary, but otherwise the park slopes gently and uneventfully down to the river. Apart from the bridges and cascades on the river, most of the incident is packed into the 15-acre (6ha) pleasure ground and, while the flower gardens are historically most interesting, the layout on the west of the house is also noteworthy. Leading away from the side of the house is a short avenue, or perhaps the remains of a previous

Fig. 67. Woods's plan for Cannon Hall, redrawn for clarity by Jane Furse. Like a number of his plans, the original is faded and difficult to read, and does not reproduce well. Another very similar plan, undated, is a survey with Woods's improvements added.

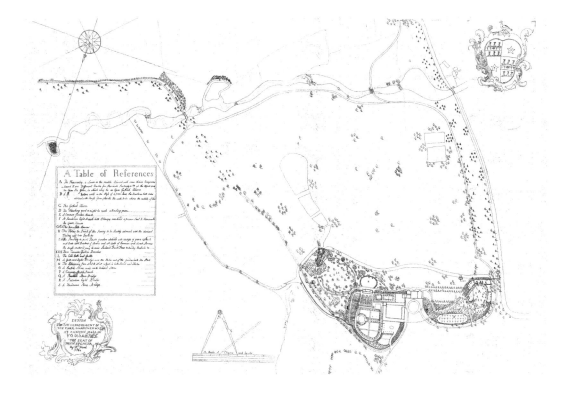

longer one, described on the references as a 'green Terase', closed by a 'handsome light bench with a canopy overhead'. Just beyond but screened by planting is a pheasantry with 'a Lawn in the middle adorned with some choice evergreens' surrounded by the 'courts' for the birds, and at the upper end a fir grove 'in which may be an open Gothic alcove'.

Pheasantries and menageries, which were often more properly aviaries, were popular additions to the pleasure-ground scene through the eighteenth century, and Woods tried to sell the idea to Lord Arundell. Although there is a reference in the Wardour correspondence to a probably purely functional pheasantry in the Lady Grove, on the 1770 plan (Plate 11) the oval lawn is again backed by menagerie pens, which here would have had a decorative purpose. This proposed (unexecuted) pleasure garden on the west of the house was as unusual for the period as the ornamental kitchen garden. The first of the two oval lawns it contains carries the standard mix of irregular clumps, scattered trees or shrubs and a few studs for flowers, but the second, interconnected, lawn is atypical. The menagerie pens are arranged in a curved band above the lawn, set in plantation, while the centre of the lawn is taken up by an oval pond symmetrically surrounded by short oval flower beds and regularly placed shrubs in a triangle round them, giving the effect of a series of small garlands. Such a design would hardly look out of place in a Repton Red Book.

Distinctive as this is, the design for Wormsley in 1780 is astonishing. The lack of references, lost some years ago, leaves the plan wide open to interpretation, but the surprising layout, scattered with circular formal gardens (which would have had to be carved out of the steep hanging wood behind the house) and including a rather tortuous open grove, is more reminiscent of Thomas Wright than of Capability Brown. Woods's plan as a whole could be interpreted as a hybrid design whose formality adumbrates aspects of Repton while harking back to Southcote's or even Switzer's *ferme ornée*: the house and gardens look out over parkland (depicted by Woods as grazed by horses) sandwiched between arms of 'sheep lawn' and enclosing fields (at least one of them arable) still retaining their ancient boundaries. Woods's client John Fane was an enthusiastic agricultural improver, which might explain the retention of fields within the designed landscape, while Woods was not only inclined to the *ferme ornée* but was also at that date a farmer himself and therefore even more receptive to the inclusion of fields in his plans.

Lingering traces of formality can be seen in many landscape plans of the later eighteenth century, and all the improvers – Brown included – made use of existing features where they did not compromise a new design, both for reasons of economy and to give an air of maturity to a fledgling layout. Woods undoubtedly on occasion incorporated remnants of the previous landscape, such as one of the two bastions in the pleasure ground at Goldsborough, and even sometimes introduced new formal aspects. It is not

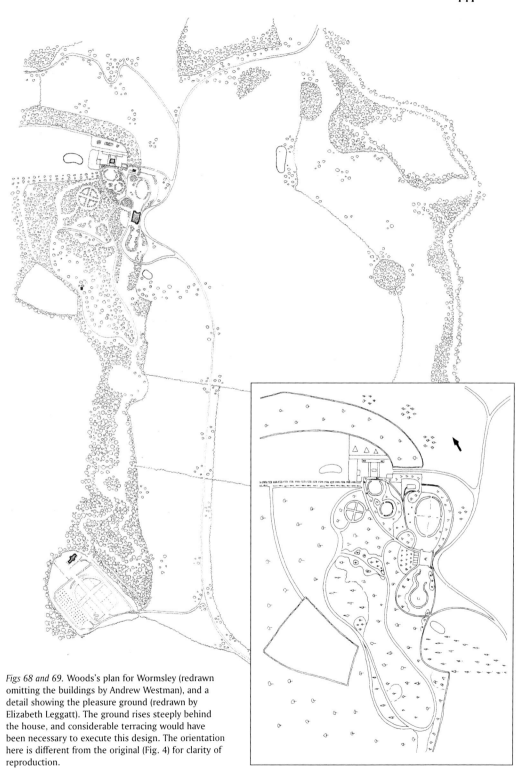

Figs 68 and 69. Woods's plan for Wormsley (redrawn omitting the buildings by Andrew Westman), and a detail showing the pleasure ground (redrawn by Elizabeth Leggatt). The ground rises steeply behind the house, and considerable terracing would have been necessary to execute this design. The orientation here is different from the original (Fig. 4) for clarity of reproduction.

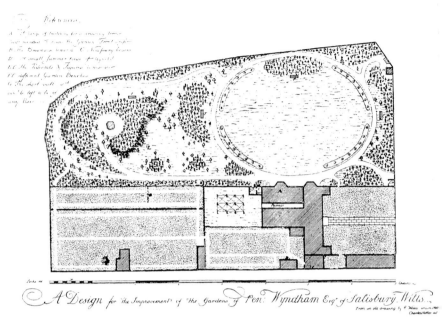

surprising that his only known design for a town garden, at Wyndham House
in Salisbury, should contain a regular oval lawn banded by a narrow belt
containing evenly spaced shrubs and possibly flowers, but it is more
unexpected to find the form virtually replicated at Cannon Hall (1761) in front
of the pinery and at Wormsley (1780) in the middle of the pleasure ground.

Copford, especially when taken with the later plan for the adjoining part
of the estate at Stanway (see Plate 6), combines many of Woods's design
preferences. His plan was partly adaptation, partly creation: the two existing
geometric ponds were softened in outline by making them oval, and the
smaller was surrounded by a rose garden. Flower borders and studs were set
out at the side of the house, which retained its view over farmland across ha-
has; a circular bowling green formed a 'salon' within a grove, which was the
former Hawbridge Wood partly cleared and opened up. A wide lawn
(somewhat resembling that at Little Linford) was bordered with scattered
trees and scalloped-edged woodland screening the public road. The cascade,
complete with bench perched on it – as at Cusworth – and a grotesque mask
as keystone harking back to Wardour, linked two of the four small pieces of
water. The unexecuted additional landscaping at Stanway would have formed
a *ferme ornée* of the whole. The end result is unmistakably Woods, and equally
unmistakably not in the style of any other improver practising at the time.

Cusworth remains one of Woods's outstanding achievements, and is rare
among his commissions in that it survives and has been extensively restored.
Although there is no design to show what Woods initially visualised the
memoranda fully compensate for this lack; even the absence of a pleasure

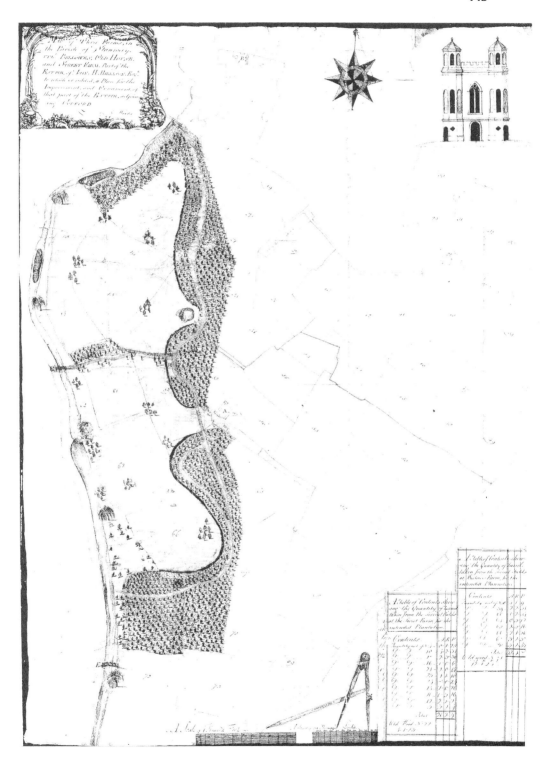

garden as such does not place it outside Woods's typical work, in that the whole park can be seen as pleasure ground. The overall effect was unreservedly praised by Loudon, who in general had little time for Brown's 'imitators and followers'. Woods's subtle use of different levels to add interest to the three small pieces of water; his winding walk down the side of the hanging lawn, bordered with flowers and flowering shrubs; his grotto-boathouse, cascade and bridge-cum-dam, all similar to features he designed for other estates; and his very distinctive planting in the park beyond the water (discussed on p. 46) all combine to make this one of his most delightful and successful commissions.

These examples show that Woods did indeed have a distinctive manner, which encompassed elements from an earlier, more intimate idea of designed landscape while also including aspects closer to Brown. The most significant point raised by a study of Woods is that his designs can variously look old-fashioned or ahead of his time. In view of his apparent attraction for and adherence to the architecture and layouts of the 1740s and 50s, it seems unlikely that he was breaking ground in other respects. His Cannon Hall plan, although rare in the work of the improvers, is now accepted not as a new departure in pleasure-ground planting, but as proof of the continuum of pleasure-garden creation, alteration and maintenance.[83] The fact that part of his 1770 design for Wardour looks Reptonian while there are hints of Thomas Wright in his 1780 plan for Wormsley shows the extent of the danger of being too categorical about the progression of fashions in style and their acceptability to clients.

CHAPTER 7

LABOUR DEMAND, SUPPLY AND ORGANISATION IN THE EIGHTEENTH-CENTURY GARDEN

T HE WORKFORCE NEEDED TO CREATE THE LANDSCAPES designed by the improvers was composed of unattached labourers from a class which, in the period 1700–75, has been reckoned to have comprised between two-thirds and three-quarters of the population. An annual income of £20 was 'generally thought necessary for mere subsistence'.[1] They were hired and fired from week to week as necessary, and were supplemented by the team of 'garden men' – also casual labour – employed for the day-to-day upkeep of the grounds. Garden hands had long been employed on these terms, but the explosion in population and changing farming practices from the mid century onwards were resulting in a larger flexible agricultural labour force (as described by Tom Williamson[2]). This meant that more unattached labour was available when extra hands were required on a sporadic – and indeed short-term – basis for the creation of designed landscapes.

As garden history is still a relatively new discipline, there are as yet no in-depth studies investigating the composition and lifestyle specifically of the garden labourer, but it may be assumed that the majority if not all of the casual day-labourers employed to execute garden improvements were in essence farm workers. The same skills or strength were required to dig a ha-ha as a field drain; to scythe a lawn as a hayfield; to construct temples as to repair farm buildings. The two sets of activity were in many cases so closely related that at Wivenhoe it was the farmer who was employed to thatch the new deer house built by Woods's men, and Woods's foreman who was given extra piece work felling trees at the nearby estate of Alresford.[3]

Whereas the labourers could be agricultural men-of-all-trades, it was assumed that the foremen were conversant with laying out grounds, and anyone describing himself as 'gardener' would be expected to have some specialist experience and/or training in horticultural practice. In the kitchen garden this was even more necessary, and was made clear when an applicant was being considered for a vacant position in this part of the garden.[4] Where men were required for more permanent work than the day-labourer satisfied, probably in a nursery, an advertisement in the local press might attract the right sort of recruit: 'Wanted immediately, a Number of Hands that understand Gardening in its several Branches … to apply to Robert Simmonds, Gardener in Brentwood, where they will meet with constant Employ and Great Encouragement.'[5]

WAGES

In an age of no statutory minimum wage and little communication among men in different localities at the lowest end of the social scale to compare working conditions, the variation in labouring wages was considerable. This can be partly explained by regional differences in rates of pay (with the west generally lagging behind the London area and northern counties, where commerce and industry kept wages up[6]), but where accounts survive for the estates where Woods worked, it is clear that generalisation is dangerous. Rates for labourers varied between 10d a day at Hartwell in Buckinghamshire (1744–65) and Kirklees in West Yorkshire (1766) and 1s a day at Cusworth in Yorkshire (1762–63) and Wardour in Wiltshire (1764).[7] Thomas White wrote in 1767 that 'it is not more than Twelve Months since the standard Wages of this Country was not more than 1s per day, I have already advanced the wages to 14d [1s 2d]',[8] showing that there was a notion, even if one not adhered to, of a 'fair rate'. Workmen apparently employed on the same or similar tasks recorded on a worksheet are sometimes earning different rates of pay, presumably reflecting age, strength or experience. Whereas for about the first sixty years of the century there was little upward movement of wages, prices also were generally low and static, but from shortly after the mid century grain prices started rising significantly. At Hartwell the garden labourers in 1765 were still earning the 10d a day they had commanded in 1745, but by the following year the daily rate had been increased to 1s in line with White's comments.[9]

By the late 1770s and 1780s, estate accounts for Woods's commissions show that the labourer's rate of pay had risen materially, for instance to 1s 8d in the summer and 1s 6d in the winter at Wivenhoe in 1778.[10] A surprising attitude to his labourers is found in a letter (not dated, but probably written in autumn 1780) from the Wivenhoe foreman Lupton to Colonel Rebow.[11] He reported to Rebow that 'wee have had a good set of working men and has kept good time and laboured hones[tl]y for their wages' but suggested that as 'work is scarce and men plenty as after this work shou'd think 9s pr. week will be soficient as ye Days grows short … last year they had 10s pr. week thro Novr'. The worksheets show that Lupton had himself been on labourer's wages at the beginning of the improvements, and was only promoted to foreman a few months into the work, which makes him look very much like 'poacher turned game-keeper'. Nevertheless, 9s a week – 1s 6d a day – through the winter was not a mean rate of pay. Where it was acknowledged that some of the men's tasks were unusually disagreeable, they were

147

LABOUR DEMAND,
SUPPLY AND
ORGANISATION
IN THE
EIGHTEENTH-
CENTURY GARDEN

generally rewarded with beer or beer money, as at Hartwell, where the accounts for 1744 show payment for ale to eleven men making the serpentine river 'while they stood in the water to remove the earth',[12] and at Kirklees, where the accounts for 1766 show 1s for 'the workmen opening the Water course (a dirty jobb) to drink'.[13]

THE ECONOMY OF THE LABOURING CLASS

It may well be wondered how a workman could keep himself and family in such uncertain conditions. It is difficult to be sure of making a true comparison of the standard of living between the highest- and lowest-paid garden labourers, but no workmen of this sort expected to subsist only on their wages. The traditional progress for a boy from about the age of eleven was from farm-servant, living with or housed by the farmer, to day-labourer after marriage in his twenties, when he set up in some sort of cottage of his own.[14] From that point, he earned his wages on a week-to-week basis, whether working as farm hand or garden labourer. In both categories men were sometimes employed over several years by the same farm or estate, but on an *ad hoc* basis.[15] The harvest bonuses probably did no more than offset lean times during the winter, but a degree of self-sufficiency could be achieved in various ways.[16] A wife and children brought in supplementary cash by such menial tasks as weeding or scaring birds, or by taking on extra work such as spinning, weaving and knitting – at least until the effects of the Industrial Revolution started to bite. On the small plot surrounding their cottage, produce would be grown and possibly even a pig or chickens kept, as noted by Adam Smith: 'the poorest occupiers of the land can commonly maintain a few poultry, or a sow and a few pigs, at very little. The little offals of their own table … supply those animals with a part of their food, and they find the rest in the neighbouring fields without doing sensible damage to anybody.'[17] Gilbert White described the rushlights made by poor Hampshire families to use instead of candles, with the rushes being collected by 'decayed labourers, women and children' and 'the coarser animal-oils [which] come very cheap' used as the fat, although even the 'scummings of the bacon-pot' served the purpose if necessary.[18] For much of the century modest poaching was tolerated, and most farmers allowed gleaning, which was a vitally important part of a labourer's subsistence. The rent demanded for the labourers' dwellings also varied, and might account for some of the apparent discrepancy in wage rates between estates. Young in 1771 noted a labourer's house rent in the east of England as being 40s (i.e. £2) a year,[19] but much depended on whether the parish was 'close' – that is, with a restricted number of cottages available (on the grounds that 'they harbour the poor that are a charge to the parish'[20]), so that labourers working in that parish probably had a long journey from a house elsewhere to their place of employment – or 'open' – with an unrestricted number of dwellings, resulting in a parish that was 'over-crowded, insanitary, and ill-regulated, with numerous small proprietors who let tumbledown cottages at exorbitant rents'.[21] Either way, the labourer was at a disadvantage.

In spite of no security of employment and no certainty of stable wages, even the casual labourer was not necessarily servile, and, as Switzer experienced, could be 'insolent and insufferable'.[22] This had been observed a generation previously by Timothy Nourse, who warned that unless labourers were 'in a settled Estate, such as that of Marriage … they will upon every turn be taking a rambling Frisk'.[23] The craftsmen and skilled workers were equally independent-minded, and Woods moaned on 20 December 1768 that the mason employed at Irnham to turn the arch over the moat 'shuffles off, and will not get about it till affter the Hollydays'.[24] On a visit to Wivenhoe a decade later he was annoyed to find that 'the carpenters, was stoptd and gone, and which was still more vexatious, I could get only one hand, till Tuesday next.'[25]

There was unquestionably a very fluid labour market at this level, and it is immediately noticeable when looking at estate accounts that the number of men employed varied considerably from week to week, even during periods of routine garden maintenance. While improvements were under way, the worksheets kept by the foreman show this trend to be even more marked, and correspondence often includes instructions to employ more men 'to advance the works' or to lay some off if the labour bill was thought to be too high or conditions in any way unsuitable.[26] During the first months of activity at Wivenhoe in 1771, the number of men working under Lupton (recently promoted to foreman) varied from five to fifteen; by May 1780, towards the end of the commission, Lupton wrote that 'wee are onely 4 hands at the work now and 2 is mostly imployed in watering trees.'[27]

Workmen in search of employment usually stood in the local marketplace waiting for the like of the local farm bailiff, estate steward or improver's foreman to engage them for the following week. White instructed Stones, his foreman at Newby, to 'make all the Enquiry you can for men in the neighbouring towns, and if your Number is not encreased I would have you get … [an] advertisement printed in the York paper'.[28] Woods wrote disparagingly, 'I find good hands very scarce everywhere nowadays', and, when he ordered the foreman at Irnham to employ what men he could locally, added 'bad as they are'.[29] He also told the foreman working at Diddington in Huntingdonshire to 'engage as many hands as possible as soon as the harvest is over and send them to Irnham', a distance of some 50 miles (85km).

The annual hiring fairs, usually held after harvest, were traditionally where men in search of work might be taken on as farm servants, with rather more security than as labourers, and although this form of agricultural employment was in decline from the middle of the century, it was obviously a chance that no labourer would want to miss. The most fortunate might be housed, as those at Halston in Shropshire were, 'in a neat little village …

149

LABOUR DEMAND,
SUPPLY AND
ORGANISATION
IN THE
EIGHTEENTH-
CENTURY GARDEN

chiefly built by the Mytton family for the accommodation of several labourers employed on the estate.'[30] During the improvements at Wivenhoe, Woods warned his employer in July 1778 that he would only be able to advance work satisfactorily and end his supervisory visit 'if New Fair don't take off too many of his hands'. Presumably the labourers not lucky enough to be offered better employment would then be available to resume the improvements at Wivenhoe, and had had a few rare days of enjoyment at the fair into the bargain.[31]

Although it has been impossible to discover any detail, it seems that Woods had at his command a certain number of his own 'companies' of workmen, who – like the foremen – could be sent where required. He obviously arrived with them at the beginning of some commissions, as at Boreham House in 1763, when beer was charged at 7s 8d 'for Mr Woods & Com[y]', and he sometimes felt the lack of their presumably reliable labour: in 1769 he wrote from Irnham to Lord Arundell of being so far away from any of his own companies that he had to make do with such labourers as were available in the neighbourhood, although he would send 'some good hand from home for finishing'.[32] A reference in the landscaping accounts for Boreham House in 1771 to 'Yorkshire men' suggests that Woods might have retained some of the labourers employed on his Yorkshire commissions in the 1760s for work elsewhere in the country.[33] Whereas hiring and firing of labourers (other than those in one of his 'companies') was left to the foreman, Woods seemed to have more direct control over supply of craftsmen and specifications for their jobs; he acted as go-between for Lord Arundell and a carpenter for Irnham ('I think I have now settled your Lordship with a Carpenter, if we can but agree upon Terms')[34] and at Alresford in 1776 he reported that 'the plaisterer will be down within a few days'[35] – that is, he was not recruited locally.

From 1759 a new factor temporarily affected the balance of the labour market. The Duke of Bridgewater, acting on the rebound after an unfortunate love-affair, started what would prove to be a major improvement to inland transport through England, devoting his energy and money to initiating the canal system. The Bridgewater Canal, linking the duke's coal mines at Worsley with Manchester, opened for navigation in 1761, and thereafter acts enabling the building of further canals were passed regularly through the century. Initially the workforce of 'navigators' (the term 'navvy' was not used until the early nineteenth century) was drawn from the floating labour market of the locality[36] and their influence spread no further. Nevertheless, if an improver, and probably a farmer as well, was looking for hands near the line of one of the new canals, he may have found prices being driven up. White, engaged on the improvements at Newby, gives an early indication of this: 'I have already advanced the wages to 14d and some you give more … If all they now have will not suffice, I can not think of giving more, as I should be very sorry to run myself into difficulty in order to keep pace with the navigators who do not seem to have well considered what they are doing.'[37] White's reaction to pressure for higher wages was to instruct his foreman to employ men on piece work as much as possible, so that rather than raising the daily rate, which was never easy to lower again, a more generous bargain could be struck for measured work. By about 1780 the navigators had become a body of specialised men who followed the canal-building round the country and therefore had less impact on local labour supply.

DISCONTENT

The rate of pay commanded by the canal diggers was just one minor factor in the inexorable upward pressure of prices caused mainly by the rapidly increasing population, resulting in general discontent in the 1760s among those who felt that increasing costs were whittling away their standard of living.[38] The year 1768 saw a series of disturbances in London, including demonstrators outside the House of Lords chanting, 'It is as well to be hanged as starved', and news of such disaffection must have trickled into the market towns where men were waiting and hoping for employment. White's experience at Newby in 1767 was echoed in a more extreme form at Irnham in April 1769, where improvements had just started: having arranged several teams of men to begin work, Woods made a quick visit to a nearby commission, and on his return was furious and disconcerted to be faced by a strike. He wrote to Lord Arundell:

> I found some of my chaps, going on in a very bad way, and for all I cou'd do and say, found it was not in my power to do anything with them, but disscharge them, which I did. I cou'd scasely in a sheet of paper, describe the dissposition and behaviour of those unaccountable Creatures, in human shapes indeed but yt. is all, for in all other respects are Bruits. The first Monday morning affter I arived the[y] all draw'd up in a body, swore they wou'd not tutch a tool unless I wou'd give them 18d a day, the planting being in hand, I was oblig'd to comply being at so great disstance from any of my own Companeys yt. I could have no suplyes nor help myself any ways. Affter the harry of that Branch was over, I then parceled out the work in the manner I before observed, and agreed with em by measure, and as I just above observed, when I returned out of Nottinghamshire found them going on in such a way yt it was quite unbearable and so disscharg'd some of the very worst and Ringleaders of em, and the Rest I have bound to thire good behaviour if it is possible, which indeed is doubtfull, for no Laws can bind them, as they fear neither God nor man'.[39]

151

LABOUR DEMAND,
SUPPLY AND
ORGANISATION
IN THE
EIGHTEENTH-
CENTURY GARDEN

No local canal was under construction at that time, and without further information it must be assumed that the ringleaders were working up a general rather than specific discontent. It might have been the absence of the foreman at that moment that emboldened the labourers to go on strike.[40]

Later in his career, as tenant of a sizeable farm at North Ockendon, Woods joined a group of local gentlemen and farmers in an association formed in 1779 for the preservation of their property 'against the Depredations of Divers Loose and Disorderly Persons',[41] probably a reflection on the rising tide of mob action against what was seen as artificially inflated wheat prices.[42]

SEASONAL ADJUSTMENTS

In trying to calculate how much time would be necessary to achieve any particular portion of a landscaping commission, haymaking and harvest were the most important factors affecting progress. It goes without saying that no estate hands would be available for work on a ha-ha or ornamental plantation until haymaking was over and the crops brought in, and one example will serve for hundreds: at Wivenhoe in August 1778 Mary Rebow wrote to her husband, 'I am sorry I cannot continue ye good account of [Woods's foreman] Lupton's people, but this fine Weather has set Harvest in, & of course they have all left him except one.'[43] If men were retained on the garden improvements during harvest, they could expect a temporary rise in wages to compensate: at Boreham in 1771 the foreman noted on the ledger on 19 August 'NB the harvest month, 1s 6d per day' where the usual wage was 1s 4d.[44] Spring activity on the farm could also affect the progress of improvements: On 3 April 1780 Lupton wrote 'if I could have got workmen [the planting] wou'd aibeen finished before now labourers as been very scarce till now'.

Work obviously advanced much faster when spoil or building materials could be loaded onto horse-drawn carts rather than being wheeled in barrows. It was a standard article in an agreement that the client would provide horse labour, but that established an inevitable clash from time to time with the estate farmer and the demands of the agricultural year. On occasion Woods had to tell Lord Arundell that slow progress at Wardour was being caused by lack of horses.[45] The initial agreement was that Woods was 'to find … 3 horses as a constant team & to have yours at proper times to help on the great jobbs'; he was to have money to buy horses and corn; the hay would come from the estate, and the horses would be put out to grass 'at the time you take the stock into the Park'. Unfortunately that arrangement does not seem to have lasted. Even Woods's own companies would have no access to horses and carts during the weeks of high summer, when they were needed continuously on the farm. Again, the problem was not confined to harvest time. In April 1769 the steward at Irnham was worried about demanding horses for the carriage of gravel for the coach roads, 'as it is a busy time with the farmers'. Woods pointed out that by the time the gravel was actually needed 'the farmers will so now have don sowing and so yt. I hope he [the steward] will not be much disstressed'.[46] The extent to which horses were used on large-scale improvements is shown on a single surviving account, 'A Bill of Horse Labour' submitted by Woods's foreman for September to December 1771: out of a 104 possible days, the horses were used on 87 at tasks such as 'work at the pond', 'drawing timber', 'drawing trees and stones' and 'drawing plants and stakes' – and this was in autumn and winter.

Garden improvements, particularly where they involved building or water features, were most easily undertaken in the clement weather when farming needed most hands, although only the most extreme conditions stopped work entirely. While Woods in August 1767 urged that 'the remainder of the ha-ha wall may be finish'd this autumn otherways the banks will fall', and in June 1770 that 'the present work at the pond … shou'd be done before the winter comes on',[47] there were still a few jobs that were not brought to a standstill in bad weather. At Scone in December 1784 'although the snow lay pretty thick upon the ground, the frost did not penetrate so far as to hinder Mr White's people from working on the sunk fences'.[48]

PIECE WORK

It was noted in Essex in 1796 that in farming 'the practice of letting work by piece is rapidly expanding',[49] but in garden improvements this method of employment was certainly already widespread by the 1770s when Woods was working at Wivenhoe. Whereas White had advised his foreman to use it as much as possible in order to mask a higher rate of pay without actually raising wages, the Norfolk farmer Randall Burroughes favoured it in the 1790s for exactly the opposite reason, calculating that piece work would cost him less than employing the labourer by the day.[50] Piece work was also a convenient way of keeping the labourers to time on an occasion when supervision might be lacking. This occurred when Henry Stevens, the foreman at Irnham, had to be absent: 'before he went he had let some parcles of work to the men to do by measure', although in general the improvements at that estate were being executed on day rates. Woods's advice to Lord Arundell was that in general it was better to 'employ his old workmen upon measured work where neither party can be wronged', whereas 'jobing work will not be done without paying 1s for every 3d worth of work'.[51]

The foreman at Wivenhoe worked out an ingenious way of combining aspects of both methods of payment:

> I go upon a new plan with the carpenters every different
> jobb they do when they work by the day, and how long with
> it, I explane it in the book under theire weekly acct. so that

153

LABOUR DEMAND,
SUPPLY AND
ORGANISATION
IN THE
EIGHTEENTH-
CENTURY GARDEN

> every jobb may be easly known what it lies in and by so
> doing it makes them keep better time and work closer than
> ever I know'd them before as I tell them the Col. [Colonel
> Rebow, the owner of Wivenhoe] may very likely have all
> theire jobs valued to know if he have justice don him as he
> had not been well used time past.[52]

At Boreham in 1771, Woods's foreman Pugh also used a mixture of day wages and piece work, and men who in one week were leading their 'company' on measured work might well be on day wages another week.[53] There is no indication of the number of men in any company, making it impossible to calculate whether they earned significantly less by this method than the 1s 4d they received in the normal way.

THE FOREMEN

Brown was above all a contractor, supplying the plan for improvements, advice, and sporadic supervision of the foreman he established to execute his design. His ex-foreman Nathaniel Richmond had initially, after he became independent, retained personal responsibility for the execution of his suggestions, but in 1765 switched 'from a design and build contract basis to a design and inspect role'. From this time, he employed John Hencher as his single works contractor rather than calling on any one of a number of foremen in the market or co-operating with the bailiff of his employer, as at Compton Place.[54] Woods, like Brown and in common with most of the other major improvers, was heavily dependent on his foremen for the successful execution of his designs. The surprisingly uneven quality of these key figures reflects the struggle to find, employ and keep men with the ability to interpret and conduct the progress of the improvements, in addition to maintaining a sometimes delicate relationship with the head gardener or steward of the client. Estate accounts sometimes suggest a certain amount of resentment in the head gardeners towards 'Mr Woods's man' or 'Mr White's man', who had been inserted into their working structure. It is not unusual to find the steward, who was on a higher level than the foreman within the estate hierarchy, reporting to his employer on the conduct of the improver's man: Benjamin Dutton, John Spencer's steward at Cannon Hall, wrote rather pompously to his master that he had 'no reason to complain of [Thomas Peach's] conduct since you left us'.[55] Anthony Sparrow, Woods's foreman at Harewood, incurred the displeasure of the estate steward Popplewell, who considered that Sparrow 'does not want knowledge so much as conduct' and wrote to Edwin Lascelles, 'It is lately I have observed this conduct in Sparrow; since you was last here he has frequently gone to Harewood Bridge when he ought to have been with his labourers.'[56] Lupton at Wivenhoe even roused the suspicion of Colonel Rebow's wife herself, who noticed that he had not 'done a stroke of work these two Saturdays' and sent the steward to ask the reason, which proved to be that he had 'gone to Colchester for change and is writing out his accounts'. Mary Rebow asked her husband, 'Should it be so or would you have me speak to him about it?' The foreman was answerable to both Woods and to the estate owner, and it is not always clear who took priority.

A bad choice of foreman could have disastrous results for the commission, as White found to his cost at Scone, where for lack of anyone more suitable he installed a man who was 'no regular agent of mine and tho' an excellent rough workman has no idea of compleating anything'.[57] A sound foreman was all the more important in view of the difficulty of communication with a landscaper perpetually on the move between commissions and short of time to answer his post, although mailed letters seemed to be delivered within a week.[58] Woods's foreman William Lapidge complained in 1760 during the improvements at Hartwell House: 'I finds there is sixteen [stakes] upon the Lawn … but what Mr Woods intended them to be I cannot tell … I have heard nothing of Mr Woods since I see him at Hartwell.'[59] Stones at Goldsborough wrote to Woods in 1765, 'I made bould to trouble you with a line as i never had any letter from you sins last Christmas was a yeare',[60] and the steward at Harewood reported in the same year that the foreman 'says he can hear nothing of Mr Woods'. White had similar problems in visiting all his clients punctually, and admitted to 'having always more engagements upon my hands than I can find time for',[61] while Brown's clients frequently recognised that he would have to work in a visit on one of his pre-arranged circuits.[62] There are several instances (and there must have been many more unrecorded) of a letter chasing Woods round on his travels, as when he explained to Colonel Rebow, 'I arrived at home on Wednesday evening last & find your letter of ye 19th ult. here, wch was sent for me at St James's Place; my having left town before it arrived there, & left home before it arrived here.'[63]

Less information is available about the successful foremen running a commission smoothly than about those instances when problems necessitated correspondence to resolve them. Little is known about Richard Creswell, the foreman at Wardour, who was one of the few in whom Woods had complete trust, describing him to Lord Arundell as 'that carefull and honest man … who will never leave a stone unturned to obay my orders and have your Lordship's business done'. Another reliable foreman was Edward Pugh, who was left by Woods in complete charge of the improvements at Boreham House for fourteen months before being moved to a new commission at Wynnstay. Even taking account of the conventional effusiveness of the time, Pugh's signing-off of the Boreham account suggests that his employer had been entirely satisfied with him: 'Sir, I wish you Health and Return you thanks for all favours', and his rate of pay at 3s 6d a day doubtless reflects his abilities as well as including a housing allowance.[64] Complete silence surrounds the character of Thomas Coalie, the foreman

155

LABOUR DEMAND,
SUPPLY AND
ORGANISATION
IN THE
EIGHTEENTH-
CENTURY GARDEN

sent to Cusworth in 1762 to supervise Woods's improvements there, but as he was retained for a year after Woods was paid off, and with his final wages given two guineas (£2 2s) 'over and above by order',[65] he was presumably found perfectly satisfactory.

William Stones, Woods's foreman at Goldsborough, was of a different calibre entirely, although he subsequently found employment with both White and Brown. Within six months of employing him in June 1764, Woods was writing

> Mr Lascelles is not so well satisfied as you seem'd imagin,
> for he has found out what an eternall Drunkard you are, &
> this you may assuer your self yt. if you do not refrain from
> that Beastly Custom, yt. you will be but short lived with him.
> … I am determined, to incurrage nor imploy no man yt. will
> not behave in all respects as he ought to do, for I get more
> Discredit, for bad foremen than by any other means.[66]

Perhaps surprisingly, when Woods was shortly afterwards replaced at Goldsborough by White, Stones was retained as the foreman and subsequently followed White to Newby, where he continued to give trouble by submitting inadequate or even misleading accounts.[67] John Simpson, an early foreman at Wardour, was removed within a few months, apparently leaving his accounts in less than good order. Woods wrote to the Wardour steward, 'I have not as yet seen Simpson, but yesterday … got the Book from him, and am afraid I shall not find all to my satisfaction therein.'[68] Even at the height of his career in 1765, Brown complained, 'When I am galloping in one part of the world my men are making blunders and neglects which [make] it very unpleas't'.[69]

Once Woods had made up his mind about the character of his men, he stood by them loyally. When Lapidge was dismissed from Cassiobury in 1759 Woods recommended him to Sir William Lee of Hartwell and wrote that he believed him to be 'a down right honest man', in spite of the fact that he had left Lord Essex under a cloud.[70] Woods also requested employment for Lapidge's two sons, one of whom, Samuel, later became foreman to Brown. Similarly, when Henry Stevens, who had acted as a foreman for Woods over many years, was accused of 'losing' (stealing?) £68 by Thomas Wood when working at Littleton, Woods leapt to his defence.[71] As he explained to Lord Arundell, at whose Irnham estate Stevens was then working, the missing balance was eventually proved to be only £7 9s 7½d, caused by 'intangling & confusing the accts. no part of wch. I hope was done willfully'.[72] Seven years later Woods firmly claimed to another employer that in the twenty years Stevens had worked for him he had 'never once misbehaved'.[73] The improvers obviously kept their eyes open for hopeful material, and at the time of the strike at Irnham Woods noticed among the men he retained 'one of out of the whole Extraodenry, both as a good hand, and worthy young man, and of whom I will something more at a proper time'. The records do not relate whether this promising youth was eventually taken on by Woods in a more responsible position.

The disparity in ability, intelligence and probably ambition among the foremen of all the improvers also accounts for the fact that while some remained in that category for their entire career, others used the experience gained under Brown, Emes, Richmond, White or Woods to set up in business on their own account. Two of Emes's foremen subsequently made names for themselves: Thomas Leggett (*fl.* 1760s–1810), whose work included the layout for Brockhampton (Herefordshire) in 1769 and who is even found working alongside Woods at Wynnstay,[74] and John Webb (1754–1828), who provided a design for Maer Hall (Staffordshire).[75] Capability Brown's one-time foremen Nathaniel Richmond and Thomas White, to name the best-known, practised on their own account from 1759 and 1765 respectively. The better sort often stayed on at the estate where the improver had placed them as foremen: for example, in the 1770s, after Woods's dismissal, Creswell was earning as Lord Arundell's gardener £30 a year plus 4s a week board wages, with a house supplied just outside the park.[76]

Some of Woods's foremen aspired to independence, but the evidence for their success is weaker. Two are known to have advertised in local newspapers, using their experience with Woods as a recommendation: William Gooch took space in the *Norwich Mercury* on 4 February 1764 to announce

> That William Gooch now arrived from London is settled in
> Norwich with an intention to undertake New Work in all its
> Branches relative to Gardening. Land Survey'd and a Map of
> the same drawn with the greatest Accuracy. Any Gentlemen
> that please to make a Trial will find their Work faithfully
> executed in the neatest Manner … N.B. Gentlemen's Gardens
> taken by the Year, or executed by the Day in the True Method
> of Gardening by the above, many Years Foreman to the
> eminent Mr Richard Woods, Land Surveyor and Designer of
> new Work.

Joseph Golding, who was directing works at Thorndon Hall while Woods was employed as the estate surveyor at the end of his life (see pp. 227–9), envisaged an independent but less ambitious career: he bought the well-established nursery of George Sangster in Brentwood, and advertised in the *Chelmsford Chronicle* in October 1794 that 'having also been nine years with the late Mr Richard Woods, surveys estates, manors etc. with accuracy and maps with neatness', but without aspiring to designing new work. His advertisement in addition claimed that he was able to give 'plans, elevations, sections and estimates for hot houses etc.', which suggests earlier employment where he gained this knowledge, which was not included in the work at Thorndon.

157

LABOUR DEMAND,
SUPPLY AND
ORGANISATION
IN THE
EIGHTEENTH-
CENTURY GARDEN

Anthony Sparrow is described in the Wardour house accounts for March 1764 as 'Mr Woodses Surveyor',[77] and was presumably responsible for measuring the park and perhaps also for drawing up Woods's plan for improvements. By October that year he was at Harewood as foreman in charge of Woods's work, but in May 1765 an altercation took place which illustrates a different aspect of the fluidity of labour agreements. Woods, who by that date was withdrawing from commitments to the Lascelles, had an argument with Sparrow that was reported by the Harewood steward, Popplewell, to Edwin Lascelles:

> Sparrow tells me this morning that he has rec'd a letter
> wherein Mr Wood [sic] has ordered him immediately to leave
> your work and go to … Northumberland, and if he did not
> go directly he sh'd have no more to do with him, and desired
> **an** immediate answer. Sparrow has desired me to present his
> duty to you and inform you that as you have always behaved
> to him so very civilly that he would not leave your works in
> so rude and abrupt a manner; for Mr Woods or any
> gentleman in the kingdom, not doubting that he could
> execute your plan to your satisfaction. Therefore wd. not
> send Mr Woods an answer before he had learned your
> pleasure therein.[78]

Clearly Woods felt that Sparrow was answerable to him and employed by him, whereas Sparrow (possibly also with an eye to the main chance) considered himself a free agent.

The correspondence concerning Sparrow is illuminating in another way. It reveals that the improver's client (and his staff) had to accept the foreman thrust into their midst, whether his character would have been acceptable as an employee or not. While Sparrow was eager to continue at Harewood on a new footing, Popplewell was less certain about his calibre and wrote to Lascelles:

> I wish he be not too much addicted to liquor nor has he paid
> that attention to his men lately which I think they require all
> this I have told him. I added at the same time that you
> detested a drunkard and that he must consider what he was
> to undertake & if he thought that he cou'd serve any other
> gentleman that wou'd overlook these things he had better
> not engage here.

In the event, Sparrow continued at Harewood, initially to implement Woods's plan but also as foreman under White after December 1765. He also undertook separate pieces of surveying both within the Harewood estate and outside it as a separate contractor, as at Hawksworth in 1768. Alone among Woods's ex-foremen, he is known to have produced a plan for improvements, for Lartington Hall in County Durham for John or Henry

Maire.[79] The plan (undated and rather simplistic and clumsy in execution) is far closer to Woods's style than White's, and perpetuates features probably observed while working for Woods, such as the half-circle of 'back ground for the use of the Hot House and Kitchen Garden'; 'retired Grotesque Seat'; 'Building in the Character of a Hermitage'; and greenhouse facing pleasure-ground lawn. An intriguing detail is the range of buildings drawn below the outline of the park, entitled 'For hiding disagreeable objects'. This is taken straight out of Timothy Lightoler's *Gentleman's and Farmer's Architect* (1762), which also appears to have been used by Woods at Wardour as part-inspiration for the restoration of old Wardour Castle.

Clearly the foremen were a mixed bunch, and it would be useful to have more information on their training and early employment. Did they all rise from the ranks of the day-labourers as Lupton seems to have done at Wivenhoe, or was there some other means of progression, possibly via the nursery trade? Brown's 'overseer of works' at Burton Constable, who was paid the handsome wage of £50 a year, was replaced in 1782 not by the head gardener (on the grounds that he was ignorant about how to lay out grounds) but by one of the workmen landscapers,[80] which suggests promotion along the same lines as Lupton's.

SUPPLY AND DEMAND

The improvers and nurserymen acted as a sort of clearing house for head gardeners and foremen, and were frequently called upon to recommend a man for a vacant position. Conversely, gardeners seeking a new place would apply to improvers or nurserymen for information on what employment was available where.[81] Henry Hewitt of the celebrated Brompton nursery conducted much of his business by taking orders on an annual circuit of his customers, acting on the side in a very modest way as money-lender to some of their gardeners.[82] His account book notes who is working for whom: for example, among his creditors in 1763 were 'Mr Thomas Fillis … now engaged to serve ye Countess Waldegrave at Windsor Park' and 'Ed. Richardson (now in ye service of Mr Richard Woods)'.[83] Hewitt would thus have been in an excellent position to know who was ready to move to a different estate. A typical transaction of this sort is illustrated in a letter from William Perfect of York to John Spencer (Woods's employer at Cannon Hall), who had asked the nurseryman 'to recommend a good Gardener … that understood the Management of a Stove, Hotbeds & Firewalls'. Perfect found a suitable candidate 'brought up at Charles Leigh's Esq. at Adlington, at which place are good Stoves, Hotbeds, Fire Walls & neat Pleasure Grounds which are always kept in good order'.[84]

The letter of recommendation written by Woods in 1759 to Sir William Lee on behalf of William Lapidge, already mentioned, gives the standard assurances of probity and ability, but Woods also makes an interesting

159

LABOUR DEMAND,
SUPPLY AND
ORGANISATION
IN THE
EIGHTEENTH-
CENTURY GARDEN

comment: 'In case it shoud. not be agreeable to you, to asstablish him for some time, I can imploy him for any time', illustrating the fact that the improvers were employers in their own right, and always in need of good foremen. Lapidge was taken on by Lee, but also doubled as Woods's foreman during the improvements. Woods also placed the new kitchen gardener at Wardour in 1768, and was later called upon to intervene in what had apparently been an accusation by Lord Arundell of extravagance: 'I went up to the kitchen garden with him and talkd the matter over with him there, and he gave me for answer, yt. it was imposible for him to do with fewer hands at this season … and yt. he was desirous of carrying the business, at the lest expence it could posible.'

Perhaps the most famous example of an improver placing an applicant is the case of Michael Milliken, who while working for Brown at Chatsworth made known his wish to move south, and was installed at Richmond. Brown must have been impressed by his worth, as Milliken wrote to his wife: 'He have advance my wages more than I expected But that must be intirely a secret … as he never give so much to any man before. Nor am I to charge it in my accts. but receive it from his own hand that his Clark may not know of it as it would raise a murmoring amongst his other men.'[85]

The wages of a gardener in a responsible position could vary in the same way as the pay of the labourers. The term 'head gardener' does not seem to have been used at this date, and it is sometimes difficult to establish exactly where any one man stood in the ranking of precedence. The kitchen gardener recommended by Perfect in 1769 was unhappy about 'the smallness of the wages which are only £15 pr. ann.' but was persuaded to accept it for the first year providing his washing was done in the house. Clumber Park provides a different set of figures: there 'a Fourman to act in the capacity of Gardener' was calculated at £35 in 1763, while twenty years later the 'Gardener' earned £30, at the same time as the labourers were given rather less than on many other estates.[86] Most of Woods's foremen were earning 2s 4d a day (a little over £30 a year) and since some are known to have been housed (at Cannon Hall and Wivenhoe, for example) it may be assumed that lodging was generally included in the bargain. To set against this relatively high rate of pay was the fact that, unlike the gardener employed on an estate, a foreman was only paid while actually in work.

PAYMENT FOR IMPROVEMENTS

In principle, the system of payment for improvements was simple enough: Woods, or any of the contracting practitioners, drew up a specification and estimate for all or part of the work envisaged, which was then signed by both parties. The sums were doubtless arrived at in the same way then as now, by a rough calculation of the time and labour involved, with a margin for errors and mishaps. Occasionally, in a large commission such as Wardour, the official contract was dispensed with for some items 'not being able to ascertain the expenses', and Woods even offered Lord Arundell the option 'for Woods to take the chance of the whole, according to the different estimations, or otherways for Lord Arundell to take to the whole, & Woods will opin the accounts to his Lordship'. Arundell preferred the first alternative. In addition, Woods charged for his time and expenses, plus any extras like drawing of plans or designs for buildings, and in addition made a percentage profit on the work if this was not already built into the estimates. There is no reference to the size of this percentage in any of Woods's bills or correspondence – two entries in the Cannon Hall accounts for 'Mr Woods a prop.[ortion] of his bill' are left blank[87] – but where Woods seemed very anxious to have the commission, as at Wivenhoe, he makes a point in a preliminary letter of waiving that extra payment:

> you may rely upon it, that I will conduct [the work] in the best manner I am able, & at the least expence, to do it justice … In case we meet with no cross circumstances, so as to be fortunit enough, to do it for less than the estimate, … I will return, or at least, not receive any more of you than prime costs, & be paid for my own time & expences, that is to say, I will have no profett upon the work.[88]

When the accounts at Littleton became entangled, and Woods wrote a justifying and supposedly emollient letter to Thomas Wood, he made a point of saying of one of the items on the account:

> as to the difference there is, between y[r.] self & me, about the arch & other work at Rowtherford, I hope we shall not differ about that, for as I had no intention of getting anything by that Jobb, so I hope you will not suffer me to loose anything by it, I will leave it to your own Hon[r.] & generosity, as I am persuaded you will not suffer one to be hurtt, in that respect, as nothing is required but the intrinsic value of the work.[89]

On this occasion the hope was unjustified, as the client resorted to arbitration.

Where building was included in the improvements, such as a kitchen garden or temple, Woods made separate contracts with brickmakers, stonecutters, carpenters, masons and any other craftsmen required, giving precise instructions over the details (thickness of mortar between bricks, for example) and agreeing to pay them direct. The usual procedure was that Woods's foreman was advanced money by the estate steward or similar to pay the workmen, then after the foreman's worksheets had been examined and passed by Woods, that money was entered in the steward's cash book 'On Mr Woods acct'. which was then at every interim settlement deducted from the sum owing to Woods.[90] A sheet summarising the expenditure on

161

LABOUR DEMAND,
SUPPLY AND
ORGANISATION
IN THE
EIGHTEENTH-
CENTURY GARDEN

building and improvements at Cannon Hall, including the years of Woods's employment, lists the sums paid by the employer beside those paid by the foreman.[91] In 1761, one of the years of greatest landscaping activity, the employer disbursed £81 and the foreman £913, but this proportion was not consistent, and much depended on whether the greatest outlay in any one year was on labour. Naturally, it was the employer who ultimately paid everything.

The problem with the system was that it relied for smooth operation on conscientiousness and punctuality, and in the final resort on an employer willing to write drafts on his bank at reasonable intervals. The possibilities for misunderstanding and confusion were rife, as was well illustrated at Littleton, where the three-way arrangement of accounts between Woods, the employer and the foreman became 'so intangled … it confused the whole' and was eventually settled in court.[92] The difficulty of keeping track of money owed and paid is also noticeable at Wardour, which lacked an authoritative steward and where accounts were kept in a very haphazard way. As Woods wrote in a memorandum to Lord Arundell late in 1769, four years into the commission, 'whether affter Creswell [Woods's foreman] has finish'd [the current task], he should not employ & pay all the men, & charge his own time in one account to Mr Woods instead of keeping two accounts, wch. will be confused.'[93]

It was only to be expected that the improvers themselves were kept waiting for their money, but there was certainly embarrassment if there were no funds to settle up with the workmen at the end of the week. When White was working at Scone his cash flow arrangements broke down and the steward reported to Lord Stormont that 'his workmen had been about ten weeks that they had received no wages which occasioned a grumbling among them and his foreman was rather in a worse situation than the men having neither money nor credit.'[94] A similar breakdown of arrangements occurred at Irnham in March 1770, where Woods informed Lord Arundell that his foreman's 'cash is all gone, & has none to pay his men; I have wrote to Mr Angier [the steward] to furnish him with a little till I could acquaint your Lordship, & have your orders for suplyes'. The following month, Woods found that his foreman had 'received only £10 of Mr Angier, & yt. he could not spare him any more, & I gave him ten guineas (all I coud) to get on with a little longer. If your Lordship will be pleased to pay … the balance of my last years accts. then I will send some of that money to go on with at Irnham, till it may be convenient to yr. Lordship to order some more down.' Only two months later, this time at Wardour, he had to write, 'I must now make another payment to the Tradesmen, & shall want £200. If your Lordship be pleased to give me a draught.' By February the following year the tone was a little shorter: having made out draughts for what he owed various tradesmen on the Wardour account Woods wrote, 'I must beg your Lordship to transfer over to me … the sum of four hundred pounds, as soon as your

Lordship please, affter receipt of this.'[95] Lord Arundell was not the only employer who had to be repeatedly requested to settle accounts, and the potential for financial problems was always present.

The ultimate responsibility for bringing a commission to a successful conclusion lay with the improver, and if the foreman proved unsatisfactory or the workforce recalcitrant, if the accounts fell into a muddle or nurserymen failed to deliver what was promised, it was all laid at the door of the improver, whether it was his fault or not. The importance of a sound and intelligent foreman was paramount, and where archives survive it is clear that all the improvers looked after their best men. When Woods was prevented from setting out to start work at Irnham, 'stopt'd by illness and bad weather in the prograce of Business', he kept the foreman with him in his own home for a fortnight.[96]

Some of the items on the Cusworth memoranda, and instructions left with the foreman at Wivenhoe, suggest that Woods thought it necessary to make some very obvious remarks – for instance, when he points out that the top of a fence post being driven into the ground is liable to split when repeatedly hit unless protected in some way.[97] It may be wondered whether these minute instructions were really necessary, or whether it was a facet of Woods's rather fussy and precise attitude. Possibly in view of the uneven calibre of his foremen, he tailored his directions to the perceived ability of the man in charge of the commission. However masterly the landscape design, the improver could not afford for the execution to be bungled by the workforce.

CHAPTER 8

CONCLUSION

How, FINALLY, SHOULD WE DEFINE WOODS'S PLACE among the eighteenth-century improvers? He does not fit neatly into the category of landscape improver along Brownian lines, and was emphatically neither pupil nor follower of Brown. Whereas Brown was said to be happiest – most successful – in his interpretation of naturalistic embellished landscape, Woods was surely happiest in the gardens round the house, where he could combine pleasure ground with kitchen garden with flower garden, threaded through with winding paths and looking over a neat pleasure park with intimate pieces of water. He was far more skilful on a small than on a large scale, and indeed, represents a seeming contradiction: a practitioner of a version of the 'English landscape garden' who was more comfortable with the pleasure ground than the park.

Ever since the subject of the designed eighteenth-century landscape became fashionable, the single feature that has most engaged attention has been the park, which is held almost to epitomise the achievements of Brown and the other improvers. This to some extent reflects the importance attached at the time to a designed park as the newest aspect of a 'modern' landscape – and, for those who felt that they needed it, the outward and visible sign of gentility. But although the word 'park' may firmly march over an area on the estate map, the concept covers a wide range of acreage, and even the park at Wardour, where Woods came closest to parkland on a grand scale, is not comparable with a park such as Blenheim. The majority of his commissions, whether they included work on a 'park' or not, were at pleasure-ground level, and one of his identifying traits was his ability to combine the two concepts and produce what has been described here as a 'pleasure park'. This is not only a question of scale, but also of type of planting – although the two are not unconnected – and where evidence survives of his precise directions regarding what trees to put where in the park (as at Cusworth), the result must have closely resembled an extended pleasure ground, with a strong leaning towards clumps and belts of varied planting, including a large variety of conifers, and an effect more ornamental than naturalistic.

In addition to his unusual version of the park, Woods fails to conform to our view of mid–late eighteenth-century landscaper not only in his emphasis on the pleasure garden but also his use of a form of *ferme ornée* into the 1780s. In particular, his version of a kitchen garden sometimes goes beyond merely suggesting that this area was interesting enough in itself to be worth visiting, and takes it into the pleasure ground. Whether or not many other such gardens existed,[1] none of the other landscape improvers is known to have proposed a decorative kitchen garden in this idiom.

Many aspects of Woods's landscape designs seem old-fashioned. The most extreme example of this is the design for Audley End of 1780, where Woods produced for Sir John Griffin Griffin, who was hardly a country bumpkin squire, a plan for the Elysium Garden with winding paths, groves, walks and saloons (see Figure 61). It is no surprise to find that the design as executed was a simpler arrangement in line with current taste – but there is nothing in the curving piece of water and disposition of flower beds and borders in that alternative plan that could not have been by Woods (see Figure 72). As an improver who had been in regular practice for over twenty years, Woods cannot have been unaware of the shift in taste during that time, yet he was confident to present in 1780 a design that would not have looked out of place in the 1740s or 1750s, and moreover to a client of high social and artistic standing. Even leaving aside the very particular example of the Elysium Garden, Woods's plans for Hengrave (1777) and Wormsley (c.1781) include large areas round the house that are far closer in feeling to a rococo design than to a truly naturalistic layout, full of winding paths, intricacy and incident. Brown's plan for Brocklesby of 1772 is in no way comparable. The celebrated flower-petal garden by the house is a minor detail in a parkscape, not a major part of the design as a whole.

At Wardour Castle it was not so much the landscape layout as the architecture of the garden buildings that was behind the times, even though Woods knew that he was working for a young aristocrat who had just been exposed during his Grand Tour to all the classical trends and influences considered fashionable. Lord Arundell might have been expected to demand up-to-date design in garden buildings as he did for his new mansion, yet even where Woods supplied a rather more classical alternative design for the greenhouse at Wardour, the building as executed was in Woods's typical charmingly chunky style which, while never sophisticated, would have looked less surprising in an earlier layout. Lord Arundell was certainly not uninterested in the building proposals, as a letter from Woods in 1770 refers to 'the skitch whch I draw'd from that whch yr. Lordship shewd me', indicating that Arundell had a good idea of what he wanted. Perhaps we should be less surprised at Woods producing these designs if we remember how long it took for a style to become unacceptably out of date by society as a whole. Switzer's *Ichnographia rustica*, published as the latest in garden design ideas in 1718, was still being reissued in 1742, while Batty Langley's *Ancient Architecture* of 1742 (later *Gothic Architecture Improved*), which was intended 'for the ornamenting of

Gardens' as well as of buildings, was being reprinted as late as the 1790s.[2] Thomas Wright in 1766 suggested a very symmetrical and stylised design for St James's Park,[3] and even in about 1775 William Chambers produced for the King of Sweden a garden design full of rectangular parterres and formal enclosures.[4] Woods's career illustrates the fallacy of perceiving the march of fashion as an inexorable and smooth process.

Woods's client base is difficult to categorise exactly. The clients for three of his best-documented commissions – Cannon Hall, Wardour and Wivenhoe – were very different, although all formed part of polite society: Spencer a bachelor with a passion for the chase, enjoying considerable wealth and local standing owing to mineral extraction on his properties, but still with strong links to his merchant lineage and industrial fortune; Lord Arundell, from the ancient Catholic aristocracy, super-rich (at least at the time of inheriting) and moving in the highest circles of society; and the Rebows (originally clothiers in Colchester), well-off gentry who had been armigerous for nearly a hundred years, politically aware, not extravagant or spendthrift. William Dolby and John Wright were on the lower rungs of the gentry ladder, and the majority of those clients who could be loosely described as 'established middling gentry' retained present or past trade or entrepreneurial connections, and as might be expected had houses set in genteel but relatively modest surroundings, even if they also owned other land. Such families accounted for about half of Woods's patrons. The other half, mainly belonging to the earlier part of Woods's career, were higher gentry or aristocrats, ranging from the *arriviste* Melbournes to even higher levels of society, and including well-connected old Catholic names. This hotch-potch of clients, which diminished in grandeur towards the end of Woods's working life, contrasts strongly with Brown's employers, who were always at the upper end of society, even at the beginning of his career when he was being lent from one estate to another. Repton yearned for employment by the grand, ancient aristocracy with vast estates and initially enjoyed gratifying success with such patrons, but following the economic crisis of the end of the eighteenth century was eventually obliged to accept commissions from a class he despised, and particularly the *nouveaux riches* speculators who had made fortunes during the troubled times of the Napoleonic Wars. As Woods had never given an indication of aiming as high as Repton, so the decline over the years in the status of his clients was less dramatic.

Political affiliation, be it Whig or Tory, seemed to be of no significance in determining whether to call in Woods. Perhaps one of the factors influencing a choice – but this was, perhaps surprisingly, by no means a constant rule – was his religion. Personal recommendation must have accounted for some of Woods's work, although evidence is hard to find. It is very likely that John Spencer of Cannon Hall was responsible for introducing Woods to a number of Yorkshire commissions, and Lord Arundell might have been instrumental in gaining him work at Lulworth,

Wynnstay and possibly Chillington and Wyndham House. Apart from these, no specific link between clients has been found, and it is tempting to surmise that quite early on Woods was recognised, and employed, as the improver with a particular skill for a modest estate and/or a pleasure garden. In addition, a further division can perhaps be made into clients who were attracted by his particular style, and those wanting only small adjustments or additions to an existing design. Woods was clearly not above accepting a minor commission. Calling in Brown or Repton conferred a *cachet* which was independent of the quality of the design, whereas Woods lacked the fashionable status that they enjoyed and was probably employed more for what he could do than for who he was.

Except in the rare cases where adequate documentation survives or – as at Copford Hall and Goldsborough – where a recent estate map preceded Woods's work, it is hard to be sure exactly how he found the grounds, how his plan related to existing features and to what extent his landscaping was part of a programme of general improvement. A number of his commissions were associated with major building or alterations to the house, and Hare Hall and the very much grander Wardour Castle were new houses on previously unlandscaped sites. This probably also applied to Brizes and Buckland. Brocket, Cannon Hall and Hartwell were all undergoing building or extensive refurbishment around the time of Woods's employment, while in other instances the house had recently been built or altered and only the landscape was receiving attention: Boreham, Cusworth, Goldsborough, Kirklees, Old Alresford and Wivenhoe fall into this category. Documentation makes it clear that Woods's work was often part of an ongoing evolution of a garden landscape, involving different improvers perhaps over many years, and here Woods was commissioned for specific items: a pleasure garden at Audley End; a bridge and probably an alteration to the piece of water at Bretton; a kitchen garden and waterside flower garden at Brocket; a pheasantry as well as some improvement to the landscape at Kirklees; a bridge and widening of a small flow of water at Great Myles's; a pleasure garden and modest piece of water at New Hall. At Thorndon and Belhus, and possibly at Nuthall Temple, Woods was asked to complete or amend an already existing feature, and at Copford the before-and-after surveys make it clear that Woods's contribution was merely to bring an old-fashioned garden more in line with fashion. In some places – such as Haigh Hall, Alresford and Chillington – Woods was employed only to add a single architectural feature. However, this list is not absolute or complete: there are many instances of a lack of full documentation, and the foregoing text of this book is littered with 'possibly' and 'probably' in connection with the extent of Woods's landscaping at any one property.

While some of Woods's designs were reasonably realistic in terms of what was likely to be achieved, both the Hengrave and Wormsley plans included ideas for many more garden buildings than he can possibly have expected to have seen built. As Edward Harwood has pointed out, only at the highest end of the social scale could one expect to find 'the more elaborate associative structures', which were not made in the majority of gardens.[5] While neither Sir William Gage at Hengrave nor John Fane at Wormsley could be classed as impecunious or minor gentry, they were hardly in the same class economically, nor indeed of the same generation, as the clients for whom Rocque had surveyed Chiswick and Wanstead, with the multiplicity of little buildings arranged round the map. Was Woods hoping to tempt his prospective employers to commission at least one? Or was he just indulging himself with making an attractive plan? Given how little was done at either of those properties, one might even wonder whether the extravagance of buildings had the effect of frightening the clients away from embarking on what might have risked being a very expensive undertaking.

The gradual decline of Woods's reputation can be ascribed to several causes, starting with the social basis on which his practice was founded. There is little doubt that Brown's early employment at Stowe, one of the most famous and fashionable gardens of the time, stood him in very good stead both professionally and socially. If indeed Woods worked during his formative years at Wooburn Farm, it is relevant that Southcote had far less influence in the upper echelons of polite society than Lord Cobham, even though his *ferme ornée* was visited and discussed. With his own gifts, and with Cobham's approbation and supportive nudges up the ladder, Brown was unlikely to fail. As the arbiter of horticultural taste, he was eventually even forgiven for forgetting the subservience expected of a man in his position, as illustrated by a comment by Horace Walpole: 'The moment a fashionable artist, singer or actor is insolent, his success is sure. The first peer that experiences it, laughs to conceal his being angry, the next flatters him for fear of being treated familiarly, and ten more bear it because it is *so like Brown*.'[6] White and Richmond, as sometime associates or employees, benefited from some of Brown's reflected glory, but Emes and Woods had no such advantage and had to make their own way. Nowhere is there any hint of the kind of reception for Woods that Brown could expect from at least some of his clients, such as Lord Digby, who keenly awaited his arrival at Sherborne and certainly expected him to join the family dinner table.[7]

There remains the unanswered question of why William Angus in 1787 in his *Seats of the Nobility and Gentry* gives Woods due credit for his work at Brocket Hall and Hare Hall, but does not mention him in connection with Cusworth, one of Woods's most successful designs. In the absence of any research on the subject, it must be assumed that Angus collected information for his texts from the proprietors of the houses he featured; if this were the case, it is significant that Lord Melbourne and John Wallinger were both still alive at the date of publication and were presumably ready to name Woods in glowing terms as their landscaper, while at Cusworth John Battie Wrightson had died soon after the completion of Woods's work, and the young son who succeeded him might not have been brought up to acknowledge the author of the delightful grounds over which his house looked.

Another factor to be taken into consideration in the decline of Woods's renown is the possibility that, at least from the late 1760s, his whole heart was no longer in his profession. This is evinced by his application to Lord Arundell for the position of land steward in 1766, and, more dramatically, by his attempt to combine farming and/or market gardening on a serious scale with landscape improving. His landscaping practice should have been a full-time occupation, and there can be little doubt that he was overstretched. While his second career eventually ended in failure, it seems unlikely that he had the time to concentrate fully on his first practice, and thus he simultaneously lost money in farming and suffered a decline in popularity as an improver.

Woods's lack of Brown's easy manners might also go some way towards explaining the fact that his promising practice of the 1760s failed to develop further. An evaluation of Woods's character is made difficult through the almost total absence of surviving comments about him, and it is therefore worth quoting the only two pieces of evidence that throw light on his temperament. They both occur in letters by Mary Rebow to her husband, who was often away on militia duty in 1778 while their estate at Wivenhoe was being improved.[8] In July the Rebows had a friend's daughter staying with them (Fanny, apparently about twelve years old from the context), and of her Mary wrote, 'You cannot think how much Fan & he [Woods] are charmed with one another, & set & Prose to that degree, that they almost stupify me.' This paints a rather charming scene of the improver, then in his sixties, sitting and chatting to the little girl during one of his supervisory visits. The other anecdote paints Woods in a less favourable light, and concerns their neighbour, who had apparently asked for some minor advice:

> Mr Corsellis made me laugh yesterday, for he says when
> Woods rode down last time he ask'd his opinion about a
> couple of Trees, & he told him to trim up one, & cut down ye
> other, for which he gave him a Guinea & a Dinner, this time
> he went down one Day about ye Ice House (which by ye by I
> find is not likely to succeed at all) & upon his asking him
> what he was indebted to him, he told him, as he had been
> so generous to him before for nothing, he shou'd only
> charge him five guineas.

Woods's standard rate was two guineas a day, and if all he had done was indeed spend a few hours discussing the abortive ice house, his demand does seem unreasonably high in the circumstances – and more to the point, Mary Rebow obviously found it so.

Other clues have to be gleaned from Woods's own letters to various employers through his career, and here one trait stands out consistently. Woods comes across as a direct man, who seldom bothers to pen an elegant letter or use a clerk to write it for him unless on a very important subject; he apparently scribbles down his thoughts or instructions as they enter his head, without considering his spelling which for the same word is sometimes right and sometimes wrong, with long or difficult words spelt phonetically. Ansell was sometimes employed to draft the Wardour accounts neatly during the years that he was acting as Woods's assistant, but did not write his correspondence. Woods also gives the impression of being a less likeable character than Brown or White, and his letters hint at a certain querulousness and self-righteousness with his employers, and a peremptory tone with his employees, although the very different style of expression in the eighteenth century must not be forgotten.

There is also some indication that, while there is no suggestion of dishonesty, Woods was inclined to be careless over his account-keeping. A comment has survived from the widow of Thomas Martin, Woods's deceased client at Alresford in Essex, who wrote to her son-in-law Colonel Rebow, 'Must I put my Faith in Mr Woods so much as to pay what he pleases to demand of me, without his producing the least acct. or Information to guide me, nay where even you acknowledge there are several Matters that require Explanation.'[9] On occasion he resorted to borrowing from the steward or even his own foreman and sometimes forgot to keep an exact note of it, as, for instance, in the Wivenhoe accounts: 'To cash Recd by the hand of Thos Lupton I am not certain but think it was 2 guineas.'[10] Whereas Brown, White and Richmond were all earning enough to be reasonably relaxed over chasing small sums, it seems that Woods did not even always travel with sufficient funds: an entry in the Wynnstay accounts for £10 10s 0d notes: 'Pd. Mr Woods on acct. by paying the money Mr Lawrence of the Raven in Salop lent him' – presumably because he had not received a settlement that he had hoped for. Woods apparently also had commitments to creditors, and as early as 1765 he told Lord Arundell that the draught (for an unspecified sum but probably £50) 'has made me very happy, as it hath enabled me to keep my word and save my credit'.[11]

There is no evidence that anyone was influenced by Woods's style. Even during his most active working years he was elaborating on a form of landscape already past its peak of popularity which, while still attractive to a number of clients, was unlikely to be emulated by forward-looking competitors. In later years and after his death, the decline in his status and the shifting of taste towards a more Picturesque style effectively ruled out a band of followers. Of the improvers of consequence in the latter half of the eighteenth century, Woods alone appears to have been completely forgotten by the dawn of the next century. Repton never mentions him, although he must have been aware of his existence through his friendship with the Wallingers of Hare Hall, where Woods designed the grounds of the new mansion, if for no other reason. Repton included Richmond's works among 'the places of [his] worship'[12] but Woods was not on the list of names he admired. By the end of his career Repton was focusing on small flower gardens as Woods had done all through his life, but although some of their designs look surprisingly similar there is no evidence that this was anything other than fortuitous. They were coming from different directions: Woods working in the tradition of the flower gardens of Southcote and 'Dickie' Bateman; Repton presaging the rise of the middle-class villa garden, with the two concepts nudging each other where they met. Even if Repton had admired Woods's work, he was anxious to disassociate himself from the designer/contractor class represented by Woods and establish his calling as a genteel and artistic profession. Richmond, as the 'gentleman improver',[13] was acceptable to Repton, while Brown's social and financial success took him into a class of his own. Woods could claim neither of these advantages.

Emes and White were mentioned rather slightingly by Loudon as practising an 'affectedly graceful, or modern style' which compared unfavourably with his own,[14] but at least their names were kept alive into the nineteenth century. Thomas Shepherd in 1836 praised White in the same sentence as Brown and Repton as the three men who 'did more for British Landscape Gardening than has been done in any country perhaps in the world'.[15] No reference to Woods has been found in the nineteenth century, and not until the 1920s was his particular talent recognised again, by Avray Tipping in *Country Life*, when writing about Brocket and Hengrave.

Woods's career well illustrates the financial uncertainty of the improver. With great talent and in addition great good fortune, Brown was able to scale the heights and die a lord of the manor, a well-off man and a household name. Richmond, at a more modest scale and helped by the profits of his nursery, could also claim material success and a socially complimentary title; White attained the status of 'gent', considerable prosperity and a near-monopoly of improving in Scotland, and built up an estate in County Durham.[16] Woods, in spite of making a bid for a sounder income and more elevated social standing by entering farming, failed to reach a comfortable financial level. In a letter to Lord Arundell in 1771, in which he is indignantly countering the accusation of charging very high for his visits, he explains:

> What makes it so, my Lord, is, the multiplissity of Business
> I've allways had to settle, each time, which generally keeps
> me 9 or 10 days or sometimes more. Your Lordship thinks of
> a guinea a day, which wou'd not be sufecient to keep myself,
> horses & servant, considering how many broken days, in a
> year I have, for example, take out Sundays, many days ill by
> getting colds etc. how many days & nights, in Town at
> expences, mearly to wait on Gentlemen without ever
> charging anything for it, how many days in a year are spent

at home, only in answering letters, & add to that, ye great
expence in a year for postage, let all these dissadvantages
be balanc'd, against all the days I could make at a guinea pr.
day, & I believe it wou'd be easley prov'd yt. I shou'd soon
be oblig'd to give over traveling, unless like a Tom Tinker. If
the Gentleman your Lordship is pleased to mention [Brown],
had done business upon those terms, I know not how he
could have Raised a fortune of £2500 pr. annum. If a man is
to be for ever upon the Tatter, allways from home
neglecting his domestic affairs, & wareing his life out by
fateagues, & can not make some thing worth his while, his
fate is hard. Give me leave to observe to yr. Lordship, that
all architects are paid for their designs, & journeys, & so
much pr. cent; & there is no one of them, yt. has done as
much business in that way, as I have done in mine, yt. does
not get a pound to my crown & more … I must beg leave to
mention a certain circumstance, viz. that many of my visits
both to Wardour & Irnham, has been attended not only with
the expences of the road, but also of the place, when the
family was absent, the last Journey to Wardour while I stay'd
there cost me £6 14s 0d for myself, assistant & servant, the
last journey to Irnham, while there paid £3 3s 0d, this I say
besides the expences of going & returning, no part of which
I ever did, or shall charge.[17]

He does not add that he was usually kept waiting a considerable time for
his bills to be settled, and that the final account was often rounded down to
his disadvantage. The prompt payer, such as John Spencer of Cannon Hall,
was a rarity. It must of course be recognised that the improvers were by no
means the only profession to suffer in this way, as it was normal eighteenth-
century practice for the client to settle his debts to trades and professions
with reluctance. But Woods was not without pride, and when rebutting Lord
Arundell's suggestion that he should charge only a guinea a day, wrote
passionately, 'It is a tender point to me, the same as it wd be to your
Lordship to have the half of yr estate curtailed. My science is my estate, & as
long as I am able to do business, I will do justice & deserve all I have from
every Imployer.'

Plate 1. The kitchen/pleasure garden and flower garden at
Brocket Hall, where Woods worked between 1770 and
1775, from a survey by Thomas Pallett of 1798. The
garden laid out along the bank of the Broadwater is
reminiscent of that at Hatfield Peverel (see Figure 5).

Plate 4. Detail of a painting by John Luttrell of New Hall, 1775, with a glimpse of the 'new garden' recently designed by Woods, described in the *New and Complete History of Essex* of 1768. The 'exceeding good greenhouse' is faintly visible on the far left, but Woods's 'noble sheet of water' is out of sight behind the house. The highly ornamental mix of trees in the pleasure garden is typical of Woods's planting style.

Top left: Plate 2. A panorama of Cannon Hall, painted probably within ten years of Woods's commission. Woods's 'rustick Stone bridge' can be dimly seen on the left, with the first cascade a little further down the river. See Figure 65 for an enlarged detail of the pinery.

Left: Plate 3. One of a set of paintings of Audley End House by William Tomkins in 1788, showing the Elysium Garden looking west towards Adam's Tea Bridge. Although the garden was not laid out exactly following Woods's plan, the depiction of the flowerbeds gives a vivid impression of eighteenth-century planting style, and would have resembled Woods's pleasure-garden planting elsewhere.

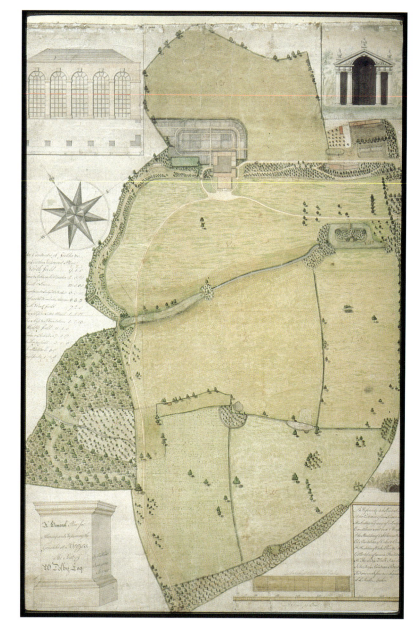

Plate 5. Woods's plan for Brizes, his last executed commission of 1788. This design combines several aspects of his style: the ornamented walk round a small park still retaining old field boundaries, with the bed of mixed shrub and flower planting in front of the bench in the Lady's Walk. This is one of three designs produced by Woods after his move to Ingrave in 1783, which all retain a clarity and freshness of colour often missing from his earlier plans.

Top right: Plate 6. Woods's plan for Copford Hall, 1784. By this date, Woods was drawing his plans himself without the help of a draughtsman, and the inset sketches are relatively crudely executed. The rock-arch cascade with bench on it echoes the boathouse at Cusworth, and both were perhaps taken from a similar feature in Wooburn Farm.

Right: Plate 7. Woods's 'Elysian Walk' at Hare Hall, raised with the spoil from the canal. The pleasure ground was restricted to a narrow strip round two of the boundaries, with the remainder of the 70 acres (28ha) left as fields. This is the painting from which Angus engraved the plate for inclusion in his 1791 volume of *Seats of Noblemen and Gentry*.

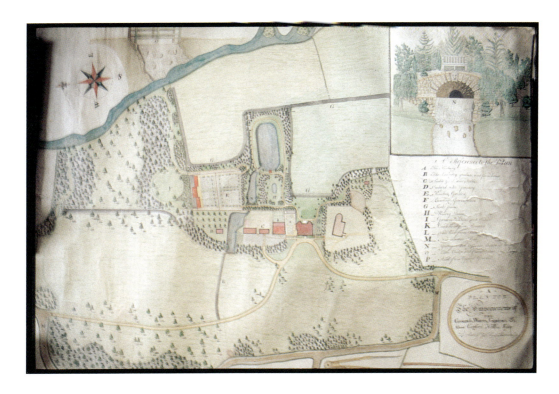

RICHARD WOODS
(1715–1793)
MASTER OF THE
PLEASURE GARDEN

Top left: Plate 8. The remains of the 'Gothick alcove' referenced on Woods's plan for Little Linford at the eastern end of the canal. It is likely that it resembled the alcove designed for Wormsley (see Figures 25 and 26).

Left: Plate 9. John Constable's painting of Wivenhoe Park in 1816, showing Woods's long piece of water, bridge-cum-dam and boathouse at the tail. The bridge, with the same purpose of disguising a change in the water level at Cusworth, probably looked much the same.

Above: Plate 10. Interpretation by Mark Laird of 'Order of Planting after Mr Southcote's manner' (Figure 3), assumed to refer to boundary planting at Wooburn Farm.

Plate 11. Design submitted by Woods in 1770 for the grounds around the new Wardour Castle, which had not been started when he produced his first plan of 1764. The signature on the drawing is that of James Ansell, Woods's son-in-law, whom he employed as his draughtsman. None of the new work on this plan was executed.

GAZETTEER

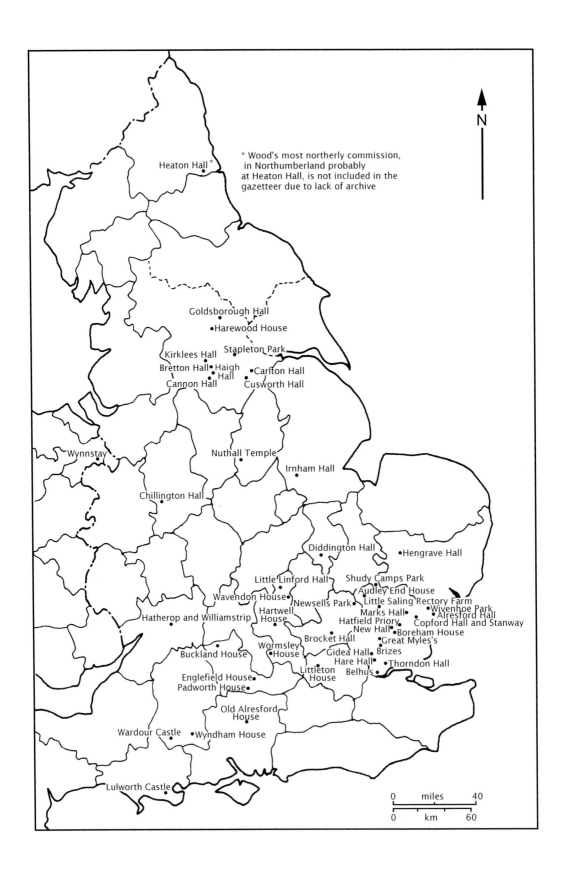

N

* Wood's most northerly commission,
in Northumberland probably
at Heaton Hall, is not included in the
gazetteer due to lack of archive

Heaton Hall *

Goldsborough Hall
•Harewood House
Stapleton Park
Kirklees Hall
Bretton Hall •Haigh
Hall •Carlton Hall
Cannon Hall Cusworth Hall

Wynnstay
Nuthall Temple
Irnham Hall

Chillington Hall

Diddington Hall •Hengrave Hall

Little Linford Hall Shudy Camps Park
Wavendon House •Audley End House
•Newsells Park •Little Saling Rectory Farm
Hartwell Marks Hall• •Wivenhoe Park
House •Alresford Hall
Hatherop and Williamstrip Hatfield Priory• Copford Hall and Stanway
New Hall•Boreham House
Wormsley Brocket Hall •Great Myles's
Buckland House •House Gidea Hall •Brizes
Littleton Hare Hall• •Thorndon Hall
Englefield House• House Belhus•
Padworth House•

Old Alresford
House

Wardour Castle •Wyndham House

Lulworth Castle

0   miles   40
0   km   60

ALL WOODS'S KNOWN COMMISSIONS ARE LISTED HERE, but the more important for the understanding of his oeuvre are treated in greater detail.[1]

Four commissions mentioned in correspondence by Woods have proved elusive. In May 1765 Woods's foreman at Harewood was ordered to go immediately to 'Mr Ridleys in Northumberland'. Of the possible Mr Ridleys in this county at that date the most likely was Matthew Ridley of Heaton Hall, but no archive has survived and the site has long been under Newcastle's suburbs. This probably most northerly of Woods's commissions cannot be investigated further, except to say that, on Fryer's map of Northumberland of 1820 and Greenwood's of 1827, Heaton Hall is in a landscape that could quite easily have been designed by Woods.

In a memorandum of 1767 to the Wardour foreman, Woods described the sort of fence he had in mind by referring to 'such rails as Sir John Shaws, with nails on the top bar'. This was unlikely to have any meaning to the foreman unless he had also been working at 'Sir John Shaw's', possibly Eltham Lodge, then in Kent, which was 'fitted up and greatly improved' in the 1760s.[2] Again, no relevant archive for this property is extant, and it will probably never be known whether Woods was improving the grounds while Robert Taylor was making internal alterations.

Woods wrote to Colonel Rebow of Wivenhoe in March 1779 that he was setting out for Sussex and Oxfordshire for almost three weeks, but while the latter commission can probably be identified as Wormsley, it has been impossible to find a candidate for Sussex. It must be hoped that the evidence will come to light in connection with another subject.

The Wivenhoe correspondence also reveals that Woods spent three days in 1777 with Captain Daniel Harvey, neighbour of Colonel Rebow and owner of the *Repulse*, one of the country's largest revenue ships. His property is described in his will as simply 'at Wivenhoe',[3] but no further archive survives and it is not one of the named estates on Chapman and André's map of Essex. The nature of Woods's involvement there, and whether he spent any further time, remains in question.

The bank accounts of potential clients can be frustrating as well as useful. 'Richard Woods' was not an uncommon name and unless there is supporting evidence for a promising-looking entry the possibility of a commission can be taken no further. This is the case for two payments in Drummonds Bank ledgers to Mr Wood or Woods from the Hon. William Cheywynd in May 1753: the first is 'Paid Mr Woods bill £181 2s 0d' and the second is 'Paid him in full £518 18s 0d'. Chetwynd at this date was living at Ashley (Staffordshire), but there is little archive for the property and virtually nothing on estate expenses and management.

Many landscape improvements – by Woods, any of the other practitioners, or talented amateurs – are probably recorded on the various large-scale county maps of the second half of the eighteenth century, but remain unidentified without their associated documentary evidence. It is unlikely that Woods was supporting his way of life with only the commissions listed in this gazetteer.

ALRESFORD HALL, ESSEX:
THE CHINESE TEMPLE (now Quarters House)

6 miles (10km) south-east of Colchester, Essex

DATE AND CLIENT
Before 1772–6, for Thomas Martin (d. 1776) followed by his nephew and
son-in-law Isaac Martin Rebow, who inherited the estate

PLAN
Fold-out plans for the interior of the Chinese Temple (Figure 33).

Woods prepared a plan for the improvement of Rebow's own estate at
Wivenhoe in 1765, although work did not start until 1776. In the
meantime, he was commissioned to alter and extend a small building
beside the pond in the woods (known as The Quarters) at Alresford Hall.
Apart from his undated estimates and instructions, there is little
documentation relating to this commission.

Woods's detailed estimate for the Chinese Temple specifies demolishing
and rebuilding the kitchen, probably the pre-existing construction. The
fishing lodge proper – the Chinese Temple – comprised an ante-room and
passage leading to an octagonal banqueting room and gallery over the
water. The support for the gallery and banqueting room foundations is the
subject of a separate drawing and instructions.

The widow of Thomas Martin wrote two acerbic letters to Rebow while
she was settling the estate, asking to see Woods's contract and accounts
and suggesting some irregularity. The outcome is not recorded, but as
Rebow went on to employ Woods at Wivenhoe he was presumably satisfied
over his reliability.

SOURCES
ERO
– Estimate and letter from Woods (D/DHt B1)
– Plans for the interior of the Chinese Temple (Acc. C47 Box 2)
– Letters from Dorothy Martin (Box 2)
– Single receipt from Woods (Box 8)

Pers. comm. Sir William Boulton, current owner of Quarters House

Fiona Cowell, 'The "Chinese Temple" at Alresford, Wivenhoe, Essex', *Follies*,
9/1 (1997)

AUDLEY END HOUSE

1 mile (0.5km) west of Saffron Walden, Essex

DATE AND CLIENT
1780, for Sir John Griffin Griffin

PLAN
*A Design for the Elysium Garden &c with the proper Ornaments for S*ʳ *John G. Griffin K.B. By R. Woods* (Figure 61).

As a contrast to the Brownian landscape[4] surrounding the house, Sir John in 1780 embarked on a small enclosed pleasure garden adjoining the kitchen garden, and employed Woods to survey the area and produce a design. The plan is undated, but Woods was paid £35 in full 'for time and drawings' in November 1780, with the account book entry 'for surveying & drawing the intended Cascade etc.'

Woods's design was far tighter than a Brown pleasure ground, and included elements that by then were hardly in fashion. A plan of 1757[5] shows a network of small streams in the area with two bigger branches flowing through the garden and connecting to the mill race. Woods incorporated these arms of water into his design and used them to create three contrasting divisions, with paths and 'saloons' within the divisions, to create greater variety. The garden was entered via a 'subterraneous Passage', a stratagem that combined emphasising the feel of seclusion with the advantage of taking the visitor under the track used by the dung carts. A 'green Lane' led into the garden itself, where the 'Cedar walk' connected with the 'exotic Saloon' while the Rosery lay to the left. Each of the discrete compartments had a focal point as well as a theme; from the Rosery the eye was drawn to a rock cascade which carried the path into the next part of the garden, offering a choice between the 'Orange Walk' and 'The Ladies Fruitery'. Where the path had to cross the piece of water as it flowed under the public way, with no possibility of screening plantation, Woods designed a simple version of a Palladian bridge with a Doric arcade and a high solid back to the road. In the last compartment, thickly screened to the north and east, and with a clear view down to the cascade, the path curved down to meet the 'exotic Saloon' again, passing in front of the 'Bath and Tea Room' and completing the circuit.

A competing design for the Garden was also produced, possibly by Placido Columbani, a Milanese architect who was intermittently employed at Audley End at that date. The 'Columbani' plan appears to be based on Woods's but much simplified, and with the important difference that the eastern arm of the water has been suppressed and the main arm fattened and given a more pronounced curve. This creates an entirely different effect from Woods's busy and intricate design. Woods's cascade was executed and is still extant, and the idea behind his bridge also survived, although reworked by Adam in the built version of 1782 (the Tea Bridge). The entrance into the garden under the track and through a rustic arch was also retained, and comparison of the two plans and the survey of 1783 by Thomas Warren[6] suggests an amalgam of the designs. Columbani's writing is not on the plan ascribed to him, and the similarity of this plan to designs by Woods for other locations raises the question of whether it could have been produced by a draughtsman in Woods's employ, even though there is no further entry for him in the accounts. William Tomkins painted two views of the garden in 1788 (Plate 3), from which it can readily be believed that Elysium was considered by a visitor in about 1795 as *le chef d'oeuvre d'Audley*.[7] But the garden was short-lived – by the 1830s the screening plantations were overgrown and the garden had become dark and unattractive. It was taken apart, leaving just the cascade and Adam's Tea Bridge.

Fig. 72. An unsigned, undated plan for the Elysium Garden, usually attributed to Placido Columbani, although the handwriting on the extensive references (not shown) does not resemble his. The final layout, as recorded on a survey of 1783 by Thomas Warren, appears to be a simplification and amalgamation of the two designs.

SOURCES

ERO
– Voucher from Woods (D/DBy A38/11)
– Entry in account book (D/DBy A211)

Audley End House: English Heritage
– Maps, plans, sketches

Mark Laird, *The Flowering of the Landscape Garden* (Philadelphia, 1999), pp. 341–50

Michael Sutherill, 'The Buildings of the Elysium Garden at Audley End', *The Georgian Group Journal*, 7 (1997)

BELHUS

Aveley, 4 miles (6km) north-west of Grays, Essex

DATE AND CLIENT
1770 – 71, for Thomas Barrett Lennard, 17th Baron Dacre

PLAN
No plan

This is the only landscape improvement where Woods worked while the client was still in touch with Brown. The nature of Woods's commission is guesswork, based on the progress of Brown's landscaping between 1752 and 1763, on payments through Drummonds Bank and on map evidence. Although Dacre had planned a piece of water as early as the 1750s, it is clear from correspondence that it had still not been finalised when Brown left. In January 1770 the first of six payments was made to 'Rd. Woods' or James Ansell (his assistant), the last one in January 1771 bringing the total to £275 – a relatively important sum compared with Brown's £668 14s 0d. Although Lady Dacre's account book for the period has survived, that of her husband has not, and possibly both Brown and Woods received more money in cash. The main evidence for Woods's work is the presence on Chapman and André's map of Essex of 1777 (surveyed 1773–4[8]) of the Long Pond in its completed form, and it is generally accepted that the payments to Woods were for this feature.[9]

SOURCES
ERO
– Payments to Brown and Woods in Lord Dacre's bank book with Drummonds (D/DL F133/1, 2, 3). These payments are corroborated by Drummonds Bank ledgers.

BOREHAM HOUSE

4 miles (6km) north-east of Chelmsford, Essex

DATE AND CLIENT
1763–66 and 1771–72, for Richard Hoare

PLAN
No plan

On Woods's first visit in 1763 beer was charged at 7s 8d for 'Mr Woods and Comy', followed three months later by beer for his surveyor Sparrow. The first recorded work was in the kitchen garden, where a sizeable hothouse with cistern and pump were built. Later that year a pleasure ground was staked out and the nurseryman Christopher Harvey supplied £122-worth of (unspecified) plants 'on Mr Woods's acct'. The most important part of the landscaping was deferred until 1771, when a stream at the bottom of the lawn was enlarged to create a 'river'. Woods's foreman Edward Pugh, who was in charge of this work, kept a detailed account of the work and expense involved, complementing the memoranda concerning the making of the pieces of water at Cusworth.

Woods was creating at Boreham House a small pleasure ground of about 11 acres (4.5ha), containing the essential elements: a lawn bordered by pleasure garden plantations and sloping down to a piece of water clearly visible from the house, with a distant view brought in by a ha-ha.

SOURCES
Hoares Bank
The archive for Boreham House is in Tin Box 21
– The accounts of Hoare's steward include references to garden labour and supplies, etc. although many of the bills on the summarised list for the year do not survive
– Richard Hoare's private ledger records payments to Woods, Ansell and Edward Pugh

ERO
– Microfilm of the landscaping of 1771–72 (T/B 511), original in Hoares Bank
– Tithe map 1838 (D/CT 40B) and untitled estate map 1852 (D/DGe P35)

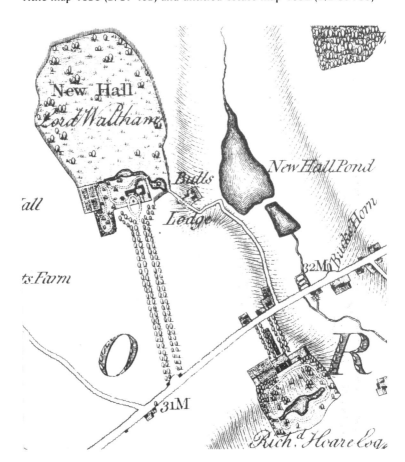

Fig. 73. Two properties landscaped by Woods, New Hall and Boreham House, on the 1777 map of Essex. In spite of the scale of 2 inches to the mile, the essentials of Woods's layouts are clear, as is the limited acreage of these commissions.

BRETTON HALL

West Bretton, 5 miles (9km) south-west of Wakefield, West Yorkshire

DATE AND CLIENT
1764 (and possibly for a further period), for Sir Thomas Wentworth, 5th Bart

PLAN
No plan

Bretton is one of several Yorkshire commissions probably obtained for Woods through John Spencer of Cannon Hall, who recorded in his diary in March 1764 that 'Mr Woods went to Bretton Hall'.[10] Woods obviously submitted a plan during this visit, and in July Spencer 'din'd at Sir Thos Wentworths … walked over the Park and view'd his intended Improvements'. After further visits by Woods that year, Spencer wrote on 15 December that Woods's bridge had been destroyed by a violent flood. Spencer made no further comments about Woods at Bretton, but in October 1767 noted that 'Sir Thos Wentworths new finished lake was a second time burst' by a massive flood. This suggests that Woods might have been working on a piece of water created after 1750, as no lake is shown on Dickinson's map of Yorkshire of that date. It also suggests that Woods's bridge might have been a cascade bridge built as a retaining wall, or a disguised dam, as at Cusworth and Wivenhoe, the collapse of which would have caused the lake to burst.[11] There was insufficient time for Woods to have created a new lake between March and December.

SOURCES
I am indebted to Dr Stephen Wright for help in establishing the chronology of the landscape, and ideas about Woods's contribution to it.

The Bretton Estate Archive, including Lord Allandale's loan collection, is in the Lawrence Batley Centre for the National Arts Education Archive (Trust), Bretton Hall. No material relevant to Woods was found.

BRIZES

Kelvedon Hatch, 3 miles (4km) south of Chipping Ongar, Essex

DATE AND CLIENT
From 1788, for William Dolby

PLAN
General Plan for Altering and Improving the Grounds at Brizes the Seat of W. Dolby Esq. By Richd. Woods Surveyor &c 1788 (Plate 5)

This was Woods's last executed design. Apart from a few deeds, no archive has survived for the property to provide any details about the commission. Woods no longer had access to studio draughtsmen, and his plan is recognisably in his own hand (as is that for Copford of 1784), with the two drawings for suggested buildings stuck on to the sheet. The temple bears such a close resemblance to some of the designs for Wardour that it was perhaps first produced for Lord Arundell in the 1760s.

Chapman and André's map of Essex of 1777 shows very clearly the modest walled garden around the house before Woods's work, while later maps prove that his landscape design was executed. Woods took advantage of some planting described on a deed of 1767, and the 'Lady's Walk' seems to have been cut through pre-existing woodland. Woods's design is a prime example of the way that a small modern park, with all appropriate decorative details, could be achieved without massive expenditure on its creation, and retaining the farming activity at its centre.

A view-line is marked from the centre of the garden façade of the house down to the swell in the south plantation, which was the place for 'an Alcove Seat or a Temple'. A rock arch is placed off-centre to avoid the sightline, and a large clump encloses a round pond, which breaks up the angularity of four field corners meeting.

SOURCES
ERO
– Woods's plan (D/DRo P1)
– Brizes deed 1767 (D/DHr T149/9)
– Tithe map (D/CT 197B)

BROCKET HALL

On the western outskirts of Welwyn Garden City, Hertfordshire

DATE AND CLIENT
1770/3–1775, for Sir Penistone Lamb, 1st Bart. Created (Irish peerage) Baron Melbourne 1770; Viscount Melbourne 1780

PLAN
No plan

The documentation for this commission consists of a letter from Woods to Lord Arundell in December 1770 announcing his preliminary visit to Brocket Hall,[12] and the account book of the Brocket steward. These accounts do not start until 1773 and there are therefore two years for which no information on possible activity by Woods is available. No differentiation is made in the ledger between labourers working on buildings by Paine, who was employed at the same time, and those under Woods in the grounds. Woods spent six weeks on site in the year February 1773 to 1774, and another seventeen days later in the year. What he achieved in that considerable time has to be deduced from indirect sources.[13]

William Angus, writing in 1787, still in the client's lifetime, states unequivocally that Melbourne made 'very considerable Improvements … in

the Park and adjacent Grounds, which are some of the most picturesque
and beautiful in the Kingdom … The Water and Out-grounds were laid out
by Mr Wood of Essex in the most luxuriant and masterly Manner' (see
Figure 58).[14] The 'out-grounds' in this context would seem to refer to the
park rather than to land outside it, but Woods appears to have
concentrated only a limited amount of planting in the southern and central
portions, including screening for farm buildings.[15] The bold, irregular but
formal planting blocks on the east and north-east, featured on a survey of
1752,[16] do not seem to have been softened. H. Avray Tipping – most
unusually for the date of 1925 – complimented Woods handsomely on his
work at Brocket, possibly even crediting him with a wider remit than he
was in fact given.[17]

Woods's main contributions to the Brocket landscape can be seen on
three almost identical surveys by Thomas Pallett, all of 1798. In addition to
the reshaped river, these surveys (Plate 1) show a walled kitchen garden of
a Woodsian irregular shape, quite different from the long rectangular
kitchen garden north-east of the house shown on the earlier survey. Since
the hot-house and pinery are both included in the accounts under a new
heading of 'Pleasure Garden' and not 'Kitchen Garden', and are shown by
Pallett to be on an ambitious scale, the walled garden may well have been
conceived as an integral part of the pleasure garden, to which there is
direct access, with the ordinary vegetable-growing area in the wedge shape
to the north beyond. The concept is similar to that seen in Woods's
gardens at Hartwell, Little Linford and Wardour, where productive and
ornamental aspects are blended.

Woods's style can additionally be seen in the riverside flower garden,
which has close affinities, on a different scale, to that at Hatfield Peverel
(see Figure 5). The combination of the gently winding swell of the river, the
pleasure garden laid out along a bank and the walled enclosure containing
elements of both kitchen and pleasure gardens is Woods at his best and
most typical.

Woods's brief probably also included re-siting the approach to cross the
river over Paine's elegant bridge with the water cascading below. To the
visitor arriving along this route, the view of the house as the corner is
turned remains one of the great visual experiences of a designed
landscape.

It is perhaps surprising that the Melbournes, who had the money and
the social ambition to command the best, turned to Woods rather than
Brown – by 1770 the acknowledged master in his field. It is possible that
Brown was contacted, but was too busy and evasive about a visit to please
the determined and imperious Lady Melbourne, forcing her to choose an
improver from among the other names available. But another possibility is
that Woods's skill with, and perhaps preference for, the pleasure garden
was recognised and influenced their choice. If they wanted a setting for the
new house rather than an entire park layout, Woods might well have had
the reputation as the leading designer in that sphere.

SOURCES

I am indebted to Esther Gatland for information about the development of the Brocket landscape.

HALS

– Single surviving series of estate accounts running from 1772 to 1835 (63828 for the volume 1772–90)
– Survey by Thomas Pallett, 1798 (D/EP P15)

H. Avray Tipping, 'Brocket Hall' in *Country Life*, 4, 11 and 18 July 1925.

David Jacques, 'Brocket Hall: draft outline of the history of the park' (unpublished study, 1991).

Esther Gatland, 'Richard Woods in Hertfordshire', chapter 7 in *Hertfordshire Garden History: a Miscellany* (Hatfield, 2007).

BUCKLAND HOUSE

4 miles (6km) north-east of Faringdon, Oxfordshire[18]

DATE AND CLIENT
From 1758, for Sir Robert Throckmorton, 4th Bart

PLAN
No plan

Sir Robert had been closing footpaths and roads from 1749, and the main boundaries of the park were probably established by the time Woods was commissioned, transforming the surroundings of Buckland from the patchwork of the 1750s[19] to a neat near-rectangle.

The earliest map recording Woods's work accompanies the enclosure award of 1803 (Figure 56). The thin river originally flowing north of the house had been shaped by 1794[20] into a 7-acre (3ha) multiform piece of water very reminiscent of the ponds intended by Woods for Wardour.

The brief entries in the single surviving account book, which covers only the early period of building to the end of 1759,[21] prove Woods's presence at Buckland on three occasions during 1758 and 1759, but there is a complete lack of information about his instructions. The evidence for what he did here lies in the remaining parts of the circuit walk,[22] the long list of plants supplied by Henry Hewitt from his Brompton nursery on Woods's orders, and the buildings in the grounds. Although there are neither plans nor accounts for these, they can be attributed with some certainty to Woods on stylistic grounds (see Chapter 5).

Buckland is an interesting commission in that the estate accounts show that the architect, John Wood the younger, and the landscape designer, Richard Woods, were on site together in June 1758, recorded by the consumption of ale 'when ye two Mr Woodses were at Buckland'. Considering how difficult employers found it to ensure a visit on any particular day, this is a strong suggestion that they arrived together by design. It is known that Sir Robert Throckmorton chose John Wood as his architect while staying in Bath and admiring the work of Wood the Elder (who in fact annotated his son's designs for Buckland House before his death in 1754), and it is conceivable that Woods may have also been in Bath at that time, and was introduced by the architect as a suitable landscaper. The 'Bath Guide' in Woods's library suggests at least one visit.

SOURCES
BRO
– Single surviving account book 1747–59 [1762] (D/EWe A3)
– *A plan … of the Estates … belonging to Sir John Throckmorton* [1803], no surveyor (Photograph T/M 90/1; the original is unlocated)

WRO
– Hewitt's list of plants sent to Buckland (CR 1998/box 57)

John Phibbs, 'Buckland House: survey of the landscape with restoration and management plan' (Debois Landscape Survey Group, 1993).

CANNON HALL

4 miles (6km) west of Barnsley, South Yorkshire

DATE AND CLIENT
1760–5, for John Spencer

PLANS
A Design for the Improvement of the Park, Gardens, & Water &c at Cannon Hall in Yorkshire, the Seat of John Spencer, Esq. By R^d Woods 1760 (Figure 67)

A Survey of Cannon Hall …with Improvements by Rich'd Woods (No date, no surveyor)

There is no recorded contact between Woods and John Spencer prior to the statement in the latter's diary for 1 April 1760: 'Mr Woods came to Cannon Hall to plan my Grounds, Park etc'. Between that date and 19 September 1765, when Spencer settled the final accounts, Woods spent some 140 days[23] at Cannon Hall, making roughly two visits a year and often using it as a base from which to attend to other nearby commissions.

After the preliminary riding 'over all Grounds' and 'viewing and planning' with Spencer, Woods immediately initiated the diversion of a highway and bridleway to give the park more space to the west. This was followed by laying out grounds, signing contracts with the carpenter and bricklayer to build the pinery and the choice of a site for a new kitchen garden.

As in a number of other commissions (see p. 132), Woods gave the kitchen garden an irregular shape, with a roughly oval north wall for maximum advantage from the sun. The interior of the garden was designed to contain decorative features incorporated into the functional layout, but these were not all executed.

Woods's pinery was erected between June and August 1760, and by September Spencer was receiving pineapples plants from his acquaintance. The pinery appears on a painting dating from before 1794 as a very plain, functional structure in spite of its prominent position in the pleasure ground (Figure 65). A pinery conferred enormous social status at this date.

Other work in hand included two pleasure gardens (see p. 55), one in front of the pinery for 'exotics' and the other, far larger, 'best flower garden' or shrubbery (Figure 13). Most of the plant material was supplied by Perfect's nursery at Telford.

The park wall was set out by Woods in April 1761, and his 'rustick Stone bridge' (Figure 44) to carry the diverted road over the water was completed in 1762 at a cost of £300.[24] An estimate for groundwork gives details of forming the lawn to the south of the house and a 'terrace walk'. There is no evidence that Woods altered the existing ha-ha.

In 1762 Spencer was occupied with planting in the park, following instructions left by Woods. The overall effect can be seen on a panorama (Plate 2) and in plan on the survey, which differs only slightly from Woods's original suggestions.

Spencer's diary entries for 'planting in the Pleasure Garden' probably refer to the grounds on both sides of the house, including but not exclusively the shrubbery. Woods's plan also shows a short length of avenue leading from the side of the house to an alcove seat and the pheasantry beyond, which received '4 portugal partridges' in 1763.[25]

The 'new intended Piece of Water' below the bridge was staked out in June 1762, and the outline duly admired by a guest the next day. Associated with the bridge and water was a cascade of wide, shallow steps (Figure 60), which played for the first time in October 1762, followed the next year by the second cascade further down the newly shaped river. The second piece of water, with a 'Palladian bridge' over it, was started in February 1764. Here, 'Palladian' indicated a simple single-span construction, not a bridge with superstructure, as at Stowe.[26]

It is clear from the fragmentary correspondence of the steward that much of the written detail of the landscaping has been lost. The archive contains sketch drawings that appear to relate to the 'Gothic Alcove' and 'A Rustick alcove made with unshav'd stone' or possibly the 'Cold bath and grotto' on Woods's plan; there is some slight archaeological evidence that the latter at least was executed. In spite of this incompleteness, Cannon Hall was a commission where Woods's plan was largely implemented.

A plan by Francis Richardson, produced for Cannon Hall some time between 1756 and 1760, makes an illuminating comparison between Woods and an improver at the end of his career still designing in the style of the previous generation. The sparse decorative garden details seem to consist of a formal semi-circular lawn in front of the house, bounded by a terrace and counter-terrace in late geometric style. Woods's plan, only four years later at most, is a version of a fully-fledged informal layout.

Spencer's diaries provide valuable information on the progress and order of the work, and also throw interesting light on the relationship Woods enjoyed with his employer, who took a particularly keen interest in his landscaping, was proudly describing the proposals to his friends straight after Woods's first visit and showed off his improvements as soon as there was anything to show.

A notable change to Woods's landscape was made c.1814 with the replacement of his pinery, by then very old-fashioned, by a handsome greenhouse on the same site.[27]

SOURCES
Jane Furse has been a constant source of guidance and information, and I am very grateful for her unstinted help.

SA
– Richardson's plan (Sp.St. 100), and two connected with Woods (Sp.St. 101 and 102)
– John Spencer's diaries for the years 1760–1765 (Sp.St.60633/13–18)
– Estate correspondence and vouchers (Sp.St.60543 and /60686)
– Book of mensuration, 1760–2 (Sp.St.60674–2)
– Building and landscaping accounts and contracts (Sp.St.60686–25E)

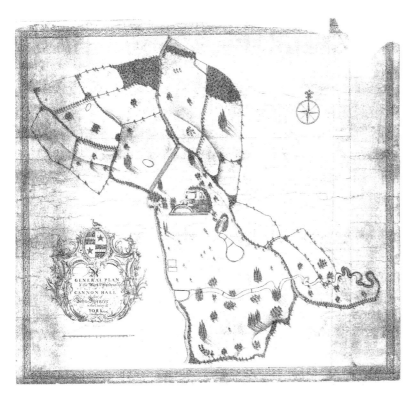

Fig. 74. The undated plan for Cannon Hall by Francis Richardson. This could have been produced any time between 1756, when John Spencer inherited the property, and 1760 when Woods started work. Although 'A General Plan' is an ambiguous title, that is how Richardson described his design for improvement at Kirklees (1757) for which he also produced a survey in the same year. Even in the 1750s, the pleasure ground design has a surprisingly tight formality.

CARLTON HALL

3 miles (7km) north of Snaith, North Humberside

DATE AND CLIENT
1765, for Thomas Stapleton

PLAN
A Design for the Improvement of Carlton in Yorkshire. The Seat of Thomas Stapleton Esq. By Richard Woods, 1765[28] (Figure 62)

Woods prepared his plan for Carlton Hall towards the end of a group of Yorkshire commissions, which had started at Cannon Hall in 1760 and ended somewhat lamely at Goldsborough in 1765. Unfortunately, the sparse surviving archive[29] includes nothing for the year in which Woods presented his plan. Thomas White prepared an alternative plan for improvement[30] which has been dated to 1780/1.[31] It is generally accepted that White's plan was executed, but while the piece of water and general layout of the park follow his proposals, an overlay of his plan on Woods's reveals that the area round the kitchen garden and the narrow plantation down to the west entrance are virtually the same. It is a reasonable suggestion that Woods did indeed start work at Carlton, and that the kitchen garden and surrounding pleasure ground was to his design. Possibly when White took over he was told, as at Goldsborough, that nothing finished should be altered; or perhaps while Stapleton was unimpressed by Woods's plan for the water, he liked the kitchen garden arrangement and the plantation down to the entrance, and told White to incorporate them. This must remain a hypothesis due to lack of archive evidence.

SOURCES
John Martin Robinson, 'A Catalogue of the Architectural Drawings at Carlton Towers, Yorkshire', *Architectural History*, 22 (1979).

CHILLINGTON HALL

6 miles (10km) north-west of Wolverhampton, Staffordshire

DATE AND CLIENT
1770, for Thomas Giffard

PLAN
No plan

The employment of Woods in this landscape, which had been improved by Brown in about 1760 and surveyed by Thomas White in 1761, might be explained by the close links of the Giffards with the Throckmortons, whose park at Buckland was Woods's first known commission, or with the Arundells, for whom Woods was currently working.

Woods wrote to Lord Arundell in December 1770 that he had been 'detained by Mr Gifford [sic] at Chillington'. Woods is described as 'architect' as well as 'designor' and 'gardener' in the single entry in the accounts for five guineas – he had produced drawings for garden buildings before, but in 1770 was perhaps presenting himself as an architect proper, with building projects recently finished at Irnham and ideas submitted (although ultimately rejected) to Lord Arundell for Wardour Castle. The probable reason for his presence at Chillington is a now-demolished Gothic belvedere (Figure 30) resembling drawings for Wardour in the 1760s and Stanway in 1792. There is no further entry relating to Woods in the accounts, and five guineas could have covered a day's visit and drawing, with the building being constructed by estate labour.

SOURCES
SRO
– account book, heading 'More Improvements' (D/590/619)

COPFORD HALL and STANWAY

4 miles (6km) west of Colchester, Essex

DATE AND CLIENT
1784 and 1793, for John Haynes Harrison

PLANS
A Plan for the Improvements of the Grounds, Waters, Gardens &c. about Copford Hall in Essex … by R. Woods 1784 (Plate 6)

A Map of Three Farms in the Parish of Stanway, viz BELLOWES, OLD HOUSE *and* STREET FARM *… to which is added a Plan for the Improvement and Ornament of that part of the Estate adjoining Copford, by R.Woods* [1792] (Figure 71)

The evaluation of Woods's work at Copford Hall is made easier by the sequence of maps: a survey of 1766;[32] Woods's plan for improvements of 1784; and another estate survey of 1817.[33] Copford Hall in 1766 had a charming but already old-fashioned garden, and by 1784 the layout was undeniably antiquated. Woods's instructions were probably to bring the grounds immediately round the house – some 28 acres (11ha) – into line with modern design to celebrate the marriage of the heir, and the most interesting aspect of this commission is how little was thought necessary to achieve this, mainly by softening the outlines of the earlier layout and adding a few of his own details (see p. 142).

In front of the house, the fields shown on Skynner's survey were taken in to make a landscaped approach, while the road was diverted to make this possible.[34] Behind the house, Woods advocated opening the views towards the river along the entire boundary of the gardens with lengths of sunk fence. The block of woodland on Skynner's survey was to be thinned and cut through with a path leading to a 'Bowling Green Saloon' behind the kitchen garden wall. Similarly, the wood on the west side of the property was to be thinned at the edges and given a sinuous outline.

The 1817 survey reveals that Woods's executed work was mainly in the garden, although some of his suggestions for giving the outlying pieces of ground a more park-like look were also taken up. The cascade shown on Woods's plan was made (although there is no evidence of the carved keystone), but the feeder pond above it dried up, leaving the arch as a decoration in its own right.

Eight years after employing Woods at Copford, Harrison again called on him for what was to be his final commission, still at the design stage at the time of his death in 1793 and not executed: the projected landscaping of the Stanway addition to the estate adjoining Copford Hall on the other side of the river. This last plan made by Woods, so visibly overlaid on a field survey, in many ways epitomises his entire output. If the plan is laid beside that for Copford, which it was intended to complement, a clear design emerges for a *ferme ornée* by visually attaching the pasture fields of Stanway with those in Copford, and embracing them within bands of plantation threaded through with a decorated walk. This landscaping would have much enhanced the Copford gardens, which stop very abruptly at the river.

The Stanway design is simple, but contains all the details and variety to be expected in a Woods design. The boundary defined by the little river adjoined the Copford property and was therefore left open, with two bridges, both vaguely 'Chinese', giving access across the water. The banks were further enlivened with a cascade and weeping willows. The wooded belt on the east boundary was pierced opposite the cascade to give a vista up to 'Bellowes Farm House, to be Ornamented', while the curving wings of plantation embracing the opening were enclosed by lengths of ha-ha. A clearing in the northern section of plantation was the setting for 'A Tower or Castle, to be erected', for which a design – very similar to one already used at Wardour some thirty years earlier (Figure 30) – was stuck on the plan. There is no reference for the Gothic bailiff's lodge, which was possibly intended for Copford.

Woods died before work on the Stanway commission started, and his widow was left attempting – largely unsuccessfully – to persuade Harrison to settle the small outstanding account.

SOURCES

Mr Brian Harrison, until recently the owner of Copford Hall, has allowed generous access to Woods's plan for improvement.

ERO

Copford – mention of improvements in correspondence (D/DU 161/234)
Stanway – Woods's plan (D/DEl P27)
– correspondence (D/DU 161/223–225)

CUSWORTH HALL

2 miles (3km) north-west of Doncaster, South Yorkshire

DATE AND CLIENT
1761–5, for John Battie Wrightson

PLANS
– Plan and cross-section for excavation of the three pieces of water [early 1762] (Figure 54)

– Plan and elevation of boat house with rock arch [1762] (Figure 40)

– Plan of drying ground, wood yard and stable yard, showing tree screening. N.d. but probably early 1762 (Figure 10)

John Battie Wrightson came into possession of Cusworth in December 1760, and from January 1761 a new heading appears in the steward's general account book, for 'Levilers and Stubers Wages'.[35] However, it has recently been established that this activity, which continued through the year, was not Woods's work but that of Francis Richardson, who was paid in March 'in part for setting out Grounds at Cusworth', although there is no specification about the nature or location of the work. Thus the sketch maps of the grounds showing viewlines[36] and existing planting, dated January 1761 and generally attributed to Woods, are in fact almost certainly Richardson's plans. This raises the interesting possibility that if Richardson had survived, Cusworth might have been his creation rather than Woods's. Richardson died before October 1761[37] and 'Mr Woods, land surveyor' first appears in the account books in December that year as receiving ten guineas on account, for 'planning and setting out Grounds at Cusworth'. By February 1762 Woods's foreman Thomas Coalie was established on site.

The eight memoranda written by Woods to the foreman between early 1762 and September 1765 allow a unique insight into the creation of a designed landscape. Woods apparently did not produce a 'plan for improvements', but the memoranda are occasionally illustrated by sketches to clarify a point.

The first memorandum (late 1761/early 1762) deals with the screening of the drying ground and wood yard, situated immediately to the west of the house, with a 'great screen' to the south (see pp. 43–6), followed by the coach road and ground forming near the house.

The major undertaking of the pieces of water (frequently referred to as the First or Great River, the Second River and the Third or Lower River) was then set in motion. Although work started on the first pond and ended on the third, they were conceived as a unity from the start and Woods supplied a plan and section for all three.[38] The main work on the water was completed by the end of 1764.

From anywhere along the north bank, the 'Great River' appears to terminate in a boat house entered through a rock arch. Woods's plan and elevation of the boat house corresponds very nearly to its present (restored) appearance (Figure 41). The mount on top of the arch was to be made 'like a natural swelling hill with the bases lost at a great distance', with a bench on top of the arch backed by planting.

Woods gave detailed instructions for the pond head to ensure that it did not give trouble in the future. A trunk was constructed through the head to drain the first pond when required.[39] In October 1763 work started on the cascade and its foundations which constituted an integral part of the head, with the wall and earthwork holding back the weight of water where it joined the second pond. Woods apparently supervised personally the arrangement of the large stones of the cascade.[40] A supplementary water supply for the ponds was found to be necessary, and unsuccessful attempts were made to harness a spring. Ultimately it was decided to raise the water with a pump designed by John Whitehurst, who was engaged at Clumber Park in erecting an engine there for the same purpose.[41] It is not clear whether this pump was made. By July 1763, Woods was planning the bridge/dam acting as the head of the second river, which was illustrated in a memorandum (Figure 45).

While work on the plantations and excavating the ponds was in hand through 1762, the 'hanging lawn and terras' on the south front were also being formed (see p. 114). The front of Temple Hill was protected from the fallow deer by a ha-ha, for which Woods provided a sketch of the section (Figure 63). The deer also had to be prevented from crossing the water to the pleasure ground, which Woods achieved by an underwater ha-ha to prevent them mounting the bank on the north side. All the plantations near the house were fenced.

In order for Wrightson to enjoy his improvements, walks had to be made through the grounds. Coalie was instructed in 1764 to finish the gravel walks in the garden, and through the park and field, so that Wrightson would be 'so far compleat in a fine range of walk'.

The pieces of water and hard landscaping were the skeleton of Woods's design, but the planting was the flesh and clothing, and every memorandum includes directions for the species and placing of the trees composing the various plantations, and the plant material for the more intimate planting through the garden.

Woods's last memorandum, of 17 September 1765, refers to work not yet started which was doubtless to be organised and supervised by the foreman. The early death of Wrightson the following year, and the succession of his fourteen-year-old heir, halted any further embellishments.

The subtlety and sophistication of the landscape at Cusworth places it among Woods's greatest successes, while for the historian the remarkable detail provided by the memoranda makes the commission unique. Woods's design is mentioned favourably by Angus and Loudon, although neither credits him with the creation.[42]

SOURCES
I am much indebted to Julie Harrup, Assistant Curator of Cusworth Hall Museum, for information and help.

– Woods's memoranda to the foreman (DD/BW/H/104–110, plus bound version with an extra memorandum H/113)
– Ledgers of John Battie Wrightson (DD/BW/A/2 and 3)
– Steward's estate accounts (DD/BW/E3/1, 6–7, 8–9, 20)
– Map of Cusworth estate, n.d. but probably late 1760s. Shows landscaping after improvements, but omits third piece of water (DD/BW/H/165)
– Plans and sketches associated with Woods's improvements (DD/BW/H/164, 166, 167)
– Correspondence and sketch concerning pump (DD/BW/H/117, 118)

Judith Roberts, 'Cusworth Park: the making of an eighteenth-century designed landscape' *Landscape History*, 21 (1999)
– '"Well Temper'd Clay": constructing water features in the landscape park', *Garden History*, 29/1 (2001)

DIDDINGTON HALL

4 miles (6km) north of St Neots, Cambridgeshire (Huntingdonshire)

DATE AND CLIENT
1769, and possibly before and after, for George Thornhill

PLAN
No plan

Woods wrote to Lord Arundell on 16 October 1769 that he had a man working 'at Mr Thornhill's near Bugden [Buckden] in Huntingdonshire'.[43] The Thornhills' main estate was at Fixby in Yorkshire, and it may be relevant that John Spencer of Cannon Hall reported in his diary for November 1765, when his improvements by Woods were just finished, that 'Mr Thornhill of Fixby dined with me'.

An absence of estate archives or maps for the period,[44] and little evidence on the ground, make an evaluation of this commission difficult. The mansion, now demolished, lay beside a pleasure ground of 10 acres (4ha), divided from the park by a ha-ha. The handsome kitchen garden has the two south corners rounded, and appears to be constructed of eighteenth-century brick, suggesting a possible area of activity by Woods. The account books of a nurseryman in Brampton show that in the 1760s Thornhill was apparently in the middle of a major planting programme of forest trees, which included just a few pleasure-ground plants in 1767 and 1770.[45]

With so little evidence, it may only be surmised that Woods was probably creating or altering the pleasure ground and enclosing it with a ha-ha, and possibly constructing a kitchen garden.

SOURCES
I am grateful to Edmund Thornhill for information on his family and for conducting a visit round Diddington; and to John Drake, Chairman of the Cambridge Gardens Trust, for arranging the study day and providing help and guidance.

ENGLEFIELD HOUSE

6 miles (10km) west of Reading, Berkshire

DATE AND CLIENT
Before 1781, for Paulet (also spelt Powlet) Wrighte

PLAN
No plan

Englefield lay less than 5 miles (8km) from Padworth, where Woods may have worked before 1767, and for which he produced a large survey in that year. Wrighte was on friendly terms with his Padworth neighbour, Christopher Griffith, and was related by marriage to Richard Benyon, Woods's landlord at North Ockendon from 1768.

An estate survey of 1762[46] shows that Wrighte's grounds, with radiating avenues in the park, an elaborate late-geometric series of canals and a plain formal garden, had not been modernised at that date. The detailed accounts of the steward for 1758–77 reveal the name of no known surveyor or improver between those dates, and Woods's name appears only once in the otherwise very sparse eighteenth-century documentation for Englefield, among the executor's accounts for Wrighte in 1781, two years after his death. This records a payment to 'Mr Woods surveyor' of £10 10s in January, and is followed in November and December by £60 and £70 on account to 'Clement Read surveyor'.

Improvements recorded on later maps are not in Woods's style, and the ten guineas probably represent visits and/or suggestions that were not taken up, perhaps owing to Wrighte's unexpected death in 1779. Alternatively, the payment could have been for a survey, which has not survived, rather than for a plan for improvements.

SOURCES
BRO
Englefield archive catalogued under Benyon
– Steward's accounts 1758–1777 (D/EBy/A132)
– Wrighte's executor's account 1781 (D/EBy/A4)
– Estate vouchers (D/EBy/A21)

GIDEA HALL

Romford, 1 mile (1.5km) north-east of town centre. Greater London

DATE AND CLIENT
1776, for Richard Benyon, snr

PLAN
No plan

Richard Benyon senior and junior were the successive landlords of Woods's farm at North Ockendon (see pp. 29–31) between 1768 and 1783, and it might be supposed that Woods would be employed if improvement of the park at Gidea Hall was being considered. The steward's accounts cover this period, but while they include payment to garden labourers and nurserymen, they contain no reference to Woods or to any known improver, or to unusual garden activity. Benyon's personal account book has a single relevant entry, in January 1776: 'Mr Woods for Plans of Ice house £2 2s 0d'. The accounts show that Gidea Hall already had an ice house before 1776,[47] but possibly Benyon was taking advantage of his tenant's expertise and experience to build a more up-to-date version shortly after inheriting the estate in 1774. There is an entry later in January 1776 for £4-worth of ice-house bricks.

The design for an ice house is the only documentary evidence for Woods working at Gidea Park, although later volumes of Benyon's personal accounts, if they had survived, might have included further payments. Harrison's *Picturesque Views* of 1788 states that 'the house … has long been a well-known object from the turnpike road; from whence, however, some judicious plantations now begin to conceal it … The grounds and gardens have been lately much improved by extensive plantations, as well as a fine piece of water.' The map of Essex by Chapman and André, surveyed in 1773 and 1774,[48] shows the remnants of a formal layout with avenues radiating into the park but also includes signs of more recent work: an informal pond, flanked by plantations cut by a winding path. By 1807[49] the remaining avenues had been softened. Thus the possibility remains that Woods partially improved Gidea Park, either for Benyon snr before his death in 1774 to create the informal canal and wilderness to the east of it, and/or for Benyon jnr in addition to the ice-house design. The shape of the canal is certainly in Woods's style, as is his willingness to retain earlier features. With the evidence available, this is as firm an attribution as can be made.

SOURCES
ERO
– steward's cash books 1768–1783 (D/DBe/A3–10)
– Gidea Hall sale catalogue 1797 (D/DHe E14)
– estate survey 1807 (D/DQb P1)

BRO (most items relating to Gidea Park have been transferred to ERO)
– Benyon's personal accounts 1775–1776 (D/EBy A2)

GOLDSBOROUGH HALL

2 miles (3km) east of Knaresborough, North Yorkshire

DATE AND CLIENT
1763–65, for Daniel Lascelles

PLANS
A Design for the Improvement of Goldsborough the Seat of Daniel Lascelles, Esqr. By R. Woods 1763 (Figure 15)

A Plan of Alterations designed for Goldsborough the Seat of Danl Lascelles Esqr by Thos White 1765 (Figure 52)

All three Lascelles – Daniel, his brother Edwin, later Lord Harewood, and his cousin Edward – had their estates managed together by the Harewood steward Popplewell. Both brothers were forthright, but Daniel was also impatient and irascible, as is evident from his correspondence.[50]

Woods's plan for improvements of 1763, complemented by a memorandum to the foreman William Stones the following year, set out his objectives. A comparison of his plan with an earlier survey[51] suggests that his brief was to modernise the earlier pleasure ground rather than to create a large-scale designed landscape, possibly owing to Daniel's concern over the expense of construction and landscaping.

Woods's memorandum covered digging the ditch for the ha-ha wall (perhaps enclosing the pleasure garden to the south-west), forming and planting the pleasure garden, forming the ground in front of the house and creating the kitchen garden and the piece of water. Although there is no evidence that the pleasure ground was made, the design provides a useful pointer to Woods's presence at Newsells Park (Hertfordshire) at about the same date.

Woods's attitude to the commission is illustrated by a letter to Stones in December 1764, which suggests that the latter had not been communicating regularly with Woods over progress, and that Woods had not been making proper enquiries of him: 'Mr Lascelles ... wants to know of me how forward his Business is advanced at Goldsborough, suposing yt. you offtin wrote to inform me. I therefore desier you will as soon as posible ... give me a perticuler account, how far you are advanced in each part of the work.' There is no subsequent surviving correspondence and within the year Woods had been replaced by White. In spite of deficiencies in book-keeping and a fondness for the bottle, Stones stayed on as foreman under White.

White's plan of 1766 is in complete contrast to Woods's: the kitchen garden moved, pleasure garden and intimate wilderness walks all swept away, and in their place an uncluttered landscape on a more generous scale. White's design was largely implemented, and in spite of two years' work between 1763 and 1765, nothing of Woods's work is apparent on a map of c.1796.[52]

Did Woods lose the commission through neglect, or because Daniel Lascelles had a change of heart? Lascelles lived mainly in London in high society, and may have been persuaded that an extensive landscape was more fashionable than Woods's design with its strong emphasis on the pleasure garden. The two improvers that he chose in succession were at opposite ends in landscape design: Woods, who was the master of the pleasure ground/garden, lover of detailed design and floral effects, and White, whose career reveals little interest in this aspect of design, who painted with a broader brush on a larger scale and whose passion was for parkscape and tree-planting.[53]

SOURCES
WYAS, Leeds
– ledger for Goldsborough, 1763–73 (Harewood 287)
– Woods's and White's plans (Harewood DB/M 285 and Estate Building No. 12 respectively)
– Memorandum from Woods to Stones – two versions (TN/C/23a/144 and TN/EA19/1)
– Correspondence in Harewood steward's letter book 5

GREAT MYLES'S

Kelvedon Hatch, 1½ miles (2km) south-east of Chipping Ongar, Essex

DATE AND CLIENT
From 1771, and 1778 for John Luther

PLAN
– sketch by Woods to accompany the application in 1778 for a road diversion

Woods's commission in 1771 was to make 'a new river' and form the ground on both sides – i.e. dam and widen the existing little stream below the house – at a cost of £600; then to build a brick bridge over the new piece of water for £250 (Figure 46); and finally to provide 'a collection of plants to furnish the ground about the water' for £53 14s 0d. These amounts suggest that Woods was providing the labour and possibly also the materials.

It seems unlikely that the 'river' and bridge were the sum total of Luther's landscape improvements. Seven years later, in 1778, an application for road diversion was made, accompanied by a plan drawn by Woods, to remove the sharp corner biting into Luther's lands and give the park a smooth south boundary. A survey of 1800 records these improvements and shows that other minor work had been undertaken, probably before Luther's death in 1786. An inventory of 1787[54] refers to a summer-house in Myles's Wood, 'Icehouse field' is newly marked on a map of 1800[55] and a 'Summer House Seat or Alcove' in a shrubbery or walk to the house is specified in a lease of 1805.[56] Whether any of these features can be attributed to Woods is uncertain; however, road diversion applications were frequently made at the same time as landscape improvements, and the fact that Woods provided the sketch suggests that Luther had been employing him after

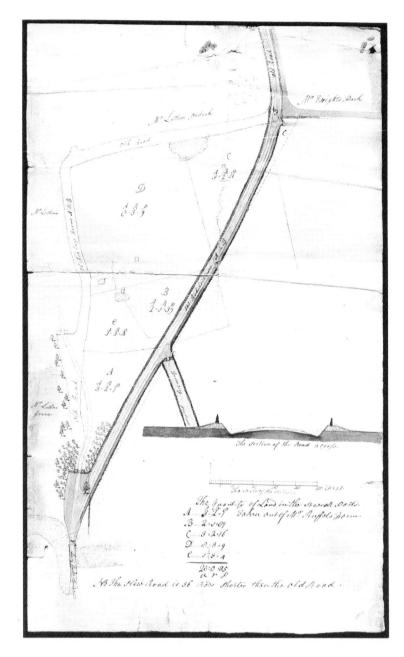

Fig. 75. Woods was employed in 1778 to draw the plan to accompany the application for a road diversion at Great Myles's, where he also built a bridge and re-shaped the river. This carefully drawn and coloured plan is far more finished that the rough sketches usually found with such applications. It also shows the camber thought suitable for a public road, which Woods was so anxious to avoid when making the carriageways through the park at Cusworth.

1771. Woods's drawing of the intended road diversion was far more finished than the rough plan usually accompanying such applications.

Luther's nephew and ultimately heir, John Fane of Wormsley in Oxfordshire, employed Woods in 1780 to make a full-scale plan of improvement for his property, and it is reasonable to suppose that Luther had provided the recommendation.

SOURCES
I am grateful to Judy Cowan for her help and encouragement.

ERO
– Maps of the Myles's estate: late seventeenth century (D/DFa P1); 1800 (D/DFa P6)
– Plan by Woods for road diversion, 1778 (D/DFa E43/38), with associated Quarter Sessions documentation (Q/RHi 3/5)
– Woods's itemised account (D/DFa E43/32)

HAIGH HALL

5 miles (8km) north-west of Barnsley, Yorkshire

DATE AND CLIENT
1765, for Thomas Cotton

PLAN
No plan

Fig. 76. The summer-house built into the wall of an enclosed garden at Haigh Hall, probably the commission for which Woods was invited to call on Thomas Cotton in 1765, while he was working at Cannon Hall. The design has a strong resemblance to a building drawn on the plan for Hengrave in 1777 (see page 209).

Very little is known about this apparently minor commission. In the diary of John Spencer of Cannon Hall the name of Thomas Cotton appears as a dining companion, and he would therefore have been aware of the improvements by Woods. Spencer noted in his diary for 20 August 1765 that 'Mr Cotton gave Mr Woods orders to come to him on Monday', but does not follow up the statement. Cotton's property of Haigh ['Hague'] Hall lay just south of Bretton Park, where Woods had also been employed. The Hill Sketches of 1839,[57] the earliest map to show sufficient detail, marks a walled garden with an integral summer-house at one of the corners. This is very much in Woods's style.

In addition to the circumstantial evidence for attributing this building to Woods, its similarity to a drawing on his plan for Hengrave of 1777 supports the claim. There are other instances of Woods re-using the designs originally intended for Wardour: an alcove seat is replicated on the Hengrave plan, a domed 'Ionic temple' reappears on the plan for Wormsley, and the cold bath at Wardour has a strong likeness to that on the plan for the Elysium Garden at Audley End. Woods was obviously not a man to waste a good design.

SOURCES
No surviving archive.

Fig. 77. One of the garden buildings drawn round Woods's plan for Hengrave. There are several instances of Woods re-using architectural designs with slight differences, so that they are not exact copies. Redrawn by Andrew Westman.

HARE HALL

Hare Street, on the north-eastern outskirts of Romford, Greater London

DATE AND CLIENT
c.1770, for John Arnold Wallinger

PLAN
No plan

Hare Hall is an elegant villa built between 1768 and 1770 to James Paine's designs and lying in about 70 acres (28ha). According to *The New and Complete History of Essex*, Wallinger was 'disposing the grounds about [the new house] to the greatest advantage and with much taste' in 1771.[58] The evidence for ascribing the landscaping to Woods comes from Angus's *Seats of the Nobility and Gentry*, which includes a description and an engraving made after a painting by Thomas Day (Plate 7). The text describes a very typical Woodsian layout:

> This beautiful Structure … was erected under the Direction of Mr Payne, the Architect, and the Garden and Pleasure Grounds laid out and improved by Mr Wood, of Essex … The Piece of Water has the Appearance of a winding River, over which is a Stone Bridge at one of its Terminations, and at the other End are some remarkable fine weeping Willows. On the opposite side of this Canal is the Elysian Walk, raised with the Earth which was taken up to form the Piece of Water, which has added considerably to the beauty of the Grounds, by giving a pleasing Elevation to the opposite Bank; and from thence is a Communication at the Back of the high Elms to a serpentine Terrace, near a Mile in length, whose sides are planted with a Variety of flowering Shrubs and Forest Trees, and extends to the Lodge by the Side of the Great Road.

Neale, in his *Views of Seats* some thirty years later, virtually repeats the text, but with a more handsome acknowledgment to Woods (with the 's') as earning 'the merit of the arrangement of these beautiful grounds'. Loudon includes a mention of Hare Hall in his *Encyclopedia of Gardening* (1822), with the comment that 'the pleasure grounds are well laid out by Mr Wood, a local landscape gardener.'

The walled kitchen garden shown on the Ordnance Surveyors' Drawings of 1799 and subsequent maps, but not on an earlier map,[59] was possibly constructed at the same time as the landscaping round Paine's house. It is therefore likely to have been part of Woods's commission.

Hare Hall illustrates how skilfully Woods could develop a relatively small site in scale with the house, creating a pleasure ground while retaining the productive land at its centre. It is in the spirit of a *ferme ornée*, with the single fashionable feature of a curved canal with associated planting near the house on the east boundary, plus a 'serpentine terrace' running along the south and west boundaries which, unlike the other two, adjoined open country.[60] The slightly curved canal was here remarkably effective in creating an illusion of a larger, grander, piece of water, with the spoil used to make a shield from the busy road beyond the boundary even before the trees grew up, and also to prevent a direct view to the end of the water.

The 'stone bridge' presents a conundrum. Wallinger was a stone merchant who had just built a stone-faced villa, and it is surprising that the small bridge disguising the end of the canal was not also of Portland stone, considering how relatively little it would have needed. The present sad remains are of flint-faced brickwork with a stone coping, vermiculated on the sides, and it may be surmised that Woods was aiming for a rustic or grotto-like impression.

SOURCES

I am very grateful to John and Rosamund Wallinger for their generous help and co-operation.

No estate archive.

HAREWOOD HOUSE and STAPLETON PARK

Harewood: 7 miles (11km) north of Leeds, West Yorkshire

Stapleton: Darrington, 2 miles (3km) south-east of Pontefract, West Yorkshire

DATE AND CLIENTS

1764–65, for Edwin Lascelles – later Baron Harewood (Harewood) and

Edward Lascelles – later Viscount, then Earl of Harewood (Stapleton)

PLAN

No plans

HAREWOOD

Edwin Lascelles started landscaping to his own ideas almost immediately after inheriting Gawthorpe (the old name of the estate), subsequently consulting Brown in 1758 without employing him. Woods went to Harewood in March 1764; the only recorded payment to him is in October, when he received £56 14s 0d for 'setting out Grounds etc.' His foreman Anthony Sparrow, who had been surveying at Wardour, arrived at Harewood in September[61] to supervise Woods's plans.

The sparse references in the steward Popplewell's letters to the activity of Sparrow and his men suggest that the landscaping was concentrated in the pleasure grounds. As Popplewell wrote only when his employers were away, there are long gaps in the correspondence.

Until White took Woods's place at Harewood at the end of 1765, Sparrow was executing Woods's plans on his own. In 1766 Popplewell reported that 'Mr White has set out most of what remains [of the intended ha-ha] but has contracted Mr Woods scheme a good deal, he says to save the mowing.' Woods seems to have soon realised that this commission was unrewarding, as in March 1765, only six months after his arrival, Sparrow reported that he had 'rec'd orders from Mr Woods to go to Lord Arundells so soon as the planting season is over in case he shall in the meantime have no further commands [from Lascelles].' Woods again tried unsuccessfully in May to send Sparrow to another commission, but in the event he stayed on at Harewood under White.

Whatever the extent and appearance of Woods's plan in the pleasure ground, it was amended by White and subsequently absorbed into Brown's design. The pleasure grounds were described in 1819 as 'long and deservedly celebrated as the first in the north of England, they were partly laid out by Mr Brown of Hampton Court, and a part of them by Mr Sparrow, a part by Mr White, and very great additions have been made of late years by Mr Webb ... one of Mr Brown's pupils.'[62] In spite of so many acknowledgments, there is no credit to Woods for having supplied the design that Sparrow was executing.

STAPLETON

Although Woods might have been at Stapleton earlier, the only reference to his presence is in March 1764, when Popplewell reported that he had 'staked out the Ground and the Road in such a manner as I think the gardener cannot possibly err.' Edward, like Edwin, did not lack his own ideas on landscaping, and it seems possible that Woods's influence on the landscaping was limited just to setting out and supervising new carriageways in the park, where his skill as a surveyor would be as desirable as his taste in suggesting the proper positioning of the roads. The earliest map of Stapleton is the Ordnance Survey, from which it is impossible to guess which of a number of carriageways through the park might be ascribed to Woods.

SOURCES

WYAS, Leeds
– Correspondence to Popplewell 1763–1782 (Harewood steward's letter book 4)
– Copies of Popplewell's outward correspondence (Harewood steward's letter book 5)
– Estate and household accounts for Harewood 1749–81 (Accounts 269)

Ian Firth, 'Landscape Management: the Conservation of a Capability Brown Landscape – Harewood House, Yorkshire', *Landscape Planning*, 7 (1980).

HARTWELL HOUSE

2 miles (3km) west of Aylesbury, Bucks

DATE AND CLIENT
1758–60, for Sir William Lee, 4th Baronet

PLANS
– 'Design for the new Garden Greenhouse and Pinery' charged for in Woods's account[63] (missing)

– 'Plan of the Mansion House and Pleasure Ground' from a book of surveys of the Hartwell estate by Robert Weston, 1776[64] (Figure 17)

The magnificent garden of the 1730s, depicted on eight paintings by Balthasar Nebot,[65] was already being altered by 1744 to comply with changing taste,[66] although it is not clear how much was done through the 1750s.

While Woods's own design is missing, Weston's survey of the estate gives a clear picture of the park and kitchen/pleasure garden after Woods's employment. Mid-eighteenth-century documentation for Hartwell is patchy, but Woods's first visit in August 1759 is recorded in his account to Sir William.[67] The most interesting aspect of this document is a list supplied by Woods of 640 forest trees and some 2200 varied ornamentals, many in small numbers, arranged in such a way that they were probably for different parts of the grounds.[68] The plants were supplied by Woods but he might have been acting as a contractor, perhaps for Henry Hewitt who supplied the Buckland order on Woods's behalf, and whose nursery had been used by Sir Thomas in 1737–8.[69]

Woods's account records a total of thirty-five days at Hartwell up to October 1760, but further visits are suggested by a letter in November from Lapidge, the head gardener/foreman, complaining of not having seen Woods recently and being held up for lack of instructions. Other correspondence is certainly missing, as a note at the top of the plant list refers to an item not in the archive: 'See the letter of Mr Richard Woods, Chertsey. 28 February 1760.'

The 'new Garden Greenhouse and Pinery', created on land that was not within the garden on an earlier map,[70] can be identified on Weston's survey. Entry was through an arch and via a way under the road, a stratagem Woods calls a 'subterraneous passage' where he suggested it for Audley End in a similar situation. The Weston map shows a built structure at this point, now restored and known as the 'triumphal arch and folly walls'.[71] The layout of the garden, although obviously including beds of produce, places unusual emphasis on its other function as a pleasure garden (see pp. 134–5).

It is probable that Woods was also responsible for the layout of at least some of the park. Lapidge told Sir William that 'there is sixteen [stakes] upon the Lawn before the Green House and stove, and 26 upon the Grass plott above the lawn, but what Mr Woods intended them to be I cannot tel' (the 'grass plott' was probably immediately west of the fruit-garden walls).

Lapidge continued: 'there is one Red Cedar wanting at the Church yard and one Cedar of Libanus and one Cedar of Libanon at the Drying Yard paile and three cypresses. ... I have wrote to Mr Woods.'

The small-scale, closely integrated pleasure park recorded by Weston is strongly reminiscent of Woods's style. The bastions in the ha-ha have been retained, as at Goldsborough, and the scattering of little buildings provides the variety typical of a Woods landscape. Continuing activity in the grounds through the 1760s is suggested by the annotations on some of the gardeners' wage sheets.

The garden buildings shown on Weston's map did not survive into the nineteenth century, and there is no clue about their form, purpose or authorship. Woods was an enthusiastic supplier of designs for such buildings, but in view of Henry Keene's employment at Hartwell on both church and house, he is the more likely architect.

SOURCES
CBS
– List of plants supplied by Woods and charges for his visits (D/LE/11/10)
– Garden labourers' wages 1763–6 (D/LE/11/11a-e and 13–19)
– Correspondence (D/LE/11/61; 11/6/1 and 2)
– Book of maps of Hartwell estate by Robert Weston (D/X/1045)

Michael Cousins, 'Hartwell House, Buckinghamshire' in *Follies*, no. 11 (1991).

Admiral William Smyth, *Aedes Hartwellianae* (privately printed, 1851).

HATFIELD PRIORY

Hatfield Peverel, 5 miles (8km) north-east of Chelmsford, Essex

DATE AND CLIENT
After 1765, for John Wright

PLANS
A Design for the Improvement of Hatfield Peverel Priory in the County of Essex, belonging to John Wright, Esq. by R. Woods [1765 or later] (Figure 5). The original date has been trimmed from the edge of the plan, and '1765' added in a different hand. This date is unlikely to be correct, as Wright did not buy the Priory until 1766, and there is no evidence from the extant bundles of leases or court books that he took a lease on the Priory[72] prior to buying it.

On an abstract of title of 1859,[73] there is a reference to 'An ancient Survey made in 1763 called A Survey of the Capital Messuage Farms Land Woods & Tenements of Hatfield Priory in Essex', but this has not survived.

The plan of the Priory is the simplest of all surviving by Woods. The c.40-acre (16ha) park is divided very clearly into four portions: the top (north-west) quarter contained two irregular ponds linked by a stream of varying width, with some ornamental planting at the top pond. A ha-ha divided this quarter from the south-west section of pasture and a little grove fitting into the south boundary corner, which to judge from its regular shape was probably pre-existing. This western half of the park would have provided the view from the front of the house, with land falling gently down to the ponds and the fields beyond the park, also owned by Wright. The north-east portion of the plan, bounded by the entrance approach, held the house, offices, kitchen garden with orchard and a long thin canal typical of Woods's style, probably incorporating the old Priory stewponds and flanked by a triangular pleasure ground. The remaining, south-east, section contained arable fields. Paths are shown all around this uncomplicated but pleasing park, one of whose main attractions (of which there is of course no hint on the plan) was the magnificent south view to Danbury Hill. Possibly to take advantage of this prospect, Wright rebuilt the house in its present position a few years later.

A salient feature of the plan is the presence of arable fields clearly within the park boundary, making this an undisputed *ferme ornée*; there was no attempt to plant out the agricultural activity, which instead was brought into the designed landscape.

SOURCES
ERO
– Woods's plan (D/DBr P2)
– Deeds and wills relating to Hatfield Priory (D/DBs/T)
– Court books of the Manor of Hatfield Priory (D/DBs/M4)

No archive has survived relating to the building of the house or managing of the estate.

HATHEROP AND WILLIAMSTRIP

Hatherop: 7 miles (11km) east of Cirencester, Gloucestershire

Williamstrip: adjoining Hatherop to the north, in Coln St Aldwyns

DATE AND CLIENTS
Before 1778, for Sir John Webb, Bart. and Samuel Blackwell

PLAN
Referred to in an indenture but missing

This apparently unexecuted plan by Woods is known only from an indenture of 1778[74] drawn up by Sir John Webb and his neighbour Samuel Blackwell, MP for Cirencester. Their properties shared a boundary, with Webb's Hatherop lying immediately to the south of Blackwell's Williamstrip, resulting in such a logical single unit that joint landscaping was contemplated. The indenture clarifies their possible intentions to avoid future misunderstandings, and formalises their agreement, should either ever wish it, to 'make such plantations … as in a plan of mutual improvements some time since [was] drawn out and settled by Mr Woods'. They also gave each other advance permission to execute 'a scheme … proposed and drawn out in writing by the said Mr Woods for a lake or piece of water to be made below both the said houses from Hatherop River [i.e. the River Coln] … and carried into execution … in such manner as by the said plan of Mr Woods is expressed.'

The vague date of 'some time since' suggests a number of years before 1778. There is no cartographic evidence of any landscape improvement after the date of the indenture.

One of Woods's possible birthplaces is Hatherop (see p. 6), where the Webbs established an active centre of Catholicism, and the miller Richard Woods – a candidate for Woods's father – was one of the seventeen papists recorded in the parish. It is possible that in looking for a landscaper to suggest alterations to his park, Webb turned to an erstwhile protégé and native of the village.

SOURCES
GRO
– Indenture (D540/E3)
– Surveys of both estates (Photocopies 64A, 64B, 64D, and 64H – originals in the possession of Earl St Aldwyn)
– Plan of Hatherop estate 1785 (D540/P2)

HENGRAVE HALL

3 miles (5km) north-west of Bury St Edmunds, Suffolk

DATE AND CLIENT
From 1777, for Sir Thomas Gage, 5th Bart

PLAN
A Plan for the Improvements of the Park, Water & Gardens with proper Buildings for Sir Thos. Gage, Bart. at Hengrave in Suffolk by R. Woods 1777[75]

A survey by Thomas Warren of 1769 compared with Woods's own plan of 1777 allows a clear understanding of Woods's intentions for the grounds, and a survey of 1816, even though probably inaccurate in some respects,[76] makes it possible to guess what was actually executed. There is no surviving documentation for this period.

Sir Thomas Gage undertook considerable interior and exterior alteration between 1775 and 1780, including reducing the house and partially filling in the remnants of the moat, shown on the Warren survey. Woods's instructions for the 300-acre (120ha) park were presumably to modernise the existing strongly linear layout, which he appears to have interpreted as minimum work in the park as such, with detailed

Right: Fig. 78. A survey by Thomas Warren of the grounds of Hengrave Hall in 1769, shortly before Woods submitted his plan for improvement. (Note: this has been reproduced upside down for ease of comparison with fig. 79.)

Opposite: Fig. 79. Woods's plan for Hengrave of 1777 (note that north is to the bottom). Although Woods proposed modernising the whole park, his most detailed work was in the pleasure ground around the house (see Figure 14).

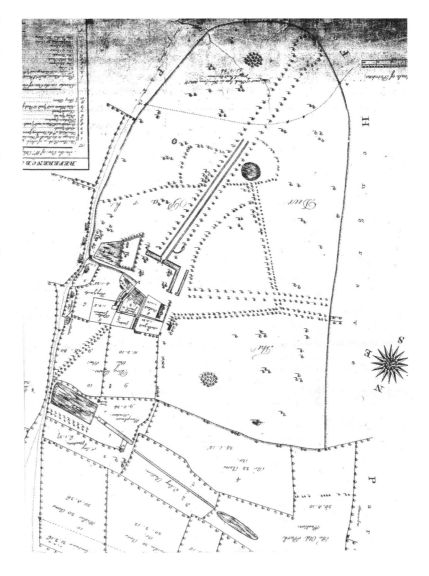

concentration on the grounds round the hall. Woods proposed replacing the long, straight avenue with a gently curving approach entering the park from the south-east, in addition to an existing entrance on the east. His plan also includes a third approach, from the west, flanked by clumps very similar to those on his plan for Wivenhoe. Two of the main blocks of plantation suggested by Woods seem to have been made, although possibly at a later date.

Woods's plan proposes combining the earlier rectangular pond and associated narrow canal to make a more natural-looking piece of water, with possibly the cold bath depicted at the top left of the plan built at the

tail. Although the pond was not made, this plantation was called 'Bath House Covert' on the first edition Ordnance Survey map (1882).

The most interesting part of Woods's design is around the house, taking in the old moat, kitchen garden and pleasure grounds. This is very typically Woods. The remnants of the moat and Dovehouse Pond (shown by Warren as a trapezoid) have been amalgamated into a single piece of water, resulting in Dovehouse Piece forming an island threaded with a winding path, and clumps and beds for shrubs or flowers. An arm of the moat, here apparently extended, curves round a pleasure-garden lawn containing a snaking border and spots (here very probably for flowers), which is almost identical to the shrubbery on the Cannon Hall plan of 1760 (see Figure 13). The rectangular enclosures of 1769 for orchard, garden and kitchen garden have given way to flowing lines, curvaceous paths, an apsidal-ended kitchen garden and what appears to be a salon in the plantation behind it, with circular segments of border – again, echoing the semi-circle of lawn and narrow flower beds in front of the pinery at Cannon Hall. The 1816 plan suggests that little of this pleasure ground arrangement was executed as Woods suggested, although an oval garden west of the house might have been based on his plan.

Arranged round the edge of the plan are insets showing the 'proper buildings' referred to in the title, including a 'Gothic Temple', a 'Stone Bridge', a 'Chineas Bridge & Cascade', a 'Dovehouse improved', a 'Cold Bath' and a very elaborate 'Garden Bench'.[77] In addition, there is a replica of the alcove seat designed for Wardour Castle c.1766 and a pavilion closely resembling that built at Haigh Hall. It is impossible to tell from the photograph of the plan whether Woods gives positions for these, although some of them, such as the cold bath and stone bridge, can be guessed.

SOURCES
The Hengrave archive was in Cambridge University Library, but that for the eighteenth century is almost entirely missing. The archive has recently been reclaimed by the owners.

SROB
– survey by Thomas Warren, 1769 (Hengrave 712/60)
– survey 1816, no surveyor (Hengrave 712/61)

Anthea Taigel, 'Report on the development of the park and gardens of Hengrave Hall', part of a survey of Suffolk Parks and Gardens commissioned by Suffolk County Council, 1993. This is a very thorough and detailed account of the history of the grounds.

IRNHAM HALL

8 miles (13km) south-east of Grantham, Lincolnshire

DATE AND CLIENT
1768–71, for Henry, 8th Baron Arundell

PLAN
No plan

Irnham was the secondary residence of Lord Arundell of Wardour. Woods was still in favour at Wardour, and at that date his talents were sufficiently well regarded for the work at Irnham to proceed without a design and with the detail of the pleasure-ground layout left to his judgement. He was also employed to alter, demolish or rebuild certain of the buildings, although his proposals were only partially executed. The original plan for a new courtyard with stables and (illegal Catholic) chapel was dropped in favour of retaining an inside room for worship and building the stables freestanding. Woods assured Arundell that they would be 'built very plain but strong and convenient'.[78]

The other main building project was to create a new drawing room, illustrated on an estate map of 1850 (see Figure 48). Following a fire in 1887, Woods's bland classical façade was replaced with a Tudor-style remodelling.

In the pleasure ground a bowling green was set out, and the ground and walks within the garden 'rectified and formed'. Woods enquired in 1769 whether he should order plants from a Newark nursery 'to fill up the plantations properly'. Other plants ordered from a Sleaford nursery specifically included some 'proper to help fill up the borders in the pleasure ground' (see p. 67). New coach roads are mentioned in correspondence and shown on the Ordnance Surveyor's Drawing of 1824.[79]

Woods was dismissed in 1771, but his design was probably clear enough for the foreman to finish it, and a letter from Arundell to his agent in 1773[80] giving instructions for planting are so similar to Woods's that it is possible that Arundell was referring to an old memorandum.

Although Woods suggested some planting in the park, and forming new coach roads, this commission was primarily for the pleasure ground.

SOURCES
I am very grateful to Sir Simon Benton Jones for his help and encouragement, and to Steffie Shields of the Lincolnshire Gardens Trust for her assistance.

WSHC
The Irnham archive is an integral part of that covering Wardour. Woods's accounts submitted to Lord Arundell are found passim among these papers.
– Irnham vouchers and the steward's account book (2667/19/6)
– estimates and correspondence (2667/22/1B/3)
– designs for chapel (2667/18/21)

KIRKLEES HALL

2 miles (3km) south-east of Brighouse, West Yorkshire

DATE AND CLIENT
1760–1 (but work executed only 1766–70), for Sir George Armytage, 3rd Bart

PLAN
'A General Design for the Improvets of Kirklees' [1760], charged for in Woods's account (missing)

Kirklees is another of the commissions probably triggered by the improvements at Cannon Hall, where Armytage was a regular visitor.[81] Spencer recorded in his diary that Woods 'went to Sir G. Armytage' on 5 August 1760 and stayed for five days, was there again for an unspecified time before 23 October 1761, and finally between 28 and 30 October of that year.

At the time of Woods's visits, Sir George had inherited Kirklees Hall recently and unexpectedly, at a time when alterations to the grounds were already being considered: in 1757 Francis Richardson had produced a survey and plan for improvements but there is no indication that anything had been started.

Woods's plan of 1760 is missing, and the next plan, by William Crosley in 1782, is entitled 'An attempt to improve Kirklees Park'. For this reason the survey of the whole estate in 1788, also by Crosley,[82] could be recording work suggested by Richardson, Woods or Crosley himself.

Following his visit, Woods submitted a bill for plans for a kitchen garden, a pheasantry, and the design for improvements. However, the estate ledger of the steward records only general garden maintenance until 1766, when headings appear for 'New Gardens and New Walls' and 'New Road and Park Wall'. Work under these two categories continued until 1770.

The 'new gardens' doubtless refer to the great walled kitchen garden and presumably follow Woods's proposals. In addition to the outside walls a 'Garden House' was built (shown on the 1788 survey) and borders and walks were dug. Melon frames were made, gravel walks set out and hot walls built with two associated 'houses'. In 1770, when the new garden was operative, 'levelling Old Gardens' is recorded, probably meaning the walled enclosure previously lying between the hall and the road.

The road replaced one from Clifton, marked on Richardson's survey, and at this date is likely to have been suggested by Woods. Stone pillars and iron gates were erected at the park entrance. A new wall enclosed a generous sweep of parkland round the house, replacing the previous fields.

As well as the kitchen garden, road and park wall, there are also a number of entries in the accounts for tidying and/or remodelling the park, including levelling and draining, and a ha-ha ('wall-fence') around a plantation.

In the absence in the accounts for 1760 to 1771 of any reference to the chain of ponds, they must have been a later creation from some time before 1788. It is a strange coincidence that this feature so closely resembles Woods's executed design for Cannon Hall.

The delay between commissioning a design from Woods and starting work might be explained by circumstances. Armytage was a financially prudent man, and while enthusiasm for improvement fostered by Spencer at Cannon Hall could have persuaded him to invite Woods to submit his ideas, he was in 1760 still funding building alterations by Carr. By 1766 the accounts record less activity on the house, and income would have available for landscaping.

SOURCES
I am indebted to Lady Armytage for showing me the maps which have not been deposited in WYAS, and for allowing me to photograph them; also to Peter Goodchild for arranging the visit, for obtaining documents and for advice.

WYAS: Calderdale
– Woods's receipted account (KMA/732/15/1)
– bills and vouchers 1747–1958 (KMA/732)
– estate cash books, 4 vols. 1751–83 (KMA/733)
– estate accounts 1757–60 (KMA/736)
– ledger recording payments to workmen (KMA/737)
– survey and plan for improvements by Richardson (KMA/1215)

LITTLE LINFORD HALL

2 miles (4km) west of Newport Pagnell, Buckinghamshire

DATE AND CLIENT
From 1761, for Matthew Knapp

PLAN
A Design for the Improvement of Little Linford the Seat of Matt. Knapp Esqr in the County of Bucks. By R. Woods 1761 (Figure 64)

All that is left as a guide to this commission is Woods's plan of 1761 and later maps. The sparse archive does not include any accounts or documents on estate management.

No map earlier than Woods's exists to show the layout of Little Linford before 1761, but the marriage settlement of Matthew Knapp and Catherine Uthwatt in 1750 includes a written survey of his recently inherited property. From the names of the parcels of land, and the lack of reference to 'park', 'grove', 'garden' or similar, it seems unlikely that any landscaping had taken place by that date. Out of over 500 acres (202ha) listed in the survey, Woods's plan, which appears to be a pleasure-ground design, covers about 30 acres (12ha), and does not include the 69-acre (28ha) 'park' marked on Ordnance Survey maps. As at Carlton Hall, Woods's plan retains the old avenue to the house, even though the approach has been realigned.

Woods's design falls into three sections: a lawn south of the house, bounded by a curling piece of water; a fenced 'sheep-lawn' to the north; and a slightly irregular canal within an ornamented plantation, associated with a semi-circular kitchen garden, to the east. In addition to the prominently placed greenhouse, the plan includes a pinery and melon ground[83] as well as the functional support buildings. The role of the kitchen garden in this design is discussed on pp. 132–3. At one end of the canal, where it would have joined the larger piece of water, Woods placed a 'Palladian bridge', almost opposite a 'Grotto over the Spring' on the other bank. The remains of a little Gothick alcove positioned at the eastern end of the canal, referenced on the plan but not illustrated, survived until recently (Plate 8).

The fenced walk round the perimeter of the sheep lawn (therefore by definition grazed) gives it a feeling of *ferme ornée*, with a 'light Doric or Ionic Alcove' in direct view of the house from the edge of close plantation at the northern boundary. Within the pasture, groups of trees were to stand 'upon soft waves'.

If any estate archive survived, this commission could probably be considered as one of Woods's more important designs, not for its size or grandeur, but because it encapsulates his thinking so neatly in several aspects.

SOURCES
I am greatly indebted to Paul Woodfield, the retired Conservation Officer of Milton Keynes Development Corporation, who gave me much help and information with this site when I was first researching it.

CBS
– Woods's plan for improvement (Ma 275/R)
– Marriage settlement of Matthew Knapp and Catherine Uthwatt (D-X 1457/1)

LITTLE SALING, RECTORY FARM

Little (Bardfield) Saling, Braintree, Essex

DATE AND CLIENT
1781, for Mr Thomas King

PLAN
Plan of Rectory Farm in the Parish of Little Saling … Surveyed March 1781 by Richd Woods

Thomas King was a London merchant who acquired Rectory Farm in 1776 by inheritance from a distant relative. Shortly afterwards he raised a mortgage on the property and, after settling a dispute over the title, he sold Rectory Farm in 1783. The survey by Woods seems to have been a valuation for a sale or letting.

This is one of two known straight surveys by Woods, without suggested improvements. A note on the map in Woods's hand concerning the plantations is obviously a valuation consideration, not a suggestion for an embellishment.

An interesting aspect of this simple survey is the information it provides about Woods's family. The mortgage on Rectory Farm was taken out by the auctioneer James Christie with some funds being supplied by Gabriel Laroche, who had been one of the witnesses at the marriage of Woods's daughter with James Ansell in 1765. This coincidence suggests that the James Ansell who later went into partnership with Christie might have been Woods's son-in-law.

SOURCES
ERO
– Woods's survey (D/DMd/39)
– Deeds, etc. concerning Alice Plampin's Bardfield Saling estate (D/DMd)

LITTLETON HOUSE

Shepperton, 2 miles (3km) north-east of Chertsey, Surrey. Previously in Middlesex

DATE AND CLIENT
Before 1768–70, for Thomas Wood, Treasurer of the Inner Temple

PLAN
No plan

Littleton lies not far from Chertsey, and the main interest of this sparsely documented commission lies in the light it throws on, and the questions it raises about, Woods's possible employment at Wooburn Farm. James Parnell left a description of Wooburn Farm in 1763 (see pp. 16–17), which is closely followed by a comment on 'a very Pritty Seat and Improvement of Mr Wood's at a Village call'd Littleton … I never was in the gardins, but he has ornamented his farm with a Gothic Barn, an Obelisk, and other embellishments that have a very Pritty Effect.'[84]

Woods's presence at Littleton is known only because there was trouble in the course of the work. Among the very sparse surviving eighteenth-century archive for Littleton, a letter from Woods in October 1770, explaining and justifying a muddle in the accounts, provides some clues about his employment. The work 'from the beginning to 9 April 1768' cost £809 2s 2d, and by the time Woods was writing had risen to a total of £1,260 10s 6½d, indicating that this was not a minor commission. The foreman, Henry Stevens (later employed at Irnham), 'so intangled' the accounts between Wood, Woods and himself that 'it confused the whole' and he was accused of embezzling £68,[85] although he was subsequently cleared of wrongdoing. Hoping to avoid the expense and unpleasantness of arbitration, which was one of the options, Woods wrote a summary of the accounts. These included his own charges for 'surveying, planing [sic], journeys, plants Barrows, Pumps Colums &c', and there is also a reference to the arch at Rowtherford,[86] which must have been a substantial structure as it cost £73 10s. These shreds of information fall into place in the light of a description of the grounds in *The Beauties of Middlesex* (1850), where William Keane writes disparagingly of 'a stone archway which is neither ornamental nor useful, and only attracts attention to condemn it in its isolated and incongruous situation.' He also mentions mature trees in the park and a grove by the stream.

While it is impossible to know what can be attributed to Woods, the emphasis on mature planting, and with species known to have been favoured by Woods, makes it very likely that he was responsible for planning and planting the shrubbery round the river, and the clumps and plantations in the north lawn.

An intriguing detail of the otherwise prosaic layout of the Littleton grounds is an 'appendix' tail given to the thin, canal-like, River Ash flowing through the shrubbery, which somewhat resembles 'Mr Wood's design for 'New Cut from Canal' among the Spence papers[87] (discussed on pp. 18–19).

SOURCES
I am grateful for help and information from H. L. Brooking, Secretary of the Sunbury and Shepperton Local History Society.

LMA
– Letter from Woods to Thomas Wood (Acc. 262/43/181)

LULWORTH CASTLE

5 miles (8km) south-west of Wareham, Dorset

DATE AND CLIENT
1769–72, for Edward Weld jnr

PLANS
– (attributed to Woods) plan for Park Lodge and surroundings, n.d.
– Plan and elevation of ice house, with directions for construction written by Woods (Figure 36).

Edward Weld inherited Lulworth in 1761 but did not return from the Grand Tour until the following year, when he married Juliana, daughter of Woods's eventual employer the 9th Baron Petre. Weld continued his father's planting programme in the park, but presumably felt a professional improver was needed to redesign the parkland setting and grounds around the castle.

Woods was first paid £18 18s in February 1769 'for his journey and trouble here', and by November 1771 had received at least a further £623

5s, with very probably more payments in the months for which no accounts survive (July–December 1769; June–December 1770; and 1772–4). For instance, Woods is known to have been at Lulworth in October 1769, as he wrote from there to Lord Arundell, and the last recorded payment of £10 10s in November 1771 was still 'on account', not the final settlement.

The initial payment would have covered not only Woods's travelling expenses but also seven or more days' work planning, setting out and instructing. Unfortunately the survey of the estate by John and Thomas Sparrow[88] was completed by March 1770, with the area west of the castle, where Woods was probably most active, left blank and marked 'Part of the New Park &c'. The vignette on Isaac Taylor's map of Dorset of 1765,[89] depicting the castle in a very uncontrived setting, probably shows the grounds shortly before Woods's arrival, with the main approach running through a hedged field to the entrance. On Sparrow's survey a neat turning-circle and approach from the side appears in this position. This might be one of Woods's contributions to the improved landscape, which from the dating would also have been one of the first, as the last payment to Thomas Sparrow was in March 1770 – although this does not specify 'in full'.[90] References in the estate accounts to work on the 'new road' in 1769 might relate to this.[91]

Woods's design for an ice house, and directions for its construction, have been discussed on pp. 91–2. The instructions include the observation that the ice house is 'to be exicuted afft er the garden walls are finishd', which suggests an attribution to Woods of the walled kitchen gardens, built to replace an earlier one on two levels.[92] This attribution is supported by the apsidal end of the northern enclosure, identical to the shape Woods used for Wormsley some ten years later. This walled garden was taken down long ago, but enough brickwork and mortar remain to identify the construction as eighteenth-century.

Apart from the Sparrow surveys, the only plan of the mid eighteenth century shows Park Lodge and its surroundings, which sufficiently resembles drawings in the Wardour collection to be attributed to Woods. The first edition 25-inch Ordnance Survey suggests that most of the plain and practical design was implemented.

For the rest of Woods's work at Lulworth, engravings by Basire give the fullest information. Although it is dangerous to place too much dependence on the individual details of an engraving, the general impression is that between 1765 and 1774 the castle has been given a far more polished and naturalistic setting.

All the evidence points to Woods gaining this commission through Lord Arundell, whose family had been closely allied to the Welds by marriage and friendship for 200 years.[93] It is not known whether Woods's employment at Lulworth was abruptly terminated after he fell from favour with the Arundells, or whether his name continued in the missing account books for 1772–4.

LULWORTH CASTLE the SEAT of EDWARD WELD ESQ.
South West View taken from the Grove.

Fig. 80. One of two engravings by Basire of 1773, showing Lulworth Castle in its landscaped setting. This probably gives an impression of Woods's work in the park between 1769 and 1772.

SOURCES

DHC

– Estate and personal accounts (D/WLC/D10/AE15)

– Plan for Park Lodge (D/WLC/P81)

– Plan for construction of ice house (D/WLC/P86)

Debois Landscape Survey Group, 'Lulworth Castle: a survey of the landscape' for English Heritage (1986).

David Lambert, 'The folly of conservation: conservation in practice at Durlston Country Park, Tyneham and Lulworth Castle', *New Arcadian Journal: four Purbeck Arcadias*, 45/46 (1998).

MARKS HALL

Coggeshall, 9 miles (14km) west of Colchester, Essex

DATE AND CLIENT
1779 (and possibly earlier), for General Philip Honywood

PLAN
No plan

Woods is known to have visited Marks Hall from evidence connected with his commission at Wivenhoe. On 14 June 1779 Woods wrote to Colonel Rebow there, 'I was to^{ve} gone to Marks Hall as today or tomorrow but I can't make two journeys of it so have postponed my going thither till Friday, & so go from thence to [Wivenhoe] park on Saturday night or on Sunday.'[94] He was also intending to return to Marks Hall on his way home on 2 July, but eventually decided against it. The June visit was for three days,[95] and he charged Rebow the cost of the post-chaise from Marks Hall to Wivenhoe on 21 June. There is no further reference to Marks Hall in the Wivenhoe archive, and the slightly casual attitude towards attendance there suggests the closing stages of a commission. When Marks Hall was demolished in 1951, 'cartloads of documents were carried off for destruction',[96] so the full story of Woods's involvement there is lost. John Luther may have introduced Woods to his close friend Honywood after employing him at Great Myles's in 1771.

Chapman and André's map of Essex (1777) records a formalisation of the last stretch of the approach to the house ending in a carriage-turn not present in 1764,[97] which is perhaps the area of Woods's activity. Other features for which he could have been responsible appear, disappear and re-appear on the series of maps between 1764 and 1842, and cannot be taken as serious evidence.[98] In short, it very difficult to guess from cartographic evidence the exact nature of Woods's work at Marks Hall.

SOURCES
ERO
– Survey by Timothy Skynner, 1764 (D/DCm P14)
– Chapman and André, map of Essex, 1777
– Ordnance Surveyor's Drawings (facsimile), 1799
– Rebow papers Acc. C47 Box 2

NEW HALL

Boreham, 4 miles (6km) north-east of Chelmsford, Essex

DATE AND CLIENT
1767–79, possibly not continuously, for Drigue Billers Olmius, 2nd Baron Waltham

PLAN
No plan

The first volume of Peter Muilman's *New and Complete History of Essex* (1768) states that Waltham 'is now laying out the gardens and park with such taste, as to render the situation delightful. He is making a noble sheet of water in the new garden behind the house, and erected near it an exceeding good green house. He has likewise, at a considerable expense, added to the other buildings a new wing for stables, coach-houses etc. which being situated near the front, have a very good effect.'

In 1767 Woods had an account with Hoares Bank from March to December which records payments from Lord Waltham of £250; this is followed by a six-year gap after Woods closed his account and before Lord Waltham opened one himself at Hoares in 1773. Between 1775 and 1779, Woods and/or his assistant Ansell received from Waltham another £795, making a total of £1045. There were probably further payments during the missing years, but even on its own such a sum indicates a considerable amount of landscaping.

Considering the date of the first payments to Woods, and the fact that Muilman wrote in 1768 that Waltham was in the middle of alterations, the 'noble sheet of water' – a thin pond running the length of the pleasure grounds, with a swell opposite the garden façade of the house – is probably Woods's design. It lasted only until 1799, when the Canonesses of the Holy Sepulchre partly filled it in after their arrival at New Hall, finally draining it in the 1890s.[99] Muilman also mentions the 'new garden behind the house', which is partially visible in a painting of the house by John Luttrell, Waltham's brother-in-law, to the left of the façade (Plate 4). There is also the faint delineation, near the edge of the painting, of the 'exceeding good green house', of a standard style with round-arched windows and pedimented front.[100]

This is a typical Woods layout, both in style and scale. A small pleasure ground of c.12 acres (5ha), a modest pond and a greenhouse of some architectural pretension placed in a prominent position within the 'new garden', which (judging from the corner of it depicted by Luttrell), seems to contain varied ornamentals. In 1763 Woods started work at Boreham House, which lay across the road from New Hall (see Figure 73); possibly Waltham had seen Woods's style in his neighbour's grounds and decided to modernise his own on the occasion of his marriage in 1767.

This commission emphasises the importance of bank accounts in piecing together the history of a property where the estate accounts have not survived. Without the bank ledgers, there would be nothing to link the landscaping described by Muilman and illustrated by Luttrell with Woods.

SOURCES
Hoares Bank
– Ledger for Woods's account, 1767 (ledger 76/27)
– Ledgers for Waltham's account, 1775, 1776 and 1779 (ledgers 87/294 – 103/122)

ERO
– Survey c.1750 of New Hall and immediate surroundings (T/M 396 – photocopy)
– Sketch associated with title deeds, 1799 (T/B 165/23 – microfilm)
Originals of microfilm and photocopies owned by the Canonesses of the Holy Sepulchre

NEWSELLS PARK

3 miles (5km) south-east of Royston, Hertfordshire

DATE AND CLIENT
1762–3, for George Jennings

PLAN
No plan

Two small pieces of evidence point to Woods's presence at Newsells Park in 1762 and 1763: an entry in George Jennings's account at Drummonds Bank for 8 April 1762 to 'Rd. Woods' for £15,[101] and the heading 'Newselles park' on a letter of 1 November 1763 from Woods to John Spencer of Cannon Hall.[102] As these two clues are nineteen months apart, Woods was probably employed by Jennings for more than just a site visit, even though there are no further entries in his, admittedly very sparsely used, account at Drummonds.

In the absence of any estate accounts, two maps serve as the only supporting evidence: the printed map of Hertfordshire by Dury and Andrews of 1766,[103] which shows a very rococo landscape, and a Newsells

Fig. 81. Detail of the trapezoid kitchen garden at Newsells from a survey of 1788. This was built after 1766, as the kitchen garden on Dury and Andrews's map of Hertfordshire is a different shape and in a different position.

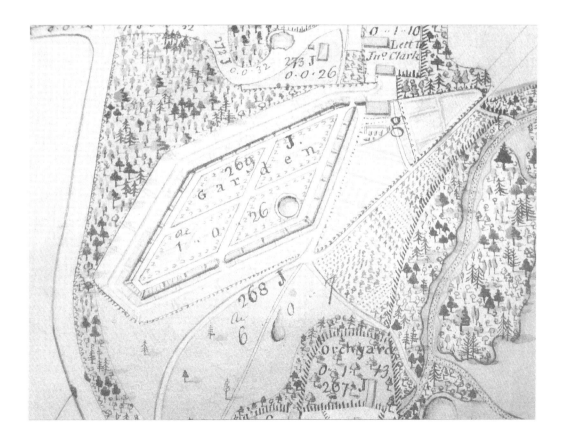

estate map of 1788.[104] The surveying for Chapman and André's map of Essex of 1777 was completed in 1773–4,[105] so a gap of three years between survey and publication for Dury and Andrews's map is quite likely, taking it back before Woods's appearance on the scene. Thus the 1788 plan would be a candidate for the record of Woods's work. It shows the park extended to the north, and the frantically curvaceous aspects of the earlier map replaced by a more naturalistic layout. A continuous shelterbelt around the whole property is described in the book of reference as young planting, which the first edition 25-inch Ordnance Survey shows as an equal mix of deciduous and conifer, very much Woods's style. This contrasts with the more formal, solid blocks of planting elsewhere in the park, perhaps left from the earlier layout.[106] The kitchen garden has been repositioned and given an interesting trapezoid shape, which could be a strong indication of Woods's hand. Other features on the list of references which could have been to his design are an ice house and hermitage. However, the feature most strongly pointing to Woods is not visible on the map but on the ground: the pleasure-ground lawn to the north of the house was formed into just such an open-ended scoop as he designed for Goldsborough. George Jennings was still alive in 1788 and, although possible, it is unlikely that he would have changed improvements of the 1760s within twenty years.

SOURCES

I am indebted to Anne Rowe, Hertfordshire Gardens Trust, for help and information, and for photographing the 1788 estate map.

HALS

– Estate survey 1788 (D/ERy P3)

The Royal Bank of Scotland: ledgers of Drummonds Bank for 1762

Site visit and discussion with Debois Landscape Group, 2000

NUTHALL TEMPLE

4 miles (7km) north-west of Nottingham (under the M1)

DATE AND CLIENT
1769–1770, for Sir Charles Sedley, Bart

PLAN
No plan

Nuthall Temple, tragically demolished in 1929, was Thomas Wright's most famous house, built for Sedley in 1754–7. There can be little doubt that Wright would have laid out the original garden around his most prestigious architectural achievement and the castellated summer-house/dovecote can confidently be attributed to him on stylistic grounds,[107] but no contemporary observer mapped, drew or described the grounds in the 1750s or 1760s.

Woods wrote to Lord Arundell on 11 April 1769 from 'Nutall Temple', where he had been for two days.[108] There is no further direct reference to him being there, although a round-trip in the vicinity in August 1770 could have included a visit. There is therefore no information on the amount of time Woods spent at Nuthall, and indeed his commission there is frustratingly vague. A written survey of 1778 survives,[109] but the first map after his visit is dated 1817 and it is impossible to say what changes might have been made since the original layout, including at the time of Wyatt's internal work around 1778. Certainly the landscape in 1817 bears no particular resemblance to Wright's style of gardens, and it is possible that the more naturalistic design was Woods's re-working of Wright's original.

As Wright was still alive and available in 1769, it may be wondered why Woods was called in. The two most likely reasons are that Sedley wanted some, perhaps minor, alterations to bring his grounds into line with current taste; and in addition that he needed some landscaping to hide his coal workings in the park, which had opened in 1764.

SOURCES
Much information was provided by Roger Hadfield, who has been researching Nuthall Temple for many years.

Eileen Harris, Introduction and gazetteer to the facsimile of Thomas Wright's *Arbours and Grottos* (London, 1979)

OLD ALRESFORD HOUSE

5 miles (8km) east-north-east of Winchester

DATE AND CLIENT
1764, for Admiral Sir George Brydges Rodney, Bart

PLAN
A Design for the Improvement of the Seat of Sir George Bridges Rodney Bt. at Old Alresford in Hampshire. By R. Woods 1764 (Figure 6)

Alresford House, with its surrounding land, was bought by Rodney with prize money gained during the War of the Austrian Succession. The impetus for a landscaping scheme of the 20-acre (8ha) grounds, as for the refurbishing of the house, probably came from Rodney's second marriage in 1764, the date of Woods's plan. The first series Ordnance Survey maps suggest that whereas a certain amount of Woods's design was retained in spirit, his main feature – the pleasure-ground lawn contained by a ha-ha swelling into the pasture – was not executed. A ha-ha in front of the house made in 1926 has only recently been replaced with one on Woods's line.

The ground from the south (garden) front of the house slopes down to the boundary road, beyond which, and not portrayed on Woods's plan, is a marshy area bordering Alresford Pond, a large piece of water created in the

Middle Ages. It appears from the openness of the south boundary on Woods's plan that it assumed a view of the water.

Woods's design is masterly in its simplicity, and is an example of the ease with which the *ferme ornée* principle merged at this scale with a naturalistic landscape. In front of the house, beyond the pleasure-ground lawn, the plan shows a generous area of pasture enclosed by ha-ha, within which two splayed arms of scattered trees lead the eye to the open view south. The tree distribution on the lawn to the west screens the churchyard; that to the east gives access to a bowling green or 'saloon', resulting in informal visual symmetry. While retaining the existing (and current) entrance to the house from the courtyard, Woods also proposed 'another coachway if it can be had' bringing carriages to the garden side of the house as the main access. This was not executed, possibly owing to the cost, but Woods's design works equally well without it. The new coachway, after providing a branch to the stables, would have merged with the circuit walk, leading through open grove and scattered planting, all behind the ha-ha, and following the two slightly curving east and west boundaries. A gate at the southern extremity of both paths gave access to a walk across the grazed parkland to pick up the return east (or west) walk back behind the ha-ha. There is no ornament beyond the hint of an urn or statue in the bowling green, and 'various kinds of benches to the different prospects'. The outbuildings lay beside the house, hidden behind the service wings.

This commission covered roughly the same area as that at Goldsborough, but the treatment is entirely dissimilar. At Old Alresford Woods devised a self-contained little park, relying for effect on the differentiation that could be achieved inside and outside the ha-ha. The ability to call in long views over the single boundary left open allowed the curving arms of the side boundaries to be made into planted corridors without inducing a feeling of claustrophobia. Variety was introduced by pushing a piece of lawn in front of the house out into the grazing, and creating a planted feature within it. There is no hint on the plan or references to a pleasure garden or flower beds, although they could easily have been created in the walks or bowling green.

The recent change of ownership heralds a major change of fortune to the landscape. The Halls have restored and where necessary created Woods's design: the 400m-long ha-ha has been built on the line in his plan, supplemented by a sunk fence down the two sides of the plantations, which have been made where he proposed them; while the extended lawn now encompasses the 'bowling green', with a statue in the centre where Woods placed it. The grazing cattle in the central meadow are an old breed, and the new trees are all species known to have been used by Woods. Within the parameters of what is practical in the twenty-first century it will be possible to see the full effect of a Woods landscape.

SOURCES
I am most grateful to Michael and Shuna Hall, and to Simon Hoare of Colvin and Moggridge, for their help and advice.

PADWORTH HOUSE

8 miles (12km) south-west of Reading, Berkshire

DATE AND CLIENT
1767, for Christopher Griffith

PLAN
A Survey of the Estate & Manor of Chris^r Griffith, Esq. at Padworth in Berks. By R. Woods 1767

This is one of two known surveys by Woods (the other at Little Saling) with no suggestion of proposed improvements in the title. It was made two years after Christopher Griffith inherited the estate. A survey of 1762 by Josiah Ballard[110] compared with that by Woods shows that in the intervening years the grounds appear to have received some attention, but there is no archive for this period to allow speculation to be taken any further. The Gothick fishing lodge in the grounds had features obviously inspired by Batty Langley, but the authorship and even the date of its design are unknown.

The value of a survey must rest on its accuracy and the neatness of its execution, and in both these respects Woods fulfilled his commission admirably: comparison with the first edition 25-inch Ordnance Survey shows the Padworth survey to have been extremely precise.

An attractive feature of Woods's survey is the unusually ambitious little drawing around the cartouche, with its engagingly skewed perspective,

Fig. 82. The whimsical decoration round the title of Woods's survey of Padworth, 1767. The large sheet is signed at the bottom by James Ansell, Woods's assistant and son-in-law, who was probably responsible for this drawing.

which has no relevance to a matter-of-fact record of landscape features and acreage. The style is not that of Woods, and the discreet signature at the bottom of the large sheet is that of James Ansell, Woods's assistant and son-in-law. Ansell also signed the design for Lady Arundell's garden at Wardour (Plate 11), but there is no information on whether he was employed as a draughtsman or as a designer as well.

SOURCES
BL
– Woods's survey (Maps 188.b.1)

SHUDY CAMPS PARK

13 miles (21km) south-east of Cambridge

DATE AND CLIENT
1763–4 for Marmaduke Dayrell

PLAN
No plan

The name of Marmaduke Dayrell occurs frequently in the diaries of John Spencer of Cannon Hall[111] as a guest in Yorkshire and fellow-diner in London, and there can be little doubt that it was through this contact that Woods gained the commission to work on Dayrell's property at Shudy Camps. Spencer seems to have taken a close interest in the landscaping of his friend's garden, as Woods wrote to him on 1 November 1763, 'I will now according to my promise tell you how Mr Dayrell & I have settled the operations of his plan.' A letter of 9 November informed Spencer that they had signed articles, and Dayrell's account at Hoares Bank shows a payment to Woods of £20 in June 1763, with a further £80 in March 1764.

Woods's first letter provides the only detail about this minor commission, and even that is very meagre. It appears that bad feeling had initially arisen between them: Woods wrote, 'We did not meet very good friends but parted as much so, as ever we where [sic] since we knew each other', followed by an agreement 'to finish all that was begone', suggesting a gap in the improvements caused by the disagreement. In addition, they decided 'to make a very small garden behind the house, & to take in the first Lane, & lay it to the Lawn.'[112]

On the first edition 25-inch Ordnance Survey (1885) the 'very small garden behind the house' (about 4 acres (2ha)) seems to extend as far as the pond, while the 'first lane' has become a curling approach through parkland. There are no extant archives for the Dayrell family, and no further correspondence between Woods and Spencer on the subject. Woods's reference to a 'garden' suggests a kitchen garden or possibly a pleasure ground.

SOURCES
Hoares Bank
– ledgers for Marmaduke Dayrell, 68/4 (1763) and 70/396 (1764)

SA
– Two letters, Woods to John Spencer (Sp.St. 60537)

THORNDON HALL

4 miles (6km) south-east of Brentwood, Essex

DATE AND CLIENT
1783–93, as surveyor for Robert Edward, 9th Baron Petre

PLAN
No plan

Woods was appointed surveyor to Lord Petre soon after his move from
North Ockendon to Ingrave, a village close to Petre's estate of Thorndon
Hall. Much of the Petre archive for the eighteenth century was burned in
1878, and the surviving documents give patchy coverage for the period.
The only General Account Book for the Thorndon estate runs from 1791 to
1804, and in that Woods is listed as earning £100 a year under 'Salaries
upon the Estate Account' – one of four men including the land agent – an
entry which continues until the year of his death in 1793. The previous
volumes are missing, but the *Chelmsford Chronicle* of 7 November 1783
carried a notice describing him as 'Surveyor to the Rt. Hon. Lord Petre at
Thorndon Hall', and as he was still at North Ockendon until September he
was presumably taken on sometime in the autumn. Although the lack of
earlier accounts makes it impossible to be certain that this was not a
vacancy filled by Woods, in the years following his death (up to the end of
the book in 1804) no new name takes the place of his in the short list of
salaries. This suggests that the position was created for him.

Apart from the measuring and checking of work expected of a surveyor,
another single survivor in a series of account books, the Weekly Estate
Account Book for 1788–92, reveals that a considerable amount of
groundwork was being undertaken at this time. It seems that although
Capability Brown's sensitive reworking of Thorndon's magnificent layout of
the 1730s was less than twenty years old, Lord Petre wanted to make some
adjustments to the landscape. Had Brown still been alive perhaps he would
have been called back, but an acceptable alternative in the person of
Richard Woods, experienced and available, was almost literally on his
doorstep. The case for arguing that Woods was in charge of the work
described in the account book is strengthened by the fact that the foreman
in charge of 'groundworks' was Joseph Golding, who in an advertisement in
the *Chelmsford Chronicle* in 1794 stated that he had been with Woods for
nine years. Again, the absence of earlier books means that the start of this

burst of activity is unknown, but it dwindles noticeably after February 1792. Woods's name is nowhere mentioned, and only the fact that Golding later advertised that he had worked for nine years with Woods links his name to the new work being undertaken.

A comparison of a survey of 1778 by Brown's draughtsman, John Spyers, with an estate map by Henry Clayton of 1808[113] suggests that some features surprisingly absent after Brown's departure had been implemented in the interim, and not that Brown's landscape was being re-worked. In particular, some of the tighter plantations remaining from the early eighteenth century have been softened, leaving just six surviving platoons as remnants of the 8th Lord Petre's layout. A significant 'new Plantation' was being made in the 1780s on the eastern boundary of the park, first mentioned at the beginning of the account book in March 1788, although the trees themselves must have been planted before this date.

In the same part of the park, slightly south of the house and bordering the open view down the esplanade, Brown's pond was being re-shaped. The long tail which petered out in a northerly direction on Spyers's map was turned in a right angle to the east and given a more precise outline.[114] Repton made a drawing of the pond in about 1790[115] – possibly because it

Fig. 83. The cartographic evidence for Woods's probable work at Thorndon Hall lies in this survey by Henry Clayton, 1808. Brown's pond (centre) has been reworked to give it a more precise form, and some of the remaining formal plantations of the early eighteenth century have been softened.

was a new feature – which seems to show the view of it from the house looking slightly to the south-east. It can be surmised from the lie of the land that turning the tail in this way greatly improved the visual impression of the water from the building. Work 'On acct. of the Pond' was already under way when the Weekly Estate Account Book opens, with the final entries in October 1789.

The new plantation and better-delineated pond gave this small section of the park greater definition than as left by Brown, and both features are closer to Woods's style than his. The pond is far more precise in outline, less truly naturalistic, than what it replaced, and the plantation includes insets of oval clumps and a walk leading to a loosely defined oval lawn projecting into the parkland, both reminiscent of Woods's work elsewhere.

'Work and levelling in the West Garden' during 1788 probably refers to the ground adjacent to the walled garden. By 1805 the long narrow pond north of the walled garden had been backed by a loose plantation and given a south aspect on to a band of planting flanking a small garden building. This again is a feature very much allied to Woods's kitchen/pleasure gardens, as at Wardour and Hartwell.

The scanty information given in the Weekly Account Book, and the fact that it starts only in 1788, five years after Woods was engaged as surveyor, means that evaluation of this period involves much guesswork. Golding and his team of between ten and twenty-five labourers were continuously engaged on unspecified groundwork until March 1791, but after Golding left the team, headed by the new foreman, was noticeably reduced. It is possible but unlikely that Woods was responsible for the design of the Octagon Lodge which replaced the pair of avenue lodges at the north entrance to the park: there is no very close stylistic link with any of his other work. The letter and memorandum from Woods dated July 1784, concerning measuring the new lodge and rectifying the framing of the roof, gives no suggestion that the design was by him.[116]

SOURCES
ERO
– Weekly Estate Account Book, 1788–92 (D/DP/A59)
– General Account Book, 1791–1804 (D/DP/A90)
– Survey attributed to John Spyers, 1778 (D/DP/P30)
– Survey by Henry Clayton, 1808 (D/DP/P43)
– Letter and memorandum from Woods (D/DP/E68)

Chris Collis, 'Thorndon Park: Phoenix of an Age' (unpublished MA dissertation, Architectural Association, 1994).

WARDOUR CASTLE

1.75 miles (3.5km) south-west of Tisbury, Wiltshire

DATE AND CLIENT
1764–71, for Henry, 8th Baron Arundell

PLANS
*A Design for the Improvement of Wardour, the Seat of the Right Hon*ble *Henry Lord Arundel [sic] Bar*n. *of Wardour, and Count of the Sacred Roman Empire. By R. Woods, 1764* (Figure 50)

Design for grounds around new house, 1770. Untitled, signed 'Jas. Ansell, delin.' (Plate 11)

*A Plan for the intended Alterations at Wardour in Wiltshire, Seat of the Rt. Hon*ble *the L*d *Arundell, by L*[ancelot] *B*[rown] *1775* (Figure 51)

Wardour Castle was Woods's most prestigious, longest-running and potentially most extensive commission, although paradoxically it is not his most successful or harmonious design. It is clear that he regarded it from the outset as an opportunity beyond the sphere of his normal practice. The size of his plan (some 5 x 7ft [1.5 x 2.1m])[117] and its intricacy, and the unusually effusive opening of his first letter to Lord Arundell ('My Dear & Hon'd. Lord'), indicate his excitement and enthusiasm for the commission.

In 1754 Brown submitted a General Plan for the Alterations, now missing, for the 7th Lord Arundell, which included measuring 620 acres of land adjoining the old castle, thus indicating a full landscaping scheme. Lord Arundell died two years later, having paid £40 on account, and Brown presented his bill again in 1757, without having started work. The landscaping for the new mansion, which started ahead of the building, was initially to Woods's design (1764–71), with a short period of involvement by Brown (from 1774) after Woods's dismissal, but was never fully implemented to the plan of either. In view of past confusion in deciding what to attribute to Woods and what to Brown, it is fortunate that two surveys exist in addition to the improvers' plans: a map of 1753 by 'WD' (pre-dating Brown's first, unexecuted, plan) and a survey by George Ingman of 1773, which neatly falls between the end of Woods's employment and the start of any work by Brown. Ingman's map is also useful as a safety device against assumption that work estimated and agreed was actually carried out. A 'General Abstract of the Accounts between Lord Arundell and Richard Woods' specifies sums paid at different times that can be matched with agreed estimates for certain articles of work, and here it has been assumed that the work paid for was indeed executed. Unfortunately the sixth and last entry, post-1769, is for £1425-worth of 'extra work neither by estimate or agreement', so that for this later period information contained in letters has to be patched together, although this may not result in the complete picture.

It is clear from Brown's original bill that no major work had been undertaken between the production of his plan and 1757, when he submitted his account again for settlement. Little if any change, at least in the wider landscape, is likely to have been made at Wardour between the survey of 1753 and Woods's first visit eleven years later, with the probable exception of a new kitchen garden above the Old Castle.[118] Following visits by Anthony Sparrow, his surveyor, in March and April 1764,[119] Woods spent twelve days at Wardour in May, possibly discussing the plan with Lord Arundell and the order of work. Minor changes had already been decided by February 1765.[120]

The Old Castle had been reduced to a shell in the Civil War, leaving the estate with no proper family seat. Following his marriage in 1763, Arundell started to consider whether to build on the old site or a different one, and had asked Joseph Spence's opinion. An unsigned sheet of 'Memorandums for Wardour Castle' is not in Woods's hand but could have been written by the unnamed clerk accompanying him to Wardour in January 1765. This same person penned a list of 'Articles of Business to be done at Wardour, previous to the Large Works', discussing details of groundwork, which makes it extremely likely that Woods was the author, if not the writer, of both pieces. The 'Memorandums' urge that the house be built not on the site of the Old Castle but 'at the proper Spott' which from the text is clearly its present position, and there are references from 1765 to 'the field where the new house is intended'. Woods submitted designs for the mansion, but Arundell eventually chose James Paine and building started in 1771.

From 1765 work on the landscape shifted towards the north where the mansion was already planned. Woods's early work was in Lady Grove,[121] where clearings were being opened and sand walks with grass margins cut in May 1764, all specified in a memorandum and 'according to a Sketch or nearly like a Sketch drawn for that purpose', probably referring to a very faint drawing differing somewhat from the Grove as originally drawn. The little piece of water within the Grove was to be made (where the ice house was later positioned), a ha-ha built round the south-west and south-east sides and £100-worth of plants to be provided by Woods 'according to a catalogue' (missing from the archive). In essence that first year's work transformed the close-planted grove cut with a star of rides shown on the 1753 survey into the wilderness/pleasure ground recorded on Ingman's map. The design for the Grove on Woods's large plan included a 'menazery house', which was possibly reduced to a pheasantry, far smaller and in a different position, mentioned by Woods in a memorandum to Creswell in 1767.

In June 1764 work started on the first of the new pieces of water, planned by Woods like a necklace thrown round the park. In the event, this was the only one executed, and it sits in slightly incongruous isolation linked to the neck of the Great Pond (now called Swan Pond). The 'intended Cold Bath' (see pp. 94–5) is also mentioned, perhaps to take the place of the 'bathing house' which had been attached to the Old Castle at least since 1729.[122]

While the landscape for the new mansion was being created, the family lived in Wardour House by the Old Castle when visiting, and the castle garden was still being cultivated. This must have been the destination for 'Perennial herbaceous flowering Plants' and a 'Collection of annual & perennial Flower seeds' provided by Woods in December 1764.

A path running along the foot of the steep, wooded bank known as the Hangings (or Hangers), shown on the 1753 survey, was transformed by Woods into a dramatic walk known as the Great Terrace.[123] The first section, started in February 1765, ran from Lady Grove 'to a Stake mark'd finis', and cost £100 9s 3d including making sand walks. The measurement is expressed as 'about 5a. 2r. 13p or 983 rod' presumably reflecting the width as well as length of the walk and associated groundwork; as the estimate for a later section specifies a width of 9 rods (nearly 50yds [49m]) it is obvious that this was no mere path through the woods. More work on the Great Terrace is itemised in an estimate of 1770, in which Woods contracted 'to grub, trench, levil & form, plant & sow with proper grass seeds the grand Terrace at the foot of the Hangers' for a further section.

Visitors commented on the beauty of this walk, and Loudon on his gardening tour of 1833 described it in detail:

> The fine feature of the place is the terrace walk or drive, a mile in length, on the side of the wooded ridge. It is as fine a thing of the kind as is to be met with any where; and being open to the south and south-west, and completely sheltered from the north and north-east, it forms an admirable winter walk, or drive. It has been originally planted with oaks, silver firs, elms, beeches, hollies and some other trees, with a general undergrowth of laurel … The views from it, down the steep grassy slopes between the trees … are grand, varied and interesting.[124]

Preparation for the building of the mansion, which was not started until seven years later, was made in 1765 by the establishment of a 'great Skreen in north of the intended new house', involving moving a quantity of earth and then planting. This screen was to enclose the house in a solid shelter belt, visible on Ingman.

A major change by Woods to the orientation of the landscape was the creation of a new approach through the park. The Old Castle had been served by a road entering from the east, but Woods suggested a long approach from the south boundary. His original version was moved slightly east, taking a serpentine line through the park to the Old Castle, with a projected extension to the new mansion that was completed only after Woods had left. This eventual 2-mile (3km) progression through the superb scenery (even before improvements) of Wardour Park revealed the magnificence of the garden front of the house before taking the visitor around to the equally magnificent but plainer entrance façade. Woods's 1764 plan placed a Gothic belvedere across the road halfway up, presumably to act as a gate and/or inner lodge, but the plain 'gate in ye new Coach Road' being made by Woods's orders in August 1767 acted merely as a simple stock barrier.

Of the ten buildings in the park (excluding bridges) on Woods's plan, only four were built. After the Cold Bath in 1766, the next to be made was the ice house, which was being discussed early in 1767 (see pp. 91–2). This decorative but useful feature was part of the reorganisation of Lady Grove. It was placed at the end of the small pond almost on the border of the woodland, but facing back into the grove. From a practical point of view it was about the same distance from both the Old Castle and the new mansion, but from the architectural importance given to the portico it seems that much of its purpose was as a decorative feature in the pleasure ground.

While the Ice House turned its back on the park, the Gothic Temple (see pp. 80–1) was placed in the Grove but looked out over the landscape, with an unparalleled view down to the Great Pond and Old Castle. The building was probably completed in 1768, as in February 1769 work was already starting on the single most expensive part of Woods's plan.

The kitchen garden serving the Old Castle was retained well into the nineteenth century either as a nursery or kitchen garden for coarser produce, but was inconvenient for the new house, and Woods designed a new walled kitchen garden which, like the ice house, was clearly meant to have aesthetic appeal as well as a useful function. The contract of February 1769 between Woods and two of the workforce to build the walls round the garden included detailed specifications by Woods about the quality of the bricklaying and width of the mortar joints. Woods managed to get the greenhouse, pineries and hot walls finished by the end of that season, but insufficient bricks could be burned to achieve more than the foundations of the walls. Woods also contracted to lay out and plant the new kitchen garden for £108 (see p. 134).

As well as work on specific features, time and money were spent on general groundwork. In 1766 all the 'parts of the lawns as are spungey' in the north-east section of the park were to be levelled and drains to be made of stone, or elmwood for the smaller drains. At the same time, old hedges were grubbed up and their banks levelled, and the new landform sown with grass. In total, 626 lime and ash trees were taken down 'about the lawns', their roots grubbed out and the holes filled.

Woods was working on a new plan when his employment at Wardour came to an end. His last surviving letter to Lord Arundell, of 4 September 1771, mentions 'the sketch (which your Lordship desired) of the ground about the new house', which he promised to send within a few days. This is not in the archive, although there is a plan, signed 'Jas. Ansell delin.' and clearly dated 1770 (Plate 11), that answers this description, and possibly the missing sketch was an amended version. The main new feature on the Ansell plan was a pleasure garden behind the house, but there is no sign of it on Ingman.

Lord Arundell was one of the employers of Woods most likely to have been influenced by his Catholicism. There was no reason why Arundell should not have used Brown, who had already been employed by his father in 1754, and who would doubtless have been delighted to realise the capabilities of such a magnificent site for so eligible a client. The Arundells were ardent Catholics, supporting the largest Catholic community outside London in the first half of the eighteenth century,[125] and were closely connected by friendship and/or marriage with the rest of the aristocratic Catholic network. Possibly Henry Arundell heard about Woods from Sir Robert Throckmorton, another Catholic grandee for whom Woods had worked in 1758. It is also possible that Woods was suggested by Joseph Spence, who wrote 'Hints for Wardour' in July 1763 for the newly wed Arundells, following the theory of a connection between Spence, Southcote and Woods (see pp. 17ff).

It is unclear why Arundell dismissed Woods in 1771. With only one side of the correspondence surviving, and that obviously incomplete, no certain answer can be given. Although Brown by 1763 was in the full flood of success Woods had also built up a flourishing practice (but mainly at a lower social level), and the difference between them was unlikely to have been so obvious at the time. Arundell may have initially employed Woods as a fellow Catholic, but he was sufficiently satisfied with what was achieved at least until 1768, when Woods was given a supplementary commission at Irnham Hall, Lady Arundell's estate in Lincolnshire. In December 1770 Woods received what he at least construed as a 'kind Letter' from Arundell, who had sent him good wishes and 'express[ed] a pleasure, in knowing yt. I was imploy'd by Sir Watkins Williams Wynn', and there is no hint of a rift in the rest of the letter. Disenchantment only appears in September 1771, when Woods wrote a passionate justification of his charges in reply to an accusation from Arundell 'that you think I charge very high for my visits'. This is the final surviving letter from Woods, and the last entry in the steward's house book for 'Creswell on Mr Woods acct.' was in January the next year, Creswell thereafter being entered as a direct employee. It seems most likely that Arundell spoke to someone, or saw something, in the latter half of 1771 to make him finally decide to break with Woods, who by that date had spent some £4521 on the landscaping. However, he did not contact Brown straight away, as his first letter of August 1773 suggested no previous communication. Still hoping for a visit from Brown that December, he wrote that he was convinced 'it is needless to go on with anything in ye grounds till you have taken a view of it, and I flatter myself you will find room to show your fine taste.'[126] This points to the conclusion that Arundell had come to feel that he was not using the most fashionable improver, and that Woods's ideas were no longer in the 'fine taste' admired by society. Brown did not visit until 1774, and produced a plan the next year, but the only entry in his account book is for £84 in 1780, covering his plan and visits to that date, with later visits still unpaid.[127] There is evidence from the vouchers that Creswell and his team continued to work on the landscape after Woods's departure, and it certainly seems that Woods assumed that what was begun would be finished. A note to the steward as late as April 1774 requests him to pay Creswell £7 on Woods's behalf 'in part of cash left in Lord Arundell's hands for finishing several articles of work which whare left unfinish'd at the settlement of accts. for Wardour'.

The accounts are too imprecise to be certain, but it seems likely that Woods was left with some payments outstanding; most of the account by the middle of 1771 seems to have been paid,[128] but a fulsome letter of thanks from Ansell in January 1773 for Arundell's 'friendly and generous Compliance with our Request' suggests an application for money still owing. It must have been a bitter ending for Woods of a story that had promised so fair in 1764.

SOURCES
WSHC
– House Book 1763–73 (2667/12/148) and Estate accounts 1767–73 (/12/200)
– Landscaping and building plans (2667/18/21, 22)
– Vouchers (2667/19/2, 3)
– Bills and letters re landscaping (2667/22/1B/3)
– Maps and plans (2667/21/9, 10, 11, 12, 13, 14)
Two letters from Lord Arundell to Brown, quoted by Dorothy Stroud[129]

Barry Williamson, *Lord Arundell's Park at Wardour* (Bristol, 1997).
– 'The Ruin of a Great Wiltshire Estate: Wardour and the Eighth Lord Arundell' in *Wiltshire Archaeological & Natural History Magazine*, 94 (2004)

WAVENDON HOUSE

4 miles (6km) north-west of Bletchley, Buckinghamshire

DATE AND CLIENT
1768–72, for Thomas James Selby

PLAN
No plan

Woods informed Lord Arundell in December 1770[130] that he was visiting 'Mr Selby near the Duke of Bedford's', a reference that can be traced on Thomas Jefferys's 1770 map of Buckinghamshire to Thomas James Selby of Wavendon.[131] The evidence from the Ordnance Surveyor's drawing of 1815, supplemented by the more detailed first edition Ordnance Survey of 1885, shows Wavendon House with a landscape obviously 'improved' since Jefferys's map. Selby's account with Hoares Bank includes small payments to Woods from March 1768, starting with £35 which would have covered a plan and site visit. Between that date and 11 June 1772, shortly before Selby's death, a total of £166 12s 6d was received by Woods, although more might have been paid in cash. This sum suggests occasional visits, with the labour force being paid direct by Selby.

The main pond, in clear view of the entrance façade, was constrained by the line of the water supply to lie at right angles, rather than parallel, to the house (Figure 57). Woods made a long bank in front of the house with a view down the narrowing tail into the end plantation, which from the house exaggerates the extent of the pond while at the same time giving pleasant views on either side of the banks.[132] A second pond above the house is similarly laid out, but with the wider section furthest away, and two modest bridges, one with a little cascade beneath it, provide access over the water.

Although lacking an archive to fill in the details, Wavendon is an excellent example of the transformation of the setting of a house by skilfully laid out pieces of water.

SOURCES

Pers. comm. Paul Woodfield, retired Property Management Director, Milton Keynes Development Corporation

Hoares Bank
– ledger 75 for 1768; ledger 77 for 1770; ledger 83 for 1771 and 1772

WIVENHOE PARK

2 miles (3km) east-south-east of Colchester centre

DATE AND CLIENT
1765, 1776–80, for Colonel Isaac Martin Rebow

PLAN
A Design for the Improvement of Park [sic] in the County of Essex, the Seat of I. M. Rebow, Esq., by R. Woods 1765 (Figure 11). The original of this plan is lost, and it is known only from a monochrome photograph in the Essex Record Office.[133]

Wivenhoe is a well-documented commission, with a plan for improvement, estate accounts and correspondence. Woods's detailed plan of 1765 pre-dates by ten years the start of work in earnest on the park, although it is possible that the pleasure garden on the south front of the house was made straight away. During that time Woods was employed by Rebow's father-in-law at Alresford, an estate inherited by Rebow in 1776, possibly providing funds for the landscaping of Wivenhoe Park.

Woods and Rebow were discussing the resumption of work at Wivenhoe in June 1776. After a preliminary visit in November, Woods sent the estimate in January 1777 and by March a foreman was in residence. Woods spent about seventy-six days over four years in planning, supervising and setting out work. His estimate covers the creation of the ponds and the bridge–dam between them, the little canal in front of the kitchen garden, the two coach roads through the park and the conveyance of water to the house from a spring. Correspondence and map evidence show that far more of Woods's plan of 1765 was executed than the estimate would suggest, but it is obvious that the pieces of water constituted the central feature of the design, to which other details were subordinate.

Woods must have soon realised that in place of the single pond he had suggested in 1765 it would be 'necessary to make several Heads or Dams, as the Water must be in several different Levels'. The head of one of the existing ponds was adapted as the basis for a bridge–dam – similar to the one he had constructed for Cusworth – with several purposes: it disguised the different levels of the water either side of it, it broke up the long slug-like shape of the water on Woods's original design and gave it a focal point, and it carried the new approach through the park over the water towards the house. Constable's painting of 1816 shows it as an unassuming decorative feature (Plate 9). Mary Rebow adds some charming detail in a letter of 9 August 1778: 'The Carpenters & Painters, go on apace with ye Railing of the Bridge … & you cant think what delight Mary [their five-year-old daughter] takes in carrying every body to see what she calls her prospect.'

Cusworth also provided a model for the boat house, although the craggy rock arch in Yorkshire was translated into a more constrained brick structure suited to Essex materials. It is illustrated in the background of Constable's painting.

Once the bridge and boathouse had been made, work started on the laborious task of shaping the ground for the ponds. On 19 July 1778 Woods wrote that the upper pond was almost completed, although the dry weather prevented it filling straight away.

Two new coach roads through the park were part of the 1777 estimate, but the cartographic evidence indicates that neither was built on the routes suggested in 1765. The only new approach entered the park halfway down the east boundary, with the section from the house to the bridge set out in July 1778.

Chapman and André's map of Essex of 1777 clearly shows the unimproved landscape prior to Woods's arrival (Figure 53). The groundwork of the landscaping included filling holes, levelling banks and forming the lawn between the house and the water, which was of crucial visual importance.

In 1779 Woods sent Rebow a sketch of a forcing pump, apparently of his own design (Figure 55), which he commissioned 'Mr Hadley' in London to make.[134] Correspondence makes it clear that the pump was associated with the 'sispool which we had proposed & had begun at the spring' which in the context must mean a sump for sediment from the spring water rather than anything connected with sewage. It therefore seems that the pump was needed to supplement the pressure at the spring to push water to the house, for which Woods had quoted.

An '**Elysian Grove**' is marked on the 1765 plan and, although the temple proposed there was not built, later maps show the unmistakable pattern of Woods's suggested tree planting. The parkland south of the house was apparently not included in Woods's improvements,[135] and information from correspondence shows that the plantations were in areas near the ponds, with Woods choosing the plants or leaving instructions about species.

The arrangement suggested for the adaptation and alteration of the offices and outbuildings was largely followed, to judge from later maps.

From 1780 the remaining work was conducted on a different basis, with the foreman reporting directly to Rebow although referring to 'my master Mr Richard Woods'. Rebow was already suffering ill health by this date, and died soon after paying Woods off in 1781.

It is interesting that Woods originally proposed a single piece of water where the landform clearly required a dam in the centre, but this criticism can also be made of Brown's plan for Wardour (Figure 51), on which he drew a large single lake which on the ground covers a considerable change of level from north to south. If constructed, it would certainly have required damming at some point.

SOURCES

ERO
– Section of pump by Woods, coloured and annotated (Acc. C47 Box 2)
– Lupton's worksheets, vouchers between 1777 and 80 (Acc. C47 Boxes 7, 8 and 9)
– Correspondence between Woods, Lupton and Rebow (Acc. C47 Box 2)
– Letters from Mary Rebow to her husband, 1778 and 1779 (Temp. Acc. C39, photocopies of originals Washington State University Library)
– single account book for 1766 and estimate for landscaping (D/DHt B1)
– photograph of Woods's plan (T/M 271)

Rosemary Feesey, *A History of Wivenhoe Park, the House and Grounds* (1963)

WORMSLEY PARK

2 miles (3km) south-west of Stokenchurch, Buckinghamshire

DATE AND CLIENT
c.1780, for John Fane

PLAN
A general Plan for the Improvement of Wormsley the Seat of John Fane Esqr with proper Buildings. R. Woods [1779 or 80] (Figures 4 and 68)

The Fanes were closely connected with the Luthers of Great Myles's and it is likely that John Fane was introduced to Woods by John Luther, his uncle, who had employed Woods in 1771.

The Wormsley estate was surveyed in 1759, at which date the house was surrounded by fields, with a formal, simple garden layout. Soon after inheriting the estate, John Fane commissioned an ambitious plan for full-scale improvement of the landscape from Woods. In a letter to Colonel Rebow of Wivenhoe Woods mentions a journey to Oxfordshire in March 1779 and two entries in Fane's account with Coutts Bank to 'Richard Woods' for £50 each in 1780 make it probable that this was to Wormsley. The modest sum suggests that the work eventually commissioned was not extensive, and the cartographic evidence indicates that only the kitchen garden, with a typically apsidal end, is clearly in Woods's style. Other features which might have been made following his suggestions are an ice house marked on the first edition 25-inch Ordnance Survey (1880) and a grotto, remains of which were discovered during archaeological investigations in the 1980s. The 'proper buildings' inserted round the edge of his plan include what could be designs for these.

The references to the plan are missing, which makes it difficult to understand fully this intriguing plan. In the absence of a description for the circular gardens behind the house, which were not executed, they look as though they were intended for flowers or some other specialist display (Figure 69). From the two-dimensional plan it is also difficult to visualise how they were intended to be made, as the ground rises sharply behind the house and the gardens would have had to be terraced into the slope, while the grove shown to the west of the house is in an even steeper part of the wood. Perhaps Woods had in mind Whatley's comment that 'a hanging level often produces effects not otherwise obtainable'.[136]

Woods proposed to incorporate all the existing woodland in his plan, with only a little planting or softening of an outline in places. The splendid chestnut avenue was also retained in Woods's plan, and remnants of it were still discernible in tangled woodland as late as 1991.

The ten little buildings around the plan include a chapel, a castellated lodge, two gateways, a hermitage, a grotto, a domed temple and an alcove seat, while either of the remaining two could be an ice house. The temple – admittedly a fairly standard design – is virtually the same as one Woods produced for Wardour in the 1760s.

SOURCES
Elizabeth Leggatt gave me generous access to her detailed and scholarly research on the archaeology and history of Wormsley, for which I am most grateful.

I am also indebted to Bryan Maggs for his help.

Coutts Bank
– ledgers of John Fane for 1780. The account was searched from 1777 to 1793, the year of Woods's death.

WYNDHAM HOUSE

(previously St Edmund's College; now known as Bourne Hill, the offices of Salisbury District Council)

St Edmund's Close, Salisbury, Wiltshire

DATE AND CLIENT
Possibly c.1771, for Henry Penruddocke Wyndham

PLAN
A Design for the Improvement of the Gardens of Pen: Wyndham, Esqr of Salisbury, Wilts. By R. Woods (Figure 70)

This is the only known design Woods produced for a town garden. A date for his employment is suggested in Charles Haskins's *History of St Edmund's College* (1927): 'In 1771 and 1772, when Mr H. P. Wyndham was levelling a portion of the ramparts to form the lawn on the east side of the house …'. It is possible that the ground on the garden front might have been levelled before Woods was called in, but in 1771 he was still working nearby at Wardour and a commission in Salisbury around that date makes sense. There is a tenuous connection between Lord Arundell, Woods's employer at Wardour, and Wyndham, whose father-in-law Thomas Penruddocke is mentioned by Arundell in correspondence in 1767,[137] suggesting that Penruddocke might have been aware of the landscaping at Wardour Castle.

Stylistically, the plan belongs to the period before Woods's move to Ingrave in 1783, after which all his drawing was in his own hand and has a fresher, more naïve appearance, and although Wyndham did not inherit the house until 1788, he was occupying it from 1768.[138]

Woods's plan is an exemplary exercise in town garden design, including within the 2 acres (1ha)[139] of dressed ground a graceful formality beside, but not jarring with, a section of irregular plantations, and incorporating the dramatic section of rampart (to the left on the plan) rising into a considerable mound. He saw that the house as it stood presented an ungainly side to the garden, and his plan includes the addition of 'a range of building recommended to make the garden front uniform' with a bay window matching the one already there. This symmetrical façade looked over a level oval lawn bordered with narrow beds reminiscent of those enclosing the oval lawn in front of the Cannon Hall pinery. The contrast between the regularity and smoothness of the lawn and the rugged remains of the ramparts within the plantations gives movement and interest to a small space. The northwards extension of the east wing was not made until 1790 under S. P. Cockerell, but whereas his design was for a flat façade Woods's second bay seems to have pleased Wyndham, as it appears on all subsequent maps.

Another feature on Woods's plan which foreshadows later events is the 'Summer house if required' tucked into the south-east corner. Although not built at the time, a fifteenth-century porch from Salisbury Cathedral, removed during Wyatt's restorations, was erected in the garden in 1791 in the south-east corner of a newly acquired extension to the east.[140]

The late-eighteenth-century addition to the garden makes it more difficult to judge how much of Woods's plan was executed, but the first edition 25-inch Ordnance Survey suggests that his design was followed to a considerable extent.

SOURCES
I am grateful to Fridy Duterloo-Morgan of English Heritage for information and useful discussions.

Haskins, Charles, *History of St Edmund's College* (Salisbury, 1927)

WYNNSTAY

5 miles (8km) south-west of Wrexham, Clwyd

DATE AND CLIENT
1770–4, for Sir Watkin Williams-Wynn, 4th Bart

PLAN
No plan. (A schedule of drawings in the house, since destroyed by fire, lists 'Wood's plans and elevations' and 'Wood's bridges'.[141] There is no evidence that Williams-Wynn was ever in contact with John Wood the younger of Bath, and as the schedule lists 'Byres's' as 'Byre's', it is probable that the designs were by Richard Woods.)

In December 1770 Woods wrote to Lord Arundell, thanking him for a letter expressing his pleasure 'in knowing yt. I was imploy'd by Sir Watkin Williams Wynn' and outlining his ideas 'wch I hope to have the pleasure of showing to yr. Lordship, in gratitude, for yr. kind wishes towards me'.

Unfortunately for Woods, Sir Watkin's new wife was the daughter of one of Brown's most enthusiastic employers, George Grenville. The new Lady Williams-Wynn was probably instrumental in ending Woods's career at Wynnstay in 1774, before he had done more than re-shape the formal pond in front of the house. The earliest map to record whatever Woods achieved in his four years is of 1820,[142] and after Woods's departure Brown was employed from 1777 to 1783 in both the pleasure grounds and the park. The only relevant pictorial records are a watercolour by Paul Sandby of c.1775[143] giving a vague impression of the remodelled canal, and another by John Ingleby of 1793.[144] The estate accounts provide an imperfect and undetailed record.

The first reference to Woods's work is February 1771, 'for a team working sundry days in the new Canal', but in 1772 two surprising and unexplained operators appear in the account book: Thomas Leggett and his foreman Edward Keithley. Leggett had been a foreman to William Emes, but had started his own practice before 1769. Whether he was working in conjunction or in competition with Woods at Wynnstay is not clear.

The heading 'Payments on account of the Ground and Water Improvements' in the steward's book suggests that work was also in hand elsewhere. Keithley and his men were paid in 1773 'for takeing down of the old Boat House',[145] and the still-surviving remains of a double rock-arch boat house at the end of the canal is very similar in feeling to the one by Woods at Cusworth.[146] Sir Watkin's agent wrote in March 1774 that the canal was almost finished 'and the Garden will now be forwarded'. This new kitchen garden can be ascribed to Woods not only on stylistic grounds – the apsidal end shown on the 1820 map is very typical of Woods – but also on indirect evidence from the accounts: the mason (who had already been subcontracted by Woods in 1772)[147] was at work in 1775 – two years before Brown's first visit – in the kitchen garden making coping for the wall, cornice for the hothouse, and flue stones 'to hot wall in gardain'.[148] This strongly suggests that the kitchen garden was being built to Woods's plan after his departure, possibly supervised by Pugh, who remained at Wynnstay until May 1775. The pleasure ground was certainly by Brown and it is assumed that the cascade was made later to his designs, but his plans do not include a kitchen garden.

A bill from Sandby of June 1771,[149] where he charges for a post chaise 'after Mr Woods to Hoxendon [Ockendon] Hall', suggests that he might have collected one of Woods's designs for inclusion in the watercolour which shows a little bridge over the canal. This is the only evidence (apart from unspecified work by the mason in 1772) that one of 'Mr Wood's bridges' might have been built.

SOURCES
I am very grateful to Elizabeth Whittle for help and information.
NLW
– Wynnstay account books and disbursements, with a sheet of 'Payments to Mr Edward Pugh on account of the improvements at Wynnstay' for 1773 and 1774 (Box 115/2–4, R40–42)
– Loose vouchers including a receipt signed by Edward Pugh, establishing that he was the same man as the Boreham foreman (Box 115/20)
– Correspondence Vol. 1 (1768–76) and Vol. 8 (1753–91)
WSHC
– Letter from Woods to Lord Arundell, 11 December 1770, announcing his employment by Sir Watkin and outlining his plans (2667/22/1B/3)
Wynnstay Estate Office
Map of Wynnstay Demesne … no surveyor, 1820
CADW
Register of Parks and Gardens in Wales (1994), register no. PGW (C) 64

NOTES TO THE TEXT

CHAPTER 1: WOODS IN CONTEXT (pages 2–11)

[1] *Country Life* (22 November 1930).

[2] 'Your dryads must go into black gloves, Madam: their father-in-law, Lady Nature's second husband, is dead!' Horace Walpole's flippant command to the Countess of Upper Ossory in a letter of 8 February 1783 following Brown's death. Mrs Paget Toynbee (ed.), *The Letters of Horace Walpole* (Oxford, 1904), vol. 11, no. 2388.

[3] Hoares Bank, ledger 76/27.

[4] Payment from Lord Waltham of £150, which on investigation elsewhere proved to be part of a commission at New Hall in Essex.

[5] Eileen Harris, introductory section to the facsimile of Wright's *Arbours & Grottos* (London, 1979).

[6] Jennifer Meir, *Sanderson Miller and his Landscapes* (Chichester, 2006), p. 15.

[7] This date has recently been established from an entry in the account books for Cusworth. DA: BW/E3/1.

[8] Entry by Keith Goodway in *The New DNB* (Oxford, 2004).

[9] Paul Langford, *A Polite and Commercial People: England 1727–83* (Oxford, 1989), p. 4.

[10] Richard Wilson and Alan Mackley, *Creating Paradise: the building of the English country house* (London, 2000), pp. 282–3.

[11] Tom Williamson, *Polite Landscapes* (Stroud, 1995) pp. 4–5.

[12] Letter from Sir Thomas Robinson to Lord Carlisle, 23 December 1734. Quoted in Timothy Mowl, *Gentlemen and Players* (Stroud, 2000), p. 117.

[13] Quoted in Mark Bence-Jones, *The Catholic Families* (London, 1992), p. 45.

[14] Langford, *Polite and Commercial People*, p. 291.

[15] All surviving Catholic registers have been transcribed, and are listed in Michael Gandy's five volumes of *The Catholic Missions and Registers* (Catholic Record Society, 1993/2002) covering the whole of England.

[16] House of Lords Record Office, reference no. 2249, contains the initial request from the House of Lords to the archbishops and bishops, their individual replies, and bundles of letters from parish priests.

[17] GRO: D540/E3. Nicholas Kingsley kindly drew my attention to this document.

[18] It is known that Webb maintained a domestic chapel from the seventeenth century, but no registers are extant.

[19] TNA: PRO: IR 1/50 p. 8, Apprenticeship Books kept by the Board of Stamps. I am indebted to Keith Goodway for this information.

[20] This is the spelling used for Southcote's property in his signed will of 1757 (ERO: D/DP/T358), although the second 'o' was later dropped.

[21] An article in *The Gentleman's Magazine* of May 1766 carried a report on Catholic children at school abroad. Discussed in Leo Gooch, 'The religion for a gentleman' in *Recusant History*, 23/4 (1997), p. 548, where the total number is estimated at about 750 in any one year.

[22] Surveys of Padworth in Berkshire in 1767; for Great Myles's in Essex in connection with a road diversion in 1778; and of Little Saling Farm in Essex in 1781.

[23] Nicholas Hans, *New Trends in Education in the Eighteenth Century* (London, 1951), p. 189.

[24] Catalogue of household effects sold by auction in 1783 when Woods left North Ockendon (Christies, London).

[25] See a steady flow of advertisements for various titles in, e.g., *The London Chronicle*, *The St James's Chronicle* and the main local newspapers such as the *Chelmsford Chronicle*.

[26] Woods retained a number of volumes (sold after his death, but with no titles given), which might have included further books on surveying.

[27] J. Anthony Williams, 'The distribution of Catholic chaplaincies c.1705', *Recusant History*, 12/1 (1973), p. 4.

[28] Letter quoted in J. Anthony Williams, '"Our Patriarch": Bishop Bonaventure Giffard', *Recusant History*, 26/3 (2003), p. 457.

[29] Gordon Rupp, *Religion in England, 1688–1791* (Oxford, 1986), p. 184.

[30] Brian Foley, *Some People of the Penal Times* (Lancaster, 1991), Appendix 8, p. 142.

[31] Frank Crisp, 'The Catholic Registers of Cheam', *Miscellanea*, 4 (Catholic Record Society, 1906).

[32] Frank Crisp, *The Registers of Woburn Lodge Chapel* (privately printed, 1888). The registers are very sparse, mainly baptismal, and start only in 1750.

[33] Joseph Hanson, 'The Catholic Registers of Isleworth', Catholic Record Society, *Miscellanea* 8 (1913).

[34] The Cheam mission was attached to the Portuguese Embassy from at least 1755, and from 1761 to 1768 was served by a priest sent direct from the Embassy.

[35] ERO: D/DP P145A. Discussed by Charles Clay, 'Father John Tempest S.J.' in *Essex Review* (1918), p. 81.

[36] Foley, *Some People*, p. 112.

[37] The case of Anne Fenwick of Hornby. See Rupp, *Religion*, p. 185.

[38] Foley, *Some People*, p. 109. The chapter on the 9th Baron Petre (pp. 105ff) describes Petre's efforts on behalf of his co-religionists.

[39] Foley, *Some People*, p. 111, where all the entries for the Oath Roll of 14 July 1778 are listed. The presence of Woods's name on this list alerted Nancy Briggs, then Assistant Archivist of Essex Record Office, to the fact that he was a Catholic, thus opening a whole new line of enquiry and research.

[40] Foley, *Some People*, p. 116, for the list of 1791.

[41] References to other commissions, which have not been traced, bring the number to about fifty.

[42] For instance, William Constable at Burton Constable; Lord Stourton at Stourton House; Thomas Fitzherbert at Swinnerton; Lord Clifford at Ugbrooke.

[43] See Bryan Little, *The Life and Work of James Gibbs, 1682–1754* (London, 1955) *passim*.

[44] Joseph Berington, *The State and Behaviour of English Catholics from the Reformation to the Year 1780* (London, 1780), pp. 121–2. The families are named in Bence-Jones, *The Catholic Families*, p. 32.

CHAPTER 2: INFLUENCES (pages 12–24)

[1] SHS: 2327/3/1.

[2] John Harvey, *Early Nurserymen* (London and Chichester, 1974), p. 97. The term 'nurseryman' was starting to come into use at this period, but 'gardener' was more commonly used to describe both activities. Timothy Oxley, advertising in *The Bath Journal* in October 1754, describes himself unusually as 'nurseryman and gardener', selling 'a great variety of fruit and forest trees'.

[3] Article on 25 June 1712. Henry Morley (ed.), *The Spectator* (London, n.d.), p. 598.

[4] Switzer had already in *The Practical Husbandman* (1733) talked of 'an ornamented

farm', but his descriptions do not follow the pattern of Southcote's creation. The additions to the first edition of *Ichnographia rustica* were probably written c.1729, although publication was delayed until 1742.

[5] The inclusion of arable fields within an intricate garden design can also be seen in Lord Petre's plan for Thorndon of 1733 (ERO: D/DP P23).

[6] Peter Martin, *The Gardening World of Alexander Pope* (Hamden, Connecticut, 1984), p. 134.

[7] Horace Walpole, 'History of the Modern Taste in Gardening' from *Anecdotes of Painting in England* (Twickenham, 1780, p. 42 in Ursus Press edition, New York, 1995); Peter Willis, *Charles Bridgeman and the English Landscape Park* (London, 1977), p. 102.

[8] James Osborn (ed.), *Joseph Spence's Observations, Anecdotes, and Characters of Books and Men collected from Conversation* (Oxford, 1966). These observations and sayings by and about his friends were not collated until this edition, and were therefore not available to eighteenth-century readers.

[9] For a full discussion of Southcote and Wooburn Farm see R. W. King, 'The "*ferme ornée*": Philip Southcote and Wooburn Farm', *Garden History*, 2/3 (1974), pp. 27–60.

[10] The earlier date is given by Spence in Observation no. 1126.

[11] (Sir) John Parnell, 'An Account of the many fine seats of nobles I have seen' etc. Folger Shakespeare Library, Washington, DC (MS M.a.11). Section on Wooburn Farm, pp. 159ff.

[12] Shenstone's letters (LXXXVII and LXXXIV) 1749. Quoted in Christopher Gallagher, 'The Leasowes: a history of the landscape', *Garden History*, 24/2 (1996), p. 206.

[13] Visit of 29 April 1757, BL Add. MS 23001, quoted by Laura Sayre, 'Locating the Georgic: from the *ferme ornée* to the model farm', *Studies in the History of Gardens and Designed Landscapes*, 22/3 (2002), p. 172.

[14] The James Marshall and Marie-Louise Osborn Collection, Beinecke Rare Book and Manuscript Library, Yale University. These papers are described and reproduced by R. W. King in articles on Southcote and Spence in *Garden History*, 2/3 (1974) and 8/3 (1980). This interpretation of the three Spence papers is accepted by Mark Laird in 'Ornamental planting and horticulture in English pleasure grounds 1700–1830', in John Dixon Hunt (ed.) *Garden History: Issues, Approaches, Methods* (Dumbarton Oaks, 1992), p. 251. Laird also discusses them in *The Flowering of the Landscape Garden* (Philadelphia, 1999), pp. 102–3.

[15] '… through the walk of flowering shrubs'; '… the walk of flowering shrubs is continued all round this cornfield'; '… the top of the hill has … different greens and flowering shrubs'.

[16] Laird, *Flowering*, p. 102.

[17] Parnell, 'An Account of the many fine seats', p. 169.

[18] George Mason, *An Essay on Design in Gardening* (London, 1768), p. 113.

[19] Sayre, 'Locating the Georgic', p. 169.

[20] E.g. see design for Nostell Priory (illustrated in Gervase Jackson-Stops, *An English Arcadia 1600–1990*, Washington D.C., 1991), p. 47, with 'A diagonal visto from the North Front Eastward' taking the eye right through the landscape into the countryside beyond.

[21] Anhalt Provincial State Library HS 10012. 'Travel notes from the year 1764' by Friedrich Wilhelm von Erdsmansdorff. Quoted by Thomas Weiss in 'J'eus le bonheur de vous accompagnez…' in *For the Friends of Nature and Art* (Ostfildern-Ruit, 1997), entry for 12 September, p. 51.

[22] Richard Sulivan, *Tour through Parts of England … in 1778* (London, 1785), vol. 1, p. 215; Richard Warner, *Excursion from Bath* (Bath and London, 1801), p. 150; John Claudius Loudon, *Notes of a Gardening Tour* (London, 1833), p. 504.

[23] The fields incorporated into Woods's design are Great and Little Voginton, with Homefield, Hawfield and Cow Pasture taken into parkland.

[24] William Mason, *The English Garden: a poem in four books* (London, 1772), lines 21–22.

[25] This is particularly noticeable in his plan for Brocklesbury, illustrated in Deborah Turnbull, 'Thomas White (1739–1811): Eighteenth-Century Landscape Designer and Arboriculturist' (unpublished PhD thesis, University of Hull, 1990), p. 449.

[26] Letter from Spence to the Rev. Mr Wheeler, 19 September 1751, transcribed in Spence, *Observations Anecdotes*, p. 645.

[27] Horace Walpole in a letter to George Montagu, 22 July 1751. Mrs Paget Toynbee (ed.), *The Letters of Horace Walpole* (Oxford, 1903), vol. 3, p. 66.

[28] Letter from Spence, 1750, quoted in King, 'The "*ferme ornée*"', p. 46, referring to Wooburn Farm, 'Where the old place of Paradise was I know not; but where the present is, I know full well.'

CHAPTER 3: IMPROVER, FARMER, SURVEYOR (pages 25–36)

[1] Ledgers for the years 1740–1760 have been searched in Childs, Drummonds and Hoares Banks, and where an entry for Rd Wood(s) has been found, the relevant estate has been investigated. Although ledgers survive for Coutts, searches may only be made of a known name.

[2] HALS: D/ERy P3.

[3] John Wright became 'Esq.' instead of 'Mr' in the middle of the ledger for 1761 at Hoares Bank.

[4] Westminster City Archives. A full range of various rate and tax books survive for St Anne's Soho for this period.

[5] LMA: Acc. 262/43/181, letter Woods to Thomas Wood of Littleton.

[6] *Survey of London: parish of St Anne, Soho*, vol. 34 (London, 1996), p. 508.

[7] *VCH Middlesex*, vol. 7 (1982), p. 59. See also *Plan of the Parish of Ealing*, 1777 (Chiswick Public Library, Local Studies Department) which gives the Chiswick boundaries and shows the area known as London Stile.

[8] There is no entry for Woods for this period in the Middlesex Deeds Registry. The inference is that his property was neither freehold nor a lease/copyhold of over twenty-one years, as the Registry only covers transactions relating to these categories. Woods's name is also absent from the Sutton Court Manor court rolls, although London Stile lay within the manor. This may be explained by the number of licences granted to major tenants to sub-let at will (Guildhall Library: MS 25343 'Copyhold properties within the Manor of Sutton Court, 1715–62').

[9] Macleod Yearsley (ed.), *Diary of the Visits of John Yeoman to London in 1774 and 1777* (London, 1934). Quoted in James Hamilton, *Turner: a life* (London, 1997), p. 14.

[10] The Kew/Twickenham/Isleworth area had contained several more nurseries between 1720 and 1750, and possibly Woods in 1762 felt that there was room for a new name.

[11] John Harvey, *Early Nurserymen* (London and Chichester, 1974), p. 83.

[12] See chapter 4 for a discussion of the nurserymen used by Woods.

[13] CBS: D/LE/D/6/2, letter William Lapidge the gardener to Sir William Lee, 16 November 1760.

[14] CBS: D/LE/11/10.

[15] The general practice was that the occupier rather than the owner of a property paid the rates, so that leaseholders as well as freeholders would be taxed, although the assessment was left largely to the discretion of the vestry. W. E. Tate, *The Parish Chest* (Cambridge, 1960), p. 28.

[16] WRO: CR 1998/box 57.

[17] WSHC: 2667/22/1B/3, letter Woods to Arundell, 20 December 1768.

[18] As n.17.

[19] Following Hardwicke's Marriage Act of 1753, no marriage was considered legal unless performed by an Anglican minister. Martha and James were married by licence at St Nicholas, Chiswick. I am indebted to Carolyn Hammond of Chiswick Local Studies Centre for photocopies of the entry.

[20] First reference to his assistant is in June 1766, letter to Lord Arundell (WSHC: 2667/22/1B/3). By the 1770s Ansell was living in St James's, where Woods mentions visiting him.

[21] The destruction of all the archive of Christie's in the war makes it impossible on current evidence to prove or disprove this theory. I am most grateful to Lynda McLeod, Librarian of Christie's archives, for help in trying to identify the various James Ansells.

[22] WSHC: 2667/22/1B/3.

[23] ERO: D/DBe/T10.

[24] WSHC: 2667/22/1B/3, agreement between Lord Arundell and Richard Woods 'of North Ockendon, surveyor', dated 16 July 1768.

[25] ERO: D/DBe/P5, with farm book E17 giving tenants' names, acreage and crops for 1782.

[26] WSHC: 2667/22/1B/3, letter of application for position of land steward.

[27] Colin Shrimpton, 'The Landed Society and the Farming Community of Essex in the late 18th and early 19th Centuries' (unpublished PhD thesis, Cambridge, 1965), p. 213.

[28] ERO: D/DBe/E49.

[29] WSHC: 2667/22/1B/3, letter 7 October 1769 to Haylock, the steward at Lulworth Castle, where Woods was working.

[30] WSHC: 2667/22/1B/2, letter Woods to Arundell, 17 April 1770.

[31] ERO: Acc. C47 Box 2.

[32] WSHC: 2667/22/1B/3.

[33] WSHC: 2667/22/1B/3.

[34] Arthur Brown, *Prosperity and Poverty: rural Essex 1700–1815* (Chelmsford, 1996), pp. 43–4.

[35] John Mordaunt, *The Complete Steward* (London, 1761), vol. 1, p. 364.

[36] ERO: D/DBe/Z1.

[37] The White family also appeared under North Ockendon but only by virtue of their main holding in South Ockendon.

[38] 'A Catalogue of all the Neat and Genuine Houshold [*sic*] Furniture etc.' 29 September 1783. Christie's, London.

[39] Brown, *Prosperity and Poverty*, p. 27.

[40] Arthur Young, *A Farmer's Tour through the East of England* (London, 1771), vol. 2, p. 240.

[41] Joseph Blagrave Gent, *Epitome of the Art of Husbandry* (London, 1670).

[42] Timothy Nourse, *Campania Foelix, or Improvements of Husbandry* (London, 1700).

[43] ERO: Acc. C47 Box 2, letter Woods to Colonel Rebow of Wivenhoe, 8 February 1780.

[44] WSHC: 2667/22/1B/3.

[45] ERO: Acc. C47 Box 2. Rebow complied with this request, and sent a draft on Childs bank for £20 as Woods had asked.

[46] J. Stratton, *Agricultural Records AD 220–1968* (London, 1969), p. 85. This useful volume describes the weather and other influences on farming year by year, and gives the annual price of wheat. In 1779 'all farm produce … fell to almost unprecedented levels, causing much distress among farmers.' The following year the price of wheat remained low.

[47] Advertisement in the *Chelmsford Chronicle*, 5 July 1793.

[48] *Chelmsford Chronicle*, 7 November 1783: 'For particulars enquire of Mr Woods, surveyor to the Rt Hon. Lord Petre at Thorndon Hall'. His salary is known from ERO:

D/DP A90, 'General Account Book, 1791–1804', the only surviving account book of this series.

⁴⁹ ERO: D/DP M1377 and M1378, Court Books for Ingrave Manor. 1736–69 and 1770–1838 respectively.

⁵⁰ ERO: Q/RPi 3, Land Tax assessments. Woods is first recorded in 1786 as 'Mr Woods for Youngs, 8/-'. Woods was the first owner-occupier of Maxes for some time.

⁵¹ ERO: D/DBe E57, assessment for Land Tax at North Ockendon, 1779.

⁵² ERO: D/DP E68.

⁵³ Notice of Sale, 8 July 1793, in *The Chelmsford Chronicle*.

⁵⁴ ERO: D/ABAc 24.

CHAPTER 4: PLANTS, PLANTING SCHEMES AND PLANT SUPPLIES (pages 38–71)

¹ I am deeply indebted to Mark Laird for reading and commenting on this chapter, and for advice and information given over the years.

² White wrote to Lord Stormont in 1784, 'One principal article of Expence seems to have been intirely overlook'd, which indeed is often the greatest in works that are upon a small scale, which is the Expence of planting.' Scone Palace Muniments, bundle 1401. Deborah Turnbull kindly supplied this reference.

³ Rev. Richard Warner, *Excursions from Bath* (Bath and London, 1801). The relative renown of Brown and Woods is obvious from this quotation.

⁴ Full description in Mark Laird, *The Flowering of the Landscape Garden* (Philadelphia, 1999), p. 83.

⁵ What Peter Collinson called 'painting with living pencils' in a letter to Southcote, 1752 (Linnean Society, Collinson MSS). See Douglas Chambers, *The Planters of the English Landscape Garden* (New Haven and London, 1993), p. 107.

⁶ The six are Brocket, Harewood, Irnham, Lulworth, Wardour and Wynnstay.

⁷ SA: Sp.St. 60633.

⁸ Identification of species has been taken primarily from John Harvey, *Availability of hardy plants of the late eighteenth century* (Garden History Society, 1988), supplemented by information from Mark Laird, and from W. J. Bean, *Trees and shrubs hardy in the British Isles*, 8th edn (London, 1976).

⁹ WSHC: 2667/22/1B/3, letter Woods to Arundell, 17 April 1770.

¹⁰ WSHC: 2667/22/1B/3.

¹¹ WSHC: 2667/21/12. The clumps shown on Ingman differ from those originally suggested on Woods's plan in being round instead of rectangular.

¹² DA DD/BW/H/163. The mix of trees in each section of the belt reads more like a survey than a design – e.g. '18 oaks, 1 ash'; '18 oaks, 1 holly'; '1 yew, 1 ash, 21 oaks' etc. The plan is dated January 1761, whereas Woods is first recorded at Cusworth in December that year.

¹³ DA: DD/BW/H/166.

¹⁴ Horace Walpole, *The History of the Modern Taste in Gardening* (Twickenham, 1780, but written during the 1750s and 1760s).

¹⁵ Roger Turner, *Capability Brown and the Eighteenth-Century Landscape* (Chichester, 1999), p. 135.

¹⁶ This subject is discussed by Laird, *Flowering*, pp. 63–4 and Chambers, *Planters*, p. 165.

¹⁷ DA: DD/BW/H/165.

¹⁸ R. W. King, 'Joseph Spence of Byfleet', in *Garden History*, 8/3 (1980), p. 96. Tod Longstaffe-Gowan describes Spence's grove-work as 'formed by intermixed (deciduous and evergreen) trees underplanted with flowering shrubs; sometimes "thick" or closely

planted, and sometimes "thin".' *The London Town Garden* (New Haven and London, 2001), p. 123.

[19] David Souden (ed.), *The Journals of the Hon. John Byng 1781–92* (London, 1991), p. 44. Entry for 3 July 1781.

[20] *A Short View of the Principal Seats and Gardens in and around Twickenham* (1760). Quoted in *Blessed Retreats* (London Borough of Richmond upon Thames, 1984), p. 37.

[21] There are virtually no accounts for Buckland, and the only near-contemporary map is dated 1803 (BRO: T/M 90/1).

[22] WRO: CR 1998/box 57.

[23] There is a discussion of the Buckland planting in Laird, *Flowering*, p. 154.

[24] John Hill, *Eden, or a Compleat Body of Gardening* (London, 1757). A description of the publication of *Eden* and Hill's career is in vol. 2 of Blanche Henrey, *British Botanical and Horticultural Literature before 1800* (Oxford, 1975), pp. 90–109.

[25] Ware: 'Let the plantation be made of selected trees … and let them have good distance. This space of planting will also give room for flowering shrubs, which may be scattered here and there about the walk.'
Hill: 'The great Error is in planting the Grove, in general, too close, and making the Walk too narrow … Flowering shrubs should be planted to edge the Walk.'

[26] Barry Williamson in his booklet *Lord Arundell's Park at Wardour* (1997) states that the Great Terrace was not the walk along the Hangings but the platform on which the house was later built. A close scrutiny of the documents makes this unlikely in the extreme, and the theory has been discounted here.

[27] WSHC: 2667/21/9.

[28] WSHC: 2667/22/1B/3.

[29] Richard Sulivan, *Tour through parts of England … in 1778* (London, 1785), vol. 1; Richard Warner, *Excursions from Bath* (Bath and London, 1801); John Claudius Loudon, *Notes of a Gardening Tour* (London, 1833).

[30] WSHC: 2667/21/12.

[31] The Boreham House archive is held by Hoares Bank, Tin Box 21.

[32] Bill of William Francis, carpenter, dated October 1763, referring to 'getting stakes ready for stakeing out the Pleasure Ground'. The bill covers the year's work.

[33] The list is reproduced in David Brown, 'Nathaniel Richmond (1724–1784), "Gentleman Improver"' (PhD thesis, University of East Anglia, 2000), p. 211.

[34] ERO: Acc. C47 Box 2, letter Woods to Rebow, 15 February 1780.

[35] R. B. Beckett (ed.), *John Constable's Correspondence* (Ipswich, 1960–68), vol. 2, letter of 21 August 1816. Quoted in Jonathan Clarkson and Neil Cox (eds), *Constable and Wivenhoe Park* (University of Essex, 1984), p. 33.

[36] This is well illustrated at Wivenhoe, where there are a few oaks and pines, possibly of Woods's planting, remaining in the plantation near the boathouse.

[37] This subject has been dealt with in great detail by Laird, *Flowering*, chapter 6, 'Flower Gardens before Nuneham', and chapter 8, 'The Shrubbery Perfected'.

[38] This extract is from the section on 'Borders', which started in 1731 as a description of parterres, but in the 8th edition of 1768 included this revised notion of a pleasure ground. There is no entry under that word.

[39] WSuRO: PHA 6623.

[40] The *Kalendar* had first been published in 1732, but from the 1754 edition was 'adapted to the new style'.

[41] Dorothy Stroud, *Capability Brown* (London and Boston, revised edition 1975), p. 93.

[42] The first use of the term is usually ascribed to Lady Luxborough or Shenstone, corresponding about planting at Barrels in 1748. The coining of the word is discussed in Laird, *Flowering*, p. 109.

[43] Hill, *Eden*, p. 612.

[44] John Rutter and Daniel Carter, *Modern Eden, or the Gardener's Universal Guide* (London, 1767), book 2, p. 200.

[45] SA: Sp.St. Map 101R.

[46] SA: Sp.St. 60673/6.

[47] Painting of the Elysium Garden, created 1780–83, one of a set of six by William Tomkins (1788) hanging in Audley End House (English Heritage).

[48] WYAS, Leeds: TN/EA19/1.

[49] CBS: D/LE/11/10. This list is reproduced in John Harvey, *Early Nurserymen* (London and Chichester, 1974), as Appendix XI(B).

[50] CBS: D/X 1045/1: Robert Weston, 'Plan of the Mansion House and Pleasure Ground' from a book of Hartwell estate maps 1776–7.

[51] The Hartwell planting is reviewed in Laird, *Flowering*, pp. 152–4. Laird suggests that the reason for ordering so many exotics in twos was an insurance against one of them failing.

[52] Laird, *Flowering*, p. 306.

[53] John Harvey, 'The Georgian garden: nurseries and plants', *Georgian Group Annual Report* (1986).

[54] The list on pp. 93–116 presents varieties by colour and name, and gives a description of each. Prices range from 6d to 15 guineas per bulb.

[55] A few copies were produced 'curiously coloured from nature', as that belonging to Joseph Banks in the British Library.

[56] Switzer, *Ichnographia rustica*, Preface p. xxxix.

[57] WSHC: 2667/12/148 and 2667/22/1B/3: Wardour House Book 1763–73, and memorandum of 15 March 1766.

[58] WSHC: 2667/20/21.

[59] By James Canter. The engraving is undated, but the costumes place it in the 1770s.

[60] A full discussion of the Old Wardour Castle garden, with illustration, is in Laird, *Flowering*, p. 229.

[61] SA: Sp.St. 60673/6.

[62] Richard Bradley, *New Improvements of Planting and Gardening* (London, 1717), p. 45.

[63] The list is reproduced in Harvey, *Nurserymen*, pp. 202–4. It was probably related to Francis Richardson's garden work at Welbeck: see Laird, *Flowering*, p. 121.

[64] The list is reproduced in Laurence Fleming and Alan Gore, *The English Garden* (London, 1979), p. 123.

[65] Laird, *Flowering*, p. 277, quoting 'Minutes of Mr Brown's proceedings', May 1766.

[66] Pendar's list is reproduced in Harvey, *Nurserymen*, pp. 194–5.

[67] William Hanbury, *Complete Body of Planting and Gardening* (London, 1770), book 1, p. 173f. It has to be admitted that it is difficult telling some of these varieties apart, and that in spite of his claims old rose varieties have a very limited flowering season.

[68] See John Harvey, *Early Gardening Catalogues* (Chichester, 1972), pp. 97 and 109; and *Nurserymen*, pp. 109, 187, 195, 201–3 and *passim*.

[69] Keith Goodway, 'William Emes and the flower garden at Sandon', *Garden History*, 24/1 (1996), p. 27.

[70] *Oxford English Dictionary* (Oxford, 1910). No examples are quoted between 1657 and 1815, and there is no entry under either spelling for this meaning in Dr Johnson's *Dictionary*.

[71] Eileen Harris (ed.), facsimile with introduction of Thomas Wright's *Arbours and Grottos*, 1755 and 1758 (1979), reproduction of the Badminton design in the Introduction (no pagination).

[72] Thomas Whately, *Observations on Modern Gardening*, published 1770 but written and probably circulating in manuscript form from 1765.

[73] An article by Hazel Le Rougetel, 'Old but sociable and oh so sweet', *Country Life* (1 July 1999), suggests planting old roses in this way.

[74] Discussed by King, 'Joseph Spence', p. 84.

[75] A full discussion of the progression of this type of design is given in Laird, *Flowering*, pp. 200–3 and 384–5, although slightly different conclusions are reached from those expressed here.

[76] Harvey's *Nurserymen* of 1974 remains the standard work on this subject, supplemented by articles, mostly by him, since that date. This section owes much to the information he has published.

[77] Harvey has calculated that in 1700 there were 15 nurseries 'of some standing' in greater London, and 'hardly any significant nurseries in the provinces'.

[78] For example, a single bill out of many for Blenheim amounted to £1400, and included among other plants 5900 'Hornbeam, privatt and Sweet Bryer' and 2219 'large Espalier Standard Limes': David Green, *Gardener to Queen Anne* (Oxford, 1956), p. 109.

[79] Henrey, *British Botanical … Literature*, vol. 2, pp. 632–3.

[80] Full information on Collinson and Bartram in Hilda Grieve, *A Transatlantic Gardening Friendship* (Historical Association, Essex Branch, 1981), pp. 9–25.

[81] John Claudius Loudon, *Arboretum et fruticetum britannicum* (London, 1838), vol. 1, p. 71. The 'hemlock spruce' *Tsuga canadensis* was introduced only in 1736 and would have been a rarity. This may be true of some of the pines, depending on variety. Wooburn Farm is mentioned among many other estates laid out at this period, including Painshill, Bowood, Strathfieldsaye [*sic*], Claremont, Oatlands and Ashley Park.

[82] Henrey gives a list of ten names from 'a careful study of the *Hortus Kewensis*'.

[83] Among eighteenth-century nurserymen, seedsmen and florists to publish were London and Wise, Switzer, Fairchild, Cowell, Hitt, Furber, Wheeler, Abercrombie, Boutcher and Maddock. Henrey's bibliographies list 376 horticultural and botanical titles published in the seventeenth century, and 1524 in the eighteenth.

[84] Richard Weston in *The Gardener's Pocket Calendar* of 1779 claimed that 'scarce a person, from the peer to the cottager, thinks himself tolerably happy without being possessed of a garden; in consequence of this, a gardener's calendar is become almost as necessary, in every family, as an almanac'.

[85] Chambers, *Planters*, p. 81.

[86] Letter for Sir Clement Cottrell, 15 February 1740/1, quoted in Ulrich Müller, 'Rousham: the steward's letters', *Garden History*, 25/2 (1997).

[87] Harvey, *Nurserymen*, p. 86: 'Thomas Emmerton of South Mimms was … very likely the Emerton who in the previous year [1762] had sent Weymouth pines to Cusworth.'

[88] SA: Sp.St. 60543, letter Thomas Peach to John Spencer: 'I think [Scott] has not acted the part of a Tradesman as I have sent to Leeds Wakefield and Barnsley to enquire several times about [the plants] to no purpose.'

[89] Henry Scott's trade card advertised that pineapple plants could be carried weekly on the Weybridge boats. Illustrated in John Plumb, *Georgian Delights* (Boston and Toronto, 1980), p. 61.

[90] E.g. charging for a visit to Hampton Court (Lowe) in August 1759 for Hartwell; choosing orange trees for Wardour at Sesarego's 1771; visiting a Sleaford nursery for Irnham 1769; plants sent 'by order of Mr Woods' from Hewitt's for Buckland 1759; visit to Perfects' for Cannon Hall 1763.

[91] Brown, 'Nathaniel Richmond', pp. 179ff. The estates mentioned include Lamer, Badminton, Stanmer and Chalfont House.

[92] 'His deep interest in the cultivation of trees and his practical experience in planting … brought him considerable respect and great satisfaction': Deborah Turnbull, 'Thomas White (1739–1811): Eighteenth-Century Landscape Designer and Arboriculturist' (PhD thesis, University of Hull, 1990). I am grateful to Deborah Turnbull for all the information below on White.

[93] Letter from Christopher Sykes of Sledmere, February 1776. Quoted in Turnbull, 'Thomas White', p. 218. Examples of places where such gardens are indicated are Lumley (1768), which has a 'shrub garden or a bowling green or both' in the design, and Norton (1772), which includes a 'shrub garden'; only Raith (1783) specifies 'flower gardens or one of the spaces may be a drying yard' – flowers not apparently being very high in the list of priorities; while Buchanan (1789), Ardoch (1792) and Abercairny (1793) all refer to a shrubbery or shrub garden.

[94] Scone Palace Muniments B667/17. The list, which includes forest trees as well as ornamentals, amounts to more than 5000 plants.

[95] For instance at Burton Constable: see Elizabeth Hall, '"Mr. Brown's Directions": Capability Brown's landscaping at Burton Constable', *Garden History*, 23/2 (1995), pp. 151, 156, 161, 166.

[96] Cusworth memorandum no. 4.

[97] John Phibbs, *The Assassination of Capability Brown* (Debois Landscape Survey Group, 1995). A list of 29 estates is given under the section on 'Conifers' where 'there is evidence of clumps and groups of conifers'.

[98] It should be noticed that Woods's use of the word 'firs' (except where otherwise specified) seems to approximate to the modern usage of 'conifers'. In the first memorandum he gives 'a word of advice relating to the firr plantations wch are grown up', and goes on to deal with the spruce firs, silver firs, scotch firs and larches which all need thinning.

[99] Hall, '"Mr Brown's Directions"', p. 160: September 1780 'Fill up the clumps with forest trees – too many Firs at present in those last planted'.

[100] Illustrated in Stroud, *Capability Brown*, plate 18a.

[101] Quoted in Stephen Bending, 'William Mason's "An Essay on the arrangement of Flowers in Pleasure-Grounds"', *Journal of Garden History*, 9/4 (1989), p. 219.

[102] Ann Smith, 'Sherborne Castle: new evidence from the archives', *The Local Historian* (November, 1995), p. 239; Janet Waymark, 'Sherborne Castle', *Garden History*, 29/1 (2001), p. 78.

[103] The painting by William Tomkins hanging in Audley End shows flower borders in the garden, but that was twenty years after it was originally laid out.

[104] WSHC: 1300/1913, quoted in Laird, *Flowering*, p. 277.

[105] Goodway, 'William Emes', p. 25.

[106] Brown, 'Nathaniel Richmond', p. 205.

[107] Brown, '"Nathaniel Richmond', p. 186.

[108] John Harris, 'A pioneer in gardening: Dickie Bateman re-assessed', *Apollo* (October 1993), pp. 227–33.

[109] Letter to Rev. Thomas Dyer 1775, quoted in Turner, *Capability Brown*, p. 79.

CHAPTER 5: WOODS THE ASPIRING ARCHITECT (pages 72–105)

[1] SRO: D590/619.

[2] Letter from Lord Coventry to Humphry Repton, quoted in Roger Turner, *Capability Brown and the Eighteenth-Century Landscape* (Chichester, 1999), p. 60. For the design, Brown may have had a helping hand from Sanderson Miller.

[3] No drawing for or of the Sea Seat has survived, but the Lamer alcove seat survives, with later alterations. David Brown, 'Nathaniel Richmond (1724–1784), "Gentleman Improver"' (PhD thesis, University of East Anglia, 2000), pp. 187 and 205.

[4] Deborah Turnbull, 'Thomas White (1739–1811): Eighteenth-Century Landscape Designer and Arboriculturalist' (PhD thesis, University of Hull, 1990), p. 440. Other references to summer-houses or temples occur on the plans for Brocklesbury, p. 447; Raby, p. 509; Arniston, p. 541; Old Melrose, p. 624; and Raith, p. 635. This is out of a total of nearly 50 known plans by White snr.

[5] Pers. comm. Keith Goodway.

[6] The buildings are at Alresford, Buckland, Haigh Hall, Irnham and Wardour; the bridges at Cannon Hall (2), Cusworth and Great Myles's. Parts of the cold bath, ice house and Gothick temple at Wardour survive in new guises.

[7] This subject is exhaustively discussed in Eileen Harris assisted by Nicholas Savage, *British Architectural Books and Writers, 1556–1785* (Cambridge, 1990), which has been used for much of the background information in this chapter.

[8] For instance, George Edwards and Matthias Darly, *A New Book of Chinese Designs* (London, 1754); Wrighte, *Grotesque Architecture or Rural Amusement* (London, 1768); Paul Decker, *Chinese Architecture* and *Gothic Architecture* (both London, 1759); and some of the Halfpennys' publications.

[9] In the section 'An Essay of a Country House', pp. 318ff, in which he described his ideal house and its setting.

[10] For a full discussion of the effect of the Grand Tour on garden design in England see John Dixon Hunt, *Garden and Grove* (Philadelphia, 1986). Also Cesare de Seta, *Grand Tour: the lure of Italy in the eighteenth century* (Tate Gallery catalogue, 1996), pp. 13–21.

[11] John Ingamells, *Dictionary of British and Irish Travellers in France and Italy, 1701–1800* (New Haven and London, 1997) lists all the known eighteenth-century Grand Tourists, numbering some 6000.

[12] Earlier examples of classical temples can be found, e.g. at Narford, Norfolk (from 1718), and Baroque architects like Gibbs and Archer had built them, but even at a high social level temple-building only gained real momentum in the 1730s. John Harris cites Castle Howard, copying Ancient Rome rather than Palladio, as the first 'templescape' (Summer Conference 2004, Bristol University and the Garden History Society).

[13] Tobias Smollett, *Travels through France and Italy* (Dublin, 1766), book 2, p. 110.

[14] Remark by Horace Walpole, 22 August 1761, *Journals of Visits to Country Seats* (Walpole Society, 1927/28), vol. 16, p. 36. Walpole considered that Gothic designs should imitate 'something that was of that time' including a mansion, but did not recognise that Strawberry Hill was as much of an anachronism as the Painshill temple.

[15] (Sir) John Parnell, 'An Account of the many fine seats of nobles I have seen' etc. Folger Shakespeare Library, Washington, DC (MS M.a.11), pp. 97–8.

[16] A Mannerist motif illustrated by Serlio, taken up in England by Inigo Jones and then again in the early eighteenth century. I am grateful to Ian Sutton for observations on the style of Serlio.

[17] Beckford acquired the estate in 1745, and Pococke commented on the gateway in 1754. No more precise date for its construction has yet been found. See Timothy Mowl, 'Inside Beckford's Landscape of the Mind', *Country Life* (7 February 2002).

[18] Retitled for the 1747 edition as *Gothic Architecture, Improved by Rules and Proportions*. See the entry for Batty Langley in Eileen Harris, assisted by Nicholas Savage, *British Architectural Books and Writers, 1556–1785* (Cambridge, 1990), p. 271.

[19] Timothy Lightoler, *The Gentleman's and Farmer's Architect* (London, 1762), plate 25. There is also considerable similarity between Lightoler's designs for stables in this book (which had also been included in the Halfpennys' *Modern Builder's Assistant* (London, 1757) as plate 63), and those by Woods for Wardour.

[20] George Mason, *An Essay in Design on Gardening* (London, 1768), p. 26. He was referring to Temple's *Upon the Gardens of Epicurus* … (London, 1692 in part 2 of his *Miscellanea*).

[21] Probably the first built 'China house' was that at Stowe, described by a visitor in 1738. Kent's kiosk designs for Esher Place were even earlier, 1733–40.

[22] 'Description of the Villa of Mr Horace Walpole' in *The Works of Horace Walpole*, 1798. Quoted in Patrick Conner, *Oriental Architecture in the West* (London 1979), p. 57.

[23] Quoted in Conner, *Oriental Architecture*, p. 45.

[24] Charles Over, *Ornamental Architecture in the Gothic, Chinese and Modern Taste* (London, 1758). For instance, compare plates 24 and 33.

[25] Illustrated in *Country Life* (9 June 1983), in a letter by Eileen Harris, who discovered it in the Avery Library, New York.

[26] Thomas Pennant, *The Journey from Chester to London* (London, 1782). Quoted in Mavis Batey and David Lambert, *The English Garden Tour* (London, 1990), p. 178.

[27] I am grateful to John Phibbs for this information.

[28] See the engraving 'A View of Twickenham' 1756, John Green after J. H. Müntz. Illustrated in Anthony Beckles Willson, 'Crossdeep House', in *Mr Pope and Others* (Twickenham, 1996).

[29] ERO: D/DHt B1.

[30] ERO: Acc. C47 Box 2.

[31] In the sensitive ownership of Sir William and Lady Boulton, to whom I am indebted for help and information.

[32] Fate has recently given Woods an unacknowledged tribute in the form of a new 'Chinese Temple' on the banks of the lake at Abbots Ripton. The architect was Peter Foster, who based the idea on Constable's painting without even being aware of Woods's existence.

[33] See the painting by Arthur Devis, dated to just before 1755, illustrated in Mowl, 'Inside Beckford's Landscape', p. 61. The rotondo was noted by Pococke.

[34] May Woods and Arete Warren, *Glasshouses: a history of greenhouses, orangeries and conservatories* (London, 1988) p. 13.

[35] Queen Henrietta Maria's 'large garden house … fitted for the keepinge of Oringe trees' at Wimbledon. Woods and Warren, *Glasshouses*, p. 19. John Parkinson's *Paradisus Terrestris* of 1629 describes keeping orange trees by 'causing them to be rowled by trundels … [into] an house, or close gallery for the winter time'. Alternatively, they could be placed against a wall and defended 'by a shed of boards, covered over with sear-cloth … and by the warmth of a stove … give them some comfort in the colder times.'

[36] Woods and Warren, *Glasshouses*, p. 33.

[37] Richard Bradley published a design in *The Gentleman and Gardener's Kalendar* in 1718 for a greenhouse with a partially-glazed cupola, but was well ahead of general practice. Woods and Warren, *Glasshouses*, p. 57.

[38] Woods and Warren, *Glasshouses*, p. 61: 'Hot-house ranges or stove houses were widespread by the 1760s and 1770s; they were always hidden from the house and the landscaped park because of their functional appearance.' The distinction is nicely illustrated on Rocque's 'Plan of the House Gardens Park and Plantations of Wanstead' (1735), where the highly decorative greenhouse faces a formal lawn, while the stoves are in the kitchen garden. See Sally Jeffery, 'The gardens of Wanstead House' in Katherine Myers (ed.), *Proceedings of a Study Day … at Wanstead Park* (London Parks and Gardens Trust, 25 September 1999), figure 22. By 1776 the novelty had worn off, and John Kennedy in his *Treatise upon … the Management of the Hot House*, p. 273, claimed that 'the pine stove is now introduced into almost every house'.

[39] Engraving after Rysbrack c.1735, illustrated in T. Cashmore, D. Simpson and A. Urwin (eds.), *Alexander Pope's Twickenham* (Borough of Twickenham Local History Society, 1988), plate 20.

[40] WYAS Bradford: Sp.St./5/2/4, copy letter John Stanhope to Woods, 14 May 1760.

[41] SA: Sp.St. 60633/13, diary of John Spencer for 1760.

[42] The greenhouse has been called, and used as, the Camellia House since the early nineteenth century.

[43] The painting by Thomas Robins the elder of the greenhouse at Woodside c.1750 is widely illustrated. A good reproduction can be found in Woods and Warren, *Glasshouses*, p. 74.

[44] Charles Over in *Ornamental Architecture* gives elevation, section and plan of an ice house, with a note that 'The Entrance may serve well for a Grotto'. This effect is achieved in Woods's ice house at Buckland.

[45] DRO: D/WLC/P86.

[46] HALS: Acc. 3898, no. 4. I am grateful to Tom Williamson for this information, and to Anne Rowe for the references. The archive is held at Beechwood Park, but notes and photocopies have been deposited in HALS by the Hertfordshire Gardens Trust.

[47] Sylvia Beamon and Susan Roaf, *The Ice Houses of Britain* (London and New York, 1990), p. 362.

[48] By Dr William Turner in 1562. See Susan Kellerman, 'Bath houses: an introduction', *Follies Journal*, 1 (2001), p. 21.

[49] John Floyer, *Psykhroloysia, or a History of Cold Bathing*, 3rd edn, with additions (London, 1709), p. 278.

[50] Quoted in *The Oxford Companion to Gardens* (Oxford, 1986), p. 41. For a description of the grotto and its bath at Oatlands see Michael Symes, *Fairest Scenes: five great Surrey gardens* (Elmbridge Museum Service, 1988), pp. 30–3.

[51] Described by Benge Burr in 1766; see Kristina Taylor, 'The oldest surviving pleasure garden in Britain: cold bath near Tunbridge Wells in Kent', *Garden History*, 28/2 (2000), pp. 277–82.

[52] Washington State University Library. Photocopies in ERO: Temp. Acc. 39.

[53] WSHC: 2667/22/1B/3. The cold bath survives in altered form as Ark Farm, with the portico moved to the side of the building.

[54] Letter of 14 May 1741, quoted in Anthony Willson, 'Alexander Pope's grotto in Twickenham', *Garden History*, 26/1 (1998), p. 45.

[55] Illustrated in Gervase Jackson-Stops, *An English Arcadia 1600–1990* (Washington D.C., 1991), p. 55.

[56] Plan and elevation: DA: DD/BW/H/167; memorandum no. 2, DD/BW/H/105.

[57] Flints were also used to face the brick structure of the bridge at Hare Hall (Romford, Essex), described as a 'stone bridge'.

[58] ERO: Acc. C47 Box 2.

[59] WSHC: 2667/22/1B/3: letter Woods to Arundell, 10 January 1770.

[60] SA: Sp.St. 60633/17: diary of John Spencer for 1764.

[61] Stephen Wright, 'Bretton: the Beaumonts and a bureaucracy', in *Wakefield Historical Publications* (2001), pp. 19 and 25.

[62] Pers. comm. Michael Symes. See his book on *Garden Bridges* (Wallington, 2007), pp. 23ff.

[63] DA: DD/BW/H/113, memorandum to foreman, 19 September 1764.

[64] Brown, 'Nathaniel Richmond', p. 141.

[65] English Heritage, Audley End House.

[66] WSHC: 2667/22/1B/3: letter Woods to Arundell 24 April 1769.

[67] James Marshall and Marie-Louise Osborn Collection, Beinecke Rare Book and Manuscript Library, Yale University: 'Hints for Wardour' given by Joseph Spence, 29 July 1763.

[68] WSHC: 2667/22/1B/3.

[69] Richard Haslam, 'Irnham Hall, Lincolnshire', *Country Life* (15 May 1986).

[70] The estimate specifies a 'noble drawing room 40ft [12m] long by 21ft [6.4m] wide and 18ft [5.4m] high' but with only a single Venetian window, whereas the vignette shows two. Richard Haslam's article describes the drawing room as 'gilded'.

CHAPTER 6: THE WOODS LANDSCAPE (pages 106–144)

[1] David Brown, 'Nathaniel Richmond (1724–1784), "Gentleman Improver"' (PhD thesis, University of East Anglia, 2000), p. 270.

[2] Quoted in Dorothy Stroud, *Capability Brown* (London and Boston, revised edition 1975), pp. 98–9. Letter Arundell to Brown, 16 August 1773.

[3] ERO: D/DP P30.

[4] WSHC: 2667/21/10 (Woods's plan); 2667/21/13 (Brown's plan).

[5] DA: DD/BW/H/104–110.

[6] Lamer Red Book, quoted in Brown, 'Nathaniel Richmond', p. 189.

[7] Letters from Mary Rebow to her husband, in Washington State University Library. Photocopies in ERO: Temp. Acc. 39.

[8] Quoted in Stroud, *Capability Brown*, p. 90.

[9] Quoted in Stroud, *Capability Brown*, p. 159.

[10] Quoted in Thomas Hinde, *Capability Brown: the story of a master gardener* (London, 1986), p. 162.

[11] For example: White in 1781 spent 'four days looking at the grounds about Scone'; Woods and John Spencer went the rounds of Cannon Hall together for three days 'viewing, planning etc.'.

[12] Although all the improvers were surveyors in their own right, and on occasion undertook that work themselves – as Woods in his later plans and White at e.g. Abercairny – in general they employed someone else.

[13] WSHC: 2667/12/148, Wardour house accounts 1763–78.

[14] The bill for Woods's very large plan has not been found. The statement of accounts kept by Woods starts in 1765; the first estate account ledger in 1767; and the house book records only payments made through the steward.

[15] Noted down by Lord Bruce in 1764, quoted in Stroud, *Capability Brown*, p. 93.

[16] WSHC: 2667/22/1B/3.

[17] DA: DD/BW/H/162 and 163.

[18] Quoted in Deborah Turnbull, 'Thomas White (1739–1811): Eighteenth-Century Landscape Designer and Arboriculturist' (PhD thesis, University of Hull, 1990), p. 242.

[19] Anthea Taigel and Tom Williamson, 'Some early geometric gardens in Norfolk', *Journal of Garden History*, 11/1 & 2 (1991), p. 64.

[20] CRO: Red Book for Catchfrench, 1793.

[21] Elisabeth Whittle, *The Historic Gardens of Wales* (Cadw, 1992), p. 47.

[22] WYAS Leeds: Harewood papers, steward's outward letters, book 5. Popplewell to Lascelles, March 1766.

[23] Stroud, *Capability Brown*, p. 105. A dam was also needed to raise the level of the Derwent for the same reason.

[24] Hoares Bank, Archives for Boreham House, Tin Box 21.

[25] ERO: D/DHt B1.

[26] Letter to Sir Horace Mann, 22 October 1771. Mrs Paget Toynbee (ed.), *Letters of Horace Walpole* (Oxford, 1903), vol. 8, p. 96.

[27] WYAS Leeds: TN/EA 19/1.

[28] Letter to George Montagu, 4 July 1760. Toynbee, *Letters of Horace Walpole*, vol. 4, p. 405.

[29] Turnbull, 'Thomas White', p. 107.

[30] James Parnell, 'An Account of the many fine seats of nobles I have seen' etc. Folger Shakespeare Library, Washington DC (MS Ma.a.11), p. 106.

[31] Switzer, *Ichnographia Rustica*, vol. 2, p. 155.

[32] ERO: D/DHt B1.

[33] Turnbull, 'Thomas White', p. 253.

[34] Stroud, *Capability Brown*, p. 120.

[35] ERO: D/DHt B1.

[36] WYAS Leeds: TN/C/23a.

[37] Lord Coventry to Brown, 21 November 1772: 'The head is faulty, my conjurors have tried to rectify it, but find the work beyond their skill.' Quoted in Stroud, *Capability Brown*, pp. 59–60.

[38] Popplewell to Edwin Lascelles, 1777. Quoted in Hinde, *Capability Brown*, p. 161.

[39] Judith Roberts, 'Cusworth Park: the making of an eighteenth-century designed landscape', *Landscape History*, 21 (1999).

[40] This deduction was made from examination of conditions on site.

[41] Steffie Shields, 'Mr. Brown, engineer', *Lincolnshire Gardens Trust Newsletter* (May 2003), pp. 11–18.

[42] Other relevant titles include the second volume of John Theophilus Desaguliers' *Course of Experimental Philosophy* (London, 1744), and the older publication by Salomon de Caus, *Les Raisons des forces mouvantes* (Frankfurt, 1615).

[43] This largest of Woods's ponds would have been about 8 acres, calculated by comparison with the known size of the Great Pond.

[44] Illustrated in John Dixon Hunt, *William Kent: landscape garden designer* (London, 1987) e.g. pp. 119, 125, 126, 165.

[45] Anonymous account, 1738. Quoted by George Clarke, in *Descriptions of Lord Cobham's Gardens at Stowe 1700–1750* (Buckinghamshire Record Society, 1990), p. 67.

[46] WSHC: 2667/22/1B/3, letter Woods to Arundell, 11 December 1770.

[47] Vol. 11 by the Rev. John Evans, quoted in Stroud, *Capability Brown*, p. 183.

[48] See, for instance, the approach to Hylands (Essex), where a plantation was made to hide the house from the road and force the route into a curve. This concept is replicated in many places.

[49] ERO: D/DFa E43/38 for the profile of a turnpike on Woods's plan accompanying the road diversion application at Great Myles's in 1778, where he drew a section through the proposed new road (see Figure 75).

[50] WSHC: 2667/22/1B/3, letter Woods to Arundell, 24 April 1769.

[51] Turnbull, 'Thomas White', p. 258.

[52] See the discussion in John Phibbs, *The Assassination of Capability Brown* (Debois Landscape Survey Group, 1995), under 'Approaches' and 'Formality'.

[53] Brown, 'Nathaniel Richmond', pp. 126, 146.

[54] Annette Bagot, 'Monsieur Beaumont and Col. Grahme: the making of a garden', *Garden History*, 3/4 (1975).

[55] Illustrated in the engraving after Rigaud, where it is shown with a low retaining wall.

[56] Parnell mentions it in the account of his 1769 visit: 'the original fencing round the fields was a small trench and very low cheveux de frize scarcely higher than the bank. this has now decayed and the present gardener has deepened the trenches and taken away the cheveux de frize, making the bank to the field much steeper.' Quoted in James Sambrook, 'Wooburn Farm in the 1760s', *Garden History*, 7/2 (1979), p. 98.

[57] Thomas Whately, *Observations on Modern Gardening* (London, 1770), p. 8.

[58] Horace Walpole, 'The History of the Modern Taste in Gardening' in *Anecdotes of Painting in England* (Twickenham, 1780), p. 43 in Ursus Press edition (New York, 1995).

[59] Hall, Elizabeth, '"Mr. Brown's Directions": Capability Brown's landscaping at Burton Constable', *Garden History*, 23/2 (1995), p. 168.

[60] Turnbull, 'Thomas White', p. 255.

[61] Brown, 'Nathaniel Richmond', p. 233.

[62] WSHC: 2667/22/1B/3 for all Wardour and Irnham references.

[63] ERO: Acc. C47 Box 2, letter of 15 February 1780.

[64] WYAS Leeds: Harewood Maps 25/56, survey of Goldsborough by Thomas Pattison.

[65] WYAS Leeds: TN/EA/19/1.

[66] WYAS Calderdale: KMA 736.

[67] ERO: D/DEl P9, survey by Timothy Skynner, 1766.

[68] This is also true of circular gardens. I am grateful to Susan Campbell for providing this information.

[69] Quoted in Sambrook, 'Wooburn Farm', pp. 97–8.

[70] See Susan Campbell, *Charleston Kedding: a history of kitchen gardening* (London, 1996), p. 25.

[71] CBS: D/LE/11/10.

[72] CBS: D/X/1045. Robert Weston, 'Plan of the Mansion House and Pleasure Ground' from a book of surveys, 1776.

[73] These walls were heightened in the nineteenth century and now look out of proportion with the rest of the garden.

[74] This is mentioned in *Aedes Hartwellianae* as either the 'Shepherd's Bower' or 'Green Arbour' – as no orientation is given, it is not clear which is which.

[75] The relative positions of greenhouse and pinery have recently been mistakenly transposed by Eric Throssell in *Flowers in the Landscape* (Bucks Gardens Trust with the Georgian Group, 2006), p. 30. There is no evidence whatsoever that the rectangular building marked on Weston's map was a 'temple of Flora' as designed by Throssell.

[76] CBS: D/LE/11/21. Agreement between J. Margesson and Sir William Lee, 5 April 1798.

[77] Probably Lady Elizabeth Lee's flower garden of 1799.

[78] HALS: D/EP P15, survey by William Pallett, 1798. As there are no entries in the accounts for work on the grounds after Woods's departure in 1775, this survey may be assumed to show the garden layout as Woods left it.

[79] Fiona Cowell, 'Richard Woods, a preliminary study', *Garden History*, 14/2 (1986). The building now in the place of the pinery was probably designed by Thomas Allason following a visit to Greece with the young Spencer Stanhope boys at the end of the eighteenth century.

[80] This can be dated to between 1766, when Woods was paid off, and 1794, when the wings were raised, but is most likely to have been painted before Spencer's death in 1775.

[81] SA: Sp.St. 124R. *The Manor of Cawthorne* by John Walker, 1839.

[82] As shown on the survey 'with improvements by Richard Woods' (SA: Sp.St. Maps 102) which covers the park and outlying fields to the north. Acreage taken from the second edition 25-inch Ordnance Survey.

[83] See Laird, *Flowering of the Landscape*, p. 218.

CHAPTER 7: LABOUR DEMAND, SUPPLY AND ORGANISATION IN THE EIGHTEENTH-CENTURY GARDEN (pages 145–162)

[1] From hearth-tax returns the figure for the 1670s is some 75 per cent of the population (the calculation is based on the assumption that one- to three-hearth households would have been occupied by plebeian families): Robert Malcolmson, *Life and Labour in England 1700–1780* (London, 1981), pp. 18–19. The figure is likely to hold for the period 1700–75, or even be an underestimate. Dividing classes into those

able to pay the poor-rate, and those likely to be a recipient of benefit – the 'labouring' class – gives a similar result for the mid eighteenth century of between two-thirds and three-quarters of the population (depending on locality and other factors): Paul Langford, *A Polite and Commercial People* (Oxford, 1989), pp. 62–3.

[2] Tom Williamson, *The Transformation of Rural England* (Exeter, 2002), pp. 178–9.

[3] ERO: Acc. C47 Box 2, letters Lupton to Rebow, 29 May and 18 May 1780 respectively.

[4] Although an unusual advertisement in the *Chelmsford Chronicle* of 15 September 1769 suggests that the knowledge required might sometimes be quite superficial: 'Wanted, a Coachman who understands something of gardening as he must work in the Kitchen Garden and no Gardener is kept'.

[5] *Chelmsford Chronicle*, 21 April 1769.

[6] Keith Snell, *Annals of the Labouring Poor* (Cambridge, 1985). Several tables illustrating the regional differences in wages, and the way in which they relate to the 'price of composite units of consumables', pp. 29–35.

[7] Tehidy Gardens, Cornwall is the only estate for which a detailed study has been made: A. D. Boney, 'Wages and working days of labourers', *Devon and Cornwall Notes and Queries*, 39/4 (2003).

[8] WYAS Leeds: TN/EA/23a/31, letter 31 October 1767, White to Stones, working at Newby. Information about White in this chapter is taken from Deborah Turnbull, 'Thomas White (1739–1811): Eighteenth-Century Landscape Designer and Arboriculturist' (PhD thesis, University of Hull, 1990).

[9] CBS: D/LE/11/15/2 and D/LE/11/20/1 respectively.

[10] In Norfolk in the 1790s, the labourers on Randall Burroughes's farm were earning 1s 4d in the winter and 1s 6d in the summer. Susanna Wade Martins and Tom Williamson (eds), *Farming Journal of Randall Burroughes* (Norfolk Record Society, 1995), pp. 33–5.

[11] Lupton by this date was reporting directly to Rebow, not via Woods.

[12] CBS: D/X 1212/3.

[13] WYAS Calderdale: KMA 732/15/1.

[14] Gordon Mingay, *Social History of the English Countryside* (London, 1990), p. 96.

[15] Of the names on the worksheets for Hartwell, five appear from 1763 to 1766, although none is continuously employed. This point is made with reference to farm workers in Wade Martins and Williamson, *Randall Burroughes*, pp. 32–5.

[16] Susanna Wade Martins and Tom Williamson, 'Labour and improvement: agricultural change in East Anglia, c.1750–1870', *Labour History Review*, 62/3 (1997), p. 280; and Malcolmson, *Life and Labour*, p. 45.

[17] Adam Smith, *Wealth of Nations*, quoted in Malcolmson, *Life and Labour*, p. 45.

[18] *The Natural History of Selborne* (1789); letter XXVI, November 1775.

[19] Arthur Young, *A Farmer's Tour through the East of England* (1771), vol. 2, *passim*, e.g. pp. 22, 73, 204, 231.

[20] Roger North, *A Discourse on the Poor*, 1753 (but written c.1690), quoted in B. A. Holderness, '"Open" and "close" parishes in England in the eighteenth and nineteenth centuries', *Agricultural History Review*, 20 (1972), pp. 126–39.

[21] Holderness, '"Open" and "close" parishes', p. 126.

[22] *The Practical Husbandman and Planter*, vol. 1 (London, 1733).

[23] Timothy Nourse, *Campania Foelix, or Improvements of Husbandry* (1700), in the section 'An Essay of a Country Estate' p. 332.

[24] WSHC: 2667/22/1B/3.

[25] ERO: Acc. C47 Box 2.

[26] E.g. at Wardour, April 1765: 'I have wrote to Simpson [the foreman] & ordered him (immediately) to reduce the hands to the num^r of 20, so yt the weekly account … will

not exceed £8'; at Irnham, August 1768: 'be assured yt. I get up the lost time by imploying more hands, so yt. your work shall be exicuted within the proper time'; at Wivenhoe, Jan 1778: 'the Col. had stoped his works at present he not having wood soficient to compleat his fences'.

[27] ERO: Acc. C47 Box 8.

[28] WYAS Leeds: TN/EA/23a/31. The advertisement, for which the employer's approval was first to be asked, sought 'a number of labourers to work either by the day or by measure, the work is very dry and good encouragement will be given to good hands.'

[29] WSHC: 2667/22/1B/3, letter Woods to Arundell, 16 October 1769.

[30] *Picturesque Views of the Principal Seats of the Nobility and Gentry*, published by Harrison and Co. (London, 1786), no pagination.

[31] Arthur Brown, *Prosperity and Poverty: rural Essex 1700–1815* (Chelmsford, 1996), p. 69.

[32] WSHC: 2667/22/1B/3.

[33] Hoares Bank archives, Tin Box 21.

[34] WSHC: 2667/22/1B/3, letter Woods to Arundell, 20 December 1768. This carpenter commanded £30 a year with board and lodging, compared with the annual wage of a head gardener, which was unlikely to be above £20.

[35] ERO: D/DHt B1, letter Woods to Rebow, 30 June 1776.

[36] Anthony Burton, *The Canal Builders* (London, 1972), pp. 157, 160.

[37] WYAS, Leeds: TN/EA/23a/31, letter White to Stones, 31 October 1767.

[38] John Stevenson, *Popular Disturbances in England, 1700–1870* (London, 1979), pp. 68, 112.

[39] WSHC: 2667/22/1B/3.

[40] WSHC: 2667/22/1B/3, letter Woods to Arundell, 11 April 1769. The foreman was 'gone to York upon a Tryall, to which he was suppearnid by Mr Lascelles'.

[41] ERO: D/DBe Z1. The 'Barstable and Chafford Association', printed minutes of the first meeting.

[42] See a local diary entry in 1772 illustrating the point: 'The mobb was up in all the towns around us upon acct. of provisions been so very deer … Some places took the corn and made the farmer bring it to town and sell it at there price' in Arthur Brown, *Essex People* (Chelmsford, 1972), p. 45. This was by no means an isolated incident.

[43] Washington State University Library. Photocopies of originals in ERO: Temp. Acc. C39.

[44] Hoares Bank, Boreham archive, Tin Box 21.

[45] WSHC: 2667/22/1B/3, letter Woods to Arundell, 16 October 1769. This also occurred at Wivenhoe, where Lupton wrote in late 1778 'am afraid wee shall be put to a stand for horses but don't want much carting at present'. ERO: Acc. C47 Box 2.

[46] WSHC: 2667/22/1B/3, letter Woods to Arundell, 24 April 1769.

[47] WSHC: 2667/22/1B/3, at Wardour.

[48] Agent's report to Stormont, quoted in Turnbull, 'Thomas White', p. 255.

[49] Lewis Majendie of Hedingham Castle, replying to the editor's letter in *Annals of Agriculture*, 1796. Quoted in Wade Martins and Williamson, *Randall Burroughes*, p. 33 and n. 81.

[50] Wade Martins and Williamson, *Randall Burroughes*, p. 59: Burroughes considered that weeding a certain field cost him 6s by piece work and 8s on day rates (entry for 8 June 1795).

[51] WSHC: 2667/22/1B/3, undated memorandum to Arundell (c.1769).

[52] ERO: Acc. C47 Box 2, letter Lupton to Rebow, 3 April 1780.

[53] For example, 'To Starling & Co, for wheeling Clay … 261 barrowfulls at one halfpenny pr. barrow full – 10s 10d' (July 8–14); or 'Thos. Starling, 4¾ days at 1s 4d … 6s 4d.' (July 29–August 4).

[54] David Brown, 'Nathaniel Richmond (1724–1784), "Gentleman Improver"' (PhD thesis, University of East Anglia, 2000). Hencher nevertheless retained his independence, and worked for others as well as Richmond.

[55] SA: Sp.St. 60543, letter of 23 April 1763.

[56] WYAS Leeds: Harewood papers, steward's outward letters, book 5. Popplewell to Edwin Lascelles, 12 and 20 May 1765.

[57] White to Stormont, June 1784, quoted in Turnbull, 'Thomas White', p. 280.

[58] A letter from Wardour (Wiltshire) to North Ockendon (Essex) took a week in September 1768; from Wivenhoe to North Ockendon (both Essex) took up to five days in June 1779.

[59] CBS: D6/2, letter of 16 November 1760.

[60] WYAS, Leeds: WYL100/EA/19/1.

[61] White to Stormont, late June 1784, quoted in Turnbull, 'Thomas White' p. 243.

[62] See, for instance, his promise to William Constable that he 'would come if he could' to Burton Constable.

[63] ERO: Acc. C47 Box 2.

[64] Hoares Bank, Boreham House archive, Tin Box 21.

[65] DA: DD/BW/E3/1. General Account Book of Steward, under page entitled 'Foreman'.

[66] WYAS Leeds: WYL100/EA/19/1.

[67] WYAS Leeds: TN/EA/23a/*passim*.

[68] WSHC: 2667/22/1B/3.

[69] Brown to Lord Bruce 21 September 1765, quoted in Dorothy Stroud, *Capability Brown* (London and Boston, revised edition 1975), p. 94.

[70] CBS: D/LE/D6/1. An informer told Lord Essex that Lapidge had taken 'a few runaway greens' from the kitchen garden as he had been allowed to do under the Dowager Countess. When Lapidge discovered that the informer was a man he had previously befriended and helped, 'it caused a few words' for which affray he was dismissed.

[71] LMA: Acc. 262/43/188.

[72] WSHC: 2667/22/1B/3.

[73] ERO: D/DHt/B1.

[74] NLW: Wynnstay R 42.

[75] Pers. comm. Keith Goodway.

[76] WSHC: 2667/19/3. Reference to 'Mr Creswell's house at Bridzer' in 1773.

[77] WSHC: 2667/12/148.

[78] WYAS Leeds: Harewood papers, steward's outward letters book 5, Popplewell to Lascelles, 1 May 1765. Woods had already tried in March to send Sparrow to Wardour 'as soon as the planting season is over'.

[79] Hanging in Lartington Hall.

[80] Hall, Elizabeth, '"Mr. Brown's directions": Capability Brown's landscaping at Burton Constable', *Garden History*, 23/2 (1995).

[81] John Harvey, *Early Nurserymen* (London and Chichester, 1974), pp. 92–3.

[82] LMA: B/HRS/396. Account book of Henry Hewitt jnr. 1762–91.

[83] Richardson was the foreman at Goldsborough until June 1764, when he was replaced by Stones.

[84] SA: Sp.St. 60537. Letter of 19 August 1769.

[85] Brown's letter to Milliken and that to his wife are quoted in full in Stroud, *Capability Brown*, pp. 126–7.

[86] Newcastle papers, University of Nottingham: Ne C. 4443 and 4356 respectively.

[87] SA: Sp.St. 60674 (2).

[88] ERO: D/DHt B1, letter Woods to Rebow, 30 June 1776.

[89] LMA: Acc. 262/43/181.

[90] WSHC: 2667/19/2.

[91] SA: Sp.St. 60686 (25E).

[92] LMA: Acc.262/43/181.

[93] WSHC: 2667/22/1B/3. Memo of 'articles of business belonging to Wardour Castle' (n.d. but the context places it in late 1769).

[94] Blair to Stormont, letter 30 November 1784, quoted in Turnbull, 'Thomas White', p. 281.

[95] All Wardour and Irnham references: WSHC: 2667/22/1B/3.

[96] WSHC: 2667/22/1B/3, letter Woods to Arundell, 22 August 1768.

[97] ERO: Acc. C47 Box 2. Instructions on design for fence for Wivenhoe, 8 February 1780.

CHAPTER 8: CONCLUSION (pages 163–171)

[1] The anonymous painting of the kitchen garden at Ashcombe (Wiltshire) in the 1770s, in the Salisbury and South Wiltshire Museum, shows just such an amalgamation of the productive with the decorative. The scant archive for this property, which belonged to a younger branch of the Arundell family, deals only with the refurbishing of the house itself in the 1750s.

[2] Eileen Harris assisted by Nicholas Savage, *British Architectural Books and Writers, 1556–1785* (Cambridge, 1990), p. 271.

[3] Royal Library, Windsor. Illustrated in Mark Laird, *The Flowering of the Landscape Garden* (Philadelphia, 1999), p. 197.

[4] Plan for Ulriksdal, illustrated in John Harris and Michael Snodin (eds), *Sir William Chambers* (New Haven and London, 1997), p. 16.

[5] Edward Harwood, 'Luxurious hermits: asceticism, luxury and retirement in the eighteenth-century English garden', *Studies in the History of Gardens and Designed Landscapes*, 20/4 (2000), p. 289.

[6] Remark by Walpole in *Visits to Country Seats*, in connection with Brown's impertinence to the Duke of Marlborough, quoted in Thomas Hinde, *Capability Brown: the story of a master gardener* (1986), p. 118.

[7] Janet Waymark, 'Sherborne, Dorset', *Garden History*, 29/1 (2001), p. 70. By the 1830s when William Sawrey Gilpin was practising, the landscape gardener was accepted as a gentleman and ate with his employer, but this was by no means the general practice in the mid eighteenth century (information from lecture by Sophie Piebenga, OUDCE conference, 3 October 2004).

[8] Washington State University Library. Photocopies ERO: Temp. Acc. C39.

[9] ERO: Acc. C47 Box 2, letter from Dorothy Martin, 1776.

[10] ERO: Acc. C47 Box 2.

[11] WSHC: 2667/22/1B/3, letter Woods to Arundell, 6 April 1765. This was the sum owing to Woods for visits that year.

[12] Quoted in David Brown, 'Nathaniel Richmond (1724–1784), "Gentleman Improver"' (PhD thesis, University of East Anglia, 2000), p. 186.

[13] Brown, 'Nathaniel Richmond', pp. 1, 46, 53.

[14] *Treatise on Country Residences*, 1806, quoted in David Jacques, *Georgian Gardens* (London, 1983), p. 167.

[15] *Lectures on Landscape Gardening in Australia*, quoted in Deborah Turnbull, 'Thomas White (1739–1811): Eighteenth-Century Landscaper and Arboriculturalist' (unpublished PhD thesis, University of Hull, 1990), p. 3.

[16] Turnbull, 'Thomas White', pp. 61–2.

[17] WSHC: 2667/22/1B/3, letter Woods to Arundell, 4 September 1771.

GAZETTEER (pages 173–242)

[1] A fuller analysis of all commissions can be found in Fiona Cowell, 'Richard Woods (1715/16–1793): Surveyor, Improver and Master of the Pleasure Garden' (unpublished PhD thesis, University of East Anglia, 2005).

[2] Edward Hasted, *History and Topographical Survey of the County of Kent*, vol. 1 (2nd edn 1797).

[3] ERO: D/DEl B19.

[4] Griffin was one of the very few clients with whom Brown parted on bad terms.

[5] By Edward Eyre: English Heritage collection, Audley End.

[6] ERO: D/DQy 8.

[7] ERO: D/DBy Z77. *Mes Souvenirs d'Audley End* by Mr Lelyveld, Under Secretary of State to the Assembly of the States General.

[8] Pers. comm. Dr Stuart Mason.

[9] *Victoria County History: Essex*, vol. 8 (1983).

[10] SA: Sp.St. 60633/16.

[11] Stephen Wright, *Bretton, the Beaumonts and a Bureaucracy* (Wakefield, 2001).

[12] WSHC: 2667/22/1B/3.

[13] A full discussion of the complications in the account book can be found in Cowell, 'Richard Woods', Gazetteer, pp. 41–51.

[14] William Angus, *Seats of the Nobility and Gentry etc.* (London, 1787).

[15] Ex info. David Jacques.

[16] HALS: D/EP P9.

[17] In *Country Life* (18 July 1925), p. 98.

[18] Although currently in Oxfordshire, Buckland was in Berkshire until 1974.

[19] John Rocque, *Map of Berkshire*, 1752–61 but surveyed earlier.

[20] The schedule of tithes (D/EWe E10) describes Further Park Leys and Horse Leys as being 'part Pleasure Ground and Water the rest'.

[21] BRO: D/EWe A3. The ledger nominally continues to 1762, but the entries after 1759 are confined to corrections of the previous accounts.

[22] Described in detail by Timothy Mowl in 'Air of Irregularity', *Country Life* (11 January 1990).

[23] Spencer's diary occasionally omits an arrival or departure.

[24] SA: Sp.St. 60672/2.

[25] SA: Sp.St. 60537/66.

[26] See Michael Symes, *Garden Bridges* (Wallington, 2007), pp. 13–17, for an explanation of 'Palladian' bridges.

[27] The architect was probably Thomas Allason.

[28] Carlton Towers archive.

[29] Brynmor Jones Library, University of Hull: DDCA/29–12/93 estate vouchers for 1763 only, garden account 1767–73; DDCA(2)/48–22 and 23 household account books for 1760–4 and 1768–1815.

[30] Carlton Towers archive.

[31] Deborah Turnbull, 'Thomas White (1739–1811): Eighteenth-Century Landscape Designer and Arboriculturist' (unpublished PhD thesis, University of Hull, 1990). The

dating of White's design is on stylistic grounds, and from entries in White's bank account at Drummonds.

[32] ERO: D/DEl P9. Timothy Skynner, *Survey of the Capital Messuage called Copford Hall*, 1766.

[33] ERO: D/DEl P32. Cole and Hale, *Map of Copford Hall*, 1817.

[34] The diversion order for this has not survived, but cartographic evidence is compelling.

[35] DA/BW/E3/1.

[36] The view-lines concentrate on the panorama north-west of the house, whereas Woods's layout gives prominence to the views south-east.

[37] DA/BW/A/2, entry for 2 October 1761 to 'Mrs Richardson excr. to Mr Richardson'.

[38] The last pond was not made with the pronged south tail shown on Woods's plan.

[39] The remains of this trunk were exposed during the restoration.

[40] 'This foundation must be carried up to the level of the surface of the lower water before I can go to work with any large stones.'

[41] DA: BW/H/117, 118.

[42] William Angus, *Seats of the Nobility and Gentry etc.* (London, 1787), plate 16; John Claudius Loudon, *Encyclopedia of Gardening* (London, 1822), p. 1242.

[43] WSHC: 2667/22/1B/3.

[44] The only estate book for the 1760s is the short account between Thornhill and his lawyer for February 1766 (CROH: 148/4/0).

[45] CROH: 2268/1. I am grateful to John Drake for bringing the ledgers of James Wood to my notice, and giving me photocopies.

[46] BRO: D/EBy P1.

[47] ERO: D/DBe A4.

[48] Pers. comm. Dr Stuart Mason, specialist in the history of eighteenth-century Essex maps.

[49] ERO: D/DQb P1. *Plan of Gidea Hall Park and Farms adjoining … in the Parish of Rumford … The property of Alexander Black, Esq, merchant*.

[50] The most strongly worded complaint about Daniel is in a letter from Stones to Woods: '…I am Tyerd to Peses for this fortnite past i think Mr Lascelles has been Crasey not only with mee but every one.' WYAS Leeds: TN/EA19/1.

[51] WYAS Leeds: Harewood Maps 25. Thomas Pattison, *A New and Correct Plan of the Manour of Goldsborough*, 1738.

[52] WYAS Leeds: Harewood Maps 27. Unsigned, undated.

[53] Pers. comm. Deborah Turnbull.

[54] ERO: D/DFa E43/1.

[55] ERO: D/DFa P6.

[56] ERO: D/DFa T11.

[57] BL Maps 176.o.87.

[58] [Peter Muilman], *New and Complete History of Essex*, vol. 4 (Chelmsford, 1771).

[59] ERO: D/DU 162/1.

[60] See first edition 25-inch Ordnance Survey map, 1871.

[61] WYAS, Leeds: Harewood Accounts, 269. On 14 November 1764, Sparrow was paid for his journey to Gawthorpe and ten weeks' wages.

[62] John Jewell, *The Tourist's Companion* (Leeds, 1819).

[63] CBS: D/LE/11/10.

[64] CBS: D/X 1045/1.

[65] In Buckinghamshire County Museum.

[66] CBS: D/X 1212/3.

[67] CBS: D/LE/11/10.

[68] Numbers of the same species appear in different places on the list.

[69] CBS: D/LE/A1/2: bill from Henry Hewitt for fir trees. Sir Thomas also noted 'Hewett Nursery Place at Little Brompton' in his note/account book for 1741 (CBS: D/X 1212/3).

[70] CBS: John and William Brudenell, *A Platt of part of the Manners of Hartwell and Stone etc.* (1661).

[71] The structure has recently been given this name from the fragments of sixteenth-century cresting stones salvaged from the old house during alterations in the eighteenth century. The date at which they were originally placed along the top of the wall is open to conjecture.

[72] Apart from the customary 'lease for a year' taken out the day before purchase of freehold property.

[73] ERO: D/DU 517/49.

[74] GRO: D540/E3. I am indebted to Nicholas Kingsley for drawing my attention to this document.

[75] Woods's plan was included in the Hengrave sale of 1952 (lot 1590), but efforts to trace it have failed. It is known from a black and white photograph of mediocre quality.

[76] SROB: Hengrave 712/61. Anthea Taigel found this map 'probably inaccurate in a number of details, most particularly in the depiction of water … In its main outline and many of the features, however, it is supported by the 1839 Tithe Award Map and these are therefore likely to have been represented accurately.'

[77] This list is not visible on the photograph, but has been taken from the text by H. Avray Tipping in *Period Homes* (London, 1926), when the plan was still hanging at Hengrave.

[78] WSHC: 2667/22/1B/3. Letter Woods to Arundell 24 April 1769.

[79] British Library Map Room.

[80] WSHC: 2667/19/6.

[81] SA: Sp.St. 60633. Diary of John Spencer.

[82] Both Crosley's maps are in private possession, although catalogued as KMA 1219 and 1220. *An Attempt to Improve Kirklees Park* (1782); *Map of the Estate of the Manors of Clifton, Hartshead and Brighouse* (1788).

[83] The outline of the now-blocked arch leading to it is clearly visible in the semi-circular wall.

[84] Folger Shakespeare Library, Washington D.C: MS M.a.11. (Sir) John Parnell, 'An Account of the many fine seats of nobles I have seen' etc.

[85] WSHC: 2667/22/1B/3, letter Woods to Arundell, 22 March 1770.

[86] A map of 1623 by John Norden shows 'the way to Rotherford', leading into the Littleton grounds at the end of the shrubbery. The name 'Rotherford' seems to have disappeared by the nineteenth century.

[87] The James Marshall and Marie-Louise Osborne Collection, Yale University Library.

[88] DRO: D/WLC/E18; P1.

[89] BL Maps *2153 (3).

[90] D/WLC/AE15.

[91] D/WLC/AE17.

[92] See engraving by Margaret Weld, 1721.

[93] WSHC: 2667/22/1B/3.

[94] ERO: Acc. C47 Box 2, letter 14 June 1779.

[95] 14 June 1779 was a Monday (see Clifford Webb, *Dates and Calendars for the Genealogist* (London, 1989) so the following Friday was 18 June. He was at Wivenhoe from 21 June.

[96] Handwritten comment in ERO catalogue of the sparse surviving archive.

[97] ERO: D/DCm P14, survey by Timothy Skynner.

[98] A stylised open grove between the avenue and field boundaries north-east of the house; extension to the woodland bordering it; the amalgamation of four fields south of the house into parkland/pasture. These do not remain as consistent changes between 1764 (Skynner), 1777 (Chapman and André), 1799 (Ordnance Surveyor's Drawing) and 1842 (tithe map).

[99] English Heritage, *Register of Parks and Gardens of Special Historic Interest: Essex* (2001).

[100] Although this is reasonably clear on the original, it is indistinct on reproductions.

[101] I am grateful to David Brown for informing me of this entry.

[102] SA: Sp.St. 60537/71.

[103] A. Dury and J. Andrews, 9 sheets, 2in to 1 mile.

[104] HALS: D/ERy P3.

[105] Pers. comm. Dr Stuart Mason, author of *Essex on the Map: the Eighteenth-Century Land Surveyors of Essex* (Chelmsford, 1990).

[106] Esther Gatland, 'Richard Woods in Hertfordshire', in *Hertfordshire Garden History* (Hatfield, 2007), pp. 110–16.

[107] Eileen Harris, 'A flair for the grandiose: the architecture of Thomas Wright – II', *Country Life* (2 September 1971).

[108] WSHC: 2667/22/1B/3. April 11 was a Tuesday in 1769, and Woods wrote that he had left Irnham on Sunday, hence he would have been at Nuthall for two days.

[109] Nottingham University Library, Holden Collection, Hn S 2/19. *Survey Book of Nuthall Lordship* by John Sanders. I am grateful to Judy Preston for this reference.

[110] BRO: D/EBy P1.

[111] SA: Sp.St. 60633/12–16.

[112] There is no *inquisitio ad quod damnum* referring to the diversion of this lane on record at the National Archives, Kew.

[113] ERO: D/DP P41. Henry Clayton, *Map of Thorndon Park*, 1805.

[114] The pond retained this form until alterations by the Golf Club.

[115] The dating of work on the pond (pre-1788 to 1789) rules out Repton as the designer of the alteration.

[116] ERO: D/DP E68.

[117] WSHC was unable to give precise measurements.

[118] This does not appear on the WD survey and is not mentioned by Woods, although recorded on his plan.

[119] In House Accounts Book, 2 March to 3 April 1764.

[120] WSHC: 2667/22/1B/3. Comparison of details on Woods's plan of 1764 and the two first memoranda of agreements (June 1764 and February 1765.)

[121] Called Hare Grove on the 1753 map but supposedly renamed in honour of Lord Arundell's daughter.

[122] Mark Girouard, 'Wardour Old Castle – II', *Country Life* (21 February 1991).

[123] Barry Williamson states in *Lord Arundell's Park at Wardour* (Bristol, 1997) that the Great Terrace was not the walk along the Hangings, but the platform on which the house was later built. A close scrutiny of the documents makes this extremely unlikely, and the theory has been discounted here.

[124] John Claudius Loudon, *Notes of a Gardening Tour* (London, 1833), p. 504.

[125] J. Williams, 'Our Patriarch: Bishop Bonaventure Giffard' in *Recusant History*, 26/3 (2003).

[126] Quoted in Dorothy Stroud, *Capability Brown* (London and Boston, revised edition 1975), p. 98. Provenance given as the Pakenham papers.

[127] In the Lindley Library, Royal Horticultural Society.

[128] On 10 April 1771 Woods received £200 on account, out of £468 13s 6½d owing at that date. A payment to Woods was made through Hoares Bank in June 1771 for £228 11s 0d.

[129] Stroud, *Capability Brown*, pp. 98–9.

[130] WSHC: 2667/22/1B/3.

[131] Although published in 1770, the map was surveyed in 1768 before Woods's work could have been recorded. The drawing for Wavendon House on the Ordnance Surveyor's drawing is very clear, in spite of the small scale of 2 inches to the mile.

[132] This stratagem was adopted by Brown in the 1760s at Dodington, where the lie of the land necessitated the piece of water being seen end-on, contrary to his usual practice. Roger Turner, *Capability Brown and the Eighteenth-Century Landscape* (Chichester, 1999), p. 120.

[133] ERO: T/M 271.

[134] Woods himself owned a fire engine by Hadley which was among the household effects he sold in 1783.

[135] It has been claimed by Professor Gray in *Wyvern* (December 2000), that in the south park 'Woods strengthened many of the [earlier] tree plantings by planting in small clumps, using mainly oak and chestnut', but this statement springs from an incorrect understanding of the position of Wivenhoe Gate.

[136] Thomas Whately, *Observations on Modern Gardening* (London, 1770), in the section 'Of Ground'.

[137] WSHC: 2667/20/19/96 and 102.

[138] There is no relevant entry in Wyndham's bank account at Hoares between 1764 and 1792.

[139] The house, kitchen garden and offices made another 1½ acres. This compares with the 6 acres of Pope's celebrated garden at Twickenham.

[140] WSHC: 727/2/17, Wyatt's bill of 1791 for dismantling and rebuilding the porch. It survives in the garden.

[141] NLW: Wynnstay Box 115/28 (1).

[142] An earlier survey by Edward Conway of 1775 presumably perished by fire (NLW: Wynnstay R 43).

[143] Bodleian Library, Oxford.

[144] National Library of Wales.

[145] NLW: R 41.

[146] I am grateful to Elizabeth Whittle for sending me photos of this feature.

[147] NLW: Box 115 (16).

[148] The curved north wall of the kitchen garden still contains the hot walls – see CADW *Register*.

[149] NLW: Wynnstay Box 115/21 (13).

SELECT BIBLIOGRAPHY

The place of publication is London unless otherwise stated; titles and archive sources specifically relevant to individual properties are listed in the Gazetteer under the relevant entries.

PRIMARY SOURCES
Titles in Woods's library are marked *

Angus, William, *The Seats of the Nobility and Gentry in Great Britain and Wales* (1787)

Chambers, William, *Civil Architecture* (1759)*

— *Scenes in Kew etc.* (1763)

Considerations on the Penal Laws against the Roman Catholics in England, in a letter to a Noble Lord by a Country Gentleman (1764)

Cosin, James, *Names of the Roman Catholic Non-jurors of England and Wales* (1745)

De Caus, Salomon, *Les raisons des forces mouvantes* (Frankfurt, 1615)

Decker, Paul, *Chinese Architecture* and *Gothic Architecture* (1759)

Desaguliers, John Theophilus, *Course of Experimental Philosophy*, vol. 2 (1744)

Dicks, John, *A New Gardener's Dictionary* (1769)

Dodsley, Robert, *A Description of the Leasowes*, in vol. 2 of the collected works of Shenstone (1764)

Edmeades, Robert, *The Gentleman and Lady's Gardener* (1776)

Edwards, George and Matthias Darly, *A New Book of Chinese Designs* (1754)

Fullmer, Samuel, *The Young Gardener's Best Companion* (1781)

Furber, Robert, *A Short Introduction to Gardening* (1733)

Garton, James, *The Practical Gardener* (1769)

Gent, Joseph Blagrave, *Epitome of the Art of Husbandry* (1670)*

Gibbs, James, *A Book of Architecture* (1728)

Halfpenny, John and William, *Rural Architecture in the Chinese Taste* (1752)

— *Rural Architecture in the Gothick Taste* (1752)

— *Country Gentleman's Pocket Companion* (1756)

— *Modern Builder's Assistant* (1757)

Halfpenny, William, *Arithmetick and Measurement* (1748)

— *New and Compleat System of Architecture* (1749)*

— *Useful Architecture* (1752)

Hanbury, William, *Complete Body of Gardening* (1770)

Hill, John, *Eden, or a Compleat Body of Gardening* (1757)

Hoppus, Edward, *The Gentleman's and Builder's Repository; or, Architecture Display'd* (1737)

Langley, Batty, *Practical Geometry* (1726)

— *New Principles of Gardening* (1728)

— *City and Country Builder's and Workman's Treasury of Designs* (1740)

— *Builder's Jewel* (1741)

— *Ancient Architecture Restored* (1742)

— *Gothic Architecture Improved* (1747)

— *London Prices of Bricklayers' Materials etc.* (1748)*

Le Clerc, Sebastien, *A Treatise of Architecture* (1732)*

Leoni, Giacomo [Alberti], *The Architecture ....* (1721; 2nd edn but the first in English only)*

Lightoler, Timothy, *The Gentleman's and Farmer's Architect* (1762)

Mason, George, *An Essay on Design in Gardening* (1768)

Mason, William, *The English Garden: a poem in four books* (York, 1777)

Mawe, Thomas and John Abercrombie, *Every Man his Own Gardener* (1st edn 1767; in continuous publication until 1848)

— *The Universal Gardener and Botanist* (1778)

Meader, James, *The Planter's Guide* (1779)

Miller, Philip, *The Gardener's Dictionary* (1731; the 8th edn of 1768 was 'revised and altered according to the latest system of botany')

Mordaunt, John, *The Complete Steward* (1761)

Morris, Robert, *Lectures on Architecture* (1734)

— *Rural Architecture* (1750). Republished 1755 as *Select Architecture*

— *The Architectural Remembrancer* (1751)

— *Modern Builder's Assistant* (1757)

[Muilman, Peter], *The New and Complete History of Essex*, 6 vols. (Chelmsford, 1768–72)

Nourse, Timothy, *Campania Foelix, or Improvements of Husbandry* (1700)

Over, Charles, *Ornamental Architecture in the Gothic, Chinese and Modern Taste* (1758)

Overton, Thomas, *Temple Builder's Most Useful Companion* (1766)

Pain, William, *The Builder's Companion* (1758)

— *The Builder's Pocket Treasure* (1766)

— *The Practical Builder* (1774)

Picturesque Views of the Principal Seats of the Nobility and Gentry (1786)

Rutter, John and Daniel Carter, *Modern Eden, or the Gardener's Universal Guide* (1767)

Salmon, William, *Palladio Londoniensis, or The London Art of Building* (1734)*

Seeley, Benton, *Description of the Gardens ... at Stow* (Northampton, 1744)

Swinden, Nathaniel, *The Beauties of Flora* (1778)

Switzer, Stephen, *Nobleman, Gentleman and Gardener's Recreation* (1715)

— *Ichnographia rustica* (1718; new edition 1741)*?

— *The Practical Fruit Gardener* (1724)

— *The Practical Kitchen Gardener* (1727)

— *Introduction to a System of Hydraulics and Hydrostatics* (1729)

Thoughts on the Present State of Roman Catholics in England by a Protestant (1779)

Trusler, John, *Elements of Modern Gardening* (1784)

Vancouver, Charles, *General View of the Agriculture of the County of Essex* (1795)

Walpole, Horace, *History of the Modern Taste in Gardening* (Twickenham, 1780)

Ware, Isaac, *Complete Body of Architecture* (1756 – contains a considerable section on garden layout)

Weston, Richard, *The Gardener's and Planter's Calendar* (1773)

Whately, Thomas, *Observations on Modern Gardening* (1770)

White, Gilbert, *The Natural History of Selborne* (1789). Illustrated edition R.H. Davidson-Houston (Exeter and New York, 1981)

Wrighte, William, *Grotesque Architecture or Rural Amusement* (1768)

Young, Arthur *A Six Weeks' Tour through the Southern Counties of England and Wales* (1768)

— *Six Months Tour through the North of England* (1769)

— *A Farmer's Tour through the East of England* (1771)

SECONDARY SOURCES

Ashton, T., *Economic Fluctuations in England 1700–1800* (Oxford, 1959)

Aveling, Hugh, *The Handle and the Axe* (1976)

Bagot, Annette, 'Monsieur Beaumont and Col. Grahme: the making of a garden', *Garden History*, 3/4 (1975), pp. 66–78

Batey, Mavis and David Lambert, *The English Garden Tour* (1990)

Beamon, Sylvia, 'To conserve snow: early refrigeration of food in England', *Follies*, 5 (1990), pp. 4–5

Beamon, Sylvia and Susan Roaf, *The Ice Houses of Britain* (London and New York, 1990)

Bence-Jones, Mark, *The Catholic Families* (1992)

Bendall, Sarah, *Dictionary of Land Surveyors and Local Mapmakers of Great Britain and Ireland* (1997)

Boney, A. D. 'Wages and working days of labourers', *Devon and Cornwall Notes and Queries*, 39/4 (2003), pp. 113–20

Bossy, John, *The English Catholic Community* (1975)

Brogden, William, 'The *ferme ornée* and changing attitudes to agricultural improvement', *Eighteenth Century Life*, 8 (1983), pp. 39–43

Brown, Arthur, *Essex People* (Chelmsford, 1972)

— *Prosperity and Poverty: rural Essex 1700–1815* (Chelmsford, 1996)

Brown, David, 'Lancelot Brown and his associates', *Garden History*, 29/1 (2001), pp. 2–12

Burton, Anthony, *The Canal Builders* (1972)

Campbell, Susan, *Charleston Kedding: a history of kitchen gardening* (1996)

Chambers, Douglas, *The Planters of the English Landscape Garden* (New Haven and London, 1993)

Clarke, George, *Descriptions of Lord Cobham's Gardens at Stowe 1700–1750* (Buckinghamshire Record Society, 1990)

Conner, Patrick, *Oriental Architecture in the West* (1979)

Cousins, Michael, 'The Chinese House, Amesbury Abbey', *Follies*, 4/1 (new numbering, 1992), p. 5

Crisp, Frank, 'The Catholic Registers of Cheam', *Miscellanea*, 4 (Catholic Record Society, 1906)

Duffy, Eamon, *Peter and Jack: Roman Catholics and dissent in eighteenth-century England* (1982)

Estcourt, E. and J. Payne, *English Catholic Non-Jurors of 1715* (1969)

Flowers in the Landscape (Bucks Gardens Trust with the Georgian Group, 2006)

Foley, Brian, *Some People of the Penal Times* and *Some Other People of the Penal Times* (Lancaster, 1991)

Gallagher, Christopher, 'The Leasowes: a history of the landscape', *Garden History*, 24/2 (1996), pp. 201–21

Gandy, Michael, *Catholic Missions and Registers 1700–1880*, 5 vols covering the whole of England (1993)

Gillow, J. and J. Hanson, 'Convicted recusants under Charles II', *Miscellanea*, 5 (Catholic Record Society, 1909)

Gooch, Leo, 'The religion for a gentleman', *Recusant History*, 23/4 (1997), pp. 542–60

Goodway, Keith, 'William Emes and the flower garden at Sandon', *Garden History*, 24/1 (1996), pp. 24–30

Grieve, Hilda, *A Transatlantic Gardening Friendship* (Historical Association, Essex Branch, 1981)

Hall, Elizabeth, '"Mr. Brown's directions": Capability Brown's landscaping at Burton Constable', *Garden History*, 23/2 (1995), pp. 145–75

Hans, Nicholas, *New Trends in Education in the Eighteenth Century* (1951)

Harris, Eileen (ed.), facsimile with introduction of Thomas Wright's *Arbours and Grottos*, 1755 and 1758 (1979)

Harris, Eileen assisted by Nicholas Savage, *British Architectural Books and Writers, 1556–1785* (Cambridge, 1990)

Harris, John, 'Fonthill, Wiltshire', *Country Life* (24 November 1966), pp. 1370–4

— 'William Kent's Gothick', in *A Gothick Symposium* (Georgian Group, 1983), no pagination

— 'A pioneer in gardening: Dickie Bateman re-assessed', *Apollo* (October 1993), pp. 227–33

Harvey, John, *Early Gardening Catalogues* (Chichester, 1972)

— *Early Nurserymen* (London and Chichester, 1974)

— 'The Georgian garden: nurseries and plants', *Georgian Group Annual Report* (1986), pp. 55–67

Harwood, Edward, 'Luxurious hermits: asceticism, luxury and retirement in the eighteenth-century English garden', *Studies in the History of Gardens and Designed Landscapes*, 20/4 (2000), pp. 265–93

Henrey, Blanche, *British Horticultural and Botanical Literature before 1800* (1975)

Hinde, Thomas, *Capability Brown: the story of a master gardener* (1986)

Holt, Geoffrey, 'The education of Catholics from the Act of Uniformity to the Catholic Relief Acts', *Recusant History*, 27/3 (2005), pp. 346–57

Hunt, John Dixon, *Garden and Grove* (Philadelphia, 1986)

— *William Kent: landscape garden designer* (1987)

Hunt, John Dixon and Peter Willis, *The Genius of the Place* (1975)

Ingamells, John, *Dictionary of British and Irish Travellers in France and Italy*, 1701–1800 (New Haven and London, 1997)

Jackson-Stops, Gervase, *An English Arcadia 1600–1990* (Washington D.C., 1991)

Jacques, David, *Georgian Gardens* (1983)

— 'The *ferme ornée*', in *Conference Proceedings of the Association of Gardens Trusts* (Staffordshire Gardens and Parks Trust, 1998), pp. 11–18

Jellicoe, Geoffrey and Susan (eds.), *The Oxford Companion to Gardens* (Oxford and New York, 1986)

Kellerman, Susan, 'Bath houses: an introduction', *Follies Journal*, 1 (2001), pp. 21–9

Keswick, Maggie, *The Chinese Garden* (2nd edn, 1986)

King, R. W., 'The "Ferme Ornée": Philip Southcote and Wooburn Farm', *Garden History*, 2/3 (1974), pp. 27–59

— 'Joseph Spence of Byfleet', *Garden History*, 8/3 (1980), pp. 77–114

Laird, Mark, 'Ornamental planting and horticulture in English pleasure grounds 1700–1830', in John Dixon Hunt (ed.), *Garden History: Issues, Approaches, Methods* (Dumbarton Oaks, 1992), pp. 243–79

— *The Flowering of the Landscape Garden* (Philadelphia, 1999)

Langford, Paul, *A Polite and Commercial People* (Oxford, 1989)

Lavelle, T., 'Essex papists and the oath of allegiance, 1715–1788', *Essex Recusant*, 1 (1959)

Leys, M. D. R., *Catholics in England 1559–1829* (1961)

Longstaffe-Gowan, Tod, *The London Town Garden* (New Haven and London, 2001)

McCarthy, M., *The Origins of the Gothic Revival* (1987)

Magee, Brian, *The English Recusants* (1938)

Malcolmson, Robert, *Life and Labour in England 1700–1780* (1981)

Martin, Peter, *The Gardening World of Alexander Pope* (Hamden, Connecticut, 1984)

Mason, Stuart, *Essex on the Map: the 18th century Land Surveyors of Essex* (Chelmsford, 1990)

Meir, Jennifer, *Sanderson Miller and his Landscapes* (Chichester, 2006)

Mingay, Gordon, *Social History of the English Countryside* (1990)

Minton, J., *Agrarian Archives* (2002)

Mowl, Timothy, *Gentlemen and Players* (Stroud, 2000)

— 'Antiquaries, theatre and early medievalism', in Christopher Ridgway and Robert Williams (eds), *Sir John Vanbrugh and Landscape Architecture* (Stroud, 2000), pp. 71–93

— 'Inside Beckford's landscape of the mind', *Country Life* (7 February 2002), pp. 60–3

— *Historic Gardens of Wiltshire* (Stroud, 2004)

Osborn, James (ed.), Joseph Spence's *Observations, Anecdotes and Character of Books and Men Collected from Conversation* (Oxford, 1966)

Phibbs, John, *The Assassination of Capability Brown* (Debois Landscape Survey Group, 1995)

Records of the Forfeited Estates Commission, PRO Handbook 12 (1968)

Richeson, Allie, *English Land Measuring to 1800: instruments and practices* (Cambridge, Mass., 1966)

Robinson, John Martin, *Temples of Delight: Stowe landscape gardens* (1990)

Rupp, Gordon, *Religion in England 1688–1791* (Oxford, 1986)

Sambrook, James, 'Wooburn Farm in the 1760s', *Garden History*, 7/2 (1979), pp. 82–101

Sayre, Laura, 'Locating the Georgic: from the *ferme ornée* to the model farm', *Studies in the History of Gardens and Designed Landscape*, 22/3 (2002), pp. 167–92

Shields, Steffie, 'Mr. Brown, engineer', *Lincolnshire Gardens Trust Newsletter* (May 2003), pp. 11–18

Sirén, Osvald, *China and Gardens of Europe of the Eighteenth Century* (Dumbarton Oaks facsimile, 1990)

Snell, Keith, *Annals of the Labouring Poor* (Cambridge, 1985)

Stevenson, John, *Popular Disturbances in England, 1700–1870* (1979)

Stratton, J., *Agricultural Records AD 220–1968* (1969)

Stroud, Dorothy, *Capability Brown* (London and Boston, revised edition 1975)

Symes, Michael, *Fairest Scenes: five great Surrey gardens* (Elmbridge Museum Service, 1988)

— *Garden Bridges* (Wallington, 2007)

Taylor, Kristina, 'The oldest surviving pleasure garden in Britain: cold bath near Tunbridge Wells in Kent', *Garden History*, 28/2 (2000), pp. 277–82

Toynbee, Mrs Paget (ed.), *The Letters of Horace Walpole* (Oxford, 1869–1910)

Tristram, Philippa, 'Sprawling dragons, squatting pagods, and clumsy mandarines', *Georgian Group Journal* (1995), pp. 1–9

Turner, Roger, *Capability Brown and the Eighteenth-Century Landscape* (Chichester, 1999)

Wade Martins, Susanna, and Tom Williamson (eds) *The Farming Journal of Randall Burroughes* (Norfolk Record Society, vol. 58, 1993 [1995])

— 'Labour and improvement: agricultural change in East Anglia', *Labour History Review*, 62/3 (1997), pp. 275–95

White, Roger, 'The influence of Batty Langley', in *A Gothick Symposium* (The Georgian Group, 1983)

Williamson, Tom, *Polite Landscapes* (Stroud, 1995)

— *The Transformation of Rural England* (Exeter, 2002)

Willson, Anthony, 'Alexander Pope's grotto in Twickenham', *Garden History*, 26/1 (1998), pp. 31–60

Wilson, Michael, *William Kent* (London, Boston, Melbourne and Henley, 1984)

Wilson, Richard and Alan Mackley, *Creating Paradise: the building of the English country house 1660–1880* (2000)

Woods, May and Arete Warren, *Glasshouses: a history of greenhouses, orangeries and conservatories* (1988)

Worrall, E. S., *Returns of Papists 1767* (Catholic Record Society, 2 vols 1980 and 1989)

Wrigley, E. A. and R. S. Schofield, *The Population History of England 1541–1871* (1981)

UNPUBLISHED THESES

Brogden, William, 'Stephen Switzer and Garden Design in Britain in the Early Eighteenth Century' (PhD thesis, Edinburgh University, 1973)

Brown, David, 'Nathaniel Richmond (1724–1784), "Gentleman Improver"' (PhD thesis, University of East Anglia, 2000)

Kellerman, Susan, 'Bath Houses in Country House Gardens and Parks' (MA thesis, University of Leeds, 2003)

Kitching, Jack, 'Roman Catholic Education in England 1700–1870' (PhD thesis, University of Leeds, 1966)

Shrimpton, Colin, 'The Landed Society and Farming Community of Essex in the late 18th and early 19th Centuries' (PhD thesis, University of Cambridge, 1965)

Turnbull, Deborah, 'Thomas White (1739–1811): Eighteenth-Century Landscape Designer and Arboriculturist' (PhD thesis, University of Hull, 1990)

INDEX

Principal commission entries in **bold**, illustrations in *italic*